Laura Doan

Fashioning Sapphism

THE ORIGINS OF A MODERN ENGLISH LESBIAN CULTURE

Columbia University Press
New York

Columbia University Press
Publishers Since 1893
New York   Chichester, West Sussex
Copyright © 2001 Columbia University Press
All rights reserved

Library of Congress Cataloging-in-Publication Data

Doan, Laura L., 1951–
  Fashioning Sapphism : the origins of a modern English lesbian
culture / Laura Doan.
      p. cm.
  Includes bibliographical references and index.
  ISBN 0-231-11006-5 (cloth : alk. paper)
  ISBN 0-231-11007-3 (pbk. : alk. paper)
    1. Lesbianism — Great Britain — History — 20th century.   2.
Lesbians — Great Britain — Social conditions.   3. Gays in pop-
ular culture — Great Britain — History.   4. Lesbians in mass
media — History.   5. Lesbians in literature — History.   I. Title.

HQ75.6.G7 D63 2000
306.76′63′0941 — dc21   00–043161

BETWEEN MEN ~ BETWEEN WOMEN
Lesbian and Gay Studies

Lillian Faderman and Larry Gross, Editors

Advisory Board of Editors

Claudia Card
Terry Castle
John D'Emilio
Esther Newton
Anne Peplau
Eugene Rice
Kendall Thomas
Jeffrey Weeks

BETWEEN MEN ~ BETWEEN WOMEN is a forum for current lesbian and gay scholarship in the humanities and social sciences. The series includes both books that rest within specific traditional disciplines and are substantially about gay men, bisexuals, or lesbians and books that are interdisciplinary in ways that reveal new insights into gay, bisexual, or lesbian experience, transform traditional disciplinary methods in consequence of the perspectives that experience provides, or begin to establish lesbian and gay studies as a free-standing inquiry. Established to contribute to an increased understanding of lesbians, bisexuals, and gay men, the series also aims to provide through that understanding a wider comprehension of culture in general.

For Mar

Contents

Acknowledgments IX
Introduction: "It's Hard to Tell Them Apart Today" XI

One
The Mythic Moral Panic: Radclyffe Hall
and the New Genealogy *1*

Two
"That Nameless Vice Between Women":
Lesbianism and the Law *31*

Three
Outraging the Decencies of Nature? Uniformed
Female Bodies *64*

Four
Passing Fashions: Reading Female Masculinities
in the 1920s *95*

Five
Lesbian Writers and Sexual Science: A Passage
to Modernity? *126*

Six
Portrait of a Sapphist? Fixing the Frame
of Reference *164*

Notes 195
Bibliography 259
Index 273

Acknowledgments

IN APRIL 1996 I sent a letter to Record Management Services, at the Home Office in London, to request access to all materials relating to the 1928 obscenity trial of Radclyffe Hall's novel, *The Well of Loneliness*. The last time an individual had corresponded with the British government on this subject was apparently in 1948, when Hall's partner, Una Troubridge, asked that the ban be reconsidered so that *The Well of Loneliness* might be included in a new edition of Hall's complete works. At that time, according to my staff informant, the request was turned down, and the files were severely purged and closed for the maximum number of years, until 2048. Two months after my petition was reviewed, I was invited to Queen Anne's Gate on a "privileged access basis" and presented with all extant materials relating to the case. Between the luxurious working conditions at the Home Office and the severely hostile reception at a library housed in a high-security facility that I had unwittingly penetrated were dozens of encounters with very helpful people who were always willing to share their time and expertise.

I would like to thank several of the curators, archivists, and librarians who assisted me in my research: Terence Pepper of the National Portrait Gallery; David Doughan of the Fawcett Library; Michael Bott at Reading University; and the staffs of the British Library Manuscript Library and British Library Newspaper Library at Colindale, Public Record Office, Metropolitan Police Historic Museum, Museum of London, Imperial War Museum, Fine Art Society, the library of the Wellcome Institute for the History of Medicine, University College London Library, Victoria and Albert Museum, Tate Gallery, Sheffield Archives, Smallhythe Place, Beinecke Rare Book and Manuscript Library at Yale University, Harry Ransom Humanities Research Center at the University of Texas at Austin, National Archives of Canada, Ottawa, and my own acquisitions librarian, Paula Henry, and the interlibrary loan staff of Milne Library at the State University of New York, Geneseo. I would like to extend special thanks to three individuals, Roy Gluckstein, Christine Hepworth, and Kenneth Pople, who invited me to their homes to examine materials held in their private collections.

Most of my research was conducted during a sabbatical year awarded by SUNY Geneseo (1995–96), and the Geneseo Foundation provided some support for expenses incurred in the project's final stages. In light of this study's topic, I feel immensely fortunate to have received a National Endowment for the Humanities Fellowship for College Teachers in 1997–98 that enabled me to complete the project. For two years I enjoyed the lively environment of the Institute for Women's Studies at Lancaster University, England; the warm collegiality extended to me as a visiting research fellow was a welcome respite from my otherwise rural isolation.

The photograph of Mrs. Sophia Stanley (figure 3) was provided by kind permission of the Metropolitan Police Service, and the following photographs were supplied by the Imperial War Museum: figure 2, Margaret Damer Dawson and Mary Allen, c. 1916 (Q108495); figure 21, Margaret Damer Dawson and Mary Allen "rescue" a child, c. 1919 (Hn69730); figures 23 and 24, women police picking up a case, c. 1919 (Hn69729); and women police taking charge of a case, c. 1919 (Hn69728).

For permission to cite from the unpublished writings of Radclyffe Hall, I wish to thank Jonathan Lovat Dickson, literary executor of the Estate of Radclyffe Hall. Reproduced by permission of A.M. Heath & Co. Ltd. (London). Crown copyright material in the Public Record Office is reproduced by permission of the Controller of Her Majesty's Stationery Office. I am grateful to the Beinecke Rare Book and Manuscript Library, Yale University, to cite excerpts from the H.D. Papers (Yale Collection of American Literature) and Bryher Papers.

Sections of chapter 2 have appeared elsewhere, and I thank the publishers for permission to reprint here: " 'Gross Indecency Between Women': Policing Lesbians or Policing Lesbian Police?" *Social and Legal Studies* 6 (Sage Publications) (December 1997): 533–51; " 'Acts of Female Indecency': Legislating Lesbianism in a Culture of Inversion," in *Sexology in Culture: Labelling Bodies and Desires*, eds. Lucy Bland and Laura Doan (Oxford: Polity Press/ Chicago: University of Chicago Press, 1998), 199–213. A shorter version of chapter 4 was published as "Passing Fashions: Reading Female Masculinities in the 1920s," *Feminist Studies* 24 (Fall 1998): 663–700.

I am extremely grateful for the generosity of several individuals who either provided letters of support or offered thoughtful commentary on sections of the manuscript: Dale Bauer, Terry Castle, Judith Halberstam, Bill Harrison, Trevor Hope, Frances Lannon, Maria Lima, Beth McCoy, Suzanne Raitt, Marlon Ross, Jackie Stacey, James Vernon, Jean Walton, Janet Wolff, and especially Margot Backus, Lucy Bland, and Hilary Hinds. Above all, I am deeply indebted to my partner whose passion for the project was always equal to my own. This book is dedicated to her.

Introduction: "It's Hard to Tell Them Apart Today"

The close companionship which existed for 40 years between Lady Ludlow and Miss Margaret Eleanor Pryce is revealed by the will of Miss Pryce, which has just been published. Miss Pryce, who left an estate valued at £89, 473, bequeathed to Lady Ludlow a diamond ring in the shape of a heart, and in her will stated:—"I beg her to wear it in memory of me. She may select anything else of mine, but I feel I cannot leave her anything more precious than my gratitude for all the love and trust she showed me during the many years we lived together, of which I set down my most deep and loving appreciation."
—Glasgow Herald, *August 21, 1928*

The chief objection to the sort of relationship which Miss Radclyffe Hall attempts to justify is that it poisons all those other innocent, cheerful affectionate relationships, and leaves no part of life secure from the wandering dragon of lust.
—W. R. Gordon, *Daily News and Westminster Gazette,*
August 23, 1928

PUBLISHED IN BRITAIN only a few days apart, these news items in the *Glasgow Herald* and *Daily News and Westminster Gazette* represent love between women in profoundly different ways. As late as 1928 reports of women who lived in "close companionship" with others of their sex could appear in newspapers with wide circulation without *necessarily* triggering associations of sin, vice, decadence, perversion, sickness, or degeneracy.[1] On the contrary, Lady Ludlow's housekeeper blithely informed a reporter, without inhibition or social embarrassment, that her employer's commitment to Miss Pryce was long-standing. Clearly, had the housekeeper thought for a moment her comments concerning her socially prominent mistress might in any way be construed as salacious, or had the reporter found a forty-year "friendship" between two women unnatural or unacceptable, the tenor of the article would have been completely different.[2] What then *is* "revealed" by the will of Miss Pryce? Certain of the *Glasgow Herald*'s readers may have surmised that the bequeathal by one woman to another of "a diamond ring in the shape of a heart" as a token of "the many years [they] lived together" indicated a relationship more intimate than friendship, a reading possibly based on familiarity with new discursive formulations for such passions or activities. Other observers, on the other hand, as may have been the case with Lady Ludlow's housekeeper, were just as likely to believe such a relationship merely "innocent, cheerful [and] affectionate." However, in the months and years following the publication of Radclyffe Hall's novel *The Well of Loneliness* (1928), and the extensive press coverage of the subsequent obscenity trial, the possibility of reading the affection of a woman like Miss Pryce for her companion as "innocent"—or nonsexual—would become more difficult to sustain.[3]

Recent feminist historians regard *The Well*, with its insistent demand for social tolerance of lesbianism, as pivotal; its publication constituted "notoriously the great British public's introduction to lesbianism."[4] Since lesbianism—unlike male homosexuality—was never outlawed in Britain, a lesbian subculture developed more slowly and less visibly than a gay male subculture. Despite these discrepancies in the law, however, the legal controversy surrounding Hall's novel "in many ways . . . had for women an equivalent social impact to the one the [Oscar] Wilde trial had for men."[5] The figure of the male homosexual coalesced in the popular imagination as a consequence of the public trials of Wilde: "At that point, the entire, vaguely disconcerting nexus of effeminacy, leisure, idleness, immorality, luxury, insouciance, decadence and aestheticism, which Wilde was perceived, variously, as instantiating, was transformed into a *brilliantly precise image*. The effect was comparable to that produced for lesbianism by Radclyffe Hall's *Well of Loneliness*."[6] What was at stake for Wilde and Hall in the denouement of their respective legal ordeals and in the plummeting of their literary reputations may be in many ways incommensurate (imprisonment and an early death, on the one hand, and a banned book, on the other), but the intense publicity, not to mention notoriety, generated by these trials culminated in both cases in the successful grafting of a narrow set of cultural signifiers onto an ostensibly legible homosexual body; thus each constituted, as Alan Sinfield's title indicates, a "queer moment." According to most historical accounts, *The Well* and its banning profoundly changed public awareness of lesbianism as well as the way in which many lesbians came to regard what Hall, following the British sexologist Havelock Ellis, termed female sexual inversion.[7]

The highly publicized obscenity trial of Hall's novel, which is generally recognized as *the* crystallizing moment in the construction of a visible modern English lesbian subculture, marks a great divide between innocence and deviance, private and public, New Woman and Modern Lesbian. The "lesbian" had, of course, never been completely invisible in British culture. As with the circulation of any knowledge, in the early decades of the twentieth century some members of the public were undoubtedly in the know, such as the educated elite who had read, for example, the relevant works on the subject in the literatures of ancient Greece and modern France or the "scientific" literature. Practitioners in the fields of medicine and law were especially cognizant of the presence of women variously known by terms such as "Sapphist," "female sexual invert," "masculine woman," "homogenic," the "intermediate sex," or "homosexual"—though rarely as "lesbian."[8] Not all newspaper readers interested in the obscenity trial were as well-informed, however, leaving journalists with the unenviable task of rendering intelligible a subject seldom "treated frankly outside the region of scientific textbooks."[9] Between the two extremes, of those in the know and those who were utterly unknowing, was another group—the vast majority of readers, perhaps—who may have preferred to "know-but-not-know."[10] For this segment of the British public the achievement of the government's prosecution of *The Well* was "to give wider publicity to a book which is supposed to be highly pernicious, and to make a subject which decent-minded persons are *glad to ignore* the commonplace of discussion and morbid curiosity among all ages and classes."[11] Detailed and explicit information on lesbianism—often illustrated with arresting photographs of the novel's author—became suddenly accessible in most major newspapers over some six months, so that the option to deny what was known or suspected all along was less feasible; readers of the *Daily Herald* and *Manchester Guardian*, for instance, were told outright that "the book dealt with physical and sexual relations between Lesbian women."[12] Yet at the height of the obscenity trial, the lesbian journalist Evelyn Irons expressed incredulity that her own mother had not looked at her daughter carefully enough to put two and two together: "There I was in collar and tie and everything—dressed in the uniform—and she didn't realize what the hell it was about."[13]

What Irons has apparently forgotten in the intervening years is that her very sense of her own clothing as an encoded "uniform" was still not widely presumed a marker of sexual identity, suggesting how the shift from cultural indeterminacy to acknowledgement would evolve slowly. Irons's mother could hardly be blamed for failing to "realize what the hell it was about," as British culture at this time was familiar with an astonishing range of masculine and feminine dress for women. The styles of the twenties extended to fashion-conscious and "masculine" women alike an irresistible invitation to experiment—in terms of dress and manners—with near impunity, as seen in the lyrics of a popular song of 1926, entitled "Masculine Women and Feminine Men": "Which is the rooster, which is the hen? It's hard to tell them apart today. / Sister is busy learning to shave; brother just loves his feminine wave. / . . . Knickers and trousers, baggy and wide; nobody knows who's walking inside—those masculine women and feminine men."[14] Unlike the prewar era, when mannishness in women was seen in a more negative light, during the twenties the "masculine woman"—a phrase used in reference to style *or* gender deviation *or* sexuality—"was not always reduced to being a misfit or a figure of abject loneliness."[15] The song's repeated refrain, "It's hard to tell them apart today," is a cogent reminder that some of the styles and accoutrements we now associate unquestionably with lesbianism (short hair, monocles, highly tailored clothing, and so on) did not signal unequivocally something about sexuality until the cultural dissemination of Hall's photographic portrait set the masculine woman—as a category of sexuality—apart from her fashionable friends. Before public exposure, for the better part of a decade, masculine-style clothing for women held diverse spectatorial effects, with few signifiers giving the game away, and readings (whether of clothing, visual images, or stories about women living with other women in "close companionship") varied accordingly among those who knew, those who knew nothing, and those who wished they didn't know. In an era of gender normativity gone haywire, and when gender deviation became entangled with chic, certain clothing styles or haircuts may have been bound up with sexual identity for some observers, but certainly not for others; within public culture those codes were unstable and fluid—and this accounts, in part, for our view of the twenties as an exuberant and volatile decade.

Knowledge of lesbianism was, as we will see, never "common." Just as the gender lines blurred in the fashion designs catering to faddish "masculine women," so too were categories of sexuality less sharply delineated; most important, lesbianism in any formulation was not yet generally connected with style or image. This very ambiguity, in fact, facilitated the emergence of subcultural development, and so the task of the cultural historian—my task in this study—is to explore what Sinfield brilliantly characterizes as "the moment of indeterminacy":

> For it is not that our idea of "the homosexual" was hiding beneath other phrases, or lurking unspecified in the silence, like a statue under a sheet, fully formed but waiting to be unveiled; it was in the process of becoming constituted. . . . To presume the eventual outcome in the blind or

hesitant approximations out of which it was partly fashioned is to miss, precisely, the points of most interest.[16]

The events of late 1928, which culminated in the media circulation of a visible embodiment of a specimen "invert," have so permeated our own cultural consciousness that it has become extremely difficult for us to reconstruct a cultural era prior to that moment. Yet when we look at a photograph of a woman in the 1920s who appears to us cross-dressed or lesbian, we presume "the eventual outcome" and, in so doing, have already missed "the points of most interest": Hall's distinctive fashion sense, manner of self-presentation, and understanding of female sexual inversion would provide the public with a provocative image of lesbianism. But the author of *The Well of Loneliness* did not invent the mannish lesbian so much as embrace sexological theories of inversion and develop an existing style made possible by the startling degree of toleration and experimentation, of dizzying permutations of sartorial play and display. Out of the ambiguities of the 1920s a lesbian subcultural style would emerge—one that dovetailed with Hall's version of inversion—but, in each of the sites under investigation in this study, we will see that because cultural acknowledgement of lesbian existence was sporadic and erratic, some women we now refer to as lesbians flourished. Even so, despite unreserved agreement over the importance of this cultural moment, many previous studies exert a reductive, distorting effect on our reading of early twentieth-century lesbian identity formation in one of two ways. They either neglect to examine in detail the developments leading up to the ban imposed on Hall's novel, leaving discussion in a kind of cultural vacuum, or frame the events in too broad a context against other cultural phenomena, such as the New Woman's emergence before the First World War or the evolution of butch and femme roles in the 1950s.[17]

In her remarkable 1984 essay, "The Mythic Mannish Lesbian: Radclyffe Hall and the New Woman," a title my opening chapter heading echoes, critic Esther Newton produces one of the first genealogical mappings of this significant watershed in lesbian history.[18] Newton's diligent hunt for the source of the mannish lesbian leads her initially to the first generation of New Women ("who were born in the 1850s and 1860s, educated in the 1870s and 1880s, and flourished from the 1890s through the First World War") and then to the second generation (women "born in the 1870s and 1880s and [who] came of age during the opening decades of the twentieth century") and, more specifically, to Radclyffe Hall (1880–1943), who created the very prototype of the mannish lesbian in Stephen Gordon, the protagonist of *The Well of Loneliness*.[19] While the first generation of New Women were inter-

ested in education and access to the professions and gained greater autonomy in their newfound economic freedom, the second generation, women
who notably "placed more emphasis on self-fulfillment . . . and a great deal
more on the flamboyant presentation of self," plunged "into creative and
artistic fields" and "fused their challenge of gender conventions with a repudiation of bourgeois sexual norms."[20] Hall's birth date falls well within the
designated chronological boundaries of this latter generation but, unlike some
of the other lesbian literary figures Newton mentions, such as Gertrude Stein,
Willa Cather, and Natalie Barney, Hall (a late bloomer who only gained
widespread social or artistic prominence with the 1924 publication of her first
novel, *The Unlit Lamp*) was the quintessential celebrity figure of the 1920s.[21]
Newton's argument, which relies heavily on her early collaborator Carroll
Smith-Rosenberg's taxonomy of the New Woman, hinges on two interrelated
assumptions: first, that many first-generation New Women were asexual and
"turned to romantic friendships" with one another and, second, that Hall
and others of the second generation appropriated "the image of the mannish lesbian and the discourse of the sexologists about inversion" in a desperate attempt to reject "the asexual model" (283). The first assumption,
based on what has become known as the "Golden Age" of romantic friendship between women, is increasingly untenable in light of recent work on
women's sexuality in the nineteenth and early twentieth centuries.[22] For
instance, the discovery of new archival materials such as Anne Lister's wildly
erotic diaries offers, as literary critic Terry Castle convincingly argues, "a
spectacular rebuke to the no-lesbians-before-1900 myth" and banishes once
and for all "the lugubrious myths of lesbian asexuality."[23] This gradual ero-
sion of the first assumption also presents a major obstacle for the second.
Newton's insight that Hall seized "the image of the mannish lesbian" to sex-
ualize the asexual culminates in a genealogical model overly reliant on such
labels as "New Woman" and "mannish lesbian": the term "New Woman"
invariably disengages Hall from a complex and particularized social, political, and cultural milieu, while "mannish lesbian" did not, in the 1920s, have
the "tremendous power and resonance" it has in our own time.[24] Acutely
aware of the fast pace of sociocultural change in postwar England for women
of her class and sexual proclivities, Hall was in the vanguard of new developments, if not as a literary experimenter then as a trendsetter in self-presentation (fashion) and self-construction (photography). The extraordinary
sequence of events in the latter half of 1928 that resulted in the publicizing
of one formulation of "lesbian"—Hall's daring to publish a novel that treated
the subject with unprecedented frankness ("an astonishing advance in plain
speaking"[25]), the attack from a hostile newspaper editor, and the novel's

collision with the English legal system—cannot be accommodated by such labels, which necessarily efface the historical detail of such a cultural moment.

In this study I propose an alternative genealogy of modern English lesbian culture by locating in history and culture Hall and other prominent lesbians—including the pioneer in women's policing, Mary Sophia Allen, the artist Gluck, and the writer Bryher [Winifred Ellerman]—within the "constructed narrative" of English modernity through the multiple sites of law, sexology, fashion, and literary and visual representation.[26] Of course, these are certainly not the only crucial sites; other areas, such as the investigation of lesbianism and sport or the importance of pornography, might be equally illuminating. My selection of subject areas has been guided by those realms most mired in cultural myth as well as those that promise to contribute most to our understanding of the factors in the evolution of subcultural style. I am also aware of the limitations of a study that focuses on a handful of socially prominent women drawn from a narrow range of social classes (upper-middle and upper) and professions. The reason some of these women were in a position to promote new professions (Allen) or new fashions (Hall and her partner Una, Lady Troubridge) was because they had significant advantages unavailable to women from other class backgrounds; others (Margaret Damer Dawson, Vita Sackville-West, Gluck, or Bryher) enjoyed a privileged life, with substantial property holdings and/or independent incomes. The influence many of these women held was disproportionate to their numbers, just like another "very small" group in the 1920s called the "Bright Young People" (the smart set comprised of socialites and flappers), who "secured a great deal of publicity by throwing wild parties and indulging . . . in gin, sex, and drugs, which caused their faces to be printed in the Sunday newspapers."[27] Although the women I discuss represent only a small fraction of a lesbian population (most were not linked by friendship networks or other alliances), their faces appeared—sometimes regularly—in the print media.[28] A crude sketch of Hall in a young lesbian artist's 1927 diary surely demonstrates the saliency and influence of the novelist's distinctively modern iconic potential (figure 1).[29]

At the core of my project—indeed, the overarching concept unifying its seemingly disparate array of topics—is the configuration of what I call "Sapphic modernity," a phrase as troubling perhaps as it is useful.[30] Mellifluence aside, "Sapphic" efficaciously denotes same-sex desire between women and, at the same time, because it is less familiar to us today, reminds us that the "lesbian," as a reified cultural concept or stereotype, was, prior to the 1928 obscenity trial, as yet unformed in English culture beyond an intellectual elite. "Modernity," of course, is an even more difficult and contested term, and few cultural critics have mapped out its meanings as concisely as Katy Deepwell, whose formulation is informed by the work of several theorists:

> Modernity remains a complex notion, whether it is understood as the transformation of everyday life through the accelerated pace of changes brought about by (1) transformations within capitalism/industrialization, by changing patterns of work/leisure, production/consumption; (2) a redefinition of space and time brought about by advances in and the potential uses of technologies of energy/transport/mass communications/visual media; or (3) definitions of what it means to be modern in the sense of being '*á la mode*' or belonging to the zeitgeist, alongside (4) the effects of social change offered by varieties of political and intellectual avant-gardism.[31]

All these interconnected and overlapping meanings of modernity circulate throughout *Fashioning Sapphism*, which examines, from numerous perspectives, certain of the key ideological assumptions underpinning, on the one hand, the ways in which some lesbians negotiated English modernity in the 1920s and, on the other, how the conditions of English modernity contributed to the early formation, not of a self-conscious political agenda or an artistic movement as such, but of a public lesbian cultural sensibility.

If modernity entails "the practical negotiation of one's life and one's identity within a complex and fast-changing world," then Sapphic modernity in 1920s England represents one sort of negotiated settlement with a postwar society undergoing radical change in ways that continued the rupture of the separate spheres, public and private, which had hitherto excluded women from modernity.[32] Whether a reward for services rendered during the war or a government strategy to circumvent any resumption of political—and highly public—agitation for suffrage, women's new status as political subjects (partial suffrage in 1918 and full suffrage in 1928) became one marker of women's entry into modernity. At the same time, despite the gradual awareness in medical and legal circles of sexual activity between women, proposals failed to extend the Labouchère Amendment, which criminalized gross indecency between men, to women. After the First World War, which brought even more opportunities for female intrusion into the masculine sphere as thousands of Englishwomen of all classes donned uniforms, the fluidity of gender roles spilled into various realms, such as fashion, and contributed to heightened confusion and cultural anxieties that the sexes were changing places. This "disintegration and fragmentation" stemming from the "destabilizing of many nineteenth-century conventions" gave some women, especially those with independent means, permission to flirt safely with masculinity.[33] For lesbians in particular, the blurring of categories of gender and the greater dissemination of sexual knowledge made possible new paradigms for self-understanding that paved the way for subcultural formation.

Unlike late nineteenth-century France, in which the "figure of the lesbian . . . came to serve as an evocative symbol of a feminized modernity in the work of a number of . . . male French writers who depicted her as an avatar of perversity and decadence," the figure of the lesbian in England during the first decade after the war registered as paradox: invisible and visible, spectral and palpable.[34] In London, even during the obscenity trial, mothers could with perfect equanimity inculcate upon their daughters the myth that lesbianism was not English: "that sort of thing can carry on in Paris but certainly not here."[35] Although, in terms of self-presentation, self-promotion or cultural production, some English lesbians were often situated in the forefront of the "modern," their maneuvers within modernity were sometimes deeply, and disturbingly, conservative in nature, frequently hostile to the project of feminism, and marked not by a desire to overturn cultural imperatives so much as to work within the established conventions and parameters of English national culture. Critic Alison Light describes this development as "conservative modernity" because "it could accommodate the past in the new forms of the present; it was a deferral of modernity and yet it also demanded a different sort of conservatism from that which had gone before."[36] As we will see, Hall occupies a central position in this "contradictory and determining tension in English social life" called conservative modernity; like other "women of an expanding middle class between the wars," Hall also embodied "Englishness in both its most modern and reactionary forms." Such profound conservatism, a peculiarly English ability to straddle the modern and the reactionary, sets Hall's Sapphic modernity apart from its continental counterpart. Consequently, to align Hall with women such as Stein, Cather, and Barney, as is commonplace in the critical literature, neglects how "the English engagement with [modernity] developed certain unique features."[37] What appears, for instance, as transgressive cross-dressing in one national context, such as Paris before and after the First World War, may signify a slavish compliance to the dictates of high fashion elsewhere, as in postwar London. Thus it is a mistake to presume too great an interconnectedness of national cultures in relation to a lesbian subcultural style—an implicit or explicit extension of Bertha Harris's belief that lesbianism transcends national difference (what she terms the "more profound nationality of their lesbianism").[38] Such attempts to "international-ize" lesbianism often result in misunderstandings and in the development of myths, such as the myth that situates Radclyffe Hall in the Parisian lesbian scene.[39] As I discuss in chapter 4, Hall's mythic presence in Paris is asserted with such frequency that few scholars realize how little time she was actu-ally there. Several of the figures prominent in this study (including women as aristocratic as Sackville-West, as wealthy as Bryher, or as impoverished as the artist Dorothy Hepworth) spent more time than Hall in the French capital. Cross-fertilization with other homosexual subcultures in cities such as Paris or Berlin was not irrelevant to the development of an English style, but to overstate Hall's engagement with "Paris-Lesbos" skews the nature of her involvement in a modern, and peculiarly English, lesbian subculture.[40]

Another powerful myth, what I term the "mythic moral panic," offers an excellent starting point for an examination of the origins of a modern Eng-lish lesbian culture because it interconnects, as we will see in chapter 1, "The Mythic Moral Panic: Radclyffe Hall and the New Genealogy," with a com-plex network of other myths generated by scholarly accounts of lesbianism in England in the 1920s. Before the furor over *The Well*, as writers Robert Graves and Alan Hodge explain: "The Lesbians were more quiet about their aberrations . . . but, if pressed, they justified themselves more practically than the men by pointing out there were not enough men to go round in a monogamous system."[41] Similarly, the novelist Douglas Goldring assumed it was this "shortage of men" that "led, in the twenties, to numerous asso-ciations, of a more or less Lesbian character. . . . Unless purposely paraded, such friendships aroused little curiosity or comment."[42] According to another contemporary of Hall's, Beverley Nichols, neither "lesbian" nor "homosex-ual" were terms widely in use in the 1920s, until the obscenity trial:

> What is quite certain is that the word "homosexual," in the twenties, was unknown by the man-in-the-street. By the "man-in-the-street" I need hardly say that I do not mean the man in Harley Street—nor, if it comes to that, the average intelligent undergraduate. . . . [I]n the twenties [the word] was taboo, and I think it is correct to say that the first time it began to come into general circulation was during the case of *The Well of Loneliness*.[43]

Prior to 1928, and for some years after, the terms "lesbian," "homosexual," "sexual invert," or "Sapphist" often overlapped with one another and, as I have already discussed, did not generally connote a specific sexual behav-ior, identity, or appearance. In the absence of a *common* cultural understanding of lesbianism, or a coherent and stable image of *any* formulation of "lesbian," I argue that the widespread belief concerning moral panic about the lesbian menace is more likely a myth produced after the fact than a product of careful historical analysis. In chapter 2, " 'That Nameless Vice Between Women': Lesbianism and the Law," I examine the legal attempts to enact regulatory legislation of same-sex relations between women in 1920 and 1921 and the role played by sexual science in these debates, in order to challenge the widely held belief that lesbians were, in effect, hunted creatures in the 1920s, and that the weapon of choice was sexology. Such an examination not only clarifies the relationship between sexology, lesbianism, and the law, but it also attempts to begin a reclamation of this pre-*Well* period, because "We know much less about lesbianism than about male homosexuality, primarily because it was much less obvious. Not being illegal, it was—with one celebrated exception [*The Well*]—rarely brought to the public eye by judicial proceedings."[44]

In chapters 3 ("Outraging the Decencies of Nature? Uniformed Female Bodies") and 4 ("Passing Fashions: Reading Female Masculinities in the 1920s"), I explore the realm of fashion—in terms of the uniform and haute couture, respectively—as a site for self-expression and experimentation, at once serious and playful. Because modernity "highlights the complexity and danger as well as the richness and excitement of everyday life in the modern city. . . . There is a new stress on display and the visual—on looking. Modern urban existence, with its transience and uncertainty, demands new morals as well as new fashions."[45] In the decades since the 1920s, we have lost touch with the wide range of female masculinities available to women in the postwar era and have also overlooked how many women whose clothing seems to us an obvious indication of one particular sexuality may not have registered as such in their own culture. My aim in these chapters is to scrutinize the ways in which clothing is a much more complicated business than we have hitherto appreciated, rather than to examine the ways particular women in this decade negotiated their own masculinity. Even *similar* uniforms in the 1920s registered *different* spectatorial effects in the eyes of the London Metropolitan Police. While the uniform of one women's policing group might have been potentially disturbing to the men in authority in its hypermasculine cut and design, their real objective was to eliminate these women from policing. Consequently, the uniform was both the problem and not the problem. In the same way, haute couture in the 1920s was deeply inflected by the style, cut, and fabric of traditional men's clothing, although adapted specifically for women and marketed in women's fashion magazines and sold in department stores catering to women. Such highly masculine clothing may have signaled sexual inversion to some savvy viewers, but this was only one available reading among others. Experimentation in clothing and gender bending was so pervasive that one could speak of an entire culture as, in a sense, cross-dressing. Thus I stretch the concept "cross-dressing" to encompass a wide range of dressing in ways not traditionally associated with one's gender. All these clothing styles were in flux in the 1920s, giving women who might later identify themselves as lesbians an opportunity to test the boundaries of sartorial expression without proclaiming sexual preference to the culture at large.

In chapter 5, "Lesbian Writers and Sexual Science: A Passage to Modernity?," I return to the subject of sexology, but in this case in relation to literary representation, to argue that by recuperating the status sexology held in the 1920s we might better understand its usefulness and appeal to the lesbian writer in this period. This is not to suggest that other "nonscientific" treatments of homosexuality were not equally important sources of information; Hall, for instance, was as familiar with several of the key French writers on the subject. All these materials were targeted by the more reactionary quarters of the English popular press, which sought to hold them at bay for the sake of old-fashioned English morality.[46] For example, a *Daily Express* editorial, in defense of its own attack on *The Well* some days earlier, warned of the danger of Hall's novel becoming "a replica of that detestable literature which has grown up in Germany to explore the perversities of sexual abnormality."[47] In a similar vein, the *Spectator* argued that had the government not prosecuted *The Well*: "The authoress would doubtless have had many emulators and we should be confronted with a succession of books on sexual abnormality, *as is the case elsewhere*."[48] For those who knew where to look, the works of Émile Zola, Charles Baudelaire, Marcel Proust, and Colette, or the German writer Frank Wedekind were as useful as the more esoteric volumes of sexology, as seen in a reading list compiled by Patricia Preece.[49] However, the attraction of sexual science for some lesbian writers was unique for it seemed to hold prestige and a certain legitimacy or authority that could be appropriated for other literary agendas.

In chapter 6 ("Portrait of a Sapphist? Fixing the Frame of Reference"), I turn to the creative use of photography by artists such as Hall and Gluck. If such photographs had been suggestive of lesbianism prior to the publicity arising from the trial of *The Well*, as some have argued, it is extremely unlikely that these images would have been circulated so extensively in the print media. Instead, I believe that photography became an exciting and modern site of self-imaging for these women eager to exploit its capabilities for political agendas or for self-promotion. In any event, the camera's allure for these photographic subjects was short-lived, as control over the dissemination of the image proved to be a slippery affair, ultimately leading to a fixed image beyond the control of the sitter.

As each of the key terms in this study's subtitle (*The Origins of a Modern English Lesbian Culture*) suggests, my approach constitutes a new direction in lesbian historiography by its insistence on a particularized national context and temporality in interrogating anew a range of myths long accepted without question (and still in circulation) concerning, to cite only a few, the extent of homophobia in the 1920s, or the strategic deployment of sexology against sexual minorities, or the rigidity of certain cultural codes to denote lesbianism in public culture.[50] Sapphic modernity in the 1920s—as "a quality of social experience"—constituted, for some Sapphists, not a cultural condition so much as a destination, a new and better world, a coveted end point; however, modernity's emancipatory impulses were neither permanent nor substantial.[51] In the end, the aperture of social and cultural experimentation that modernity facilitated for lesbians such as Hall in the decade preceding the obscenity trial was illusory and ephemeral. Henceforth Hall's name would become the byword for a cultural figure far more threatening than the modern woman; as with Wilde, so too with Hall: "The parts were there already, and were being combined. . . . But, at this point, a distinctive possibility cohered, far more clearly, and for far more people."[52] What distances us from cultural perceptions of such relationships in the 1920s is that we no longer find tenable some of the options available to readers of that time, especially when the women in question appear to us today as "obviously" mannish and/or lesbian. After 1928 Hall's fashioning of chic modernity, published in press reports everywhere, her daring in troubling the conventions of gender, and her powerful literary representation of the female sexual invert would coalesce into a "brilliantly precise image," the classic iconic type of the mannish lesbian.

Fashioning
Sapphism

One

The Mythic Moral Panic: Radclyffe Hall and the New Genealogy

I

The moral panic crystallizes widespread fears and anxieties, and often deals with them not by seeking the real causes of the problems and conditions which they demonstrate but by displacing them on to "Folk Devils" in an identified social group (often the "immoral" or "degenerate"). Sexuality has had a peculiar centrality in such panics, and sexual "deviants" have been omnipresent scapegoats.
—*Jeffrey Weeks*, Sex, Politics, and Society

I would rather give a healthy boy or a healthy girl a phial of prussic acid than this novel. Poison kills the body, but moral poison kills the soul.
—*James Douglas*, Sunday Express, *August 19, 1928*[1]

AT THE END of July 1928 Radclyffe Hall's *The Well of Loneliness*, the first "long and very serious novel entirely upon the subject of sexual inversion" according to its author, appeared in bookshops and lending libraries throughout Britain.[2] In a matter of weeks the largely favorable response by sober reviewers was overshadowed by the journalist James Douglas's sensationalizing editorial in the *Sunday Express* condemning the propagandistic aims of Hall's project and demanding the novel's suppression "without delay." The home secretary, Sir William Joynson-Hicks, entirely agreed with Douglas's estimation and instructed the Department of Public Prosecutions to initiate legal proceedings against the novel. In November the presiding magistrate, Sir Chartres Biron, pronounced the book obscene in a trial so highly publicized that *The Well of Loneliness* was virtually guaranteed a place in literary history.

Douglas's editorial and the subsequent chain of events appear to combine all the classic elements of moral panic that, as defined by Stan Cohen, occurs from time to time as individuals or a group of individuals "become defined as a threat to societal values and interests; [their] nature is presented in a stylized and stereotypical fashion by the mass media; the moral barricades are manned by editors, bishops and politicians and other right-thinking people; socially accredited experts pronounce their diagnoses and solutions; ways of coping are evolved, or (more often) resorted to."[3] In Douglas we have such a "right-thinking" editor of a major national newspaper who found in Hall's project a representation of a group of individuals whose alleged proliferation posed a significant threat, or in his terms, a "plague stalking shamelessly through great social assemblies." Douglas's allegation had plenty of support—sexologists and others had made similar claims since the closing decades of the nineteenth century; according to Ellis, "many observers—in America, in France, in Germany, and in England—[had stated] that homosexuality is increasing among women."[4] Some so-called experts attributed the increase of lesbianism to the changes in and strains of the modern world: feminism and the women's movement had worked to "masculinize" women, while female independence meant independence from men and the restrictions of marriage. The First World War had brought even more opportunities for female intrusion into the masculine sphere, especially for middle-class women, which further intensified anxieties, especially among professionals in medicine, that lesbianism had, as a 1918 letter to the medical journal the *Lancet* phrased it, "been on the increase of late years."[5] Douglas also seemed to conjure up a familiar stereotype of homosexual behavior when he claimed that the practitioners of these "most loathsome vices" deliberately "flaunt themselves in public places." His editorial appealed to all right-thinking people to "strike down the armies of evil" and charged that "if Christianity does not destroy this doctrine, then this doctrine will destroy it." We know that at least a handful of politicians and government officials were attentive to Douglas's diagnosis of this "contagion" and agreed with his recommendation for a cure: homosexual propaganda, he exhorted, must be banished "from our bookshops and our libraries" and *The Well* "must at once be withdrawn." Douglas issued a wake-up call to the nation when he famously professed his preference to offer young people "prussic acid" rather than Hall's novel on the grounds that "poison kills the body, but moral poison kills the soul."

Nearly every analysis of the reception of Hall's novel or account of the subsequent trial features this choice "poison" passage by the editor of the *Sunday Express* to impress upon readers the intense hatred or fear of lesbianism in the late 1920s and to confirm the extent of moral panic over the encroaching lesbian threat. Critics invoke the "poison" extract to invite readers to ponder what sort of culture would find in prussic acid an appealing metaphorical alternative to the literary representation of same-sex desire between women. Douglas's editorial, which associates female homosexuality with synonyms of disease ("contamination," "degeneracy," "pestilence," "plague," "contagion," "putrification," "leprosy,"), is cited again and again to illustrate not how a single newspaper spearheaded a tendentious campaign against one particular novel but rather how English society in the decade after the First World War had come to regard the female "sexual invert" as heinously unnatural, sinful, and disgusting. Whether critical discussion focuses on the novel, the trial, the intricacies of the 1857 Obscene Publications Act under which the novel was prosecuted, or even Hall herself, just as Douglas believed it was "the duty of the critic" to alert the British public to the potential "contamination and corruption of English fiction," so too is it incumbent on contemporary commentators to reiterate dutifully how Douglas subjected *The Well* to the "prussic acid" test; as critic Jean Radford observes, "almost all the subsequent editions [of the novel] refer back to that moment—the moment when Douglas . . . said he'd 'rather give a healthy boy or girl a phial of prussic acid than this novel.' "[6] However, if the Douglas critique is as integral to a proper understanding of the novel's reception as critics generally claim, and if the latter half of 1928 marked a crucial shift in lesbian visibility, we might expect to find a fuller reading of the editorial's political agenda, or information on Douglas's own cultural status, or an assessment of the impact of print media in lesbian literary production in the postwar era. Instead, while the Douglas quotation appears with regularity, analysis of the circumstances surrounding the editorial's publication is rare, even among those cultural historians and literary critics attuned to regarding newspaper articles as themselves highly mediated. The editorial, for them, quite simply represents moral panic.

This chapter questions the commonly held view that Douglas's attack on *The Well* represents a vivid example of widespread hysterical homophobia, aggravated by feminist successes in the political arena. To be sure, the timing of the publication could not have been worse: the fallout of antisuffrage sentiment in the *Express* and other newspapers had only just begun to abate. Since 1918 (when women over thirty had been given the vote in parliamentary elections), the press (especially the *Daily Express* and *Daily Mail*) had focused public attention on what it dubbed the "flapper vote," in an effort to prevent an extension of the franchise to women between the ages of twenty-one and thirty. For years readers were bombarded with dire predictions about the damaging effects of granting suffrage to such irresponsible, independent, and masculinized women and were entertained with numerous articles on issues relating to women, such as female sexuality, womanhood, and motherhood.[7] In the spring of 1928, when the Representation of the People Equal Franchise Bill (allowing women to vote on the same basis as men) received parliamentary approval, it became clear to segments of the press that their "campaign against the flapper had failed."[8] Douglas's skillful management of his *Sunday Express* readers, some critics speculate, may have been part of a larger agenda to shift the direction of press hostility from flappers to lesbians, an even more dangerous manifestation of deviance. As literary critic Joseph Bristow writes: "Undoubtedly, the lesbian embodied a signal threat to a culture that was more and more unsettled by women's demands for autonomy."[9] Recent critics have typically viewed Douglas's editorial not as aberrant or opportunistic but as the most vociferous and vitriolic voice among a unified national press that inflamed homophobia across class boundaries, as is evident, for instance, in Bristow's assertion that "the very suggestion of lesbian sexuality was enough to unleash remarkable animosity from the British press, notably in the reactionary *Sunday Express*. . . . The ferocious public response assuredly bore out the moral message of [Hall's] novel— that lesbians would be martyred in British society." Biographer Diana Souhami also speaks of Douglas's "bigotry" in relation to the "homophobia the book uncovered in the ruling class, the men of the establishment, the government that made the rules, the judiciary that enforced them, the press that disseminated them."[10] Such a string of collectivities—"the British press," "public response," "British society," "ruling class," "establishment," "government," and "judiciary"—suggests that dissident voices rarely or ineffectually challenged a 1920s version of a moral majority. As a result, the opinions of what might be characterized as the more liberal contingent are unrepresented, even though the novel was reviewed "generously in such journals as the *Times* [*Literary Supplement*], and had been received without a flutter of protest by the majority of the subscription libraries."[11]

The Douglas editorial, with its resonant acid sound bite, is cited with such frequency because it led ultimately to a successful legal action to ban the book in Britain for decades and because it succinctly encapsulates what today's observers want to argue about the reception of Hall's novel. The emphatic, unequivocal, and "by-now-famous"—not to mention, famously misquoted— statement works easily as a kind of shorthand to dramatize the fierce homophobia apparently so pervasive in 1928 in the press, government, and legal system.[12] But does the editorial represent homophobia pure and simple, or was the editorial aiming for something else, or for something more than, as historian Deirdre Beddoe claims, encouraging "hostility toward lesbianism"?[13] When critics evoke the famous "poison" passage in a vacuum without specifying whether or not Douglas was viewed by his peers as an esteemed journalist, a crank, a shrewd opportunist, or a puritanical fanatic—or worse, when critics deploy the Douglas statement as a kind of transparent gauge to assess purported homophobia—our understanding of popular attitudes toward the lesbian, lesbianism, and the reception of Hall's novel in the 1920s is skewed or impoverished.[14] Instead, for the modern reader, all the components of the *Sunday Express*'s enterprising fabrication—the front-page hook, the damning editorial, and the well-chosen illustration of Hall—coalesce in such a way as to embody, with concision and convenience, several of the potent and contradictory myths generations of critics have continually recirculated about the status of the lesbian in English society at this time: that the "lesbian" was a coherent identifiable category; or that homophobia was rampant; or even that until the publication of Hall's novel, lesbianism was unspeakable or unthinkable. As literary critic Ellen Bayuk Rosenman puts it: "The obscenity trial in 1928 of Radclyffe Hall's lesbian novel . . . provided . . . a powerful example of the social climate. . . . Society might be ready to read and reward women writers, but lesbianism remained almost literally unspeakable."[15] Thanks to Douglas's overblown invective such cultural myths continue to haunt our own reading of this cultural moment.

To challenge these myths I first survey in greater detail the literary reviews of *The Well of Loneliness prior* to and *after* the Douglas attack to propose that the infamous "poison" quotation may itself be the aberration. Most reviewers were generally united in their sympathetic attitudes toward lesbianism and, even when critical of the tendentiousness of Hall's project, dealt with its subject matter as simply another aspect of the novel, such as characterization or narrative form. Critical response tended to be framed more by the struggle between two key constituencies—highbrow and middlebrow—or by discussions of the aesthetic tensions between "art" and "propaganda" than by the topic of lesbianism. As one reviewer put it, *The Well* was "likely to raise a different set of issues, foreign to aesthetics and outside the province of this report."[16] Hall's introduction of a political agenda, some feared, clouded literary judgment and left her project irremediably bogged down "by sentiment and by sectarian passion" (314). Politics, for these readers, negated aesthetics. An examination of the literary reviews of *The Well* calls into question the myth that Hall and her novel became subject to a backlash and shows that, on the contrary, the critical establishment was generally fair and even-tempered and, most remarkably perhaps, that the handful of reviews published after the Douglas editorial were largely unaffected by the tirade.[17]

After putting Douglas in his place, so to speak, and exploring the motivations underlying the *Express*'s actions, I look to the editorial's impact to see if other newspapers were eager to join the bandwagon, as some have suggested. Finally, I discuss lesbian visibility to propose that our own critical overinvestment in certain pertinacious myths concerning the reception of the novel or the supposed increase of lesbianism in these years plays too conveniently into the great "mythic moral panic" over the alleged lesbian threat of the 1920s. My close examination of the Douglas editorial neatly illustrates in microcosm a much larger point I make throughout the study about the risks we assume not simply in extracting a passage or episode for critical convenience but in failing to read even the most significant cultural events in a specific historical context.

II

I have read The Well of Loneliness *with great interest because—apart from its fine qualities as a novel by a writer of accomplished art—it possesses a notable psychological and sociological significance. So far as I know, it is the first English novel which presents, in a completely faithful and uncompromising form, one particular aspect of sexual life as it exists among us today. The relation of certain people—who, while different from their fellow human beings, are sometimes of the highest character and the finest aptitudes—to the often hostile society in which they move, presents difficult and still unresolved problems.*
—Havelock Ellis, "Commentary," The Well of Loneliness

ELLIS'S "COMMENTARY"—technically, the first critical response to *The Well of Loneliness*—is such an opaque and evasive endorsement of Hall's project that the uninformed reader might well wonder what the novel is about. The lack of specificity was the result of editorial tampering on the part of the novel's publisher, Jonathan Cape, whose intervention represents the first instance in *The Well*'s publication history where a professional opinion of the novel was deployed to serve multiple and sometimes contradictory purposes and agendas. In reworking certain key passages of Ellis's original, Cape took substantial liberties and effectively watered down the epistemological accuracy that is the hallmark of sexological methodology, a field obsessed with subtle variation and degree. What Ellis initially described as "various aspects of sexual inversion" was scaled back to "an aspect of sexual inversion" because Cape thought the phrasing could be construed to include male homosexuality, which was a criminal offense.[18] Cape later expunged any reference to "inversion," a term he may have thought too bold or clinically precise, and replaced it with a phrase so vague as to be practically meaningless: "one particular aspect of sexual life." This change of phrase was accompanied by an equally oblique reference not to inverts or homosexuals but to "certain people." The final version, one that prefigures later reductive readings, thus achieved little more than an anodyne echo of the plea embodied in the novel itself: even if "certain people" are different, they nevertheless deserve understanding from a "hostile society."

An intelligent and savvy publisher, Cape appreciated the commercial value of a statement by a medical expert of Ellis's stature but intervened to ensure that the wording—innocuous and bland—would interest readers without causing the slightest offense.[19] (Ellis himself later indicated privately to the lesbian writer Bryher that he found Hall's novel "a remarkable book by its frank recognition of inversion, but otherwise perfectly respectable and conventional. Not a word that anyone could object to."[20]) Ellis's participation had the desired effect: nearly half of the reviews mention Ellis, although sometimes to protest that the novel, good in its own right, did not require the testimony of the famous sexologist. For example, a glowing piece in the *Morning Post*, the paper of choice for "the retired senior officer and his family," announced: "There can be nothing but respect and admiration for the author's handling of [the theme]. Mr. Havelock Ellis's brief commentary was not required to establish its challenge, which from the first page emerges with a frankness free of offence."[21] The "most important literary periodical," the *Times Literary Supplement*, also objected to the jarring effect of a scientific preface and criticized Ellis's involvement: "*The Well of Loneliness* is a novel, and we propose to treat it as such. We therefore rather regret that it should have been thought necessary to insert at the beginning a 'commentary' by Mr. Havelock Ellis."[22] While the unusual combination of the "scientific" and the "literary" struck some as inappropriate, unlike Douglas, these reviewers did not use the occasion to dismiss sexology as a "pseudo-scientific" and "terrible doctrine." The insertion of Ellis's affirmation of Hall's "faithful and uncompromising" negotiation of sexology, although an unwelcome distraction for the *TLS* and others, nevertheless alerted the literary establishment from page one that the long novel was, in certain respects, extraordinary.

Cape was fully aware that the subject of Hall's novel might be "called into question," as he put it, and therefore proceeded with caution.[23] The large advertisements promoting *The Well* avoided its subject matter and instead noted prominently that Hall's last novel, *Adam's Breed* (1926), had received the Prix Femina Vie Heureuse-Bookman and the James Tait Black Memorial Prize (the only other previous winner of both awards was E. M. Forster for his 1924 *A Passage to India*). The volume's physical appearance and high price worked in tandem to establish the project's credentials as serious and significant: the novel "was produced in a large format, in sombre black binding with a plain wrapper, and priced at fifteen shillings, twice the average price for a new novel. . . . Review copies were sent only to the serious newspapers and weekly journals." Cape pitched the publicity, pricing and reviews not to Hall's usual middlebrow following but to a more highbrow readership—a strategy that was, initially anyway, successful: between July 27 (the date of publication) and August 19 (the date of the Douglas editorial) the novel was reviewed in fourteen of the so-called quality newspapers and journals: "serious and authoritative critics . . . commended it both for its high-minded sincerity and for its literary quality."[24] The Douglas editorial looms so large in most critical discussions of the novel's initial reception that the tenor of these early reviews has been eclipsed. True enough, some thought *The Well* "far less accomplished than her previous novels," but it is misleading to suggest that "in contemporary reviews of *The Well* and in private comment by her contemporaries, it was considered a pious and dreary book."[25] The novelist L. P. Hartley, for instance, discovered in *The Well* "passages of great force and beauty," while Leonard Woolf mentioned Hall's "very considerable gifts for novel writing."[26] The *Daily Telegraph* described the book as "truly remarkable": "It is remarkable in the first place as a work of art finely conceived and finely written. Secondly, it is remarkable as dealing with an aspect of abnormal life seldom or never presented in English fiction—certainly never with such unreserved frankness."[27] The writer Ethel Mannin, who found the book "profoundly moving and beautiful, a delicate and lovely and sensitive piece of work," pointed out that the novel "was selling . . . on the strength of the author's previous reputation and an almost *unanimously eulogistic press*."[28] The startling intervention of the *Sunday Express* has made it difficult to recuperate that short period of time when both professional critics and the public were able to judge the novel on its literary merits alone. As a result, as Margaret Lawrence lamented, Hall became "an example of the inability of the public, even of the reading public, to hold more than one idea about one writer. . . . [*The Well*] doomed her to be remembered in her own time only as a student of sexual inversion. All the beauty and power of her prose was, in general, lost."[29]

In the interregnum between *The Well*'s publication and the editorial, some of the most prominent literary journals, including the *Nation*, the *Saturday*

Review, and the *TLS*, and many respected and influential critics, such as Hartley, Woolf, and Arnold Bennett, assiduously reviewed the novel, recognized the "danger, where a highly controversial subject is being considered, that the essential qualities of a work may be overlooked," and endeavored to assess the literary qualities in a fair and balanced manner; the novel's open discussion of lesbianism never interfered with the task at hand.[30] An early commentator attributed this new sophistication in the handling of the subject of lesbianism to "an interesting development in fiction writing of late years . . . the large influx of young women, many fresh from college . . . are apt to discuss phases of sexual life, and some do not even hesitate to introduce a slight flavor of Lesbianism."[31] When the *Glasgow Herald* expressed shock it was not, as we might expect, with the subject but with Hall's uncharacteristic "lamentable inattention to style."[32] All fourteen reviews prior to August 19 identified the novel's literary strengths *and* weaknesses; some praised Hall's "beauty of style and delicate, yet vivid, presentation of character and mood," while others found the narrative structure "formless" and "chaotic," or complained of Hall's "tendency to preach."[33] Bennett thought that, although the novel was "disfigured by loose writing and marred by loose construction . . . [it] nevertheless does hold you. It is honest, convincing, and extremely courageous."[34] That the novel attracted Bennett's attention was an impressive coup in the first place for the author and publisher because Bennett had the "reputation as a maker of 'best sellers.' "[35]

Neither Bennett nor Woolf—representing, respectively, the literary middle and highbrow—had read any of Hall's previous work, even though her last novel had won prestigious literary prizes.[36] Woolf seems to have been drawn to the book because of its "extremely interesting" topic, while Bennett admits his interest was piqued by the Ellis commentary: "I ought to have guessed [the novel's] subject. It is Havelock Ellis, the essayist, to whom I am indebted for the enlargement of my outlook."[37] The novel's success in enticing reviewers from such a broad spectrum of the literary establishment was quite unusual, for it constituted a crossing over of discrete literary boundaries, or put more pugnaciously, a transgressing of lines drawn in what Virginia Woolf described as the "Battle of the Brows."[38] In her sophisticated analysis of English literary culture, Q. D. Leavis observed: "A novel received with unqualified enthusiasm in a lowbrow paper will be coolly treated by the middlebrow and contemptuously dismissed if mentioned at all by the highbrow Press; the kind of book that the middlebrow Press will admire wholeheartedly the highbrow reviewer will diagnose as pernicious; each has a following that forms a different level of public."[39] In the 1920s individual authors belonged to these distinctly separate, if not hostile, literary and inter-

pretive communities and, like the distinctions of the class system, the boundaries were seldom breached; as critic Anthea Trodd explains, "the categorization of writing by heights of brow between the wars was not simply a
media pastime; it was a means by which the literary world attempted to
interpret the changes which had taken place in the expanding and frag-
menting market."[40] Such categorization accounts for some of the mixed
responses to Hall's novel, a point feminist literary critics often overlook.

When Virginia Woolf famously declared, "No one has read [Hall's] book,"
she meant, of course, no one in her circle because, as sales figures indicate,
before the ban *The Well*'s readership was immense; it included the prolific
middlebrow writer and lesbian Naomi Jacob, who had the book on order and
received it on the first day of publication: "I read it with deep interest, and
found its sincerity very touching and fine."[41] When the initial print run (fifteen hundred copies) quickly sold out, Cape doubled that number for the second impression because, after Douglas's piece, orders for Hall's novel poured
in. By the time Joynson-Hicks initiated proceedings, about five thousand
copies "were in circulation, or available from shops and libraries."[42] Thus literary critic Gillian Whitlock is only partially correct when she speculates that
Woolf's comment suggested "the novel lacked literary merit"; Woolf meant—
more precisely—the novel lacked merit from a highbrow modernist perspective.[43] Woolf's pronouncement that *The Well* was "lukewarm and neither one
thing or the other" confirms her sense of it as thoroughly middlebrow, a phrase
fully compliant with Woolf's own definition of the term: one "who ambles and
saunters now on this side of the hedge, now on that, in pursuit of no single
object, neither art itself nor life itself, but both mixed indistinguishably."[44] Of
course, the positioning of individual writers within "brow culture" was—and
still is—a highly subjective and slippery business, but we know that Woolf
proudly claimed highbrow membership and revealed her animus toward all
things middlebrow in her ironic comment: "I often ask my friends the low-
brows . . . why it is that while we, the highbrows, never buy a middlebrow
book, or go to a middlebrow lecture, or read, unless we are paid for doing so,
a middlebrow review, they, on the contrary, take these middlebrow activities
so seriously?" (157). Woolf called on the high and low to "band together to
exterminate a pest which is the bane of all thinking and living"; for Woolf, the
detestable middlebrows were "people, I confess, that I seldom regard with
entire cordiality" (159; 155). Rosenman perceptively accounts for Woolf's disapproval of *The Well* in terms of literary style ("she found it conventional,
even old-fashioned"), but it is important to note that Woolf's uncordial comments (a "meritorious dull book" that was "pale, tepid, vapid") were directed

as much at middlebrow literary culture as a whole as at *The Well* and its representation of lesbianism.[45]

The depth of the chasm between the two literary spheres in which Woolf and Hall moved can be gauged in their differing responses to winning the Femina Prize back to back: Hall in 1927 for *Adam's Breed* and Woolf the following year for *To the Lighthouse*. Biographer Hermione Lee describes Woolf's reaction to the prize as ambivalent:

> By an irony of literary history, she took part, just before the proofs of *Orlando* arrived, in the sort of establishment prize-giving which was one of the book's targets of satire. . . . She called it . . . her "dog show prize," though her scornful embarrassment did not quite disguise some pride. . . . She thought it "a very shoddy affair, with a distinct Pen-Club atmosphere about it."[46]

Hall, on the other hand, regarded her prize as a sign that she had come of age as a writer: "Isn't it amusing," she earlier confided to a cousin, "that I should have become quite a well known writer? I sometimes cannot understand it myself. But there it is, it has certainly come to pass."[47] When the prize results were announced, Hall's partner Una, Lady Troubridge, noted in her diary that "many messages, letters & c[ongratulations] about Femina" had been sent to Holland Street, where the couple lived on the edge of London's South Kensington.[48] Ironically, the ceremony for the Femina Prize took place at the Institut Français, also in South Kensington, an area Woolf ridiculed as the home territory of the "middlebrows": "They do not live in Bloomsbury which is on high ground; nor in Chelsea which is on low ground. Since they must live somewhere presumably, they live perhaps in South Kensington, which is betwixt and between."[49]

Equally offensive to Woolf was the fact that middlebrows often made money out of their literary pursuits. Woolf rarely earned large sums from royalties generated by her novels because her books were not best-sellers; as historian Ross McKibbin notes, "the great mass of the English people were unmoved, or unmoved directly, by the culture of the country's intellectual elites. . . . High culture was not their culture."[50] *Orlando* proved an exception: its large middlebrow readership was no doubt surprised to discover that the work of a writer previously regarded as off limits was suddenly and delightfully accessible and, as a result of such unexpected success, Woolf enjoyed royalties on an unprecedented scale. Compared with sales of *To the Lighthouse* ("3,873 copies in the first year"), *Orlando*'s sales figures ("8,104 copies in the first six months") most closely approximate Hall's, which were consistently strong; *Adam's Breed* sold about 9,400 copies in the first three months of publication.[51] In the long run, however, "it was the middlebrows who lost out. The works of Woolf are still in print; so are those of [lowbrows such as Agatha] Christie . . . [and] Georgette Heyer, but the middlebrows have not survived so well."[52] Had Hall never written about lesbianism in *The Well of Loneliness*, or had the Home Office chosen instead to ignore it, few readers today would probably recognize her name—*The Well* is the only one of her eight published works to remain continually in print. The explosive topic of the novel effectively turned Hall into a one-book author and stole from her the "literary."

Anticipating that *The Well*'s frank exploration of inversion was bound to attract attention, early reviewers warned their readers that the topic might not suit everyone's taste. Still, critics strongly urged readers to keep an open mind because the failure or inability to deal with this important and timely topic would constitute a loss. I. A. R. Wylie, herself a lesbian, novelist, and close friend of Hall's, divided potential readers into two groups, "those who insist that life as a whole is not a fit subject for nice-minded people to write or think about and those who believe that most of our troubles spring from our refusal to look ourselves honestly in the face."[53] With considerable boldness and panache in light of her own sexual identity, Wylie lavishly commended the novel to "those who care for truth and who believe that somehow or other 'we are all God's chi'un,'" and concluded with a statement impressive in terms of its prescience and accuracy: "the reward of [Hall's qualities of courage and honesty] is uncertain, and it will be interesting to watch the reception of this daring study. If it is received as it was written, it will be something of a landmark in the history of human development." Wylie well understood the dangers that lay in store for a book on such a topic, as did Richard King whose long review in the *Tatler*, which described the novel as "a work of considerable art," is the most sensitive to potential homophobia; in an audacious challenge to his society-conscious readers King spoke of the "huge army of the narrow-minded" and asserted that "only the bigoted and the foolish seek to ignore an aspect of life which is as undeniable a fact as any concrete thing."[54] Like Wylie, he broke readers into two camps: "You will either be interested by [the novel], or peradventure it will make you too furious and disgusted to do more than throw the book in the fire. We will leave it at that." King gloomily acknowledged that "the majority delight in trampling under their feet the people whose nature they cannot understand, no matter how spiritually lofty, how mentally brilliant, how pitiful." This sympathetic review was the last to appear before Douglas abruptly shifted the critical framework from the narrow world of the literati to an entirely different group, some of whom had an entirely different agenda.

The most obvious and immediate result of the *Express*'s intervention was that all future critical discussion of the novel could not but engage with or refer to the controversy. For instance, before August 19 Hall's representation of the childhood of the protagonist, Stephen ("the first 150 pages") was regarded as "good," but after the crucial date *Life and Letters* found that same "episode of the story . . . comparatively restrained and *non-controversial*": the measuring stick no longer related solely to the art of the novel but to the manner in which the subject of lesbianism was negotiated.[55] Likewise, in October 1928 the *British Journal of Inebriety* generously described Hall's handling of a "poignant situation" as "vividly portrayed with real insight and without offence," but then strenuously exhorted their (professional) readers not merely to "consider" the novel but to "consider [it] *without prejudice*."[56] In a journal devoted primarily to health issues, the short review noted incongruously that Hall, an award-winning author and "enthusiastic dog-breeder," "is a woman of exceptional powers." Thus it was thought all the more regrettable and disturbing that her "remarkable" novel should become subject to government censorship, making "it increasingly difficult in the future for authors and publishers to deal with certain medico-sociological problems in works of fiction." Like other reviews produced *after* the Douglas editorial, the *British Journal of Inebriety* urges readers not to turn away from a book that is "without offence."

Another by-product of the *Express* attack was the tendency among reviewers to approach the text not as a new work of fiction by a popular writer but as a potentially titillating novel at the center of a growing controversy. After all, some readers may have reasoned, if a ban for obscene libel was in the offing, Hall's protagonist must be fast-living, hard-drinking, foul-mouthed, sexually promiscuous, or a combination of all of the above; to their disappointment, Stephen Gordon was an honorable upper-class English-woman who desired a quiet life with her female companion among the respectable county set. *The Well*, it seemed, was all too tasteful. As a result of the shift in inflated expectations arising from the hype, some critics who imagined the narrative to be more shocking or graphic expressed surprise or dissatisfaction that it was only "a sadly ordinary novel."[57] In the October issue of *Life and Letters* the anonymous reviewer speculated that if one were to "rob Miss Radclyffe Hall of her challenging thesis . . . [*The Well*] would quite naturally slip back into the category to which it belongs; it would rank, that is to say, as a simple, pleasantly written love-story with an unhappy ending."[58] In a discussion notably flippant and irascible, newspaper critic

W. R. Gordon observed that although Hall's protagonist may have had "a passion for a member of her own sex," the only discernible obscenity was the author's audacity in presenting Stephen—a woman with no "serious grievances against society"—as a figure of pity.[59] Some earlier critics had thought Hall's plea irksome in certain respects, but when Douglas mentioned "martyrdom" in referring to the novel's primary objective ("a seductive and insidious piece of special pleading designed to display perverted decadence as a martyrdom inflicted upon these outcasts by a cruel society"), others followed suit. Thus Gordon found *The Well* objectionable because "it falsifies realities, and presents as a martyr a woman in the grip of a vice."[60] In a rare class-based critique, Gordon concluded that Stephen's suffering was no different from that of any other human being because "loneliness is the human lot," and indeed, as a member of the upper classes, Stephen was better off than many others: "There is no trace of persecution. She collected her dividends regularly. She lived as she pleased."[61]

Finally, two post-Douglas reviews exhibited a new attentiveness to clothing and personal habits, indicating a heightened curiosity about the physical appearance of such women. A couple of early reviews mentioned Stephen's parents' desire for a son, Stephen's personal qualities ("athletic, clever, and scholarly"), or her aversion to men, but Stephen's manner of dress never came under discussion.[62] Suddenly, *Life and Letters*, which insisted on referring to the protagonist as "he," professed to find tedious the novel's sartorial detail: "We could have preferred a briefer account of the inessential part of the hero's life, the shirts, ties, underclothes he bought and the way he decorated his rooms."[63] Yet, as the reviewer fully recognized, the novel is no ordinary heterosexual love story, and what in part signifies that difference is the preference of the "hero-heroine" for masculine clothing. In protesting too much, the reviewer reveals not boredom with Hall's "shirted and tailored" protagonist but fascination. The complex relationship between clothing and sexuality had become a source of unease, as seen in Gordon's observation about the way in which Stephen "liked wearing knickerbockers better than skirts, riding astride and screwing her hair well out of her eyes. . . . Exaggerating the importance of clothes in a thoroughly feminine fashion, she dresses herself in clothes of masculine character."[64] Hall's description of Stephen's wardrobe forces Gordon to scrutinize the importance of clothing in a new way by associating sartorial preferences with a particular (deviant) sexuality—in what Douglas had succinctly called a "display [of] perverted decadence."

The *Sunday Express* editor may have been energetic and clever, but did he engineer a genuine moral crusade or a cynical newspaper stunt? Douglas knew full well how to pull out all the stops to achieve a desired effect: "If anybody were ever to compile an Anthology of Overstatement," the writer Beverley Nichols observed, "one sentence in Douglas's article [on Hall's novel] would deserve a page to itself."[65] Nichols may be giving Douglas too much credit though, for measured against some of his other writing, the tone of *The Well of Loneliness* editorial seems comparatively moderate. An earlier attack against so-called "modern sex novelists," for instance, reveals that his lambasting of *The Well* was not the exception but rather typified Douglas's "bombastic . . . turgidly rhetorical style," to borrow Nichols's terms. This same example also demonstrates Douglas's penchant for tropes of bodily disease, with the critic as moral exterminator:

Vermin like you are expelled from the schools when they are detected, but you are not thrown out of our drawing rooms. You crawl everywhere, and there is no insecticide with which to spray you. . . . You are the deadliest bacteria in our blood; but we have discovered no antitoxin that prevents you from multiplying. . . . Not long ago I retched over a novel by a female procuress which explored abysmal horrors that hitherto have been the monopoly of psycho-analysis. Sweet girl graduates read it and discussed its esoteric abominations and fetid mysteries. . . . In every degenerate era of history parasites like you have appeared. You are the lice of decadence.[66]

Douglas's unrestrained invective against the authors of so-called sex novels raises name-calling to a high art: "Mimes, Cads, Bounders, Sniggerers, Innuendists, Pornocrats, Garbage Mongers, Purveyors of Pruriency, Vendors of Vice, Sewer Rats, Carrion Crows, Maggots of Decadence, Hookworms of Salacity, Literary Lepers and Yahoos." The editor displayed an uncanny talent for scraping the bottom of the cultural reservoir to spin out elaborate, sensational fulminations but, as his engagement with modern sex novelists suggests, he did not require a topic as drastic as homosexuality to set him off.

Such fanaticism flies in the face of a skeptical fellow member of the Fleet Street profession, J. C. Cannell, who protested: "I have never met a journalist who believed anything with strong conviction. He meets so many of the political partisans. . . . He has to listen to them, endure them, and afterwards . . . he talks and laughs about them in his club or meeting-places."[67] Cannell insisted that since any journalist was so immersed in the creation of headlines, "illusions about most things are smashed and he becomes a humorous cynic. The platitudes of bishops and parsons, of statesmen and reformers do not stir him" (201). Biographer Sally Cline's juxtaposition of Hall's motives ("sincere and sensitive") with those of Douglas ("mercenary and malicious") lends further credence to the characterization of the journalist as opportunistic.[68] Yet contrary to Cannell's argument that real conviction is more inhibiting than enabling, Douglas's interest in religion and morality—ironically, like Hall's—was passionate and long-standing.[69] An exemplary "champion of the muscular Christian," a notion associated with late Victorian culture, Douglas embraced a form of Christianity that moved away from the public school ideology of " 'godliness and good learning' to a more vigorous and manly training suited to an expanding and dynamic Empire. . . . Athletic prowess took precedence over intellectual development. . . . Boys were supposed to be muscular *and* Christian, but the Christianity was adapted to suit Imperial aspirations."[70] Douglas regularly used his column in the *Sunday Express* to rant against the "degeneracy and decadence" of modern life, in the hope of reinvigorating an "essentially . . . Protestant and Puritanical renaissance," which he defined as "a movement of the mind, the soul, and the heart."[71] Well-read in contemporary fiction, Douglas drew selectively on such writers as Aldous Huxley and Katherine Mansfield but aligned himself with the "common people" against the "intellectuals." The writer John Middleton Murry knew Douglas to be "a serious moralist," and thus conjectured ironically that the August editorial must have been penned by Douglas's pet "smut-hound" while the journalist was away on holiday: "We suggest that Mr. Douglas should give a dose of prussic acid to his smut-hound, and quickly."[72] Rebecca West too could not resist poking fun at the editor's overzealous nature: Douglas, she chided lightheartedly, was "a cheerful newspaper man until he was overcome by a serious illness and was sent to a famous sanatorium, at which he was allowed no form of nourishment . . . save orange juice. He returned in perfect health but in a state of extreme moral delicacy."[73]

Souhami's unequivocal declaration that "James Douglas voiced his bigotry to sell his newspapers" may underestimate the depths of the editor's "moral delicacy"—it is more likely that Douglas's fervent sentiments happily dovetailed with the *Express*'s equally sincere desire to make money.[74] Douglas's masterful, if vicious, attacks on anything or anyone could not have been more advantageous for a newspaper intent on boosting sales during the middle of a sleepy August, the so-called "silly season."[75] The *Express* forced all other papers to scramble for their angle on the "story." With some "16 national newspapers, 21 Sundays and about 130 provincial papers" in operation after the First World War, "circulation wars were fuelled by more eye-catching layout, photographs, strip cartoons, crosswords, competitions and special offers for regular subscriptions. Newspapers set out to entertain in order to capture the largest market."[76] The war between the newspapers was noticeably intense in the latter part of 1928. As the *Tatler* observed: "The public always loves a fight and there is a lively public interest in the battle for public favor which is developing on all fronts between those two popular morning papers, 'The Daily Mail' and 'The Daily Express.' "[77] Lord Beaverbrook's *Sunday Express* was particularly notorious for its awesome range of ruthless tactics:

> It regales its readers each week with a confection of spicy gossip and piquant pictures. If some poor creature is lying in jail under sentence of death in connection with an especially lurid and sensational murder every effort will be made to obtain from him a literary contribution to the *Sunday Express*. . . . Also . . . we are presented with articles by charming actresses or noted athletes, ministers of the Church, or members of the peerage, and, in fact, by anybody who happens to be in the limelight. Finally, to give a literary flavor to this luscious *compôte*, we find thrown in from time to time, an article in which a book is violently denounced as immoral, or a "love-story of the great" recalling in flamboyant fashion the romances or sexual tragedies of famous men and women of the past.[78]

Such well-planned gimmickry proved immensely successful: the *Daily Express* could be counted among the winners in the circulation race with a rise in the number of its readers from "half a million in 1910 . . . to almost two and a half million in 1939."[79]

"Unabashedly capitalistic," the *Express* group's launch of Douglas's call for a ban of *The Well*, like so many of their other "campaigns," was a brilliantly well-managed affair that started on August 18 when the *Daily Express*

> carefully aroused public expectations by printing a sharply edited resumé of Douglas's piece which omitted the name of the novel and its author. At the same time posters and bill-boards gave wide prominence to the impending thunderbolt. That Saturday night the *Evening Standard* obligingly kept the world on tenterhooks by reproducing the *Daily Express* "teaser" word for word. The result was that, come Sunday the 19th, other newspapers were leaping [on the story] with gusto.[80]

Beneath the headline "A Book That Should Be Suppressed" followed by Douglas's "prussic acid" line set in bold face, the *Daily Express* promised readers that the editorial on Sunday would undertake not a literary review or thoughtful discussion of an "astounding new novel" by "a well-known woman writer," but a "vigorous exposure."[81] The article alleged that the "utterly degrading" novel was "devoted to a particular hideous aspect of life as it exists among us today," a topic "decent people" would regard with "unspeakable horror." Who could resist such a tantalizing buildup? That same day Douglas sent a copy of his editorial to Cape to give him fair warning of a possible controversy. On the following day the *Sunday Express*, confidently anticipating their hype would stimulate curiosity, perversely provided up-to-date information about the book's availability, with brief statements from four leading sources of books for the middlebrow readership: W. H. Smith and Sons (bookseller and library), "an official" of Mudie's Library, the head librarian of Boot's Library, and Jonathan Cape, Ltd.[82] To maximize publicity for a news item of its own making, the *Sunday Express* strategically inserted a short front-page article under three bold and titillating headlines ("Novel That Should Be Banned," "Story of Perverted Lives," and "Nauseating"), intimating mysteriously that the novel in question dealt "with a subject taboo in decent circles." On the issue's tenth page was the Douglas column with an opening line that simulated an actual review, perhaps confusing some readers: "*The Well of Loneliness* (Jonathan Cape, 15s. net) by Miss Radclyffe Hall, is a novel." Adjacent to the piece was the finishing touch: what some regarded as an especially unflattering photograph of Hall, "monstrous-looking . . . with short hair and a bow tie."[83] Where Cape had undertaken every precaution to ensure the book was discreetly and tastefully published with a look, price, and expert testimony underlining the project's sincerity, seriousness, and "science," the *Express* called for the book's withdrawal with a layout trumpeting all the relevant information concerning the publisher, the cost, and its acquisition—the silencing of homosexual propaganda, it seems, was a noisy business.

One week later, on August 26, the *Sunday Express*, evidently pleased that the "story" had taken off, denied that the attention they had given to the novel had resulted in an increase in sales of the offensive book and then distracted readers with a sampling from a few of the "hundreds of letters and telegrams" received "from all parts of the country" about "the obnoxious character of Miss Radclyffe Hall's new novel."[84] Of the nine letters printed, two chastised the newspaper for "stirring up the mud" and instigating a "slanderous attack." One correspondent wrote: "I feel it would be a grave injustice to the thousands whom you term 'moral derelicts' if your scathing criticism . . . were to go unchallenged. I am one of those individuals whom you so cruelly condemn, merely because you have no scientific knowledge." For this writer-invert, sexology was not coupled with the oppressors who condemn or stigmatize but was a powerful marker separating the ignorant from the informed. A second correspondent complained that the editor had gone too far: "This is the first time I have ever disagreed with Mr. James Douglas." This tolerant reader spoke of his willingness to "read an account of anything God allows to happen" and viewed the novel's subject as part of nature's diversity. All the remaining letters, of course, praised the paper for its bold moral stand against the "ever-growing menace" and commended the *Express* for its diligent efforts to safeguard innocent young people, but the inclusion of the two dissenting voices suggests that the selection of letters was designed to sustain the intensity of the controversy rather than simply to report public reaction to the "cause": the more urgent cause on behalf of an increase in newspaper sales was better served through the reproduction of opposing views.

If Douglas's self-righteous editorial truly represented the vox populi (one of whom thought the results of Hall's "gospel" could be seen in "our prisons and asylums"), we might reasonably expect a deluge of similar letters addressed to other editors and an eagerness on the part of competing newspapers to leap on what biographer Michael Baker calls "the unstoppable *Express* bandwagon."[85] An examination of a range of major newspapers and journals, however, demonstrates that few members of the public felt strongly enough about the issue to voice their opinion, and that those who did tended to be less than sympathetic toward the editor: "Mr. Douglas addresses a public . . . with an ear for superlatives and little regard for reticence, and he writes with success in the style that is popular in the ring round the journalistic soap-box."[86] Most newspaper editors were also quick to challenge Douglas's motives, and one of the first, Arnold Dawson of the *Daily Herald* and *Clarion*, wrote, "It is of vital importance that stunt newspapers and the stunt journalists and publicists who contribute to them should not be allowed to stifle and suppress serious literature."[87] Branding the editorial "abusive and hysterical" Dawson questioned, "Could fatuity go further? In the first place, who is likely to give a boy or a girl this book? In the second place, what boy or girl would be likely to read it? In the third place, if a boy or girl did read it what would they find of an exciting or inflammatory character?"[88] By taking the *Sunday Express* editor at his word, Dawson effectively deflated Douglas's rhetoric and at the same time dramatized the vacuity of his outlandish preference for prussic acid. In the *New Statesman*, editor Raymond Mortimer also launched a testy protest "in the name of decent journalism and all decent journalists" and angrily complained that Douglas's attack was "indecent, and from the standpoint of honorable journalism, disreputable."[89] Mortimer denounced Douglas's "hysterical hypocrisy," pointing out that "Mr. Douglas gave the book a flaring advertisement, introducing it to hundreds of thousands of readers who would never otherwise of [sic] heard of it."[90]

If Douglas had really cared about his readers' innocence, other editorials argued, he would have brought the objectionable book to the attention of the Home Office quietly and without sensation. In this way, the *Yorkshire Post* conjectured, the *Express* would have circumvented the "storm of publicity" that only ensured the novel "an immediate 'succès de scandale.' "[91] The *Nation* surmised pragmatically that the *Express*'s primary motivation was the difficulty in obtaining "good copy . . . at this season," and found deeply disturbing the precedent set in the government's response to a newspaper editor's call for suppression of a "serious" book.[92] Any book, even one by "a writer of refinement and distinction," "weightily prefaced" by a medical authority, and "favorably reviewed," could now be attacked by an editor keen for a palpable hit or "a successful 'stunt.' " With the exception of one or two tabloids such as the *People* or the *Sunday Chronicle*, both of which covered the controversy only briefly, "the British press" did not exude "animosity" toward *The Well*—on the contrary, most major newspapers and journals were largely sympathetic either to Hall's predicament or to her right as an author to publish without legal hindrance.[93] Neither the topic of lesbian sexuality in general, nor Hall's novel in particular, nor the controversy over the banning of that novel generated the backlash against Hall or lesbians some critics have claimed; instead, most editors condemned the *Express*'s handling of Douglas's rhetoric of outrage, identified it as "stunt journalism," and exposed the hyperbole for what it was: flat and empty.[94]

III

In my view this book would tend to corrupt the minds of young persons if it fell into their hands and its sale is undesirable. . . . My view . . . is that there would be a reasonable prospect of a conviction in this case.
—*Sir George Stephenson, Home Office*[95]

THE MID-AUGUST CONTROVERSY, whether the result of a sincere crusader, a stunt concocted and skillfully manipulated by the *Express*, or a combination of both, established a dangerous legal precedent: an editor of a publicity-seeking newspaper successfully goaded a publisher into voluntarily submitting a work of fiction for government inspection. Without consulting the author, the publisher Cape naively or unwisely forwarded a letter and a copy of the novel to the Home Office for review, together with "a selection of the serious reviews which had been published."[96] Cape inexplicably believed the Home Secretary, Joynson-Hicks, would also be incensed with "the sanctimonious hypocrisy of [Douglas's] article." Whether Cape was frightened by Douglas, as McKibbin speculates, or thought that controversy could only stimulate interest and improve sales, we cannot know for certain. A historian of the press believes that Douglas's audacious questioning of Cape's integrity (the editorial concluded "fiction of this type is an injury to good literature") so angered the publisher "that he rose to the bait."[97] In any case, Joynson-Hicks, with Cape's package in hand, conferred with Sir George Stephenson, the deputy acting on behalf of the absent director of public prosecutions, Sir Archibald Bodkin. Within forty-eight hours of the editorial Stephenson had discussed the case with the Bow Street magistrate Sir Chartres Biron (who had already read the book) and told the home secretary the book should be banned. Acting on behalf of "decent people" everywhere, a phrase Biron would later use in his judgment, a handful of men caught up in the public-spirited morality campaign Douglas promoted went on the offensive.[98]

Times had never been better for the puritanical forces of the land in the years between 1924 and 1929. During the increasingly intolerant reign of Joynson-Hicks (popularly known as "Jix"), a group of "social purists" were allowed what many now regard as undue influence over public policy: when asked about his duties for the government, Joynson-Hicks reportedly replied, "It is I who am the ruler of England."[99] Jix, affiliated with the Zenana Bible Mission, was supported by Bodkin, a one-time council member of the National Vigilance Association and the London Public Morality Council, and the attorney general, Sir Thomas Inskip, "a fervent evangelical and an active supporter of social purity causes," who was also initially consulted about Hall's case and later represented the Crown in the appeal process.[100] All three men—Joynson-Hicks, Bodkin, and Inskip—were either current or past members of fringe organizations, with narrow interests in reviving religious values and policing public morality. These are the same men Souhami takes to represent "the English establishment, the Old Boys . . . peers of the realm, oligarchs, guardians of the nation's morals."[101] Feminist critic Angela Ingram, in an otherwise complex examination of the legal and political circumstances leading to *The Well*'s suppression, also casts such men in similar terms (as the "fathers") and further contends that the banning of particular novels in the late 1920s "offers a paradigm for the Establishment's repeated attempts to suppress women by lumping us all together as blasphemers, lesbians, bad mothers, non-mothers."[102] Yet when contemporary critics settle for grand, oversimplified dichotomies (the establishment versus artists or women) or, for that matter, a succinct quotation (such as "prussic acid"), a cautious, nuanced reading of the events leading to the banning of *The Well* becomes all the more elusive. Why are some prominent establishment figures counted among the "fathers" and not others? As we have already seen, Hall's novel received positive reviews from men such as Bennett who circulated in the same exclusively male clubland as Douglas and Biron. After the editorial appeared, Bennett recalled, "I went alone to lunch at the Garrick [Club] and saw James Douglas and Chartres Biron together in the lounge, so I set violently on Jimmy at once about his attack on Radcliffe [sic] Hall's sapphic novel . . . Biron defended Jimmy with real heat; so I went on attacking. I told Jimmy to come in and lunch with me."[103] This gentlemen's disagreement reveals that even in the public space (the lounge) of a private realm (the men's club), where we might most expect a gathering of the like-minded, there was no united front. Another so-called establishment figure to support Hall was the esteemed surgeon Sir William Arbuthnot Lane who, at a literary luncheon sponsored by the bookshop Foyle's after the banning of *The Well*, told the gathering "that the heart of the public is beating in unison with hers, in spite of what has been said against her."[104] When the writer Cecil Roberts introduced Hall that afternoon, he repeated what he had said in print at the time of the ban: that the legal "proceedings were a disgrace to the English system of law." This evidence indicates that no such monolithic power existed to endorse Ingram's proposition that Hall and her novel were victimized by a coherent establishment policy mobilized and committed to crushing the lesbian vice through silencing lesbian representation.

The successful prosecution of *The Well of Loneliness* for obscene libel was the result not of an entity that could be collectively subsumed under the heading of "fathers" intent on suppressing women or lesbians but of a small group of "self-constituted guardians of . . . morality" who, in the so-called Age of Jix, were poised—like Douglas—to monitor cultural production in their search for *anything* thought immoral and therefore contrary to the interests of "decent" people.[105] This is evidenced by an almost identical incident that took place two years earlier involving the work of another author, Shane Leslie's *The Cantab* (1926) and three of the central figures in Hall's case—Joynson-Hicks, Bodkin, and Biron. The trio's modus operandi was to attempt to intimidate author and publisher into self-censorship to circumvent prosecution under the Obscene Publications Act—a strategy that failed when deployed against Hall who had resources to defend her book and a sense that her "one voice, one demand" represented "those millions."[106] Hall refused to be cowed by the sort of warning Biron issued to Leslie: authors "must realize that there were certain canons of public decency which they could reasonably be expected to adhere to."[107] The chief magistrate, who reviewed for the *Observer* on occasion and fancied himself a literary man, told the court during a preliminary hearing that he found a "great deal" of Leslie's novel absolutely acceptable, except for a few "errors of taste, and a certain undergraduate aggressiveness which was not altogether unsuitable to the subject."[108] However, there were "two or three passages of so gross a kind that he should have had no hesitation—had it been necessary—in issuing process." Further action was, as it turned out, unnecessary; to avoid the prospect of a costly court case, Leslie stated publicly that his book "was improper and ought not to have been published." In his summation Biron added: "It was much more desirable, from every point of view, that the book should be withdrawn under the pressure of public opinion rather than by the coercion of legal proceedings." This claim was obviously disingenuous, for not only had the book been withdrawn precisely because of the threat of legal proceedings but the magistrate and his moral watchdogs had little regard for or understanding of the "public opinion" they claimed to represent.

The "fathers" were in fact the "fools and bigots of their time, puffed with power, tainted with prejudice and sexual unease," as Souhami so aptly puts it.[109] Biron, "an elderly nonentity of strong views who apparently colluded with the home office before the hearing" on *The Well*, was ridiculed by Roberts, who wrote witheringly of the chief magistrate's abilities: "If he was as shocked and astonished as he professed to be, [over the novel's subject, he] should not have been a judge at all, being incredibly ignorant of human nature."[110] The same might have been said of Jix, who was as out of touch with the efficacy of his social purity agenda as with mainstream opinion. Lampooned during the trial as the "Policeman of the Lord," Jix, who "knew himself to be the chosen one, the saviour of England," was frequently ridiculed and subjected to intense criticism in the press, even in the *Express*, an indication that his campaign to restore to the nation the virtues and ideals of a past age was out of step with the times.[111] The *Daily Herald* humorously posited: "People like Hicks and Bodkin . . . [and others] inhabit that seat of learning known as Scotland Yard. They, stifling their natural horror and disgust, plough through all the naughty books, heroically risking any possible shocks to their chaste minds in order to safeguard the innocent British public from the insidious attacks of those who would hold the mirror up to Nature."[112] In a pamphlet entitled *Do We Need a Censor?* Jix responded to press criticism and refuted the charge that he and Bodkin were "conspiring to stifle genius": "I fear I have not yet fully understood the basis of the attack—whether it was launched because I ventured to give an opinion for which I had been asked, or because I had thought to find obscenity where none existed, or because I had had regard to a law which was obsolete and should have been ignored."[113] The government's actions, he continued, "provoked a storm of comment—both well and ill informed—on the supposed literary censorship in this country, and I was attacked, at times in far from moderate language"—language that included being labeled a "narrow-minded Puritan zealot."[114] The pamphlet, at once defensive and peevish in tone, becomes the mechanism for lodging a protest over mistreatment by the press and demonstrates that Jix perceptively recognized, although objected to, his own marginal status.

From the July publication of *The Well of Loneliness* until December, when the final appeal against Biron's decision failed, Hall put her literary reputation and public persona on the line in defense of her novel. The resulting publicity made it possible for anyone to discuss not only the question of censorship but also the issue of same-sex relations between women, as Virginia Woolf observed: "At this moment our thoughts center upon Sapphism. . . . All London, they say is agog with this."[115] Yet that "moment" should not have caught anyone by surprise. As feminist writer Vera Brittain points out, in all London—and elsewhere in the country—the subject of "Sapphism" had been gradually disseminating into public consciousness as part of a larger process of social change brought about by the war, especially among educated middle-class women who were "sophisticated to an extent which was revolutionary compared with the romantic ignorance of 1914. . . . Amongst our friends, we discussed sodomy and lesbianism with as little hesitation as we compared the merits of different contraceptives and were theoretically familiar with varieties of homosexuality and VD of which the very existence was unknown to our grandparents."[116] Another commentator agreed: "Ever since the war, when women displayed such unexpected ability in doing the work of men at the front, there has been a tendency to recognize and discuss [inversion] in public."[117] Implicit in this statement is a theory of causality, the notion that one kind of inversion, the introduction of women into the masculine world of work, led to an increased awareness of another sort of inversion, lesbianism.

Still, the 1920s may have *seemed* a sophisticated time, but regardless of the claim of a "well-known author and journalist" that "everybody has been aware for some time past of this condition of degeneracy among small sections of women, particularly in London," that "everybody" didn't seem to

include everyone—the social reality was far more complex.[118] As the journalist (and former police inspector) C. H. Rolph pointed out:

> As usual the sophistication touched the lives of about two per cent of
> the population, the other ninety-eight per cent playing out their lives
> on well-established lines. . . . It was here that the James Douglases occa-
> sionally, and profitably, exposed the wickedness and profligacy of the
> two per cent by writing articles about them for the horrified enjoyment
> of the ninety-eight.[119]

Knowledge of lesbianism was, for Rolph, one significant marker or index of
class separating the sophisticated from the "masses"—the unknowing
"ninety-eight per cent"—who indulged in "traditional hard work, Saturday
nights, football and the boozer." The other miniscule "two per cent" for
whom homosexuality, at the time of *The Well*'s publication, became "almost
a fashionable subject at 'intellectual' dinner parties," further subdivided as
discussants were forced to take a position on the issues raised by the novel
and the controversy; as a result, such evenings were an occasion "where the
ignorant and the informed archly skirmished."[120] In this context the designation "ignorant" signified the absence of enlightened acceptance rather than
lack of awareness. Only *after* the *Express*'s crusade against Hall's novel would
the "tens of thousands" whom Douglas sought to protect be exposed to "a
subject . . . ordinarily ignored."[121]

In the decade after the war lesbianism increasingly became a topic of private and public discussion among the educated, upper classes. The question,
however, remains: Did the terms "lesbianism," "Sapphism," "inversion," or
"female homosexuality" signify a collective or individual sexual or political
identity, or a particular sexuality, or a lifestyle organized around sexual object
choice? The persistent discursive indeterminacy exacerbated the risk of ambiguity, confusion, and imprecision. In reviewing *The Well of Loneliness* the
more elite journals, which were pitched to a well-educated and informed,
albeit small, readership, used the same terminology as some of the sexologists. Just one highbrow journal referred to "Sapphic" and "Lesbian" (specifically, Leonard Woolf who added, "Miss Hall rather strangely calls her heroine . . . [an] invert"[122]), and "homo-sexual" or "homosexuality" appeared
only in such highbrow and medical publications as the *New Statesman*, *Time
and Tide*, and the *British Journal of Inebriety*. This same group, along with
the *TLS*, *Life and Letters*, and, somewhat surprisingly, the *Liverpool Post
and Mercury*, also used terms associated with Ellis: "sex inversion," "inver-

sion," or "female invert." Two other publications (the *Morning Post* and the *Tatler*) deployed the preferred terms of the radical thinker Edward Carpenter: the "intermediate sex" and those "midway between the sexes." Yet only the *Liverpool Post and Mercury* clearly explained to the uninitiated the correct meaning of "the painful problem of inversion."[123] With textbook precision, the *Liverpool Post* article informed its readers that the term referred to "men and women who have inherited the constitution and psychology of the sex to which they do not rightly belong." This definition conforms with the Victorian medical understanding of the term "inversion," which "did not denote the same conceptual phenomenon as homosexuality" but rather "a total reversal of one's sex role."[124] As historian George Chauncey Jr. explains, " 'sexual inversion' referred to a broad range of deviant gender behavior, of which homosexual desire was only a logical but indistinct aspect, while 'homosexuality' focused on the narrower issue of sexual object choice" (116). The slow drift of medical terminology into cultural discourse meant that few of the other print media were attuned to such subtle shades of difference. For instance, throughout a *Spectator* piece several of these terms and phrases appeared as if completely interchangeable ("sexual perversion" and "sex-perversion," "sexual abnormality" and "homo-sexuality"), indicating an absence of a nuanced understanding—or a deliberate rejection—of the distinctions such medical terms denoted.[125] Douglas too coupled his only reference to the scientifically correct phrase "sexual inversion" with "perversion," creating a bizarre and oxymoronic conflation of medical and moral discourses.

More often the language describing lesbians in these publications was less clinical; for example, the phrase "masculine woman" appeared four times, while the most frequent wording (in ten reviews) was "normal" and "abnormal," although these terms were far from neutral. The *North Mail and Newcastle Chronicle* resorted to the word "abnormality" ("what . . . can only be called abnormality"), but only with evident frustration and discomfort for it seemed "offensive."[126] The prevalence of euphemistic phrases in these reviews ("her kind"; "vagaries or aberrations of Nature"; "a woman who is . . . well, who is not as normal women are"; "this particular mystery of sex"; and "study of an Amazonian soul") suggests that there was as yet no comfortable consensus about or understanding of the appropriate language, even among the most sophisticated reviewers.[127] There was also an extensive range of unscientific and far from neutral phrases in the coverage of the controversy in the popular press, including: "votaries of a sexual vice" and "one of the hidden cankers of modern life."[128] Douglas solved the problem of how to discuss what he called the "undiscussable," appropriately enough, by ignoring it. In a rhetorical style of pounding repetition, the editor demonized by a refusal to name: lesbians were referred to only by pronouns ("they" and "their")—ten times. By contrast, the editor devised numerous phrases when discussing members of society in need of protection, a gesture that underscores the otherness of the unnameable: "people of all ages"; "young women and young men"; "older women and older men"; "general reader"; "English people"; "younger generation . . . young lives . . . young souls"; and "great social assemblies." In his editorial Douglas sought to dehumanize all lesbians by reducing them to "they," but his attack on *The Well* was also an attack on its author, an elegant and high-profile literary persona, so that— unwittingly—Douglas may be the man most responsible for endowing lesbianism with a human face.

Eve: The Lady's Pictorial, which had contributed to a broadening of the social awareness of *lesbianism* by publishing a review of Hall's novel, became the first publication after the *Express* to invest, inadvertently perhaps, in an image of the *lesbian* by projecting Hall's fictional representation of Stephen onto the author herself.[129] One week after its review of *The Well*, the magazine ran a sketch of Hall sporting a short haircut and a wide-collar, open-necked shirt. Beneath the author's portrait the caption read "Radclyffe Hall . . . patronizes a severely tailor-made style of outfit, and usually wears a monocle. Her latest book . . . has been banned by the libraries." Two days after the Douglas editorial that had included a photograph of Hall without commentary on her appearance, the *Daily Express* also ran a short illustrated article on Hall as the "Monocled Authoress" in their regular gossip column, "The Talk of the Town," again establishing a link between the author, her novel on "sexual abnormality," her mannish female protagonist, and a "look."[130] In the mid-1920s the gossip columns had enjoyed prattling on about Hall as a familiar figure at London first nights, taking stock, for instance, of her stylish manner of dress; however, after Douglas the "old" press image of Hall—as a dashing figure of modernity—did not linger long. What was distinctively stylish before the editorial metamorphosed into something that was distinct and unsettling; Hall, and by implication women like her, could now be "easily recognized by her Eton crop, monocle and *unusual* clothes."[131] Hall's clothing, haircut, and monocle assumed a new meaning, one that Douglas and the *Express* carefully labeled a "display [of] perverted decadence." Consequently, the reading public would gradually come to regard Hall's look as the embodiment of one formulation of "lesbian." Just as the prosecution of Wilde marked the arrival in public culture of the male homosexual, the controversy over Hall's novel signaled the female homosexual's transition from the shadows to public visibility; the result of such publicity, according to the

Spectator, was to drag the "subject of sexual perversion . . . into the full light of day."[132] Whether the "subject" referred specifically to Hall *or* the topic of lesbianism was irrelevant—hereafter the two would eventually become synonymous, as seen in this 1929 comment reported by Bryher: "Lady Macpherson shattered [us] by saying . . . Mrs. Arthur is a . . . is a . . . well, you know, Radclyffe."[133]

In August 1928 the editor of the *Sunday Express* set in motion a chain of events that irrevocably changed the public perception—then and now—of the lesbian; the question is: Did this cultural moment represent an outbreak of moral panic? Feminist scholar Gayle S. Rubin astutely reminds us that in a time of moral panic:

> The media become ablaze with indignation, the public behaves like a rabid mob, the police are activated, and the state enacts new laws and regulations. When the furor has passed, some innocent erotic group has been decimated, and the state has extended its power into new areas of erotic behavior.[134]

But in the controversy over *The Well* "the press," as we have seen, was not "ablaze with indignation." No reviews before the editorial condemned Hall's novel for its subject matter; instead, condemnation was directed against bigotry and, though the word was not yet coined, against homophobia. Nor did a single review after Douglas's piece express concern about the novel's handling of lesbianism. Douglas's loud and strident protestations and the *Express*'s coverage succeeded in capturing headlines for months, but the campaign against lesbians as such failed to garner support from other leading papers or to rally the country, despite Douglas's warning: "The English people are slow to rise in their wrath and strike down the armies of evil," but once aroused "they show no mercy, and they give no quarter to those who exploit their tolerance and their indulgence." No doubt much to Douglas's disappointment, the great mass of English people continued to go about their daily business. Nor did the state intervene to enact any laws against lesbianism, and while the police were "activated," it was to seize and burn copies of the banned book. (*The Well* nevertheless remained available through illegal imports from France since Cape had the foresight to send the plates out of the country at the first sign of trouble.)

The publication of Hall's novel was halted by a combination of superb journalistic timing and a chain of serendipitous events. One extreme moralist—not the voice of an era—found in Joynson-Hicks a fellow crusader noted more for his overzealous hope of turning back the clock than for upholding prevailing social values. If any constituencies were galvanized over the debate stirred up by *The Well* in 1928, it was the forces against Douglas and Joynson-Hicks, who received the brunt of the attacks from those constituencies. Thus historian Sheila Jeffreys's claim that Hall's novel "was pilloried in the media" more aptly characterizes the treatment of the men responsible for the ban, who found themselves labelled narrow-minded puritan zealots and ridiculed by a largely unsympathetic press.[135] The intelligentsia, angered primarily with government interference in literary matters, demonstrated its support of Hall's case first by signing a joint letter published in a number of newspapers, then by volunteering to testify at the trial. Before and after Douglas's intervention, other commentators joined Hall in advancing her case for tolerance and understanding with more sense than sensation. King, for example, stated forthrightly that the facts about lesbianism "must be faced and, however unpleasant they may be from the normal point of view, it is better to face them—and seek to understand them—than to persecute them ruthlessly."[136] Other pools of support came from unexpected parts of the country: "a section of the National Union of Railwaymen sent a signed protest to the Home Secretary ament the suppression of the book. Another section of the South Wales Miners did the same."[137] The *Daily Herald*, firmly behind the author throughout the proceedings, reported: "Leaving court for her car, Miss Radclyffe Hall was surrounded by sympathizers, who shook her by the hand."[138] Hall was also rumored "to have received 10,000 [letters] around the time of the publication and trial. On September 1, 1928 alone she received 400 letters"—only a handful of which were negative.[139] The damaging effects of the glaring publicity—in terms of triggering a potential backlash against lesbians—would be felt, but only gradually in the coming decades.

If, as Weeks argues, moral panic is the crystallization of "widespread fears and anxieties" about "x" displaced on to the scapegoat "y," we can readily identify an "x" in the cultural anxieties circulating around the extension of the suffrage in 1928.[140] In July—the same month *The Well of Loneliness* was published—when the new franchise bill passed into law, Douglas may have thought that the struggle for a return to traditional values, such as normative gender roles, could only be sustained if shifted in a slightly different direction. With "x" representing prevailing cultural fears and anxieties related to younger women and the women's movement, what better way to control women than by pinpointing a certain group whom Douglas claimed had become pervasive in English "social life"? Such a proposition works hypothetically, but a key prerequisite is absent: an "identified social group." The very concept of "lesbian" as a specific category of identity or as a subcultural style had not, by August 1928, sufficiently cohered within the public consciousness for such women to become successfully scapegoated. This explains why Dawson's fear "that public opinion may be swayed . . . by [such] hysterical misrepresentation in widely circulated newspapers," never materialized and Douglas's one-man show remained just that.[141] If before the publication of Hall's novel and before the damning editorial the "lesbian" was not yet a stable or intelligible notion within public culture and discourse, the vital "y" factor was missing from the moral panic equation and, consequently, Douglas could not tap into existing "widespread fears and anxieties." The real significance of the banning of *The Well* was that the resulting publicity for the first time provided the public with one clear and identifiable image—not just a word—of the "lesbian" and that over the next few decades a "stylized or stereotypical" lesbian, to borrow Cohen's terms again, would emerge on the political landscape.

As others have demonstrated, witch-hunts and scapegoating would occur, but in 1928 there was as yet no recognizable "innocent [lesbian] group" to attack.[142] Douglas's hyperbole certainly packs a punch, but just as one editorial cannot neatly summarize an entire critical reception or an important cultural moment, so the "poison" soundbite, albeit highly quotable, requires far more circumspection before serving as a springboard into quick and easy conclusions about a moral panic that has undeniably assumed mythic proportions. Myths, however, have an indomitable habit of taking on a life of their own. In the chapters that follow, I therefore propose to tackle and unravel several more myths concerning lesbians in England in the 1920s and offer in their place a rich and detailed examination of the genesis of a modern English lesbian culture.

Two

"That Nameless Vice Between Women": Lesbianism and the Law

I

"The cult of the clitoris," can only mean one thing, and that is that the lady whose name is coupled with it, either in her private or in her professional life, approves of that which is sometimes described in perhaps less—I do not know whether it is less objectionable—but less gross language as lesbianism, and a more horrible libel to publish of any woman . . . is impossible to find.
—Mr. Travers Humphreys (1918)

The defendant . . . [made] against her as horrible an accusation as could be made against any woman in this country. The words used by the defendant could only mean that the plaintiff was an unchaste and immoral woman who was addicted to unnatural vice.
—Sir Ellis Hume-Williams (1920)[1]

MR. TRAVERS HUMPHREYS, legal counsel for the dancer Maud Allan, told the magistrate at Bow Street Police Court on April 6, 1918, that the radical right-wing Member of Parliament Noel Pemberton Billing had coupled the "filthiest words" imaginable with his client's name and should therefore be prosecuted for criminal libel.[2] On February 16 Pemberton Billing's private newspaper, the *Vigilante*, had published an announcement of Allan's performance in Oscar Wilde's *Salome* under the bold-type heading, "The Cult of the Clitoris." The notice of the performance itself would have been meaningless, the lawyer explained, had it not been placed beneath such a headline, for the juxtaposition indicated that there was "some connection with *that nameless vice between women* and the performance" (2, emphasis mine). Two years later, on November 18, 1920, Radclyffe Hall's counsel, Sir Ellis Hume-Williams, told the lord chief justice, King's Bench Division, that slanderous allegations had been made by St. George Lane Fox-Pitt, a member of the Society for Psychical Research (SPR).[3] In an effort to block Hall's election to the Society's council, Fox-Pitt allegedly told two prominent SPR members, including the secretary, Miss Newton, that Hall was "grossly immoral" and had spent a number of years with an "objectionable" woman, Mabel Batten, before forming a relationship with Una Troubridge that had wrecked the marriage of his friend, Admiral Sir Ernest Troubridge. Newton understood the words "grossly immoral" to have a "special meaning" implying that Hall was "addicted to unnatural vice" in her relationship with Batten.

These two fascinating lawsuits, the first late in the war and the second in the immediate postwar period, signal the beginning of an important shift in the visibility of lesbianism in English legal discourse and in the public arena.[4] In this culture of inversion Allan and Hall, like Wilde in 1895, sought through court action to clear their names and protest their innocence, even though the "evidence" suggested they were in fact what their accusers claimed, as is particularly indisputable with Hall. As a consequence of widespread and occasionally sensational press coverage of the trials, public interest in the subject of lesbianism intensified, even though references in the press to same-sex relations between women were for the most part oblique.[5] Since there was no common cultural understanding or legal definition of lesbianism in the early 1920s the discussion of "gross immorality" between women in the trials of Allan and Hall would, like the 1920 and 1921 parliamentary hearing and debates on the criminalization of lesbianism, become entangled with competing political agendas and complicated by the unintelligibility of the subject matter itself, as well as by the gendered nature of sexual knowledge. Of the many interesting links between these cases, two in particular provide an intriguing springboard into the main concern of this chapter, the lesbian and the law, by vividly demonstrating in microcosm how efforts to legislate the lesbian were regularly inhibited and complicated by contradiction and illogicality.[6]

The first parallel is that in each case the accusation of lesbianism was not an end in itself but a means to another end, political or personal in nature. In other words, the accusers' primary objective had less to do with establishing proof that the plaintiff was a lesbian than with a hunger for publicity (on the part of Pemberton Billing) or a vindictive action (as in the case of Fox-Pitt) on behalf of a friend (Admiral Troubridge).[7] In the "cult of the clitoris" case Pemberton Billing virtually admitted that he purposely sought a headline that would cause offense: "The action arose . . . from a deliberately indecent paragraph in a small newspaper [inserted] by Mr. Pemberton Billing, M.P., with the object, as he practically boasted, of forcing exposures by means of libel."[8] *The Times* reported that a writer for the *Vigilante* had telephoned a "village doctor for an anatomical term, and the doctor spelt out a word for him over the telephone."[9] In the witness box another physician confirmed under oath that "he could not, as a medical man, have suggested another title . . . unless the word 'lesbianism' might be used."[10] Allan's suit was swiftly sidelined by an immensely complex range of other subjects closer to Pemberton Billing's real concerns, all of which, in the patriotic hysteria at that moment in time, seemed more urgent and compelling; as *The Times* astutely noted, "It is hardly surprising that a week of indiscriminate mud-flinging should have diverted all attention from the real cause of [this] action."[11] Pemberton Billing deftly exploited media attention with his jingoistic rhetoric to publicize his extreme right-wing political agenda, and in one of the most sensational trials of the twentieth century, his courtroom antics invited public scrutiny of sexology, foreign influence, exoticism, and decadence—but rarely of lesbianism. The scope of Hall's suit also widened beyond sexual immorality to include aspects of spiritualism and psychic phenomena. Press coverage of the actual proceedings was extensive, but there was scant commentary on the original cause of the alleged slander; instead, most papers focused on the psychical aspects of the case with headlines such as "Seances and Slander" and "The Spirits of the Dead Slander Action."[12] *The Times* found in the trial an opportunity to critique psychical research generally: "A slander action of a very simple nature has attracted a great deal of attention, because the evidence revealed to a wondering public something of what goes on in the regions of psychical research."[13]

The fact that Pemberton Billing and Fox-Pitt suddenly rescinded their original accusations of lesbianism provides further proof that "sexual immorality" was only distantly related to their larger stratagems. Such a bizarre turn of events was possible because the defendants had elected to represent themselves—a decision that worked in Pemberton Billing's favor, who was found not guilty, but backfired for Fox-Pitt, who lost. At Pemberton Billing's abrupt retraction Justice Darling asked: "Do I understand, Mr. Billing, that you withdraw that [Allan] is a Lesbian?" to which the defendant responded, "Certainly. I never said she was."[14] As historian Lucy Bland correctly points out, "this was in fact a lie, since at the very beginning he had stated that the defamatory matters in the indictment were true, and the indictment claimed that the paragraph meant that Allan was a lesbian and consorted with lesbians."[15] More implausibly still, Fox-Pitt "denied malice and said when he used the word 'immoral' he meant, not to impugn plaintiff's chastity or honor, but attacked the character of the paper [on psychical research] she had written, which had been published, and was, he alleged, harmful."[16] He then claimed disingenuously that "he was still most anxious to find out how they [Hall and Troubridge] got this idea into their case as to the meaning of his words. It was entirely foreign from his thoughts."[17] Fox-Pitt's brilliantly feeble redefinition of "immorality" was, he insisted, based on a rejection of the word's "popular" meaning: "I am a special student of moral science . . . and we do not use the word 'immoral' in a sexual or erotic sense."[18] The lawyer-defendants resorted either to absolute denial or radical modification of the charge of lesbianism because they had stumbled across what parliamentarians would soon discover: lesbianism is as difficult to prove as it is to define. That the press directed more attention to issues such as patriotism and spiritualism suggests a persistent nervousness with the topic of female homosexuality, though such activities between women may have been less interesting than male homosexuality because the latter was prohibited under the Labouchère Amendment.[19] The accusation of "gross indecency between women" might lead to a damaged reputation but not to imprisonment and hard labor.

The second connection between the two trials concerns the gendered nature of sexual knowledge itself. Lawyers and magistrates occasionally exhibited a gentlemanly concern for any women witnesses or spectators who might find the subject of lesbianism distressing or shocking inasmuch as the subject of same-sex relations between women had hitherto been solely the purview of "men of the world." In Hall's trial, when Fox-Pitt inquired of Miss Newton, "What do you mean by unnatural vice?," the judge intervened before she could attempt an answer: "Now, now. . . . The jury are men of the world and know. You can't put such an indelicate question to a woman. I will not allow it."[20] Allan's lawyer hesitated before reciting the infamous phrase "cult of the clitoris": "I find words which I must read, [and] although I see there are some ladies in Court . . . I must read them aloud."[21] The hesitation could have been calculated to intensify the gravity of the libel, but the momentary pause nevertheless represents a deferential nod to the social propriety of exposing women to such language. Allan's acknowledgment in the court that she understood the meaning of the word "clitoris" thus became in effect an inadvertent admission of lesbianism since, as Bland argues, "a woman's knowledge of sexual terms carried different implications from a man's knowledge, for ignorant women were innocent, while women with sexual knowledge were, by definition, 'tainted.' "[22] As the verdict against Allan demonstrated, sexual knowledge was extremely dangerous for women.

In a culture of inversion the female plaintiff (whether inverted or not) involved with accusations of sexual immorality was in a no-win situation. Of Allan's immediate post-trial career biographer Felix Cherniavsky writes that she "was shunned by her public and by theater managers, who bluntly advised her not to appear on any London stage."[23] Hall fared slightly better in the immediate aftermath of her trial. Because Una Troubridge barraged the SPR with protests and threats, Hall was eventually elected to the council, even though "several [SPR] members felt that . . . [the trial] warranted keeping [Hall] off the Council."[24] In a sense, the plaintiffs were implicated before their trials even began because the very instigation of legal proceedings indicated that they fully understood the slurs leveled against them. Once in court, Allan and Hall, presumed guilty even if innocent, soon discovered that while their accusers were on trial to answer charges of libel and slander, the women's possession of contraband knowledge, coupled with the phenomenon of guilt by association, ultimately ensured that the final verdict was redundant.[25] When the subject of criminalizing lesbianism came before parliament in 1921, members who opposed the action would claim that most women were completely unaware of the existence of lesbianism and should remain so: sexual knowledge inevitably results in a loss of innocence.

To understand and assess how female homosexuality appeared in legal discursive practices during this period in Britain, scholars have carefully analyzed the 1921 parliamentary debates surrounding the Criminal Law Amendment (CLA) Bill in relation to a wider sociohistorical context. With the support of some fifty-nine national women's organizations, this "agreed" bill (meaning that the introduction of any contentious or hostile clause would sink the entire bill) sought to strengthen further the laws to protect children from sexual abuse and would have removed a major loophole in the law that allowed men to claim "reasonable cause to believe" that a minor was over the age of consent. The group chiefly responsible for coordinating efforts to ensure the passage of the bill was the Association for Moral and Social Hygiene (AMSH), whose secretary, Alison Neilans, liaised closely with the first female member of parliament, Nancy, Lady Astor, via her political secretary, Hilda Matheson. Among a small group of men opposed to the bill, dubbed by the feminist press as the "obstructionists," were three lawyers, Frederick A. Macquisten, Howard Gritten, and Sir Ernest Wild who, late in the evening of August 4, 1921, unexpectedly called for the introduction of a new (and contentious) clause, the "Acts of indecency by females," which read: "Any act of gross indecency between female persons shall be a misdemeanor and punishable in the same manner as any such act committed by male persons under section eleven [the Labouchère Amendment] of the Criminal Law Amendment Act, 1885."[26] Weeks speculates that the publication of Arabella Kenealy's *Feminism and Sex Extinction* (1920) may have influenced the attempt to legislate same-sex relations between women because Kenealy drew attention to the ways in which the women's movement fostered "masculinism" in women and posed a threat to parenthood.[27] In *The Spinster and Her Enemies*, Sheila Jeffreys subjects these same parliamentary exchanges in the House of Commons to intense scrutiny; but since her discussion is divided into two separate chapters, Jeffreys—usually a masterful spinner of conspiracy theories—fails to detect possible links between feminist support for the CLA Bill and antilesbianism.[28] As a result her discussion of the antilesbian clause, like that of Weeks, lacks a specific political context. Historian Martin Pugh, who offers a rather misleading account of the debates, attributes the Commons vote in favor of the clause to "fears over the presumed connection between the single woman, feminism and lesbianism."[29] Such readings clarify how hostility toward single women translates into hostility toward feminists, whose tactics and demands were seen by some as aggressive, and toward lesbians, whose numbers were perceived as growing. Yet the introduction of such legislation may have been bound up not only with sweeping sociocultural change but also with particular political imperatives.[30]

In the absence of a precise historical context, scholars have been unable to map how regulatory legislation of same-sex relations between women might have become the locus for conflicting agendas, such as the struggle for hegemony over the enforcement of the law and the control of public space. In other words, an antilesbian clause may not—or may not *primarily*—have constituted a direct attack on female homosexuality as an immoral behavior or abnormal sexual category but may have, like the trials of Allan and Hall, been a pragmatic strategy enacted against certain individual women or movements to achieve other political or personal aims. Thus accounts by scholars such as Weeks, Jeffreys, and Pugh, while generally valuable, have not come to terms either with the complex nature of the threat such women posed to masculine hegemony or how such a threat was discursively constructed and reproduced. Judith Butler theorizes:

> If subversion is possible, it will be a subversion from within the terms of the law, through the possibilities that emerge when the law turns against itself and spawns *unexpected* permutations of itself. The culturally constructed body will then be liberated, neither to its "natural" past, nor to its original pleasures, but to an open future of cultural possibilities.[31]

One way to test such a proposition is to reassess the lesbian's vulnerability vis-à-vis the law as well as the ostensible tool of the law, sexual science. Thus in the following sections, I propose to examine two historical moments, in 1920 and 1921, when the subject of criminalizing same-sex relations between women first entered legal discourse in England through the official record of parliamentary proceedings. In the first section I will explore one particular hypothesis focusing on how the force of law in the form of an antilesbian clause may have exerted legislative power over particular women, in this case the officers of the Women Police Service (WPS), as a response to their self-presentation and strategies for economic self-determination. The leadership of the WPS would learn, as had Allan and Hall, that the accusation or suspicion of lesbianism could wreak havoc, even if unproven, and serve diverse agendas. In the second section I will reconsider the role sexology played in the attempt to name the "nameless vice" and thus enable parliamentarians to legislate same-sex relations between women. By reading the minutes of the parliamentary hearings and debates against sexological writings on female sexual inversion we will see whether some of the current assumptions and conclusions about how "scientific" knowledge disseminated into the public sphere attributed to sexology an exaggerated and extraordinary efficacy that it may in fact never have had.

II

ON OCTOBER 21, 1920, Cecil Maurice Chapman, a London Metropolitan Police (Met) magistrate, appeared as an expert witness before a Joint Select Committee on the Criminal Law Amendment Bill.[32] The responsibility of the Joint Select Committee, comprised of six members from each house of Parliament, was to determine how best to merge three possible versions of the CLA Bill and to consider the evidence of a range of witnesses from the legal and medical professions, as well as representatives from moral and sexual reform groups. During his testimony Chapman was invited to comment further on the particulars contained in a note he had passed to the chairman, Lord Muir Mackenzie, who remarked: "I notice in the note that you gave me . . . that you desire to suggest that the clause [in the CLA Bill] should be extended so as to cover cases of gross indecency between women."[33] In the brief discussion that ensued, the subject of criminalizing sexual relations between women entered the official record of parliamentary proceedings for the first time. Although the matter proceeded no further at this stage, it would surface again on August 4, 1921, when, during a heated debate in the House of Commons on the CLA Bill, Frederick A. Macquisten, a Tory M.P., introduced the "Acts of indecency by females" clause. Thus female homosexuality and the law became the topic of parliamentary debate, first in the Commons and then in the Lords, where the clause would eventually fail on the grounds that it would be unenforce-able, would render women vulnerable to blackmail, and would only serve to increase lesbianism by advertising it.

The fact that Chapman's request coincided with a sustained, strategic assault by the Met against a specific group of women, the Women Police Ser-vice (WPS), who were bent on acquiring the force of law, might suggest that there was a good deal more going on behind the scenes. The WPS's attempted "subversion from within the terms of the law," to use Butler's phrase, did indeed engender "unexpected permutations," as their aims and appearance would compel detractors to decry them as more masculine than men. In the eyes of the Met, this independent female police force threatened to disrupt lines ostensibly differentiating normative and deviant, and their desire to play the field and pioneer modern formations of female self-determination may have forced police officials to explore mechanisms for political and cul-tural containment. As the WPS found themselves subject to a campaign of intimidation by the Met, the would-be regulators could themselves become the regulated, for the force of law might potentially construct as deviant their gender, class, and sexuality—a process the WPS would find exceptionally difficult to challenge, let alone subvert, inasmuch as their "unexpected per-mutations" replicated masculine authority too efficiently, as we will see. In their refusal to capitulate to the rules of containment set by the Met, WPS leaders put themselves on a collision course with men who may have turned from law enforcement to lawmaking in their efforts to control such power-ful and powerfully disruptive women. If so, the attempted criminalization of female homosexuality in the early 1920s must be seen as a potentially force-ful tool of *political* rather than simply *social* control.

In the early days of the First World War, as historian Philippa Levine recounts, "Women, generally in pairs, wearing lettered armlets and darkly colored clothes or official looking uniforms, began patrolling after dark in streets, parks, and railway stations and in towns close to the swelling mili-tary encampments."[34] One of the first female policing groups was the Women Police Volunteers (WPV), which was led by feminist and former suffragette Nina Boyle and by Margaret Damer Dawson, an upper-class Chelsea philan-thropist whom Joan Lock describes as "wealthy and well-connected . . . and [who] cannot have been without charm considering the vast amounts of money she managed to spirit out of wealthy friends to support her aims."[35] The WPS came into existence in early 1915 when it split apart from the WPV after Boyle asked Damer Dawson to resign.[36] Rather than step down, Damer Dawson called a general meeting and, upon receiving support from all but two women (out of fifty), launched an entirely new organization.[37] Another prominent group of women police patrols was sponsored by the National Union of Women Workers (NUWW) and directed by Mrs. Sophia Stanley.[38] Although the name might suggest otherwise, this organization consisted primarily of women from the middle classes and had no associations with militant groups. All these groups had distinct class and ideological differences, and

> from their earliest inception, both major policewomen's groups—the NUWW patrols and the WPS—were closely associated with controlling the public and even the private behaviors of working and working-class women and, by extension, working-class men. . . . Policewomen patrolled public places, separating couples thought to be embracing too closely, following those they suspected might be about to embark on unsavory courses of behavior, and warning youngsters of the dangers of overly casual behavior.[39]

While the WPV gradually drifted from the scene, the WPS and the NUWW remained active throughout the war, with the scope of their police activities expanding to include, for instance, supervising women in munitions factories and other industries. The WPS's contribution to the war effort and service to the country were recognized in February 1918 by the king who invested Commandant Damer Dawson and her then sub-commandant, Mary Allen, with the Order of the British Empire (OBE) and named Superintendent Isobel Goldingham a Member of the British Empire (MBE).[40]

Damer Dawson and Allen were both preoccupied—some might say obsessed—with establishing their organization as a permanent, independent female police force. To this end, during the war and the early postwar period, the WPS vigorously lobbied, among others, the Home Office and influential individuals it believed could help, though to no avail. When General Sir Nevil Macready, a commissioner of police of the Metropolis, launched his own female police force in 1918 (the Metropolitan Women Police Patrols or the MWPP), he chose to appoint Stanley (formerly of the NUWW) as the new superintendent, who in turn promptly recruited members of her own organization and, to Damer Dawson's dismay, rebuffed the top command of the WPS.[41] That few WPS rank and file members were accepted in the initial recruitment drive (four out of thirty) typifies their treatment and, as Levine explains, not many "complained when the WPS was utterly excluded from this new force [the MWPP] despite the enthusiastic support it had garnered from influential women."[42] One reason for this exclusion had its origins in the early history of the WPS's founding members—the so-called "Council of

Three." Damer Dawson, Allen, and Goldingham, who governed the WPS, each had prior association with groups and activities at odds with the police in one way or another. Damer Dawson had been an active member of the National Vigilance Association (NVA) and the Criminal Law Amendment Committee, both of which supported the need for policewomen.[43] The CLA Committee called for women police to repress solicitation by prostitutes, protect women from unwelcome sexual advances, assist women and children by investigating "cases of assault, indecency and incest," supervise and patrol public spaces, and inspect women's lodgings.[44] Damer Dawson adhered to NVA and CLA Committee principles and ideals and embraced an activist and even interventionist role for the policewoman as opposed to the less aggressive "preventative" approach advocated by the MWPP's Stanley. Allen and Goldingham possessed credentials even more dubious in the eyes of the police, for they were former members of the Pankhursts' Women's Social and Political Union, the militant group that advocated confrontational tactics to attain female suffrage. As a militant suffragette, Allen had been arrested by the Met for breaking windows at the Home Office, and served time in Holloway Prison where she endured forced feeding.[45] Such activities, which brought these women into direct confrontation with the police on behalf of feminist and suffragist objectives, were hardly viewed as acceptable qualifications for police work, especially as "the police were largely composed of hostile anti-suffragist men."[46] Historian John Carrier notes too that the Police Federation, created in 1919, carried out a continual campaign against women police in general, which nearly led to the disbandment of the MWPP.[47]

In February 1920 Macready confirmed this antisuffragist view when he presented the following testimony to the Baird Committee, whose task was to determine the feasibility and desirability of employing women in police duties:

> I heard that the moving spirits [of the WPS] were what in days gone by were called "militant suffragettes," and a certain number of them had got into trouble in the past when militant suffragettes did get into trouble. Now the ordinary policeman is a very conservative person, and the starting of [a female police force] was not by any means received with acclamation. . . . I knew that if we took on any women who in days gone by had got into trouble and been before the Courts for assaulting the police, I should never get this thing to run properly.[48]

Macready reasoned that if a female police force had any hope of succeeding, the women "must be very carefully selected, broad-mindedness and kindly sympathy being essentials."[49] As early as 1916 the Met deployed ideological control over women with activist backgrounds by demanding that WPS members "sign a 'Declaration of Allegiance,' which forbade them the public expression of political opinions and formally guaranteed their eschewal of what the police dubbed 'Suffragette propoganda [sic].' "[50] Macready's preference for recruits from the NUWW was a simple method of separating out more militant women because its central committee was, according to Levine, also "reluctant to engage women with a militant history, especially those who had been arrested, for it was felt that their presence would exacerbate the distrust of male officers" (47). Thus Macready's minimum requirements enforced a process of de-politicization by weeding out women with firm political convictions and by imposing his own standards of "purity" within his new female police group.

In addition to screening WPS members for his newly formed MWPP, Macready offered several reasons for rejecting the WPS as an independent female police force, casting as drawbacks what these highly qualified and experienced policewomen touted as strengths. For instance, when Allen praised Damer Dawson in a speech to the National Union of Societies for Equal Citizenship (NUSEC) for choosing "women of the right kind—educated women"—for otherwise no women police would have existed "in this country at all"—Macready apparently countered that "he did not agree."[51] Allen, however, neglected to point out that WPS members came principally from the upper and upper-middle classes, and possessed "private means," and that Macready could have satisfactorily rested his case against them on the more-or-less legitimate grounds that the Met needed to maintain some degree of educational and social parity.[52] Instead, he went significantly further in his objections to the WPS, arguing, for example, that its impressive service record was problematic and that there were profound and irreconcilable disagreements between the Met and the WPS about how to enforce the law. Allen proudly writes of the "great variety of police work undertaken and efficiently carried through by the [WPS]. . . . Our members had served during the war as traffic and probation officers; had patrolled streets, parks and public places; had been given the power of arrest in many towns."[53] She then complains that this splendid record "entirely escaped" Macready, who in 1918 informed the *Daily Mail*, "I have a great objection to the amateur in any form, and the women I enrol will be professional workers."[54] Although the WPS leaders had performed police work in exchange for a regular salary, Macready did not regard them as "professional" because their organization, in his view, operated outside official parameters: "For this reason the woman who has had no amateur or voluntary experience *in police work* may prove of greater ultimate use to the force than one recruited from any *existing outside force*" (emphasis mine). Ironically, Damer Dawson captured the source of Macready's underlying unease when she wrote in a report on the WPS, "It has been of immense advantage to the whole movement that we have worked so long 'unofficially.' We have been free to create the new precedents required by an entirely new force of trained officials."[55] Such "new precedents" ranged from accepting assignments never before undertaken by women, as in the supervision of female workers in munitions factories, to patrolling on motorcycles with sidecars. Raw recruits, one suspects, would be easier to mold than women with previous experience in an energetic and innovative organization that advocated full equality with men in every aspect of policing, including the power of arrest, as specified in their own annual report: "Women police should be attached to every police force, to act in cases where women are concerned in the same way that men constables act where men are concerned. They should be equally the agents and representatives of the law in all its bearings, and should by no means be limited to the question of the moral welfare of young women."[56]

In essence, WPS leaders were attempting to take "the law" into their own hands. For one thing, they demanded the unthinkable: nothing less than equal powers with policemen, a logical extension of their own beliefs in sexual equality. Thus Damer Dawson was "anxious [for the WPS] to take up the ordinary duties of a constable and . . . have powers of arrest conferred on them."[57] Stanley, on the other hand, was uninterested in obtaining power of arrest for the MWPP because "the work was better done by patrols, in cooperation with the police, than by policewomen."[58] Damer Dawson further informed Macready that "women police should be an entirely separate, state-controlled force and not operate under individual police authorities" (113). Instead, she envisioned a female police body answerable—in the same way as the Met—only to the Home Office. Sir Leonard Dunning of the Home Office complained with evident irritation, "The truth is that Miss Dawson Damer [sic] cannot get rid of her ideas of the Women Police Service as an independent body and does not realize that the real thing to be aimed at is the employment of women by police authorities as an integral part of the police force."[59] An independent women's police force full of independent women was not what Macready and others had in mind.

However, the WPS refused to disappear and, from Macready's perspective, both its physical presence and performance of police duties challenged the very integrity of the MWPP, not to mention his own control over the future of female policing in London. For example, Macready was unable to prevent either Damer Dawson or Allen from testifying in February 1920 before the Baird Committee, which had been appointed to establish guidelines for the employment of women in the police force. This was despite his earlier warning to Sir Edward Troup, Under Secretary of State at the Home Office: "I hope, if you have a Committee on Women Police, that Miss Damer Dawson, or any of her other satellites, will not be included thereon, otherwise there will be considerable trouble over here."[60] The fact that the women did testify shows that while the WPS faced considerable opposition from the Met and the Home Office, it clearly had influential friends. This was acknowledged by Alker Tripp, also at the Home Office, in a note to Sir Chartres Biron, the chief magistrate, which Tripp attached to the voluminous file on the WPS he had received from Sir William Horwood, who succeeded Macready in April 1920: "As there may be some sort of howl from the friends of the 'Women Police Service' [about the uniform controversy] I thought you ought to know what he [Horwood] proposes to do."[61] (I will discuss the uniform controversy in chapter 3.) One such friend was the Bishop of Kensington, who sent a letter to Horwood on October 6, 1920, protesting against the Commissioner's interference with the WPS.[62] With a formidable list of powerful patrons—a 1916–17 WPS report names over fifty such individuals in a virtual "who's who" of London's upper classes, including members of the aristocracy, the legal and medical professions, bishops, and government and military officials—the WPS was capable of launching a credible defense against the Met's attempts to shoot it down.[63] The fact that both Damer Dawson and Allen had been awarded OBEs and Isobel Goldingham an MBE for service to the nation may also have led both the Home Office and the Met to proceed with caution. Finally, WPS "friends" donated generously to the war chest so that Mr. A. L. Dixon, one of the officials directed by Mr. Edward Shortt, the secretary of state, to write a memorandum on the Baird Report, expressed concern that "the WPS who were understood to have 'considerable funds in hand' would try to carry on independently of the official police."[64] In phrasing that would have sent considerable shock waves through the Met, Damer Dawson told the Baird Committee, "We have enough funds to equip a small standing army of policewomen."[65] The WPS's powerful allies and independent means may have led the Commissioner and his colleagues to the conclusion that the WPS could not be easily controlled.

Obviously, women like Damer Dawson did not know their place and exceeded the boundaries of feminine propriety: in short, they were pushy and aggressive where they should have been demure and passive. When Macready characterized the WPS leadership as "extreme," it is clear what he had in mind: "The main point was to eliminate any women of extreme views—the vinegary spinster or blighted middle-aged fanatic."[66] Terms such as "spinster" and "man-hater" may have been euphemisms for what we now term "lesbian," a concept then familiar to some in the legal and medical professions, but other terms such as "strong," "masculine," and even "educated" could also have signaled codes frequently associated not only with single women and feminists but with lesbians, or women uninterested sexually in men. Macready's blunt disapproval of the WPS leadership invokes conventionally coded language to conceal that which could not be spoken: the perceived link between the masculine woman and the lesbian. Even other members of women police groups insinuated that the WPS had lesbians in its midst. In an exchange between Dorothy Peto of the NUWW's Policewomen's Training Center at Bristol and Damer Dawson over the role of women in the police, Peto argued emphatically that police authorities must recruit "the very best of our womanhood"—slyly implying the absence of this essential quality among WPS members (Peto must have felt secure in her own power base, for in photographs she appears in every way as "masculine" as Allen and Damer Dawson).[67] Senior Met officers, Lock informs us, concurred with this assessment: "Policewomen should retain their femininity and accept their limitations. Mrs. Stanley, the Met's charming and attractive new woman superintendent, agreed."[68] More important, Stanley, whom "men found . . . hard to resist," had "as well as charm and sex appeal . . . common sense—enough to know when not to push."[69] Never politically savvy, the hubris of the WPS leadership—the inability "to know when not to push"—intensified their conflict with the Met.

In a campaign of harassment that moved from veiled threats in correspondence, to conferring with the Home Office, to specific allegations regarding WPS members' appearance and behavior, even to briefly considering the option of arresting some of them, Horwood attempted to intimidate the WPS leadership. For example, on September 21, 1920, he wrote to Allen and warned that if WPS members did not pack it in and cease to patrol in London in full uniform, the chief magistrate "would probably deal severely" with them.[70] (The chief magistrate, incidentally, was Sir Chartres Biron who would later preside over the obscenity trial of Hall's novel.) At the same time Horwood wrote to Troup at the Home Office, declaring with exasperation that the situation had become "quite impossible."[71] In the weeks preceding the day on which Chapman passed his note to the Joint Select Committee chairman, it is clear that the minor war the Met was conducting against the WPS had reached new heights, as detailed in a list of the correspondence between all concerned—some eight letters were exchanged in a single fortnight. How far was the Met willing to go in its drive to maintain absolute control over the future of women police in London? Would more unorthodox measures be necessary to discredit and even destroy the WPS? This early attempt to criminalize lesbianism may have become in effect a weapon, enabling those who create and enforce the law to render some women—whether lesbian or not—vulnerable to intimidation, social humiliation, blackmail, and even imprisonment. Underlying the high moral tone of parliamentary circumspection of female homosexuality *and* the law may have been a more urgent and expedient agenda: to expunge female homosexuals *from* the law.

To return to the question posed at the outset: Was Chapman's request to the Joint Select Committee to extend the law against gross indecency to females part of a legal maneuver by Horwood and others to intimidate WPS members, and more especially its leaders, who might have been suspected of lesbianism? As a magistrate, Chapman was undoubtedly aware that raising the issue of same-sex relations between females in a parliamentary committee was unprecedented. Inasmuch as the function of a witness is to respond to questions posed by the committee and not vice versa, Chapman's interference with normal procedure in and of itself constitutes a violation of sorts. While the passing of notes in a court of law, Chapman's métier, was not an unusual practice, a review of the *Minutes of Evidence* demonstrates that it was uncommon in these hearings. The tactic of passing the note at the very beginning of his testimony—perhaps even before questioning commenced—points to several possibilities. For instance, while the record indicates that Chapman handed the note to the chairman, it does not specify whether the note was written by someone else. Alternatively, the magistrate might have taken the unusual step of introducing such a delicate topic in handwritten form as a gentlemanly gesture in deference to the presence of Lady Astor for, as he himself acknowledged, "People were a little shy . . . [of the subject] because not many knew that such a thing existed or could take place."[72] (Chapman refers here to a previous attempt, probably in 1913, where such shyness meant that the issue of criminalizing lesbianism in an earlier CLA Bill was never raised. Such verbal reserve is reminiscent of the reluctance to discuss "that nameless vice between women" in the earlier trials of Allan and Hall.) Finally, Chapman could have thought it more politically astute to allow the chairman to judge the appropriateness of pursuing the question; in this way the witness surrendered the responsibility of making the first move and transferred that power to the chairman, who could have chosen to ignore it. In any case, the mechanism of the note was a silent invitation to utter what was heretofore unspeakable, and thus the chairman broke the silence and named the vice, "gross indecency between women."

It is certainly interesting that Chapman's testimony took place during the height of the dispute between the Met and the WPS. Chapman first informs the committee that while gross indecency between women is "an offence which people speak of as if it was almost unknown to the public . . . it is very well known to the police." To the question, "There is nothing to make you suppose that it is on the increase at the present moment?" Chapman answers, "I can only say what the police tell me." When another committee member rephrases the question slightly, "Do they [the police] say that it is on the increase?" he replies, "Yes, they said that when I put the question." Finally, to the third question in this line of enquiry, yet another member asks if "it" had been increasing "since the war," and Chapman responds, "An Inspector said that the evil which was brought to my attention was very much on the increase lately." The choice of words here, "brought to my attention," could simply represent the formal, ritualized language of parliamentary exchange, but it might also indicate that Chapman may not have planned to raise the subject until approached by the police. Although no concrete evidence proves definitively that Chapman knowingly collaborated with the police, a close reading of his answers to the committee confirms that prior to testifying he either consulted individuals in the Met or that Met officials supplied him with details about such offenses.

Yet Chapman cannot be cast uncritically in the role of the Met's lackey. For a start, both the magistrate and his wife were long-time WPS supporters, and "were listed as patrons in WPS annual reports, and he is thanked for his lectures to them."[73] When the WPS leadership appeared before him in the uniform dispute, Chapman stated, "Personally I am very desirous that the organization [WPS] should be preserved."[74] Such a stance is entirely in concert with Chapman's solid prewar prosuffrage politics, as historian Angela John has discovered. Chapman, it turns out, had "sat on the executive committee of the largest of the men's support groups, the Men's League for Women's Suffrage. In 1911 he was elected chairman of this society though rapid intervention from the Home Office ensured that he soon stood down."[75] Chapman would have been a well-known figure in suffrage circles and among feminists generally as he was "a frequent speaker at social and educational gatherings where he would advocate developments such as children's courts and the probation acts." Why then would a magistrate with progressive leanings and no apparent hostility toward the WPS introduce the subject of "gross indecency between women" to the Joint Select Committee? Historian Lesley Hall interestingly speculates that Chapman "may have been drawing attention to the anomalous injustice of the Criminal Law Amendment Act of 1885 as it applied to male homosexuals, rather than attacking women as such."[76] Close examination of Chapman's testimony reveals that one clear motivation for raising the topic grows out of a concern for the sound feminist principle of "absolute equality": "There is no question about it that in regard to all these acts there ought to be absolute equality between the sexes as far as it is humanly possible." This sentiment was echoed by one feminist newspaper on August 12, 1921: "The new clause dealing with indecency between females is on the right lines in so far as it equalizes the sexes in this respect."[77] Chapman further underscores his commitment to the question of sexual equality near the end of a brief discussion on the question of whether gross indecency between females was increasing: "The other day I was saying that I hated the inequality of the sexes with regard to the way in which they were dealt with."

Chapman's emphasis on "absolute equality" may also explain the curious choice of cases he presented to the committee. He first describes "very serious cases . . . in which women have been in the habit of getting girls to their flats and houses in London," but rather than elaborate on any actual occurrence, he leaps immediately to another case: "I remember a case that took place at Bournemouth, where girls were practically being treated as if they were prostitutes." After relating this scenario, Chapman mentions one further incident where young women at a reform institution were being "corrupted" by a "woman controller." When pushed to clarify when exactly these events had taken place, he first responded, "Certainly within 10 years." Unsatisfied by this reply, members pressed still harder and Chapman informed them that the Bournemouth case was "a long time ago. . . . [Within ten years?] Longer than that. . . . It is more like 20 years." Such examples might indicate more a last minute rifling through his memory of past experiences for possible case histories than a thorough, systematic study. But the fact that all of Chapman's examples involve women and girls reveals that he has chosen carefully; such examples are relevant to *his* specific concerns about equality with regard to age and gender. Chapman and the WPS shared a common concern regarding the moral corruption of young girls, and his support of extending the law to include "gross indecency between women" exposes his liberal views because at this time, as Jeffreys explains, "Feminists complained that the offence of sexual abuse [against girls] was not treated as if it was at all serious and that sentences were completely inadequate in comparison with the sentences given for sexual abuse of boys."[78] In fact, Chapman's own wife was a member of the Women's Freedom League, which set up a "Watch Committee" to monitor court proceedings and "concentrated particularly on cases of sexual abuse of children," especially young girls who could be preyed upon by anyone older, male or female.[79] Such groups recognized that, as Chapman put it to the committee, "It is very well known to the police, and it is very well known to many people who are students of criminology that women as well as men corrupt girls." Chapman may have been willing to raise the subject of "gross indecency between women" because of his profound commitment to issues pertaining to the age of consent and sexual equality.

Although aspects of Chapman's testimony are vague, as is evident, for instance, in the slippage in his call for revisions from Section 5 (concerning the "defilement" of girls thirteen to sixteen years of age) to Section 11 (the Labouchère Amendment), it is highly unlikely, in light of Chapman's progressive views in matters dealing with equality and sexual behavior, that the wider issue of lesbianism and the perception of its increase in the postwar period were of interest to him (he does not offer a shred of up-to-date evidence to prove the proliferation of this aberrant sexuality). As a member of the radical British Society for the Study of Sex Psychology (BSSSP), Chapman was well informed about sexual inversion as a medical category and not only shared the society's disapproval of legislating sexual inversion between consenting adults but "denounced the senselessness and cruelty of the sentences passed on [male] inverts."[80] If Chapman was indeed pursuing an agenda congruent with feminist rather than homophobic concerns, as seems to be the case, a positive and sympathetic response on the part of the Joint Select Committee to his request might have been possible if all its members possessed an unequivocal, shared understanding of the phrase "gross indecency between women." In fact, the opposite was the case. This was partly Chapman's own fault for, although he carefully cited cases involving women and girls, he contributed to the confusion by introducing "gross indecency between women," and failed to clarify to the committee what he meant by "vice." In an exchange between the Earl of Malmesbury (who did not support the clause when it came to the House of Lords in August of 1921), Lady Astor (noticeably silent during Chapman's testimony and later in the House of Commons debate), and Chapman, Malmesbury asks whether "it is notorious that the particular vice to which you allude is extraordinarily common." Chapman replies, "I think it is fairly common." When Astor presses him to define "fairly common," Chapman answers, "I should not say that it was very frequent." This exchange is typical in its confusion because of the participants' reluctance to name the unspeakable. Does "it" refer to same-sex relations between consenting adult females, which is what some committee members appear to assume, or to sexual acts between women and girls, which Chapman evidently presumes to be the topic under consideration? Apart from Malmesbury's allusion to "the particular vice" and Chapman's mention of "the evil," every other reference in this section of the testimony is to "it"—some twenty times. The resistance to specify the act to which "it" refers allows Chapman's request for limited legislation concerning adult females and minors to slide toward a call from some members to legislate same-sex relations between women. Thus while Chapman initially advocates an extension of Section 5 (on "defilement" of girls), by the end of the committee's questioning he acquiesces to amending Section 11 (the Labouchère Amendment). The limited control that Chapman sought suddenly ballooned to include all lesbians, or women who engage in lesbian sexual acts, rather than exclusively those who preyed on minors, thus, unwittingly perhaps, reinforcing the myth of the predatory lesbian.

Chapman's concern for the welfare of young girls, leaning closer to feminism than to homophobia, inadvertently tapped into larger cultural anxieties about masculinized women and their intrusion into the public sphere: from unwomanly suffragettes to women in uniform (military or police) to masculine women as lesbians. Without question, if Chapman had not passed his note, someone else soon would have; gentlemanly reserve over the topic of female sexual inversion—the "it"—would evaporate in the explicit and open discussion of the 1921 parliamentary debates. Such episodes vividly illustrate how women who refused either to be constructed as culturally feminine or as heterosexual would be henceforth exceptionally vulnerable to the full force of political control by any institution of state. The final irony perhaps is that a predominantly lesbian WPS leadership (as I explore in the following chapter) who wanted the power to police heterosexual behavior—patrolling parks to disrupt activities of heterosexual couples, assisting in raids on brothels, preventing loitering and solicitation by prostitutes, and aiding women and children who had been indecently assaulted—were, as a result of the Met's campaign, constituted as the impure. While in the public sphere WPS members were "enforcing norms of sexual morality," in their private lives they rejected the dominant culture's valorization of femininity and family and preferred not to marry or take up conventionally feminine occupations.[81] The WPS persistently agitated police officialdom and deployed every mechanism available to become a self-governing, autonomous female police force, with its own chain of command, free of masculine control. The WPS meant business, but so did the Met—who may not have tried but would most certainly have welcomed any attempt to engineer the ultimate weapon: an antilesbian clause in the form of regulatory legislation concerning "gross indecency between women" that would force WPS leaders out of policing for fear of becoming the policed. The WPS, specimens of culturally unintelligible femininity, would be pathologized by the sexological discourses that made identification possible and displaced by alternatives the police found more acceptable, so-called "fluffy policewomen."[82] By mapping out this cultural terrain with a more rigorous attentiveness to historical detail, we can understand with far more complexity how, even in the absence of a conspiracy on the part of magistrates and police authorities, or between parliamentarians and government officials, the accusation of lesbianism, as Allan and Hall learned, would put any woman, whether lesbian or not, in a no-win situation.

III

Those who have had to engage either in medical or in legal practice know that every now and again one comes across these horrors, and I believe that the time has come when . . . on account of its civil and sociological effects, this horrid grossness of homosexual immorality should . . . be grappled with.
—Frederick A. Macquisten, M.P.[83]

SOME FEMINIST HISTORIANS who enter the contentious and politically charged debate over sexology's role in constructing lesbianism in the late nineteenth and early twentieth centuries conclude that sexual science became a kind of weapon deployed against women, particularly feminists, to retaliate against their newfound economic and political freedom. Jeffreys, for instance, writes: "The significance of the sexological construction of the lesbian must be seen in its historical context of the backlash against feminism, alarm at spinsters and celibacy, and of the importance of passionate friendships to women in this period."[84] Following Jeffreys's lead, Margaret Jackson claims that the "sexological model of sexuality" was heterosexist and "anti-feminist." "The morbidification of lesbianism," she maintains, "was undoubtedly a key factor in undermining feminism . . . in essence no more than the re-packaging, in scientific form, of the patriarchal model of sexuality which feminists were struggling to deconstruct."[85] Lillian Faderman is also highly suspicious of what she terms the sexologists' conscious or unconscious "hidden agenda," which aimed "to discourage feminism and maintain traditional sex roles by connecting the women's movement to sexual abnormality."[86] Without question, the scholarly preoccupation with the harmful effects of sexology has enhanced our understanding of the wider ideological stakes operating during this period, but this negative critique has also inhibited a strategic shift toward investigating how—or even if—sexological models of female homosexuality entered the public domain in the early decades of the century. Sexology, one presumes, must have been a powerfully incisive and devastating ideological force to undermine feminism, stigmatize lesbianism, and successfully connect the two.

The realm of law is one effective starting point in tracing how and if such sexological constructions and sexology as ideology seeped outside medical circles and, by permeating public culture, became in effect a tool of sociopolitical control. By 1920 more than two decades had passed since the initial publication of most of the influential sexological material on female sexual inversion and thirty-five years had lapsed since the Labouchère Amendment had criminalized acts of gross indecency between men. Surely, in the immediate postwar era in England, we might reasonably assume that magistrates, lawyers, police, and parliamentarians with privileged access to sexological literature could appropriate its medical epistemologies and taxonomies to devise regulatory legislation. Sexology's reservoir of case histories, its strategies of identification and classification noting the habits, behaviors, and physical appearance of sexual inverts, would enable legal experts to challenge and deflect skeptics or sexual progressives who rejected the need for a clause or law to control the alleged threat female sexual deviants posed to civilized society, especially to the institutions of marriage and family. In its methodical delineation of abnormal behavior, sexological literature could demonstrate, with the ostensible force of scientific objectivity, the imperative for such a law and its implementation.

When Chapman passed his note in 1920 to stiffen the laws to protect children from predatory adults of *both* sexes, and later in the debate on the "Acts of indecency by females" clause put before both houses of Parliament in the late summer of 1921, competing and contradictory constructions of sexual activities between females would circulate uneasily. Before examining the parliamentary debates of 1921, I will first return to Chapman's testimony before the Joint Select Committee in 1920 in order to determine how or if sexology played a strategic part in the proceedings. We have already seen that Chapman's motivation for introducing the note was precise and narrow: his overarching concern was to protect all minors from adult sexual abuse rather than to criminalize lesbianism as such. As I have already indicated, Chapman's interest in the protection of young girls explains the curious choice of cases he presented to the committee—each involving women and girls. He first mentions "a Home which was started for the reformation of girls where the police had to interfere because of the girls being corrupted by the woman controller of the Home." That same-sex institutions were frequently a breeding ground for sexual activities between females was documented by the early sexologist Richard von Krafft-Ebing, who explained that such sexual meetings were "practiced now-a-days in the harem, in female prisons, brothels and young ladies' seminaries."[87] In *The Sexual Question* August Forel concurs with Krafft-Ebing by specifying that "all these things take place chiefly in brothels or with prostitutes, in barracks, boarding-schools, convents, and other isolated places where . . . women live alone and separated from the other sex."[88] According to Chapman's testimony, however, young girls were also vulnerable outside of same-sex environments. Thus he notes, "I have had very serious cases in my experience in which women have been in the habit of getting girls to their flats and houses in London, and I remember a case that took place at Bournemouth, where girls were practically being treated as if they were prostitutes." This image of the older woman as sexual predator is reminiscent of Forel's claim to "have known several women *of this kind*, who held veritable orgies and induced a whole series of young girls to become their lovers."[89] The phrase "of this kind" is highly significant, for Forel refers specifically to "feminine sexual inversion" and goes on to suggest that "when a woman invert wishes to seduce a normal girl, it is easy for her to do so." Likewise the Berlin sexologist Albert Moll undoubtedly contributed to an exaggerated concern for the welfare of young girls when he asserted that "many women inflicted with sexual inversion practice masturbation. . . . Those who masturbate themselves think of young girls during the act. . . . There seem to be women of homosexual tendencies who desire young immature girls."[90]

Chapman's primary concern for the welfare of girls was fueled by his experiences as a magistrate, but he may have also been influenced by the work of sexologists such as Forel, Moll, and others, including the feminist and sexual progressive Stella Browne. Elected to the BSSSP in 1914, Chapman may have heard the 1917 paper Browne presented to the society where in several of the case histories she observed intimacy between women and young girls: two were devoted to children; one was involved with a girl "ten years her junior," and another was "professionally associated with children and young girls and [showed] her innate homosexual tendency by excess of petting and spoiling."[91] Browne's cases might seem to evoke the image of the predatory lesbian, but nowhere in the paper does she suggest that these activities were themselves ethically questionable. Browne and other progressive sexologists clearly differentiate between women who prey on young girls and the true or congenital sexual invert. Krafft-Ebing argues emphatically that while there are cases of teachers as "seducers" of "daughters of the high classes of society," these kinds of "sexual acts between persons of the same sex do not *necessarily* constitute antipathic sexual instinct. The latter exists only when the physical and psychical secondary sexual characteristics of the same sex exert an attracting influence over the individual and provoke in him or her the impulse to sexual acts."[92] In other words, women who engage in such practices may not be themselves inverted but may simply take advantage of the available supply. That such activities are extremely rare is underscored by the fact that in an entire chapter on female inversion, Ellis mentions only one case where a young girl was "indecently assaulted" by a woman and this case, he writes reassuringly, happened "some forty years ago."[93] Ellis generally dismisses some kinds of erotic attachments, such as those between girls and their school teachers, as "a spurious kind of homosexuality, the often precocious play of the normal instinct" (216). These attachments, he maintains, need not be of concern, for whether they occur between girls, between schoolmistresses, or between a girl and a schoolmistress, it is only if the individual is "congenitally predisposed" that her activity will persist while "in the majority it will be forgotten as quickly as possible." This notion that most women simply go through a phase would surface in the 1921 debate where one member in the Lords reminds his peers that same-sex relations are disagreeable but inevitable: "We all know of the sort of romantic, almost hysterical, friendships that are made between young women at certain periods of their lives."[94]

The cases Chapman presented to the Joint Select Committee were neither harmless nor a phase; rather, they were clear-cut incidents of sexual abuse. Yet Chapman scrupulously avoided using negative terms, such as "evil" or "vice," except when reporting what a police inspector had told him. On the other hand, although undoubtedly familiar with the clinical language for inversion, Chapman neither uttered the words "lesbian," "female homosexuality," or "sexual inversion" nor implied that his cases involved female sexual inverts. In fact, he not only failed to invoke the proper medical terminology but went so far as to devise a method to raise the topic without public speech by passing a note to the chairman. I believe that Chapman refrained from sexological language precisely because he was well informed about sexological ideas—as a BSSSP member, an organization that included Edward Carpenter, Ellis, and Browne among others, Chapman would have been exposed to the notion of inversion as a category and perhaps shared their view that sexual activities between consenting adults should not be subject to legislation. Of all the participants in the parliamentary hearing, Chapman alone, it would seem, recognized that the acts he sought to criminalize—sexual relations between women and girls—had no *necessary* relationship to female sexual inversion. Just as both men and women have the potential to corrupt minors, so too do both heterosexuals and homosexuals. Such an understanding of inversion is, however, highly nuanced, and the magistrate's subtle, even strategic, distinctions were clearly lost on most of the committee members.

Chapman's reticence, indeed his persistent invocation of the word "it" to encompass any manner of female indecency, had disastrous consequences: it caused confusion among the committee members which, ultimately, resulted in the collision of contradictory constructions of sexual activities between females. This is evident from the moment Muir Mackenzie intoned the phrase "gross indecency between women," and the subsequent lack of specificity led to some farcical and scientifically vague discussions, as we have seen. The failure to clarify the nature of the sexual behavior—indeed the collapsing or blurring of diverse sexual acts—occurred regardless of whether the participant was well informed on matters relating to sexological theories (such as Chapman) or whether the "expertise" was merely based on hearsay, indicating that the new medical knowledge circulating within the cultural realm, which should have provided lawmakers and law enforcers with clinically correct language and categories, had not yet been fully disseminated. Each committee member seemed convinced that particular people had particular knowledge, but no one was positive about what anyone else meant by "it."

Such a parliamentary exchange reminds one of what Michel Foucault, in his analysis of what he terms the "repressive hypothesis," calls the myth about Victorian sexuality: where ostensibly "on the subject of sex, silence became the rule."[95] In actuality, Foucault argues, "new rules of propriety screened out some words: there was a policing of statements. . . . Areas were thus established, if not of utter silence, at least of tact and discretion."[96] Yet both the magistrate's and the Joint Select Committee's reluctance to name the "particular offence" seems to have been confined only to the actual room—for the testimony itself reveals ample evidence of correspondence and numerous conversations on the subject occurring behind the scenes. Thus Chapman reports on conversations he had with people at the reform institution ("people told me . . . what the girls had to submit to"), with officials in Paris ("I was told that it was a frequent occurrence"), and with various policemen in England ("I can only say what the police tell me" and "an Inspector said that the evil which was brought to my attention was very much on the increase lately"). Lord Wemyss also announces authoritatively, "One has heard that it is on the increase as long as one remembers," while Muir Mackenzie states, "It has been known for centuries." That such discussions were by no means rare exposes unequivocally the existence of public secrets—in the formal setting of a parliamentary hearing, a silence of sorts ("it") coexists alongside terse, cryptic references. As Foucault notes: "What is peculiar to modern societies . . . is not that they consigned sex to a shadow existence, but that they dedicated themselves to speaking of it *ad infinitum*, while exploiting it as *the* secret."[97] The refusal or simple inability to name the act or to distinguish between nonconsensual, cross-generational sexual relations and same-sex relations between consenting adults demonstrates persuasively that sexological labels and distinctions had, at this stage, minimal impact within legal discourse.

This sort of confusion about what is under discussion or what should be criminalized dissolves when the question goes before Parliament during the debate on the CLA Bill in 1921, yet the delicate circumspection about discussing sexual inversion remains. Macquisten opened the debate by announcing that the topic under consideration—"acts of indecency by females"— could not be discussed frankly in the Commons: "One cannot in a public assembly go into the details; it is more a matter for medical science and for neurologists. But all lawyers who have had criminal and divorce practice know that there is in modern social life an undercurrent of dreadful degradation, unchecked and uninterfered with."[98] When the Lords took up the clause, Malmesbury, who had sat on the 1920 Joint Select Committee that had heard Chapman's testimony, apologizes for even initiating "a discussion upon what must be, to all of us, a most disgusting and polluting subject," and the Earl of Desart notes that it is "very disagreeable talking of these things."[99] In an earlier presexological age, one wonders if the whispers were also preceded by loud apologies, because such matters could not be discussed by "decent" people. Yet this time it is obvious none of the well-mannered gentlemen intends to abandon the "disgusting" subject; the apology is nothing more than a rhetorical device to break public silence.

The parliamentarians' next crucial order of business was to gauge the boundaries of intelligibility; in other words, to speculate on who knew what. Two constituencies, according to the various speakers, have a degree of familiarity with the "gross practices": medical men (especially neurologists and physicians who work in asylums) and legal men (in particular criminologists, lawyers, and police). In the epigraph to this section, Macquisten is quoted as saying that "those who have had to engage either in medical or in legal practice know that every now and again one comes across these horrors." Most of those who voted in favor of the clause in the Commons were "leaders of the Bar who happen to be Members of the House."[100] Yet Macquisten exclaims that "to many Members of this House the mere idea of the suggestion of such a thing is entirely novel; they have never heard of it" (1800). Colonel Wedgwood then asserts that the intention of the clause would have to be explained to members of the Labour party who, by their lack of a public school education, would not have encountered the "Lesbian vice": "For their benefit, I will tell them that the ordinary boy who goes to a public school learns at that public school from the classics which he reads about what is known as Lesbian vice" (1801). Thus, knowledge of such practices, demarcated by profession and class, can be exploited, as Foucault argues, as "*the* secret." Equally interesting is the assumption that the very group most affected by the proposed clause, women, are largely ignorant of such practices. The lord chancellor, for example, refutes the suggestion that the practice is well known and states that "the overwhelming majority of the women of this country have never heard of this thing at all. . . . I would be bold enough to say that of every thousand women, taken as a whole, 999 have never even heard a *whisper* of these practices."[101] Ironically, the knowledge of "such practices" circulated in some circles precisely in the form of whispers, which generates discourse as effectively as medical science.

Of all the members, only Sir Ernest Wild refers to specific sexologists in his speech when he relates how in preparation for the parliamentary discussion of the clause (as a cosponsor he researched the topic prior to the debate) he had consulted "one of the greatest of our nerve specialists" (1803). This unnamed "expert" affirms in his letter to Wild that sexological literature is indispensable in understanding the full spectrum of female sexual "malpractices":

> It would be difficult to recite the various forms of malpractices between women, as it would be impossible to recite them in the House. If you wish for these it would be best to obtain a copy of Kfraft-Ebing [sic] "Psychopathia Sexualis," or Havelock Ellis's work on sexual malpractices. My own feeling is simply to refer to the Lesbian love practices between women, which are common knowledge. (1803)

Curiously, according to the logic of the nerve specialist, sexology itself is unspeakable and ordinary "Lesbian love practices" are common knowledge. Sexologists may have identified a whole range of sexual activities between females but it would be wholly inappropriate to mention these in a public forum—ironically, Wild announces this not only to his parliamentary colleagues but to a gallery packed with feminist supporters of the CLA Bill.[102] In presenting to the Commons a portion of the letter that mentions two leading sexologists by name, Wild steals the prestige of scientific knowledge, its veneer so to speak, to legitimize his own political agenda. Wild thus speaks with the authority of science but cleverly distances himself from any of the arguments of these same sexologists who, as "congenitalists," argue that since true sexual inversion is congenital it should not be subject to legislation. His eagerness to cite these men by name does not signal an acceptance of their conclusions, which explains why Wild's descriptive language is at logger-heads with sexology: lesbianism, for Wild, is "a beastly subject," a "vice" and "a very real evil" (1802). Wild fails to grasp, or chooses to ignore, sex-ology's principal achievement in shifting the terms of the debate from moral-ity to modern medical discourse.

What we see here is the formation of an incipient understanding of how "scientific" objectivity could be deployed to work productively on behalf of a law to control sexual deviance. For men such as Wild sexology's real appeal is simply its guise of scientific authority. The use of sexology to call for the legislation of lesbianism thus represents not merely a *selective* use of its find-ings but the virtual turning of sexology against itself. Consider, for exam-ple, Macquisten's vaguely oxymoronic phrase, "homosexual immorality," which marries a scientific term with a moral imperative (1800). Inasmuch as the word "homosexual" operates as an adjective, the weight of the phrase leans more heavily toward immorality—demarcating simply one form over others, though the threat homosexuality poses to "feminine morality" strikes at the heart of civilization. That the preferred term for the "very real evil" is "vice," which appears literally dozens of times throughout the debates, suggests again that the central tenets of sexology have been either rejected or unassimilated. This is evident in Desart's question: "How many people does one suppose really are so vile, so unbalanced, so neurotic, so decadent as to do this?"[103] This laundry list of attributes, which slips between psy-chology, popular belief, and cultural anxiety, reflects a very real confusion about and conflation of the subject matter.

A skilled lawyer, Wild cites a number of cases to support his argument in favor of the clause, some reminiscent of Chapman's earlier testimony. First, Wild recounts how the nerve specialist told him "that no week passes that some unfortunate girl does not confess to him [the specialist] that she owes the breakdown of her nerves to the fact that she has been tampered with by a member of her own sex" (1803). Wild also produces a report from the Cen-tral Criminal Court "in which a witness stated on oath that this practice had taken place between her and an elder woman," and that any "chief officers of police" would confirm that the case was not unusual. Finally, he reports that "many asylum doctors . . . assure me that the asylums are largely peopled by nymphomaniacs and people who indulge in this vice." (Macquisten also relates how "there is . . . much victimization of young women by their own sex."[104]) Unlike Chapman, who was careful to distinguish between sexual acts between women and girls and lesbianism, Wild conflates the two because his purpose is simply to prove that the latter practices exist, with greater or lesser frequency. It is inconsequential whether or not such cases are the result of congenital sexual inversion. Thus while Wild ostensibly builds his case on behalf of the criminalization of lesbianism upon the convergence of medical and legal opinions, using such case histories as proof, careful scrutiny of his "evidence" reveals that these cases are less than persuasive and that his batch of "experts" never specifically endorses his agenda—a savvy politician would have most certainly cited them if they had. One presumes that his medicolegal "experts" were familiar with the dominant position among sexologists that homosexual acts between consenting adults should be exempt from the law. Such a position, in direct contradiction of Wild's aims, would have been in concert with the leading advanced views of the age, as articulated by sexologists such as Forel who writes: "So long as homosexual love does not affect minors nor insane persons, it is comparatively innocent. . . . Legal protection of the two sexes against sexual abuses of all kinds should be extended at least to the age of seventeen or eighteen."[105]

Just as in the 1920 parliamentary hearing, the question of whether female homosexuality was increasing was both at the forefront of the parliamentary debate and at the same time lacked consensus. Macquisten asserted that "these horrors" occur "every now and again," while Wild claims doctors say "this is a very prevalent practice," only to contradict himself later by stating, "I will not say the vice is rampant in society [but] there are people in society who are guilty of it" (1800, 1803). Opponents of the clause such as Lord Desart retorted: "You may say there are a number of them, but it would be, at most, an extremely small minority" (573). The fixation on the frequency of same-sex relations between women suggests that, swirling beneath the legal body's determination that the "vice" should be halted before it spreads too far was a growing anxiety, as feminist historians affirm, about female emancipation and increased sexual sophistication. For supporters of the clause such as Wild, female homosexuality was just one indication of the decline of civilization that "saps the fundamental institutions of society" (1804). Wild elaborates on this point by claiming that the vice "stops child-birth, because it is a well-known fact that any woman who indulges in this vice will have nothing whatever to do with the other sex. . . . [This] vice . . . must tend to cause our race to decline."[106] This idea is echoed by Macquisten who argues that it is "best to stamp out an evil which is capable of sapping the highest and the best in civilization" (1800). Chapman's earlier concern for the welfare of young girls pales in comparison with a lesbian threat that strikes out at a vulnerable society, indeed the survival of the race itself.

As I have previously mentioned, Weeks speculates that the writer responsible for establishing this "well-known" fact was Arabella Kenealy. For Kenealy, the women's movement "de-sexed and masculinized" women, and although masculinized women had always been considered "abnormal" in previous years, lately it "has become a serious Cult." Such a woman "is incapable of parenthood," and thus feminism leads to "Race-suicide."[107] Before the war, in 1909, the eugenicist couple William and Catherine Whetham warned that the "interests of active public life . . . exert such a fascination on the minds of [unmarried] . . . women that they become unwilling to accept the necessary and wholesome restrictions and responsibilities of normal marriage and motherhood. Woe to the nation whose best women refuse their natural and most glorious burden!"[108] The feminism under attack in this passage is responsible for the decline of female morality and for the increase in lesbianism. In fact, several sexologists, including Carpenter, Forel, and Magnus Hirschfeld, believed there was a strong lesbian presence in the women's movement, as Ellis notes: "[Iwan] Bloch and others believe that the woman movement has helped to develop homosexuality."[109] Ellis himself was "most concerned," but for a different reason; he believed the "Women's Movement was encouraging . . . not true inversion but its 'spurious imitation.'"[110] Female homosexuality thus becomes a significant threat to civilization and the future of the race. Pervading the parliamentary discussion is this new "fact" of modern life: same-sex relations between females signaled the decline of civilization and the undermining of the institution of marriage. To clinch this argument, Wild and Macquisten each describe a case known to them where a marriage had been destroyed either by a "wife [who] had been taken from [the husband] by a young woman" or "by the wiles of one abandoned female" (1803, 1800). In the latter situation the corrupted wife subsequently became involved with a man, which was fortunate because the long-suffering husband could then establish grounds for divorce. Neither Wild nor Macquisten clarified whether any of these activities constituted clinically defined female inversion or consensual same-sex relations between women, since legislators were uninterested in the distinction.

From opponents of the clause we find a greater sympathy, though not a particularly clear-cut understanding, for the position of groups such as the BSSSP who in 1914 published an English translation of a 1903 German pamphlet on *The Social Problem of Sexual Inversion*. This pamphlet advocated the most advanced view of its time in arguing that because "God, or Nature, has brought into being not only normal men and women but uranians . . . it is really too ridiculous to imagine that the processes of nature can be abolished, or even appreciably restrained, by pen and paper enactments."[111]

Obviously, those opposed to the criminalization of homosexuality were at a disadvantage inasmuch as the very reason for the discussion—to insert a clause into the Criminal Law Amendment Bill—already plunged the subject into a criminal context with a moral tone. But as Wedgwood explains, "You cannot make people moral by Act of Parliament" (1801). Lieutenant-Colonel Moore-Brabazon, who concedes the need for a certain "moral courage" to join the discussion, also urges his fellow members to remember "that on this subject we are not dealing with crime at all. We are dealing with abnormalities of the brain . . . [and must] decide whether it is wise to deal with mental cases in the Law Courts" (1804). He then puts an interesting twist on Kenealy's "race-suicide" argument: "These cases are self-exterminating . . . they have the merit of exterminating themselves, and consequently they do not spread or do very much harm to society at large" (1805–6). Here Moore-Brabazon maintains that the inability of such women to bear children is positive, as the failure to procreate prevents the spread of lesbianism—a point also voiced by Malmesbury: "I believe that all these unfortunate specimens of humanity exterminate themselves by the usual process."[112] This argument had been made some years earlier by Forel when he queried, "What is the use of prosecuting inverts?"

> It is comparatively innocent, for it produces no offspring and consequently dies out by means of selection. . . . It is a fortunate thing for society that . . . [they] are contented with their mutual sexual intercourse, the result of which is sterile and therefore does no harm to posterity.[113]

The feminist press branded the "small but determined group of opponents" who successfully derailed the CLA Bill "obstructionists," whose aim was to prevent at any cost the passage of a bill that would eliminate the favored loophole allowing a man to claim he had "reasonable cause to believe" a woman was over the age of consent.[114] When the "Acts of indecency by females" clause was rejected by the Lords and the entire bill returned to the Commons, the obstructionists protested speciously that wrecking the bill had never been their intention for, like the bill's many supporters, they too were motivated solely by a concern for the protection of the young, male and female alike.[115] Yet if the obstructionists had indeed been sympathetic to the larger bill, they would hardly have introduced a contentious clause, especially one so malicious and calculated to shock. Its very indelicacy undoubtedly embarrassed and humiliated some social purity advocates and feminists (including lesbians) who had campaigned actively for over a year for the CLA Bill's passage.[116] That the supporters of the bill were completely caught by surprise when the clause was proposed in the final hours of the debate is evidenced in a letter the AMSH secretary, Alison Neilans, had already written to Astor to celebrate the victory: "I am just writing to offer you my very sincere and hearty congratulations on the passage of the Criminal Law Amendment Bill."[117] Once Neilans became aware of the controversial clause, she sent a letter to several members of the House of Lords on August 12, 1921, characterizing the subject matter as "repulsive, and indeed unintelligible to many people."[118] In general, the feminist press echoed this AMSH position and further pointed out that the clause would not only expose women to blackmail "of a peculiarly revolting kind" but would be impossible to prove.[119] The one feminist newspaper to draw on sexology, the *Shield*, vigorously challenged the minority feminist view that the clause against lesbianism at least "equalized" the sexes. This editorial praised Havelock Ellis as "perhaps the greatest living authority of all these difficult and perplexing problems" and offered the most advanced and sophisticated response to the clause by reading it against earlier legislation of male homosexuality:

The truth is that it is slowly being recognized that these laws provide the most fertile source of blackmail against both normal and abnormal men; that the offences are extremely difficult either to prove or disprove, and that modern scientific opinion is opposed to laws which attempt to punish very severely, not only the vicious pervert, but also the invert who is not really responsible for his psychic abnormality, and in whom the normal development of his sexual life is impossible owing to the congenital misdirection of his instinct.[120]

Despite the obstructionists' dire warnings of the social consequences of female sexual inversion, no law was ever passed against "gross indecency between females." When the CLA Bill was reintroduced in July 1922 the obstructionists' burning concern over the lesbian menace suddenly vanished once they found they could cut a satisfactory deal "retaining the defence of 'reasonable cause' for men under twenty-three."[121] The CLA Bill of 1922 passed into law without a single mention of lesbianism. The obstructionists had won—for not only did the earlier CLA Bill fail but feminist supporters were smeared with the unsavory association of inversion, a happy by-product. This might explain the silence surrounding the clause in some feminist newspapers: the topic may have been a little too close to home. Such a heightened sense of caution is seen in a letter written by a friend to Vita Sackville-West: "One thing I did urgently want to call to your attention was 'The

Criminal Law Amendment Bill' and the clause that was inserted in the Bill at the third reading. It only makes me *implore* you to be *careful*."[122] The antilesbian clause, while basically a desperate measure to sink a bill that threatened male privilege, had the potential to wreck any woman's life.

Rather than a tool of control in the service of patriarchal hegemony, sexology served multiple functions and conflicting political agendas. Men of law who sought to protect children or to preserve a legal loophole were just as inclined to rely on hearsay and rumor, gleaned in the backrooms of police stations or in reports from unnamed sources as on sexological notions. In the attempt to impose regulatory legislation of same-sex relations between women, sexology could be abused whether one's political agenda was conservative or liberal, homophobic or homogenic, or even feminist. Historians invested in the negative critique of sexology presume—incorrectly—that it drifted into the public domain in a more-or-less pure state, and that sexologists were complicit with antifeminists and homophobes who launched a backlash against both feminists and lesbians. On the contrary, in legal discursive practices at this time we see that sexology would all too often be read against itself, its ideological force diluted through misinterpretation and simplification, its medical taxonomies ignored or glossed. Far from avidly consuming sexology, legislators would exploit its nuanced findings in ways that many sexologists would not have sanctioned. Whether articulated as an "it" or as a perversion of sexological language, as with "homosexual vice," female sexual inversion as a coherent sexological construction did not exist within 1920s legal discourse. The invocation of the medical labels never necessarily signified the unmediated acquisition of the relevant medical knowledge. Words such as "lesbian" or "invert" could refer to *any* sort of sexual act between females, without regard to the fine distinctions advanced by Ellis, whose designation "congenital sexual inversion" was intended to remove any stigma of sin, mental illness, or physical disease.

In the end, lesbianism was not the primary target, and sexology was not the effective strategic weapon its detractors claim. Thus feminist historians who view sexology as a weapon are both right and wrong; that is, they are correct in their conclusions but wrong in their method, for we must always be cautious, as George Chauncey Jr. reminds us, not to attribute "inordinate power to ideology as an autonomous social force."[123] Sexual science obliquely facilitated legislation by lending its veneer of prestige; however, the full explanatory power of sexology's case histories, its epistemologies and taxonomies, became, in the hands of the would-be oppressors, misused, adulterated, and impure. Legislative interest in lesbianism was more likely to be a circuitous and tangential route to attain other ends, such as exercising efficient control over an independently minded women's police force or conveniently preserving a legal loophole ("reasonable cause to believe"). We give far too much credit to men such as Pemberton Billing, Fox-Pitt, to the Met, or to the obstructionists if we characterize their actions as part of an elaborate, sustained, and coordinated attack on lesbianism rather than as isolated, diverse, and narrow. In the early 1920s lesbianism was not a "fact" marked on the body, nor was it commonly understood as a particular sexual object choice or sexual practice between women, nor was it (as yet) a modern identity or subjectivity—instead, lesbianism was, as Neilans argued in her letter to particular members of the House of Lords, "indeed unintelligible to many people." Nameless or not, the entering of the "vice between women" into legal discourse and public consciousness marked an important step in the formation of a subcultural identity because, as Weeks so aptly explains, "social regulation provides the conditions within which those defined can begin to develop their own consciousness and identity."[124] The potentially explosive topic of women who desired women, or women with no interest in men, was a tinderbox waiting for a spark.

Three

Outraging the Decencies of Nature?
Uniformed Female Bodies

I

ON APRIL 18, 1918, Vita Sackville-West's life "changed suddenly."[1] Although married to diplomat Harold Nicolson and a mother of two young sons, at age twenty-eight she had just discovered what she described as the duality of her nature ("in which the feminine and the masculine elements alternately preponderate") and was about to embark recklessly on a passionate affair with her childhood friend, Violet Trefusis (102). In an unpublished autobiography discovered after her death, Sackville-West attributes the sudden exuberance of "one of the most vibrant days of [her] life," not to Trefusis herself but to particular articles of clothing: "An absurd circumstance gave rise to the whole thing; I had just got clothes like the women-on-the-land were wearing, and in the unaccustomed freedom of breeches and gaiters I went into wild spirits; I ran, I shouted, I jumped, I climbed, I vaulted over gates, I felt like a schoolboy let out on a holiday."[2] "Breeches and gaiters" were the catalyst for a radical life-changing moment that culminated in an entirely new sense of self and a headlong plunge into lesbian desire. This episode captures succinctly how masculine clothing was extraordinarily transformative for women at this time—and not just any sort of male clothing but a military-style outfit "like the women-on-the land were wearing."

Sackville-West was not alone in her discovery that a uniform-like garb could trigger a sense of adventure and an "unaccustomed freedom" of movement. During the First World War, women everywhere could be seen in every sort of uniform: "in offices, shops, railway companies, banks, acting, writing, driving taxis, ploughing the land, taming vicious horses, felling trees . . . [dressed] in khaki, blue, brown, or grey, with slouch hat, round hat, or no hat at all, in skirts as short as ballet girls' or in masculine breeches."[3] In 1918 the *Sphere* commented ironically: "Quite half the feminine world must be in uniform now."[4] Uniforms on female bodies had become, as historian Angela Woollacott astutely explains, "emblems of [women's] direct involvement in the war effort. . . . Uniforms carried enormous social prestige and symbolism. A war-related uniform was an immediately recognizable emblem of patriotic engagement, of dedication to the nation's cause. To wear such a uniform was a statement at once political and moral."[5] Yet throughout the war the public response to women in uniform remained mixed, as seen in the Marchioness of Londonderry's account of the gap between her own personal pleasure and the reactions of others: "I always wore uniform, and never before was life, from the feminine standpoint of dress, so delightful. You wore it at functions, you wore it for every day, at funerals or weddings. It led indeed to some strange experiences. Some people were always rude to a woman in uniform . . . they were incredulous or laughed outright."[6] Naomi Jacob likewise recalls that all women in uniform, except nurses, were thought "strange, eccentric, and a fine target for jokes."[7] Writer Mary Agnes Hamilton, on the other hand, remembers the scrutiny of onlookers as overwhelmingly positive:

> Women wore trousers or knickers and puttees in perfect immunity from the guffaws that once greeted the brave spirits who had clambered upon bicycles in divided skirts; the lift-girl in smart boots, the driver of official car and public taxi in neat breeches and leggings, the munition girl and the land girl in trousers and overalls were not so much remarked upon by anybody. They were in uniform: uniform was immune from jeer or sneer.[8]

While such diverse recollections of the impact of a uniformed woman in the public sphere seem the inevitable product of the vagaries of personal memory, quite clearly the individual woman in uniform was as central to the overall spectatorial effect as the actual uniform itself, as we will see in the response of the London Metropolitan Police to different women's policing groups.

The *Daily Express* was more restrained in its assessment of the athletic "well-developed, powerful" girl in uniform against the prewar "lass with the delicate air": "One has only to compare any well-tailored, stoutly-shod young Eve in uniform with the vanished silhouettes of tan, teas and garden parties to judge of the aesthetic as well as the utilitarian value of the war girl. There is no 'camouflage' about her beauty."[9] The war girl, though "well-tailored" and "stoutly-shod," is every bit as beautiful as her prewar counterpart, if not more so. The article valiantly stretches the feminine "aesthetic" to encompass the war girl's vigor and strength, qualities hitherto associated with masculinity. But the attempt seems strained, and one suspects that admiration for a "well-developed" physique had more to do with wartime pragmatism than genuine appreciation. For one thing, the lyrical phrase "vanished silhouette" conjures up a lingering nostalgia for a past cultural aesthetic completely absent in "utilitarian value." While it cannot be denied that the war girl's new qualities signal a loss of traditional femininity, the *Daily Express* exhorts readers not to despair; masculine clothing cannot prevent her from fulfilling her primary role: "[The war girl] has the grace of the athlete and the reality and sanity of her charm fit her to be the ideal girl of today and mother of tomorrow." Not all members of the public were convinced by such arguments, as seen in a letter sent to the editor of the YWCA magazine by a sergeant in the Royal Flying Corps who complained, "The days are so strange now when women are doing their best to become like men in dress, smoking and drinking, that one wonders where it will ever stop. I think that women would do best to keep all that men admire, which is a womanly woman."[10]

Such strange days are illustrated in a 1918 *Punch* cartoon in which two dapper fellows in uniform survey two other figures, one also in uniform, at some distance in a garden. To the first officer's question, "Who's the knock-kneed chap with your sister, old man?" the second officer replies, "My other sister."[11] During the war such cases of "mistaken identity" could seem more amusing than anything else. A story about "Wiffs" (Women's Land Army) in the *Daily Mail* suggests that the occasional instance of gender confusion resulted not in angry hostility but gentle teasing: "The guard of the train by which the 'Wiffs' travelled Londonwards asked what particular kind of land work they did. 'We are fellers,' replied one of the party. 'And I thought you were young ladies,' said the guard with a chuckle."[12] Such jovial light-heartedness was another way of coping with the realization that female bodies were everywhere "cross-dressed" in military or police uniforms. When one exasperated reader wrote to the editor of the *Daily Express* to complain that a girl in uniform "puts her feet on the mantelpiece, sprawls on the rug, smokes, and, abomination of abominations, she whistles!," the primary objection was that most people no longer found such things objectionable.[13] Whether the sight of uniformed women inspired begrudging acceptance or wholehearted support, one message became increasingly clear: Britons slow to accept the new sort of war girl were just old-fashioned.

After the war, however, it was a different story, and women in uniform became fair game for pundits, as seen in the harsher jibes of *Punch*. In one 1919 cartoon, for example, a woman in breeches and jacket resembling the Women's Land Army uniform places her order with the butcher while those behind her in the queue barely conceal their indignation. The cartoon sarcastically dubs the woman's dress as a "favored uniform," but she has unknowingly become the object of whispers, scowls, and bemused looks. An "indignant lady" in the queue remarks, "I suppose *I'd* have had a chance if I'd had breeches on."[14] No longer a sign of women's patriotism, the uniform in the postwar era became at best a signifier of gender confusion and at worst an indisputable sign of the inappropriate appropriation of masculine power. Still, whether for greater economic opportunity, intense erotic pleasure, or access to jobs once exclusively available to men, some women wore uniforms of their own design with only a tenuous link to an officially recognized organization or with no link at all. Such women risked public censure and greater measures of social control by continuing to wear a uniform— whether police or military—in the postwar era because, unlike traditional women's clothing, such a uniform had the amazing effect of transforming their entire manner of self-presentation and interaction with others.

The uniform accelerated the trend toward more masculine fashions for women, thus posing a unique and significant challenge to conventional notions of femininity in a decade when Englishwomen were drawn to different sorts of masculine clothing for different reasons. This chapter begins by examining the uniform of the Women Police Service (WPS) as one of the most vivid examples of the ways in which uniform clothing and its accoutrements possessed the power to destabilize gender and sexuality in the immediate postwar era, even in the absence of official recognition by authoritative bodies. WPS Commandant Mary Sophia Allen's manly struggle to establish her organization as an officially recognized, permanent, independent female police force in London pitted her and other WPS leaders squarely against the London Metropolitan Police (Met), as I have discussed in chapter 2. Curiously, although the Met could have initiated legal proceedings against Allen and the WPS on any number of grounds, the policemen built their case around the problematic status of the WPS uniform. Allen's commitment to a female police force was bound inextricably to the uniform— policing itself was inconceivable to her without it, and her passion for her own uniform was thought by many to be excessive. If, as historian Angus McLaren argues, masculine women became vulnerable to social policing for gender transgression, Mary Allen was certainly a prime suspect.[15]

Since women in uniform already looked quite masculine, male impersonation for some became even more tempting. Sackville-West records how on several occasions in 1918 she dressed in men's clothing and passed as an ex-soldier, wrapping a khaki bandage around her head: "It must have been successful, because no one looked at me at all curiously or suspiciously—never once, out of the many times I did it. . . . It was marvellous fun, all the more so because there was always the risk of being found out" (105). Colonel Victor Barker (who was known by several other names, including Valerie Arkell-Smith) also risked passing as an ex-soldier until she was found out.[16] The discovery of the colonel's true biological sex captured headlines in 1929 and was "one of the few stories that have really astonished Fleet Street," as one journalist put it.[17] For nearly six years Barker had worn the uniform of a military officer and had passed undetected as a man—a "masquerade" so convincing that Barker had married a woman in a church. This audacious act resulted in a tongue-lashing by a judge who proclaimed that she had "outraged the decencies of nature."[18] In the final section of this chapter I analyze how the female body dressed in a masculine or male uniform produces surprisingly diverse spectatorial effects. By reading the ways in which Allen and Barker were construed within legal and journalistic discursive practices, I argue that women such as the leaders of the Women Police Service, who retained their uniforms *without* approval from the authorities, became vulnerable to social and legal regulation—some were accused of attempting to "masquerade" in men's clothing—a phenomenon quite distinct from both Colonel Barker's "masquerade" and, as I discuss in chapter 4, the playfully boyish or gracefully masculine fashions of the 1920s.

II

TO UNDERSTAND HOW and why the uniform became the center of the fracas between the WPS and the Met, I will first review the events that led up to the 1920–21 legal dispute. General Sir Nevil Macready, commissioner of the Met from 1918 to 1920, believed that women could play a special role in policing, but that to be successful, any such organization had to operate under the auspices of an established police force—that is, under male authority. Further, the women chosen for the new force would have to be the right sort, possessing, in Macready's terms, "broad-mindedness and kindly sympathy"—qualities Macready believed were absent in the WPS.[19] Consequently, in creating his own female force, the Metropolitan Women Police Patrols (MWPP), Macready passed over the WPS. To guarantee the future of his new organization, Macready selected the compliant Mrs. Sophia Stanley, who shared Macready's vision of a female force with limited powers (Stanley thought the power of arrest for policewomen unnecessary) as well as his prejudices against the WPS.[20] Far from driving the WPS into extinction, the creation of the MWPP had the effect of impelling WPS leaders to intensify their efforts to attain official recognition in London. From 1918 until the early 1920s the WPS remained highly visible—in full uniform—in London and petitioned vigorously anyone who might be influential in supporting their cause. Because the WPS refused to abandon its plans, the Met was forced to consider further, perhaps even unorthodox, measures to drive the women's organization out of existence. Although Macready usually resorted to code in speaking about the WPS (hence his use of the phrase "broadmindedness and kindly sympathy" to mean, among other qualities, traditionally feminine and nonfeminist), he was quite straightforward in his threat that "steps will be taken to do away with this anomaly."[21]

Once the MWPP was established, Macready, a former military officer of distinction and with a reputation as a man of action, considered the options available to deal with the WPS. Its continued visibility in London undermined not only the authority of the MWPP but also that of its overseer, the Met itself. From the Met's perspective, the presence of a rival, indeed renegade, female police force "posing," as Macready put it, "as Police Women in the streets of London," would create both "inconvenience and uncertainty in the mind of the public."[22] If we take Macready at his word, the problem with the WPS was that it constituted a viable imitation of his own force, the MWPP, and thus the public would unwittingly mistake the bogus for the official. We would expect the head of the Met to have serious objections to any group pretending to be police; however, the intensity and aggressiveness of the Met campaign that followed suggest that other factors in addition to a concern for public well-being may have been in effect. For Macready and others at the Met the WPS was an intolerable nuisance in many respects: some members' previous involvement in suffrage organizations was unacceptable as was the upper-class background of many of its members; their understanding of police procedures and powers was faulty; WPS members operated in some areas without permission from the authorities and were therefore "amateurs"; and so on. Although the list of grievances was long and varied, the Met concentrated less on such factors than on what they considered most unconventional and unacceptable: the WPS uniform. I argue that the Met seized on the WPS uniform as *the* site of contestation because of its unsettling effects, specified and unspecified. Both the Met and the WPS leadership were obsessively preoccupied with the uniform because each came to recognize how it embodied a form of masculine power hitherto unassociated with women, even if and when such power was not sanctioned by the state. Thus Macready's stated concern about the WPS uniform's potential to confuse the public masked deeper and more troubling worries about the collapse of much more, and explains why even when the Met had other grounds for attacking the WPS (no one, for instance, contested that the female group was intruding into the London area without jurisdiction and authority), it continued in an almost foolhardy way to focus exclusively on what might have been, in the eyes of the law, a gray area.

In September 1919 Macready requested verification from the Home Office that the MWPP uniform was protected under the provisions of Section 10 of the Police Act of 1919 that stated: "If any person not being a member of a police force wears without the permission of the police authority the uniform of the police force, or any dress having the appearance or bearing any of the distinctive marks of that uniform, he shall on summary conviction be liable to a fine not exceeding ten pounds."[23] After the government's assurance that the MWPP uniform was indeed "official," Macready decided on a course of action to put pressure on the WPS to surrender its uniform and, by reducing the organization's visibility, hasten its demise. With the backing of the Home Office, the Met was fully in control and confidently poised, if necessary, to prosecute the WPS under Section 10; yet it would take the Met leadership nearly a year to reach this stage in their attack. Before proceeding with the Met's grievance, Macready checked with legal experts at the Home Office not once but twice—the legal wrangling lasted several months. Carrier attributes Macready's obsessive behavior to the fact that he "wanted to be quite sure of his ground before commencing battle. He knew the WPS would be able to command the services of good lawyers on their behalf and he did not want to take any chances."[24] For a seasoned officer accustomed to the stresses of conflict, Macready seemed, as someone in the Home Office observed, "unnecessarily apprehensive."

Further evidence of Macready's extreme caution in dealing with the WPS can be seen in his craftily worded testimony in February 1920 to the Baird Committee. With regard to the WPS, Macready told the committee: "I thought it only right that the public should not be deceived by having people get themselves up in a uniform who can be *reasonably* mistaken for our own [MWPP] women."[25] The phrasing here is interesting, for Macready argues not that the WPS uniform looked exactly like that of the MWPP but that the public might "reasonably" mistake the WPS for real police. The tentativeness implicit in Macready's use of the word "reasonably" likely stems from the fact that he knew that his explanation to the Baird Committee glossed over some important facts. First, since Commandant Margaret Damer Dawson had designed the WPS uniform in 1914, if any group wore the "copy" of an "original" it was the MWPP. In fact, the Met found itself in the unenviable position of demonstrating precisely how the two uniforms were the same—a task that absorbed the better part of ten days for the investigating officer—while arguing that the WPS, not the MWPP, had copied the uniform's design. Second, since Macready and others at the Met found the WPS uniform so excessively masculine, why did they approve a similar uniform for their own female force in the first place? What remained stubbornly unacknowledged throughout the uniform controversy was the fact that neither Macready nor the WPS leaders cared for a moment that the WPS uniform looked like that of the MWPP. Clearly, what was at issue here was less the actual cut and design of any particular uniform and more the behavior performed by those wearing it; in other words, in the convoluted warfare waged between the Met and the WPS, the latter's use of the uniform was a threat, in Macready's view, to official police power because it represented that which was disturbing and culturally disruptive. All the delicate maneuvering during the hearings in the spring of 1921 was a subterfuge for a complex constellation of issues relating to gender and sexuality that neither group could articulate in a public forum: above all, the dangerous, radical potential symbolically invested in the uniform to upset normative gender roles and the interrelationship between masculine women and sexuality. To better understand the cultural significance of the WPS uniform for the individual wearer as well as the onlooker, I will examine its distinctive design and then analyze the role it played in questions revolving around gender and sexuality.

As I have already mentioned, Damer Dawson created the first WPS uniform soon after the outbreak of war in 1914. This earliest version of the uniform, Mary Allen writes, was "very simple" and "business-like . . . dark blue, plainly cut, with shoulder straps bearing . . . WPS, in silver letters. With a hard felt hat to complete their costume, the new members of the force were chiefly *conspicuous* for their sober neatness."[26] From the organization's inception, WPS leaders opted for a uniform that most approximated that of their male counterparts. No group with designs for permanence would have chosen khaki, which signaled a temporary response to the exigencies of war.[27] Allen's description downplays what would have been obvious to anyone surveying WPS members patrolling the streets anywhere: the WPS uniform made few concessions to the fact that it was worn by a female. In 1917 Damer Dawson modified the early design for the senior ranks because, as Allen explains, "it became necessary to have some distinguishing marks between the ranks" (25). Since the WPS was working more closely with the military in "munitions areas" during this time, senior officers, according to Allen, wanted to ensure that officers could be clearly distinguished from lesser ranks. Allen further justifies the change because, when the WPS became responsible for wider areas, the leaders began to patrol in "motor transport": "Commandant Damer Dawson and I were the first to use motor bicycles on police inspection duty in Great Britain" (25). Allen's account of the uniform change is not disingenuous, but it neatly glosses over the fact that officers' uniforms took on a more masculine appearance than the uniform worn by the lower ranks. Thus the design modification may have been highly significant for reasons other than those Allen offers, as we will see below.

Unlike many other kinds of uniforms that attempted to preserve femininity, such as those worn by women in some military organizations or transport workers, the police uniform—the representation of the law—remained largely unchanged for its female wearers. In wearing a uniform all too similar to that of their male counterparts, women in policing organizations were allowed freedom from the constrictions of traditional feminine clothing but were doomed to appear "as the parody of a police-man . . . The hat is absurd, the boots heavy and ridiculous."[28] To tamper with the uniform of the police was to endanger the efficacy of law enforcement. If women "wear their bodies through their clothes,"[29] the challenge for such women was to retain crucial signs of femininity because police uniforms rarely preserved those essential feminine features. The police uniform erases femininity at every turn: rigid lines flatten curves and breasts, the cap or helmet obscures the length of one's hair, leather boots appear heavy and large. Such a uniform does not flatter the female figure but instead invites the onlooker to scrutinize the body more intensely in order to discover those signs of femininity so effectively suppressed by the designers of the WPS officers' uniform. Their uniform was notably masculine: high black boots, high-peaked hats (in some cases concealing closely cropped hair), numerous brass buttons, leather straps and belts, and military insignia (figure 2). To top it off, officers wore greatcoats that further obscured what was worn underneath: breeches or skirts. Such a manifestly unfeminine uniform alerted the onlooker to the presence of women impinging on the territory of supreme masculine authority by an organization that sought such power on equal terms. Unlike the glorified "scout leader" uniform or simple armband of rival female policing groups, the WPS's uniform incorporated the symbols of military power.

Despite the uniform's inextricable connection with masculinity, certain women managed to retain something of their femininity, as seen in a photograph of Stanley in a soft felt hat and gently tailored jacket of the MWPP (figure 3). Such miniscule modifications in the fabric and the cut assist particular women in conveying a modicum of womanliness, though against tough odds. Lilian Wyles, for example, who upon the advice of Cecil Chapman decided to join the MWPP rather than the WPS, called the same uniform "unspeakable . . . Harrods made it, but it was designed elsewhere, surely by men who had a spite against us."[30] Wyles portrays the uniform as an attack by men against women. The WPS uniform was modeled on that of a police constable and, though designed for the female body by a woman, it kept the constable's "numerous pockets and belted tunic-like appearance."[31] Philippa Levine notes that the WPS uniform had a "consciously military styling . . . [that] trumpeted women's assumption of substantial war work, a shift in their role, and a new appreciation and acknowledgement of their physical capabilities."[32] This uniform marked a departure in the history of uniforms for women, which had previously "signified the servitude and domesticity associated with traditionally female work." Damer Dawson's design projected an image of forcefulness and power rather than "servitude and domesticity," as Chapman, the magistrate who would preside over the the the hearing concerning the uniform dispute, would politely summarize for the press: "I must say the officers of the [Women] Police Service have all the appearance of military officers. The only difference is that the former are ladies."[33]

Chapman's distinction is informed by class assumptions. Diana Condell and Jean Liddiard argue that "middle- and upper-class women" were attracted to "military-style uniforms" because of their own class biases regarding "the social composition of the Armed Forces. To them the 'real' Army and Navy were the 'officers and gentlemen' whose ethos they wished to share in their own organizations."[34] The same holds true for upper- and upper-middle class women in policing, where there was an association with what Condell and Liddiard describe as a "glamorous tradition." Moreover, as Allen writes, the police uniform for these women was an instrument of class power that transformed these ladies into "gentlemen" who could easily intimidate the lower ranks with working-class backgrounds: "The private soldier, for the most part, turned tail and fled ignominiously at the first sight of the familiar uniform worn by a woman he could have knocked down with one blow of his fist."[35] Thus the WPS set out to imitate the military and police in organization and dress by appropriating the titles of rank from the military or police: commandant, sub-commandant, superintendent, inspector, sub-inspector, quarter-master-sergeant, sergeant, and constable.[36] In *The Pioneer Policewoman* Allen describes the military-style organization of the WPS: "Miss Damer Dawson was Commander-in-Chief, I was in command of the actual field of battle, while Miss Isobel Goldingham was in command of the staff" (56). Allen took the military analogy one step further by asserting naively that WPS work was more challenging than military service: "Military duty in the trenches seemed, by comparison, a light and agreeable pastime" (28).

Allen linked the police uniform inextricably with power and social control at an almost intuitive level: "It was a notable fact that the policewoman in uniform (as soon as the newness of her appearance had worn off) was treated with respect by the most frivolous and incorrigible girls; . . . The uniform also earned the *instinctive* respect of the young soldier, even when drunk and inclined to be violent" (84–5, emphasis mine). A plainclothes policewoman would have far more difficulty in carrying out her duties than a uniformed officer for, "unless very insistent," the former would probably be "impertinently disregarded." Since the manner of a plainclothes policewoman is inconsistent with her clothing, the uniformed policewoman has a distinct advantage, in that uniform transforms her. Allen believed that the uniform was a "weapon": "It was evident to all those closely concerned with the maintenance of order, that the uniform was in itself a deterrent, an actual weapon of defence, and that it had also a prompt moral effect" (25). As fashion critic Joanne Finkelstein explains, changes occur accordingly for both the officer in question, whose bearing inevitably shifts in response with the power it bestows, and the onlooker: "One would certainly find oneself acting and speaking differently to the other when s/he was clad in the uniform of the constabulary, or clothed in ecclesiastical or judicial robes."[37] "Occupational clothing such as military, medical and sporting uniforms, judicial and academic robes, ecclesiastical raiment and so on," Finkelstein continues, are inherently "restrictive" for such clothing "alert[s] individuals to certain proscriptive modes of conduct." This is precisely the effect Allen claims for the uniformed policewoman, and is one that she herself exploited during most of her life with her own distinct mode of self-presentation. Allen fully appreciated how, as Finkelstein persuasively argues, clothing "is a means by which images of the self can be created and displayed" (130).

Still, Allen's sanguine depiction of the way in which WPS members were perceived by the public strains credulity. In Allen's account the public responds to individual WPS members of all ranks with deference and respect. As the uniform glides through the dirty streets of the metropolis, miscreants of all descriptions (primarily working-class) become placid and cooperative: "The uniform alone unnerves the offender, and shows to onlookers and possible sympathisers that the power and majesty of the law is behind the figure in official blue."[38] The uniform gives its wearer special powers, which in turn become "extraordinarily infectious" throughout the community: "Terrified mothers, dragging wailing children, plucked from their beds [during air raids] . . . were readily pacified by the realization that other women [from the WPS] were facing the common peril with so much coolness and equanimity."[39] WPS members were unquestionably conspicuous on the streets, but conspicuous for what? Elizabeth Lutes Hillman notes that the uniform achieves a number of effects, including: distinguishing between ordinary citizens and police; clarifying hierarchies; and literally creating uniformity.[40] In addition, and perhaps most crucially, the police (and military) uniform is by definition masculine, creating enormous difficulties for women attempting to perform their feminine role properly, whatever that role might be. Moreover, the uniformed body embodies something about sexuality, even when that something is inexpressible within the cultural imagination of the early 1920s. On some level, Allen must have recognized this fact, for Joan Lock notes that Allen "seems never to have taken her uniform off."[41] She risked public ridicule for the sake of the uniform: "In those post-war years, everyone was somewhat tired of uniform; and I was constantly heckled because my choice was unhesitatingly for it in the case of Women Police."[42] That the uniform became a mechanism for women such as Allen to express something about sexuality may explain Allen's insouciance or blindness to the way in which the uniform was actually perceived.

Allen's exaggerated account of the public response to the uniform skirts what other commentators could not fail to notice. George Howard, for instance, notes that there was an "Amazonian touch about these volunteers which had the opposite result to that desired. Formidable-looking women, with their heavy boots and mannish dress, were derided by Londoners, and they became the butt of the music hall comedian."[43] As early as 1917 policemen and the policed (prostitutes and soldiers) viewed WPS members as "frustrated spinsters or men-haters."[44] Lock speaks of Mary Allen's appearance in 1925 as "grotesquely masculine" (128). For the individual wearer the WPS uniform may have represented police power and perhaps gentleman-like chivalry, but to many outsiders the garb was the symbolic representation of a bizarre claim to masculinity itself. The uniform did not transform WPS officers into men but into mannish women, and perhaps for the most astute observer, female sexual inverts. The uniform embodied empowerment and masculine authority and also expressed (or allowed members to express) sexual identity. What Macready, Allen, and others could not state publicly was that the choice of dress and self-presentation were clearly associated with female homosexuality, as Emily Hamer argues: "The uniform is a sexual tool to the lesbian, by making her visible, as the Sam Browne belt is a tool to the workman. As a reward for her life-enhancing sexual work the lesbian deserves the uniform which advertises her sexual desire."[45] Jacob recognized the potency of Allen's uniform both as a source of power and (homo)sexuality: "I have seen hundreds of women in uniform in two world wars, but I have never seen one who carried it off better than Commander [sic] Mary Allen. Her uniform, a severe military 'frock coat' in dark blue, which fell just below her knees, breeches and riding boots, with a field service hat with a gold band round the peak, was both dignified and arresting. Her boots alone could have demanded respect."[46] Far from being put off by the outfit, Jacob finds it glamorous and charged with eroticism—for her, WPS officers were highly attractive.

In *The Sexual Question* sexologist August Forel associated female sexual inversion with a penchant for the uniform: "Female inverts have been known to wear men's uniforms and perform military service for years, and even behave as heroes."[47] Unlike Magnus Hirschfeld and Havelock Ellis, Forel did not carefully delineate between sexual inversion and transvestism; moreover, since his taxonomies were based on case histories prior to 1914, his conflation of the uniform and inversion seems dated or irrelevant because of the large number of women in uniform during the war.[48] Nevertheless, the First World War did give lesbians such as Damer Dawson and Allen an irresistible opportunity to dress in uniforms as masculine as they pleased. In fact, many of the "less orthodox sisters," as Radclyffe Hall calls them, found a way to be "useful" to their country that enabled them at the same time to crossdress with cultural impunity, though not perhaps with wholehearted approval.[49] Female inverts, Hall writes, worked alongside their heterosexual sisters, referred to in the novel *The Well of Loneliness* as "purely feminine women" (271). This uniformed, happy breed of female inverts were not passing as men but passing as women who desired women—the uniform was their lesbianism made visible, satisfying a desire to wear less stereotypically feminine garb and perhaps to signal to others within a small circle of inverts. Hall at least implies as much when she writes about such women: "One great weakness they all had, it must be admitted, and this was for uniforms—yet why not?" (271). The uniform enabled female inverts to look just like their straight counterparts, with small yet significant differences. Hall captures the nuances perfectly: the inverts "might [have] looked a bit odd, indeed some of them did, and yet in the streets they were seldom stared at, though they strode a little, perhaps from shyness, or perhaps from a slightly self-conscious desire to show off" (271).

Few dispute the claim that the top leadership of the WPS were lesbian, as well as some members of the other ranks. Allen's description of her meeting with Damer Dawson is telling: "The meeting between Margaret Damer Dawson and myself struck an immediate spark, and began a period—all too short, alas!—of close association and intimate friendship, ending only with the sudden death of the Chief in 1920."[50] We know that Damer Dawson and Allen lived together, and after Damer Dawson died in May 1920, Allen was a major beneficiary of Damer Dawson's will. Hall may have been referring to Damer Dawson herself when she wrote about a "Miss Tring who had lived with a very dear friend in the humbler purlieus of Chelsea."[51] Myra Steadman recalled meeting Mary Allen in about 1917 and found her "very good-looking and so smart and such a dominating personality. Decidedly masculine. . . . I suppose nowadays we would say she was partly lesbian."[52] In late 1930, when Allen and her new partner (a former WPS member referred to as Miss [Helen] Tagart) were introduced by Isobel Goldingham to the lesbian couple Hall and her partner Una Troubridge, the latter recorded in her diary that Allen believed "the authorities were against her because she was an invert."[53] But did "the authorities" at the Met know or suspect that Allen and other leaders were "partly lesbian"? As I discussed in the previous chapter, Macready characterized the WPS leadership as "extreme" and argued that "the main point was to eliminate [from the official police] any women of extreme views—the vinegary spinster or blighted middle-aged fanatic."[54] Thus, while never suggesting lesbianism outright, the commissioner invoked code words and phrases, such as "extreme," and lacking in "broad-mindedness and kindly sympathy." Such characteristics echo Ellis's description of the inverted woman: "The brusque energetic movements . . . the direct speech . . . the masculine straight-forwardness and sense of honor . . . and especially the attitude towards men, free from any suggestion either of shyness or audacity, will often suggest the underlying psychic abnormality to a keen observer."[55]

Macready was indeed such a keen observer, but he still proceeded by innuendo rather than by direct attack. Was the uniform specifically one such code of lesbianism for Macready? When he looked at WPS members, what did he see? Macready registers his anxieties about the WPS in his memoirs, *Annals of an Active Life*: "Another and more militant organization had also grown up during the war, adopting the title of 'Women Police' and dressing in uniform of a rather masculine type."[56] The double standard in operation here is revealing: when women from the WPS put on this uniform it is "rather masculine," but no objections are lodged when a similar one is worn by his own MWPP. The women under Stanley are, of course, never subjected to such comments by Macready, and this leads one to suspect that either he withheld criticism of MWPP women or that he thought there was something peculiar about the women in the WPS or its leadership.

Macready's objections to the WPS were complex, varied, and interconnected. He recognized how the uniform was bound up with a particular attitude toward police work, but also how it profoundly affected the way in which the individual officer carried herself. The body in uniform is externally transformed: the head is held high and shoulders erect. To wear a uniform is to change one's behavior, movements, and conduct, as Chapman observed in his final opinion (later reprinted in the WPS newsletter): "These defendants have all the appearance of belonging to a trained body. . . . There is their whole carriage and the look of them. . . . They show it in every way, in their capacity and in their bearing."[57] As we have seen, the uniform itself is a kind of presence with its own unique form of power. In part, the way in which the WPS implemented this power became part and parcel of what Macready objected to. It was not simply that the uniform itself was masculine but that the very donning of it somehow made its wearer more deeply masculinized. In Macready's exhaustive file on the WPS a memorandum describes how the senior policewoman at Grantham (Damer Dawson) was a "better man" than Grantham's chief constable.[58] In this letter both Damer Dawson and Allen were characterized as "strong ladies," which is to say they were not really ladies at all.

Macready continually circled back in his objections to the WPS to what they wore or were even rumored to have worn. After a reference to their "rather masculine uniform," Macready writes, "I was told that one of them was seen wearing a sword on one occasion, but to that I cannot vouch."[59] The qualification dangling at the end of the statement ("but to that I cannot vouch") relieves the accuser from the responsibility of establishing the veracity of the assertion. The aim in floating the innuendo is to make it so and thereby damage the reputation of the organization to which the sword-wearing woman belongs. By conjuring up an image of its officers parading around as men or pretending to be cops, the accusation also renders ridiculous anyone associated with the WPS. Such women cannot be taken seriously since, Macready implies, it is common knowledge that only real men wear swords. Any woman who wears the sword is, in effect, demanding full sexual equality, power, and privilege, which is one reason why the weapon became an effective symbol for the women's suffrage movement.[60] The patron saint of the radical Women's Social and Political Union (WSPU), whose membership included Allen and Goldingham, was none other than Joan of Arc. A 1913 cover of the WSPU journal, the *Suffragette*, depicts an armored Joan with sword upheld in readiness to slash a ferocious dragon who bears the label "indecency."[61] With her sword drawn (not worn) and her shield of purity, Joan prepares to cut down the perpetrators of evil. That evil may not have been specifically named as "men," but the hands in the illustration pushing the dragon toward the resolute Joan look suspiciously masculine. Macready's brief comment about a WPS member wielding a sword might have been a sly reference to the fact that both Allen and Goldingham were former members of the WSPU—surely the idea that former militant suffragettes would have the temerity to wear a police uniform was anathema to Macready, who in his memoirs recalls an unpleasant encounter in 1912: "When walking home one evening . . . I found myself in an excited crowd which had collected to watch the removal to the Vine Street Police Station of various suffragettes who had been amusing themselves by smashing shop windows in Piccadilly, in furtherance of their efforts to secure the vote. The forbearance of the police was as noticeable as the undignified appearance of the ladies as they were being carried off."[62]

Mary Allen, self-appointed apologist of the WPS, could have dodged Macready's allegation about the sword-wearing incident by completely ignoring it in her own book. Instead Allen stands her ground and, framing Macready's remarks with her own ironic commentary, cites his passage in her book in its entirety, even italicizing the phrase "wearing a sword."[63] Determined to set the record straight, Allen introduces the quotation from Macready's text with the following comment: "The benevolent Commissioner, secure in his isolation from facts, thus dismisses the Women Police Service" (131). If the accusation about wearing the sword was true, it would seem equally audacious for Allen to have featured it so prominently in her book. The closest she comes to repudiating the allegation is to suggest that the commissioner was isolated from the facts. Allen's reluctance to flatly deny the charge leaves an aperture in her text whereby Macready's assertion might have been true. If there were any extenuating circumstances, such as that the sword wearing was for a private ceremonial occasion, she withholds further information. Instead she uses Macready's accusation as a springboard to tout WPS achievements and to lament that "the great variety of police work undertaken and efficiently carried through by the Women Police Service had evidently entirely escaped Sir Nevil Macready's attention" (131–2). In listing WPS activities in detail, Allen argues that it is entirely inconsequential whether someone in the WPS wore a sword: nothing can obscure their splendid service record, with swords or without. Mary Allen's novelist friend, Hall, may have been alluding to this incident in *The Well* when she describes the female inverts who volunteered "their best without stint" and "rallied to the call of their country superbly": "And although their Sam Browne belts remained *swordless*, their hats and their caps without regimental badges, a battalion was formed in those terrible years that would never again be completely disbanded" (271–2, emphasis mine). Macready likely exploited the allegation because he knew the outrageous image of a woman wearing a sword was so patently absurd that even to hint of it would draw the organization into dispute.

Thus Macready's effective modus operandi was to discredit by advancing allegations against the WPS both in his own writing and in public testimony. Perhaps the most damaging attack came in Macready's testimony to the Baird Committee, where he submitted a newspaper photograph (originally from the WPS's own publicity apparatus) ostensibly depicting a WPS member cross-dressed as a man in civilian dress and posing as a "drunk." (I will discuss this incident in greater detail in chapter 6.) The accusation of cross-dressing probably damaged the WPS, but private correspondence between Macready and the Home Office reveals that the men in power were irked most by the fact that the photograph depicted women in unofficial police uniform apprehending what Macready called a "drunken bargee." In a letter to Macready, Sir Edward Troup of the Home Office wrote: "I confess I do not like the idea of your *fair lady in uniform* being impelled by her sense of legal obligation to engage in a fierce struggle for the arrest of a drunken bargee."[64] Macready responded: "I do not think—except once in a blue moon—you will have any snapshot in the illustrated Press of the drunken bargee locked in the arms of the Policewoman!"[65] This correspondence concerned the controversial question of whether or not policewomen should have power of arrest, and moreover if that power of arrest should be extended to allow women to arrest men. Thus the photograph in question displays a complicated mesh of cultural perversities, depicting two women passing as official police without Met approval and another woman allegedly cross-dressing. Macready asserted that his overarching concern was that the public might "mistake the uniform" and assume that Allen and Damer Dawson were real police; thus his interest in setting the record straight was superbly altruistic. The way in which he expresses this concern is curious, however. To assert that the photograph depicts a woman cross-dressed as a man implies perversity, though there was nothing technically illegal about such behavior for women (or men).[66] There was a law, however, about ensuring that private individuals did not dress in such a way as to be taken for the police, and it was this rather more legitimate allegation that the Met pursued further.

On September 21, 1920, Sir William Horwood (the new Met commissioner upon Macready's retirement from the force in February 1920) sent a letter to the WPS leaders informing them that WPS members had to cease at once patrolling in London in full uniform or face serious consequences. Failure to obey this police order would inevitably result in legal action, Horwood warned, and moreover, the Chief Magistrate (Sir Chartres Biron) "would probably deal severely" with them.[67] In early 1921 the Met initiated a lawsuit against the WPS for "wearing uniform resembling that of the Metropolitan Police and the Metropolitan Women Police Patrols."[68] As a result, in March and April 1921 a handful of WPS officers stood before the magistrate Cecil Chapman at Westminster Police Court. The Met was fully aware that the WPS uniform was Damer Dawson's creation, since Sir Edward

Henry, commissioner of the Met in 1914, had given "his permission . . . [when Damer Dawson] submitted to him a drawing of the uniform that [the WPS] proposed to wear."[69] Throughout the controversy the Met's firm line of attack was that the similarity of the WPS uniform to their own female force would cause confusion among members of the public. In pursuing their case to the court, the Met was convinced that legal intimidation would expunge the WPS from the capital. The magistrate expanded on the Met's concerns regarding similarity by pointing out, "The law says no one must wear the uniform without authority, or any dress having the appearance, or bearing any of the distinctive marks. I do not think it is only a question of confusing it with the Women's Police Patrol; If it was there would be a simple way out of it. It is not only that, but it is *the wearing of the uniform by these ladies*, and the wearing of the crown, and the word 'police' which must be attached to the lawful police."[70] The commissioner at the Met refused to negotiate openly with the WPS about what changes might be made to satisfy him.

The WPS was most likely unaware that the commissioner was in close consultation with Shortt, the secretary of state, who fully supported the Met. A memorandum attached to a transcript of the proceedings at Westminster Police Court states that "the Secretary of State thereupon said that no discussion was to take place with the defendants as to the kind of uniform which they should wear. He was afraid they could not be trusted, and moreover it is not the business of the Commissioner to help them to sail as near as possible to the border line between what the law allows and what it does not allow."[71] The WPS leadership was indeed sailing along the borderline on their own, as Allen remarked: "It was an extraordinary situation."[72] Technically, the Met won its suit and the WPS received a small fine because the magistrate agreed with the charge that the uniform's similarity caused confusion. This despite the fact that the lawyer representing the WPS told the court that the "question of similarity" was a nonstarter because a sergeant from the Met, who had "spent the best part of ten days in his investigation of these uniforms says that except in the case of the sergeants there is no similarity so far as he can see between the one and the other."[73] The WPS was forced to make slight modifications to the uniform by adding "scarlet shoulder straps bearing the marks of rank in black braid, a change in the cap badge, and an alteration of the title to the *Women's Auxiliary Service*."[74]

After the Met's success in the hearing against the WPS, the activities of the WPS were sharply curtailed and eventually, as the Met had hoped, the women's organization faded away. Allen campaigned on behalf of women police throughout the 1920s and into the 1930s in places such as Germany and the United States, always in full uniform and—to the chagrin of the Met and the Home Office—passing herself off as head of an officially recognized female police force. If, as McLaren writes, "masculine women" (and "feminine men") who reject their "appropriate gender role" must be "closely policed," the Met found in the WPS uniform the effective mechanism to literally police women thought to violate codes of gender and sexuality.[75] Uncompromising in its masculine appearance, the WPS uniform played an important and daring role in pioneering a startlingly new and radical form of "female masculinity" and in attempting to appropriate for (unauthorized) women the authority of the law.[76]

III

THE FIRST WORLD WAR allowed not only Commandant Mary Allen her first opportunity to abandon traditional women's clothing but also Valerie Barker, who exclaimed, "For three hectic, wartime years I dressed more like a man than a woman. In breeches and tunic."[77] A 1922 description of Barker as a young bride demonstrates how her *self-designed* uniform challenged femininity: "Although she was Mrs. . . . in name, she dressed as what was then known as a land girl: in riding breeches and open-neck shirt and coat."[78] In her next metamorphosis, as Colonel Victor Barker, she donned the uniform of a highly decorated officer in order to pass as a man. This attempt to secure male power might at first seem more dangerous than Allen's postwar passing as the official representative of a bona fide police organization for, until the disclosure of Barker's true sex, she did not, like Allen, merely lobby for such power but seized it by deception. As a result Barker enjoyed the pleasures and privileges reserved for men, from cigars to boxing. While both women eagerly put themselves on public view and relished the uniform's total absence of ambiguity, Allen's open and honest proclamation of intent to attain official recognition met with far more intense hostility and regulatory force than Barker's ruse. In Allen's case the female body in uniform, especially when the uniform included trousers, constituted a uniquely subversive and sensational performance of female masculinity, whereas for Barker the uniform facilitated the acquisition of masculinity itself. What I propose to show in this section, therefore, is that there is nothing uniform about the spectatorial effects generated by women in uniform. In analyzing the treatment of both women by the law and the press, it is evident that their assaults on the prevailing constructions of gender and sexuality in the postwar age were of a very different nature.

This section seeks to understand how—or if—such flamboyant figures of female masculinity were policed and regulated by forces of social and cultural control in the 1920s. In so doing, it is tempting to slot individuals such as Allen and Barker into medical taxonomies, such as mannish lesbian or female transvestite. However, scholarly preoccupation with claiming modern subjectivities can obscure rather than enlighten. For example, critic Nicky Hallett describes Barker and the WPS leaders as lesbians who were "attacked more blatantly" than other women in uniform during the First World War.[79] Historian James Vernon sensibly cautions that such categorization inevitably results in loss, for there is always "a sense in which . . . sexual and gender orientation has to remain indeterminate, undecidable and unknowable."[80] Speaking of Barker specifically, Vernon explains that "it is the very ambiguity of Barker's story that makes it so interesting, for it enables one to shift attention away from the classification of Barker as an object with a 'real' gender and sexuality to be discovered and revealed, to a concern with how Barker was understood and made knowable by contemporaries." I agree that there is much to be gained in resisting easy categorization, especially in the case of Barker, who slips among and between categories. At the same time the suspension of categorization may be somewhat idealistic and fundamentally at odds with an historically situated reading. Press reports in the 1920s always resorted to some form of categorizing—from masquerader to impersonator to the neologism "man-woman"—to describe Barker. I would argue that the historical project is to suspend decidability over the positioning of Barker and instead determine how such labels had currency in the 1920s.

For Allen, policework without the uniform was inconceivable and she firmly rejected as unnatural, deceptive, and insincere proposals to dress policewomen in plain clothes. She declared that she could "think of few things more contemptible . . . than for Women Police to masquerade in silk stockings, satin gowns and high heels in order to entrap male and female offenders."[81] If women were to dress as women even in undercover operations, every woman would become a potential snoop-cum-officer: "If this practice became at all general, every woman in a public place would be suspected of being what is termed in the more vulgar criminal classes 'a police nose.' " Lock argues that Allen's hostility toward plainclothes policewomen had less to do with a concern about public perception than that "she herself had the utmost aversion from dresses."[82] Lock reports that Allen was affronted during her 1924 visit to New York City when a woman "had the temerity to ask her if she ever wore pink satin." On this trip Allen in uniform, complete with monocle, took center stage and fully exploited the potential of her public exposure by exposing more still: "At my first meeting in the United States there was a considerable riot at the back of the hall because some of the audience could not see my uniform. I was wearing my overcoat, but when I learned the cause of the disturbance, I turned it back and showed my blue jacket and riding breeches beneath."[83] Allen's instincts as performance artist seem to override her instincts as law enforcer. Although she sensed the ways in which her physical presence was creating a scene, "a considerable riot," Allen threw caution to the wind and virtually flashed the audience by revealing, in the most dramatic of gestures, what was hidden underneath the greatcoat. Apparently, the serious lecture Allen was poised to deliver on the importance of women in policing was less important than the lecturer's uniformed self—Allen's adept performance belies the fact that outsiders may have been drawing other, unintended conclusions from her shocking declaration: "I haven't worn a skirt for six years."[84] (Women did not wear trousers in public until the Second World War.) The stark honesty, even recklessness, of Allen's disclosure indicates either that she was caught up in the excitement her appearance generated among the Americans or that she completely misjudged the impact it would have in some quarters. In either case her statement confirms how utterly natural Allen felt in a uniform devoid of the trappings of "pink satin."

Barker also had an aversion to feminine clothing. In her 1929 court appearance she was obviously awkward and uncomfortable in her feminine apparel ("a grey coat and skirt, thick grey woollen stockings and black shoes") and confessed in an interview with the *Sunday Dispatch*: "I am a woman again and feel strangely ill at ease. As a woman I have to face the future alone—and I am frightened."[85] In men's clothing Barker experienced a greater congruence between self and presentation: "Of course there are those who will say that it was impossible to be honorable and straightforward when I was living a lie. But I did not feel that I was living a lie. I actually felt that I was a man."[86] Barker was not satisfied though with men's civilian clothing but pushed the masquerade still further and falsely represented herself as a military officer, wore medals she had not earned, invented her own military rank, and spun elaborate tales of heroic deeds. Like Allen, Barker understood how an officer's uniform allowed privileged access to the traditions of the upper classes.

Just as Allen's WPS uniform was extravagantly masculine, even for a man, Barker's choice of uniform was also over the top. Barker's valet told the *Daily Mail* that the colonel had "a most extensive wardrobe of civilian clothing and uniforms. Generally he went out from the flat wearing uniform, saying he was going to the War Office, where he had a staff appointment. He always wore the ribbons of the DSO, the Croix de Guerre, a Belgian decoration, and the three war medals."[87] The photograph most frequently reproduced in newspaper coverage of Barker's 1929 trial (figure 4) shows her in the formal attire of an officer, with an abundance of ribbons and medals. Barker also posed in the uniform of a cavalry officer, with high peaked cap, jacket and tie, and again with numerous medals and ribbons pinned to her chest. When the *Daily Mail* conducted a lengthy interview with Barker's landlord, he reported that the colonel "had several suits of uniform, and was very fond of strolling around . . . in the full dress of a staff officer and wearing many medals. 'He' told me 'he' had to go to Buckingham Palace to receive the OBE. I dressed 'him' in a blue peace-time uniform. 'His' body was padded, and 'Captain Barker' explained that this was necessary because 'he' had been blown up in the war."[88] Such public "performances" were also cited in the *Daily Herald*, which revealed how "in full military uniform, and wearing many medals, 'Captain Barker' attended the Overseas Officers' Dinner in 1926."[89] Later, as a member of the National Fascisti, Barker wore "a black shirt, khaki trousers and puttees, and also displayed medal ribbons."[90] Barker thus had a uniform for every occasion—but how did she develop such a passionate obsession?

As I have mentioned, many women during the First World War had their first opportunity to wear masculine clothing, take on men's jobs, and taste something of the power that came with this new social position, but in the early months of the war it was not clear that such opportunities were in the offing. Both Barker and Allen were initially frustrated because they were convinced that only men would be able to do really useful war work. Barker felt intensely the limitations of her sex and characterized her wish to change sexes as the result of the highest of all motivations, patriotism: "I was nearly 19 when World War I broke out. For the first time there surged over me the wish that I had been born a man. I can recall so vividly the urge to do something."[91] Barker was offered a job training horses at a Canadian Army cavalry camp where "everybody knew me as a woman, although they treated me as a man and as one of themselves" (2)—though Barker does not explain how or why. Barker claims to have tamed wild horses better than any of her male colleagues, whom she characterizes as a "comradely bunch": "Such was my war job. In a way a man's job, and certainly I savoured the friendship of man, and became accustomed to living like a man" (2). That Barker relished being one of the boys suggests that she was psychically predisposed to masculinity, for her clothing was not yet masculine. In the first installment of her life story she informs readers that "there was nothing 'manly' in my make-up. Whenever I got home on leave I would rush up to my room . . . [and select] the most feminine garments I could to change into

'civvies' " (2). Barker mentions only in passing that she later became a driver
for the Women's Auxiliary Air Force, and she provides no details about the
uniform or the actual work.

After the war Barker married Lieutenant Harold Arkell-Smith, but after
just six weeks she left him to live with Ernest Pearce-Crouch, and in the
early 1920s she gave birth to two children: "While, for the most part I went
about in male clothes, I still retained my long hair, done up in a bun, which,
with my rounded figure made any mistake regarding my sex impossible."[92]
The war may have been the first occasion when Barker realized her profound desire to change her sex, but she would not begin to cross-dress until
she had given up her daughter for adoption, fled her second male partner,
and taken up yet another life with a woman. As a plea for the sympathy of
her readers, Barker presents her choice to "become a man" as a necessary
step to support herself and her son, and as an escape:

> I would go out into the world as a man and do a man's work. . . . Behind
> the change from woman to man I would be able to screen myself against
> all the tortures, miseries and difficulties of the past, and work out my
> own salvation. . . . I shall be free to take on any work that comes my
> way as a "man." Had I not already mixed with men and done a man's
> work in the Army? Had I not worked as hard as any man on the farm?
> Was I not used to wearing male clothes? Yes! I would become a "man."[93]

This narrative conforms to what cultural critic Marjorie Garber calls the
"progress narrative" whereby "transvestism is *normalized*, by interpreting it
in the register of socio-economic necessity . . . to get a job . . . in order to
support his family."[94] McLaren also comments on this phenomenon: "The
idea that women would seek male powers by donning male attire made sufficient sense to be usually viewed by the public as presumptuous rather than
perverse."[95] According to one newspaper report, Barker's gender metamorphosis did not take place overnight but occurred in stages: "Mrs. Pearce
Crouch's transition was slow. She forsook skirts for shorts, worn with a khaki
shirt, then came a man's collar and tie, then a man's hat."[96] Still, the transformation from "female" to "male" was not a simple exchange of clothing—
the gradual change was both a willful act and a surrender to a greater force:
"It seemed as though Fate were taking a hand. My hair began to fall out. I
had to have it cut short."[97]

At the outbreak of war Allen also realized that, after she had tasted the
exhilaration of the militant suffrage movement, the prospect of traditional
women's work was immensely unsatisfying: "To those of us who had been

leaders and organisers . . . the ordinary channels of usefulness for the weaker sex in war-time—nursing, canteen work, sewing societies, etc.—made preciously little appeal."[98] War work became another way to extend the camaraderie of women: "The sudden disbanding of our Suffragette groups was for many of us a bewildering blow. We had worked for Suffrage for so long that we did not know where else to turn when seeking to serve our country . . . I was offered a job in a Needlework Guild, which infuriated me because I wanted action."[99] War work as a member of one of the country's first female police organizations became part of an ongoing political and feminist agenda. Allen embraced her new career path with gusto and her whole persona became bound up with the uniform, which she "seems never to have taken . . . off, even wearing it for travelling and attending banquets in her honor."[100]

The uniform gave Allen and her comrades total freedom of movement, including the ability to zoom around London on a motorbike with a sidecar, collecting drunks and lost children.[101] The uniform also permitted her to wear breeches several years before it was socially acceptable to do so, since the greatcoat fell below the knee, leaving visible only her shiny black leather boots. Allen's navy blue breeches did not construct her own unique sense of female masculinity; rather, they confirmed it. A de facto policewoman, in uniform Allen stood tall next to powerful politicians, as depicted in a photograph of her beside Lady Astor. Allen reproduced this newspaper photograph in one of her three historical accounts of the WPS, *The Pioneer Policewoman*. Captioned "Viscountess Astor and Commandant Allen with Deputation to the Home Secretary," it shows Astor enveloped in a huge fur coat, clutching a bundle of papers; Allen stands beside her in full uniform. Allen's pleasure in her uniformed self-presentation is palpable in the numerous photographs of her in the print media, the WPS newsletter, in her own books, and also in her description of the New York visit when she brought the traffic to a halt: "Every vehicle that came in sight instantly pulled up, with a squeal of brakes, and the drivers leaned out, frankly stared at me, and began shouting to each other. They ignored the signal lights, they ignored the 'Stop!' and 'Go!' notices, they ignored my directions to move on."[102] Allen reports this amazing incident with ebullience, blithely unaware that some of the double takes might have been because she seemed outrageously masculine and perhaps vaguely ridiculous. Such a craving for attention was criticized by the British consul in New York who fired off a letter to the Home Office to complain that Allen "had been obtaining for herself quite a good deal of publicity going around the city in breeches, boots and a monocle."[103] It mattered little what people actually thought since the uniform confirmed *her* sense of self.

While Allen sought to exploit the uniform's power on the lecture circuit and in photographs, she failed to distinguish between illusion and reality. For example, Allen's inclusion a of photograph of herself with Astor in *The Pioneer Policewoman* was presumably an attempt to portray Astor's genuine approval and admiration for the WPS. However, a memo Astor composed to Lord Muir Mackenzie indicates that while Astor supported other women's policing organizations, she sought to distance herself from the WPS: "I should like very much to have one or two experienced policewomen called as witnesses before the Joint Committee, if you think it would be possible. I would suggest either Miss Peto . . . or Miss Tancred. . . . There is also Miss M. S. Allen. . . . I do not think their [the WPS] point of view is perhaps quite so valuable, but I understand that she is very anxious to give evidence."[104] Just as Allen never comprehended how her uniformed self was often more of an entertaining sideshow for some observers, so too she had little awareness that her persistent lobbying drove many politicians to distraction.

Allen was strangely—almost willfully—indifferent to the actual impact her uniform had on others. Although she was not taken for a man (and never attempted to pass as one), she was pleased when people noticed that she looked different, insouciant that "different" might have meant masculine. In this sense Allen was like Barker before Barker's transformation, in that while both women dressed first for themselves, a viewer was required to complete the performance. Barker seems to have had that attention at each stage in her transition from female to male; as Mrs. Pearce-Crouch her "mannish clothes and mannerisms attracted much attention."[105] Depending on the reception, Barker became increasingly tempted to push the ruse still further: "in clothes which made it difficult to tell whether she was a man or a woman . . . [she] seemed flattered when people addressed her as 'Mr.' "[106] Cross-dressing was almost a narcotic, where the risk had to be increased to get a bigger thrill; as Barker explains: "I discovered that boldness was the best way to allay suspicion, and, as time went on, I became more and more daring."[107] Ironically, once the transformation was complete, the criteria of excellence could be gauged only if people stopped looking at her. The uniform gave Barker's masculinity more authenticity as, according to one observer, " 'he' . . . looked very well in uniform, but 'his' appearance in striped trousers and a black coat was strikingly peculiar."[108] In the six years of "passing" Barker's additions to the uniform increased exponentially, ultimately changing her entire manner ("I . . . swaggered around posing as a dashing cavalry officer"[109]). By the time of her court appearance, several newspapers had commented on her demeanor and admired how distinguished she looked. The *News of the World*, for example, wrote of a "debonair officer" who "boldly adopted the role of a dashing cavalry officer . . . tall and handsome. . . . His appearance was distinguished and his bearing admirable."[110] However, women's illicit use of the uniform signaled an incursion into masculinity that would not go unnoticed by viewers better informed about the nuanced distinctions of perversion and inversion.

The admiration for Barker's successful impersonation so in evidence in the popular press was not shared, for instance, by Hall.[111] From Hall's perspective, Barker was no kindred spirit, and her case raised a number of troubling issues. First, Hall feared the notoriety following so close upon her own obscenity trial; "the exposure [of Barker] at the moment is unfortunate indeed," she writes.[112] The reason was that she felt the timing would make it more difficult to push for, as Hall phrases it, "some sort of marriage for the invert." This fear was confirmed when Sir Ernest Wild (the judge who presided at Barker's trial) addressed Barker's lawyer: "Do I understand these two women [Barker and Elfrida Haward] were living together as man and wife from 1923 for about four years?"[113] When the answer was in the affirmative, Wild was outraged that the couple chose to marry in a church: "You have falsified the marriage register and set an evil example."[114] It would have been more proper, Wild admonished, if Haward had informed her father, "We are calling ourselves husband and wife, but we are really a couple of girls."[115] Wild was less perturbed that Barker had masqueraded as an officer and war hero than by the fact that she had engineered a church wedding and had thus "profaned the House of God."[116]

Second, Hall was convinced that the public would not be sufficiently knowledgeable about the topic of sexual inversion to differentiate between women such as herself and Barker, and would conclude erroneously that all women dressed in masculine clothing were members of the same tribe, passing, that is, for the same thing. In discussing the Barker incident, one of Hall's biographers, Michael Baker, marvels in skeptical bemusement that Hall "evidently" makes a distinction "between her own case . . . and a mere masquerader like Barker." Baker dutifully accounts for Hall's anger toward Barker by explaining that since Hall drew upon the theories of late nineteenth-century sexologists, particularly Richard von Krafft-Ebing and Havelock Ellis, she views herself as a "woman with a masculine psyche," while Barker simply assumes the disguise of a man. This distinction was one that Hall's legal representative had in fact argued at the trial when he stated that *The Well* deals with "what is known and tabulated as inversion—a physical disability. . . . [The novel's] theme is not perversion. . . . The theme is inversion, and, indeed, it deals with a disability laid upon certain members of humanity for which they are not responsible. . . . But perversion, a deliberate thing done of free will and a totally different matter, is not the subject-matter of this book."[117] So, while Hall cannot help herself and has no choice about her sexual inversion, Barker—if taken at her word in the court and to the press—assumes male clothing to better herself financially and to support her child. Because of Barker's total control over her predicament, she is, by Hall's definition, a pervert rather than an invert.[118]

Most newspapers reached a different conclusion, however, and portrayed Barker not with "hostility," as Hallett surmises, but simply as a woman whose performance of masculinity was astonishingly convincing.[119] Newspapers largely concurred with the argument Barker's lawyer presented to the court: "It is only one in millions who could live as a man and deceive people over a period of years."[120] That the press coverage of Barker's trial focused on *gender ambiguity* rather than *sexual identity* suggests that by the late 1920s there was as yet no common cultural understanding that clothing could signal sexuality. In 1929 the medical discourse on transsexuality had not been clearly formulated (the word "transsexual" was coined in the late 1940s[121]). Nor did it appear even after the trial of *The Well* that many readers were familiar with the available sexological label for women who dressed in masculine clothing and had sexual relations with other women. Only the man who passed judgment on Barker seems to have been attuned to the sexological nuances of the case; Wild proclaimed the defendant was "an unprincipled, mendacious and unscrupulous adventuress . . . [who had] profaned the House of God, outraged the decencies of nature, and broken the laws of man."[122] Few legal men would have had a keener understanding of the ways in which perversion or inversion violated the law than Wild since, as I have discussed in chapter 2, he was a key supporter of the antilesbian clause in 1921 and, in preparation for the parliamentary debate on the subject, had consulted with experts in the field. While the press may have been willing to accept Barker as a "husband" to Haward the wife, Wild insisted on a reading more congruent with certain sexological theories on the subject and likely viewed Barker as a masculine woman who had formed a relationship with a feminine woman. In Wild's view Barker's immoral conduct had offended every sort of law: religious ("profaned the House of God"), natural ("outraged the decencies of nature"), and civil ("broken the laws of man"). Such a comprehensive list lends support to critic Judith Halberstam's contention that "female masculinity seems to be at its most threatening when coupled with lesbian desire."[123] The intense publicity focusing on Barker's body, conduct, and exploits would be, according to the judge, "part of the punishment for [her] perverted conduct."[124]

Wild's selective or casual use of sexology's clinical discourse in his speech before the Commons demonstrates that while he was uninterested in the fine distinction between perversion and inversion, he was sufficiently informed about sexology in ways overlooked or deliberately ignored by the press, which preferred to cast Barker as a masquerader. "In the press reports available before 1950," Dave King points out, the "common term" for cross-dressers was "masquerade": "The same mode of interpretation was conveyed in a number of similar terms—'pose,' 'impersonate,' 'hoax,' 'disguise'—but the most commonly used was 'masquerade.'"[125] Haward maintained that due to Barker's war injuries no sexual activity had ever taken place. Vern L. and Bonnie Bullough argue that Haward's

> denial of knowledge of her partner's biological sex is almost a standard characteristic of cases in which a woman cross dresser is unmasked. By the denial, both partners could escape charges of being lesbians, since the public found it difficult to believe that intercourse could take place without the "male" partner revealing "his" true sex. This allowed the cross dresser to claim, as most did, that they had impersonated men in order to get a job, accompany a loved one, or gain freedom, and this explanation struck a responsive chord in both men and women.[126]

The ubiquitous "progress narrative" resurfaces to allow readers hungry for heterosexual respectability to believe that Barker fled to Haward to escape domestic abuse and dressed as a man to better herself financially in order to care for her son.[127] Only Wild saw through this pretense to observe, as he aptly put it, that Barker and Haward were not man and wife but "really a couple of girls"—insinuating unnaturalness or sexual abnormality for anyone willing to see beyond the masquerade.

Barker's successful fabrication of a plausible and familiar narrative to account for the cross-dressing enabled the press to overlook issues relating to sexuality. This is hardly surprising for, as Ellis notes in his major study of cross-dressing (or Eonism, in his parlance): "Although this psychic peculiarity is so difficult both to name and to define, it is, strange as that may seem, the commonest of all sexual anomalies to attain prominence in the public newspapers. . . . [Because cross-dressing] constitutes no violation of our moral feelings and laws, it is easily possible to discuss it plainly in the most reputable public prints."[128] Barker supplied the public with a rationale not just for becoming a male impersonator but for passing as a military man by claiming that her "war exploits were not so much vainglory but with the set purpose of giving [her son] a manly example to follow, for my dearest wish is that he shall be a manly man."[129] Barker argued that cross-dressing enabled her to perform both male and female gender roles more fully. By becoming a man, Barker could be both the best mother and the best father—in fact, her cross-dressing was the very sign of maternal care as it signaled the lengths to which she would go in order to ensure economic security for her child. As a man, Barker provided her otherwise fatherless son with an excellent role model of masculinity. All of this was treated with seriousness by the press. Any lapse in an otherwise superlative performance of masculinity was attributed to war injuries. For example, Barker "rode very badly, but 'he' explained that that was due to shrapnel wounds received during the war."[130] Thus the military uniform rendered the impersonation more convincing, while military service at the front supplied the injury that prevented the fullest performance of that masculinity and thus derailed the issue of sexual inversion.[131]

At no time in the massive publicity for the "most embarrassed woman in London" was there any inflection of titillating scandal, scorn, scolding, or mockery; instead, press reports were filled with fascination, admiration, and even respect for a performance flawlessly executed.[132] At Barker's sentencing journalists scrutinized the defendant with careful curiosity to see whether she would react like a woman or man. At this moment of intense emotion, each reporter saw something different. The *Daily Mail* interpreted Barker's breakdown as a straightforward display of manly emotion: "She cried as a man cries, with hard dry sobs, and she used her handkerchief to dry her tears, not daintily like a woman, but vigorously like a man."[133] The *Daily Sketch*, however, concluded that Barker was a living contradiction: in her "black felt hat, like that worn by men" Barker "broke down and showed that, indeed, she was a woman."[134] The *Daily Express* too discerned in Barker traits of both genders: "Her face quivered with emotion, and, womanlike, she almost burst into tears, but manlike she just managed to restrain herself, although she could not control the quivering of her lips."[135] The quotation marks some journalists placed around male pronouns in describing Barker gesture toward an acceptance that Barker was essentially a woman masquerading as a man. But the observation that the defendant exhibited both male and female characteristics, and the inherent undecidability in the use of the phrase "man-woman," demonstrate how on the question of Barker's "true" biological sex, the jury was still out.

Allen's performance in uniform did not amaze as much as provoke, as seen in a pamphlet entitled *The Women Police Question*. In this diatribe railing against the introduction of women police, Captain A. H. Henderson-

Livesey refers to the MWPP as "Macready's monsters" and argues that all "normal men and women" sensibly regard policewomen as "psychic hermaphrodites."[136] No man "worth calling [himself] a man" would permit a female police officer to place him under arrest.[137] Thus, in his view, all policewomen are unnatural—creatures no longer female but not fully male. Henderson-Livesey then speculates on the "implications" of Allen's remark that she no longer wore skirts during her notorious trip to New York, described by Carrier as "one of the most bizarre episodes in the history of policewomen."[138] Henderson-Livesey concedes that in the mid-1920s few would regard Allen's statement as anything more than the "eccentricity" of " 'modern' woman."[139] But, the author warns, such behavior cannot be dismissed so lightly: "The discussion of a lady's garments, in public at any rate, would not in the ordinary course of events strike me as being a useful proceeding, but in the present case there is justification in that the lady started the discussion herself, and moreover the matter has certain *psychological implications* which have a very direct bearing on the question under review [concerning women police]" (7, emphasis mine). The captain refers to anyone who supports female police (from Macready to feminists) as "abnormal," but Allen's sartorial disclosure merits special consideration. Perhaps wary of a libel suit, the author backs off from positing an explicit connection between a woman who rejects female clothing in favor of a masculine uniform and sexuality and instead declares that "people who are possessed of a *congenital* desire to make fools of themselves . . . [when] left alone . . . will do little harm, but when their pretensions to a representative character are endorsed by official bodies, a protest must be made" (emphasis mine). The pamphleteer's sly allusion to the word "congenital" links Allen specifically to a disorder that in sexological discourse is an inborn condition: female sexual inversion. Allen as a private citizen is harmless enough, the writer generously implies, but she is hardly suitable for service in the police.

Allen braved the innuendoes and Barker served a spell in prison for falsifying a marriage registry, yet neither would abandon the uniform because, for them, it was not an exhilarating lark but almost a career in itself. The rigidity and seriousness of the masculine or male uniform appealed to Allen, who disdained "pink satin" and to Barker, who commented: "It is difficult to express the loathing and contempt I felt as I watched some [women] preen and trick themselves out to capture the attention of some man."[140] (This same fascination with unambiguous and rigid clothing would eventually lead to even more extreme forms of militarism as both drifted toward fascism: Allen embraced its politics whereas Barker was drawn to its style.[141]) Barker's contempt is especially understandable since she seemed cross-dressed whether as a man *or* as a woman. If, after public exposure, Barker had reversed her role and begun to dress as a woman, she argued that she would "have been more likely to attract the unwelcome attention of the police as a *man* masquerading as a *woman*."[142] The *Daily Mail* noticed too that despite Barker's "grey tweed costume" and "fur" (clothing she described as "horrid"[143]), she failed "to give a feminine touch. With her close-cropped hair, her strong, fresh-complexioned face, with the wide-set eyes, her large hands, and her powerful frame, [Barker] suggested a man masquerading as a woman."[144] Since the cross-dresser is always cross-dressed, clothing is at once the solution and the problem. What clothing confirms for the cross-dresser and observer alike is not gender but gender's status as fiction.[145]

Female incursions into the hypermasculine world of the uniform provoked cultural authority, but, as the cases of Allen and Barker reveal, the degree of reaction was relative to the nature of the perceived threat. Allen's "crime" in wearing a masculine uniform deemed too similar to the MWPP's seems hardly equivalent to Barker's impersonation as a highly decorated war hero in full dress uniform and as a baronet, husband, and father. Only a handful of observers, such as Hall, were deeply offended by Barker's masquerade and her "mock war medals [and] wounds."[146] Hall regarded Allen, by comparison, as a "fine" citizen.[147] So why was Allen the one subjected to vicious attack if Barker was the sham? Barker's narrative could be easily subsumed by the press into a familiar tradition of masquerade where for centuries women had passed successfully as soldiers and sailors.[148] Her penitence in the courtroom reassured fascinated onlookers that the masquerade was only a laudable, if pathetic, attempt to fulfill her maternal role more effectively. Any suspicions about her sexuality could be safely deflected by a prevailing interpretive strategy that reinforced gender norms and normative sexuality (except by a judge who thought himself "well-informed" about such matters). Within a culture accustomed to reading the motivations of the "exposed" female-to-male cross-dresser as a practical response to an extraordinary situation, Allen's performance as a woman in such a highly masculinized uniform was culturally unintelligible. In the end the cross-dresser was a diverting spectacle whose clothing bestowed the veneer of power. The masculine woman, on the other hand, "outraged the decencies of nature" for she represented a bid for real power.

FIGURE 1   Sketch of Radclyffe Hall by Patricia Preece. c. 1927. Collection of Christine Hepworth.

FIGURE 2   On the left, Margaret Damer Dawson OBE, Commandant, Women's Police Service, with Sub-Commandant Mary Allen OBE. c. 1916. Imperial War Museum.

FIGURE 3   Mrs. Sophia Stanley. Undated. The photograph provided by kind permission of the Metropolitan Police Service.

Valerie Arkell-Smith,
alias Colonel Victor
Barker. *Daily Mail*,
March 7, 1929.
British Library.

"The Beret Follows
Borotra from the Pays
Basque." *Eve: The
Lady's Pictorial*,
June 30, 1926.
British Library.

(a)

(b)

FIGURE 6   The County Set.
(a) Miss Wilson. *Eve: The Lady's Pictorial*, March 25, 1925. British Library; (b) Mrs. Woodburn-Bamberger. *Eve: The Lady's Pictorial*, June 16, 1926. British Library.

THE BOYETTE.

SEASIDE GIRLS WHO DRESS LIKE BOYS.

The "Boyette" has been increasingly prevalent this Easter at southern resorts where a year ago one saw only occasional specimens of this very latest type of the young emancipated female. Dozens have made their appearance during the holiday. The Boyette not only crops her hair close like a boy but she dresses in every way as a boy.

Sometimes she wears a sports jacket

Types of the boyette.

FIGURE 7
"The Boyette." *Daily Mail*, April 19, 1927. British Library.

FIGURE 8 *Punch*, February 15, 1928. © *Punch* Ltd.
"BUT HE'S NOT EVEN AMUSING. WHAT ON EARTH DOES YOUR SISTER WANT TO MARRY HIM FOR?"
"OH, WELL, I SUPPOSE HE'S THAT HELPLESS CLINGING MASCULINE TYPE THAT WOULD APPEAL TO A GIRL LIKE JOAN."

FIGURE 9 *Punch*, April 27, 1927. © *Punch* Ltd.
Aunt. "WELL, I DARESAY THEY'RE COMFORTABLE, BUT—I SUPPOSE I'M OLD FASHIONED—I DON'T MUCH LIKE THEM. WHY, ONE WOULD THINK YOU WERE A BOY."
Niece. "OH, COME, DEAR OLD THING, THAT'S ABSURD. WHO EVER SAW A BOY WEAR EARRINGS?"

The Best Ingénue as a Bad Garçonne.

AS FAY COLLEN IN " SPRING CLEANING "—AND AS HERSELF : MISS EDNA BEST.

Miss Edna Best, who has roused so much admiration by her portrayal of ingénues, and dainty, fluffy, innocent heroines in various successful productions, is now to be seen in a very different rôle, as in " Spring Cleaning," the brilliant Frederick Lonsdale comedy at the St. Martin's, she plays Fay Collen, the unpleasantly mannish girl who is one of the members of the fast, decadent set which so disgusts Richard Sones. Our photographs make an amusing contrast, as at first sight it seems incredible that they should be portraits of the same lady.

Photograph of Miss Best in " Spring Cleaning " by C. Pollard Crowther, F.R.P.S., specially taken for " The Sketch." Inset by Foulsham and Banfield, Ltd.

FIGURE 10   Edna Best. *Sketch*, February 11, 1925. British Library.

WEDDING RING GIVES THE SHOW AWAY.

It's a hard life telling which are men and which are women nowadays. These sports girls of 1927 might be mistaken for League goalkeepers.

(a)

EVE'S TROUSERED BLISS.

She doesn't look very like a girl, this up-to-date holiday-maker, "snapped" at Shoreham, Sussex—but her dainty shoes betray her secret. Obviously she finds masculine attire ideal for summer wear.

(b)

FIGURE II
Which Are Men and Which
Are Women?
(a) *People*, March 27, 1927.
British Library;
(b) *People*, June 12, 1927.
British Library.

FIGURE 12 *Punch*, March 21, 1928. © *Punch* Ltd.
Young Woman (looking at photograph of friend's fiancé). "WELL, GOD BLESS YOU, MY DEAR, CONGRATULATIONS AND ALL THAT. HE CERTAINLY LOOKS TWICE THE MAN YOU ARE."

FIGURE 13   Radclyffe Hall and Una Troubridge. 1927.
Hulton Getty/Liaison Agency.

FIGURE 14 Radclyffe Hall in Spanish Hat by the photographer
Douglas, 1926. © A. M. Heath & Co.

THE
NEW EVENING DRESS
FOR WOMEN

FIGURE 15   *Tatler*, April 14, 1926. British Library.

Modes Approved for the Petite

Featured at Harrods

AILOR-MADES with a hint of mannish severity in their trim lines—Two-piece modes of feminine grace ! Both types are smart for Spring, both enhance the charm of the petite figure. The models sketched hint at the variety to be found in Harrods Salon for Small Sizes

FIGURE 16 *Eve: The Lady's Pictorial*, March 31, 1926. British Library.

FIGURE 17 Una, Lady Troubridge by Romaine Brooks, 1924. National Museum of American Art, Smithsonian Institution.

FIGURE 18   Gluck by the photographer E. O. Hoppé, 1926. Permission courtesy of the E. O. Hoppé Trust, c/o Curatorial Assistance, Inc., Pasadena, CA © 1995 Curatorial Assistance.

FIGURE 19   *Punch*, February 29, 1928. © *Punch* Ltd.
"I'LL TELL YOU WHAT, OLD THING, THIS NEW FEMININE TOUCH IS ALL RIGHT, BUT YOU'LL
HAVE TO ADOPT A NEW STANCE."

FIGURE 20 *Punch*, October 6, 1926. © *Punch* Ltd.
The New Feminine Photography
Fair Sitter (to Photographer). "I DON'T WANT ONE OF THOSE SLOPPY PICTURES. JUST GET THE CHARACTER AND LET IT GO AT THAT."

FIGURE 21   Margaret Damer Dawson (right) and Mary Allen (left) "rescue" a child. c. 1919. Imperial War Museum.

Photo by Lambert Weston, Folkestone.

BABIES AT THE DAMER DAWSON MEMORIAL HOME WITH INSPECTOR SAUNDERS.

FIGURE 22   "Babies at the Damer Dawson Memorial Home with Inspector Saunders." c. 1924. *The Pioneer Policewoman.*

FIGURE 23   Women Police Picking up a "Case." c. 1919. Imperial War Museum.

FIGURE 24   Women Police Motorcyclists Taking Charge of a "Case." c. 1919. Imperial War Museum.

FIGURE 25   Gluck by Douglas. Undated. Collection of Roy Gluckstein.

FIGURE 26   Gluck by E. O. Hoppé, *Royal Magazine*, December 1926. Permission courtesy of the E. O. Hoppé Trust, c/o Curatorial Assistance, Inc., Pasadena, CA © 1995 Curatorial Assistance.

FIGURE 27   Mrs. Tudor Wilkinson. *Eve: The Lady's Pictorial*, March 25, 1925. British Library.

FIGURE 28　Miss Elizabeth Ponsonby and her fiancé, Mr. Denis Pelly. *Eve: The Lady's Pictorial*, April 17, 1929. British Library.

FIGURE 29
Radclyffe Hall
with her dog,
Colette.
Daily Mirror,
April 13, 1927.
British Library.

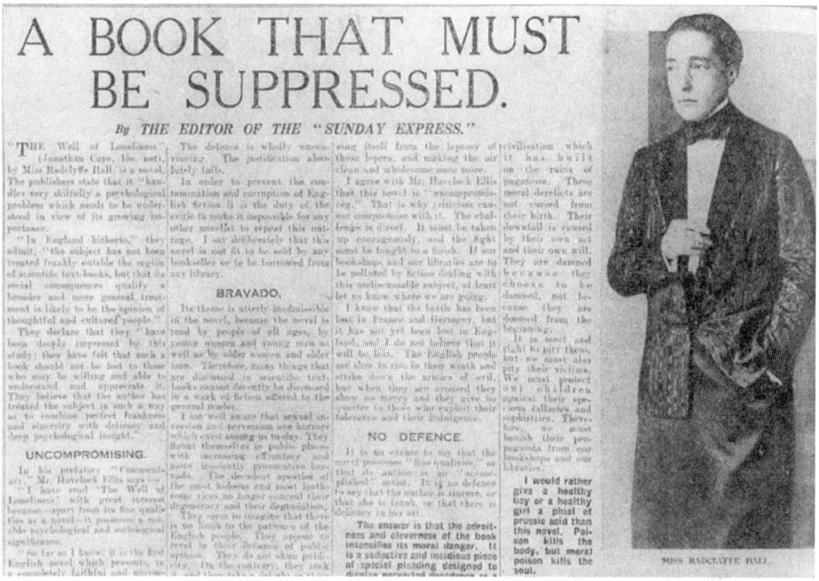

A BOOK THAT MUST BE SUPPRESSED.

By THE EDITOR OF THE "SUNDAY EXPRESS."

"THE Well of Loneliness" (Jonathan Cape, 15s. net), by Miss Radclyffe Hall, is a novel. The publishers state that it "handles very skilfully a psychological problem which needs to be understood in view of its growing importance.

"In England hitherto," they admit, "the subject has not been treated frankly outside the region of scientific text-books, but that its social consequences qualify a broader and more general treatment is likely to be the opinion of thoughtful and cultured people."

They declare that they "have been deeply impressed by this study; they have felt that such a book should not be lost to those who may be willing and able to understand and appreciate it. They believe that the author has treated the subject in such a way as to combine perfect frankness and sincerity with delicacy and deep psychological insight."

UNCOMPROMISING.

In his prefatory "Commentary," Mr. Havelock Ellis says:—

"I have read 'The Well of Loneliness' with great interest because—apart from its fine qualities as a novel—it possesses a notable psychological and sociological significance.

"So far as I know, it is the first English novel which presents, in a completely faithful and uncom-

The defence is wholly unconvincing. The justification absolutely fails.

In order to prevent the contamination and corruption of English fiction it is the duty of the critic to make it impossible for any other novelist to repeat this outrage. I say deliberately that this novel is not fit to be sold by any bookseller or to be borrowed from any library.

BRAVADO.

Its theme is utterly inadmissible in the novel, because the novel is read by people of all ages, by young women and young men as well as by older women and older men. Therefore, many things that are discussed in scientific text-books cannot decently be discussed in a work of fiction offered to the general reader.

I am well aware that sexual inversion and perversion are horrors which exist among us to-day. They flaunt themselves in public places with increasing effrontery and more insolently provocative bravado. The decadent apostles of the most hideous and most loathsome vices no longer conceal their degeneracy and their degradation.

They seem to imagine that there is no limit to the patience of the English people. They appear to revel in their defiance of public opinion. They do not shun publicity. On the contrary, they seek

-sing itself from the leprosy of these lepers, and making the air clean and wholesome once more.

I agree with Mr. Havelock Ellis that this novel is "uncompromising." That is why criticism cannot compromise with it. The challenge is direct. It must be taken up courageously, and the fight must be fought to a finish. If our bookshops and our libraries are to be polluted by fiction dealing with this undiscussable subject, at least let us know where we are going.

I know that the battle has been lost in France and Germany, but it has not yet been lost in England, and I do not believe that it will be lost. The English people are slow to rise in their wrath and strike down the armies of evil, but when they are aroused they show no mercy and they give no quarter to those who exploit their tolerance and their indulgence.

NO DEFENCE.

It is no excuse to say that the novel possesses "fine qualities," or that its author is an "accomplished" artist. It is no defence to say that the author is sincere, or that she is frank, or that there is delicacy in her art.

The answer is that the adroitness and cleverness of the book intensifies its moral danger. It is a seductive and insidious piece of special pleading designed to

civilisation which it has built on the ruins of paganism. These moral derelicts are not cursed from their birth. Their downfall is caused by their own act and their own will. They are damned because they choose to be damned, not because they are doomed from the beginning.

It is meet and right to pity them, but we must also pity their victims. We must protect our children against their specious fallacies and sophistries. Therefore, we must banish their propaganda from our bookshops and our libraries.

I would rather give a healthy boy or a healthy girl a phial of prussic acid than this novel. Poison kills the body, but moral poison kills the soul.

MISS RADCLYFFE HALL.

FIGURE 30 *Sunday Express*, August 19, 1928. British Library.

FIGURE 31
Sunday Chronicle,
August 26, 1928.
British Library.

MISS RADCLYFFE HALL, whose new novel, "The Well of Loneliness," was withdrawn from publication yesterday at the Home Secretary's request.

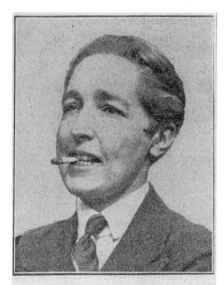

FIGURE 32
London Calling.
September 8, 1928.
British Library.

Miss Radclyffe Hall.

*D*ISTINCTIVE people have a queer way of reminding you irresistibly of other distinctive people. This sounds a contradiction, since the statement apparently cancels the distinction.

When I first saw Miss Radclyffe Hall some years ago, I thought of the late Lewis Waller in *M. Beaucaire*—something to do with the poise and shape of the head, no more, yet sufficient.

The first impression is blurred. She continues to remind me of a French aristocrat. I feel she would have graced a tumbril, and defied a whole mob with supreme tranquillity and much secret zest.

Perhaps she could *meet* a great moment more adequately than achieve one. I am aware in her, perhaps inaccurately, of an eternal, watchful defiance of life.

At the moment, the muck-hounds are on her track, and her latest book (reviewed on this page) has been withdrawn at the instance of the Home Secretary. Yet her earlier work, *Adam's Breed*, achieved the Femina Vie Heureuse Prize for 1925-26, and the James Tait Black Memorial Book Prize for 1926.

Four

Passing Fashions: Reading Female
Masculinities in the 1920s

I

IN MARCH OF 1929, just months after the banning of *The Well of Loneliness*, Radclyffe Hall, a woman many assume to be the supreme embodiment of female masculinity, complained to her literary agent about Colonel Victor Barker, "I would like to see her drawn & quartered. . . . A mad *pervert* of the most undesirable type."[1] As I discussed in the previous chapter, the shocking revelations of Barker's case, like the earlier obscenity trial of Hall's novel, received massive publicity: reporters scrambled to obtain as many details and photographs as possible about the extraordinary woman who masqueraded not only as a man but also as a husband and decorated military hero. How strange that Hall, whose own masculine appearance was the source of continual comment throughout her life, would invoke the "p" word to vilify another woman drawn to masculine clothing and to members of the same sex. Hall's intense derision seems even more anomalous when read against the dominant reaction of the tabloids, which ranged from amazement to curiosity, not to mention admiration. Most newspapers reduced the life story of Colonel Leslie Ivor Victor Gauntlett Bligh Barker, DSO, to headlines such as "Exploits of Man-Woman" and "Secrets of Six Years' Masquerade: Amazing Impersonation" and peddled sensational accounts of Barker's life based on evidence presented in court by her legal defense or garnered through investigative reporting.[2] At first glance it seems unimaginable that the press covered Barker's perjury trial without alluding to the recent banning of a novel in defense of lesbianism. Equally surprising, most reporters did not connect Barker's superb performance of masculinity to the decade-long cultural phenomenon of fashionable female masculinity, except the lone journalist for the *Daily Herald*: "in her new feminine attire," for Barker was compelled by the court to dress in accordance with her sex for the duration of the trial, she was "the typical woman of 1929, with her manly stride and Eton-cropped hair."[3] The journalist wrestled with the remarkable incongruities the dressed and cross-dressed body represented, but like his colleagues stopped short of relating Barker's awkwardness in women's clothing, mannish physical movements, or haircut to sexual identity.

That anyone in England—especially in the print media—missed the link between (masculine) dress and (homo)sexuality presented in the figure of the cross-dressed woman, or a woman who seems cross-dressed, is incredible to us today. Yet what was obvious to Hall after the 1928 publication and subsequent banning of her novel—and, of course, what seems "obvious" to us now because we share Hall's post-*Well* perspective—had not by 1929 been thoroughly disseminated throughout the public domain. This leads me to the central argument I wish to advance in this chapter: in the decade prior to the publication of Hall's novel, and even for a short time after, boyish or mannish garb for women did *not* register any one stable spectatorial effect. The meaning of clothing in the decade after the First World War, a time of unprecedented cultural confusion over constructions of gender and sexual identities, was a good deal more fluid than fixed. If we impose our current assumptions about the requisite association of clothing and same-sex desire, we risk misreading female masculinities in the 1920s, for *in* the 1920s, as the tabloid response to Barker indicates, such connections were not yet consolidated.

This point is underscored in the June 30, 1926 page from *Eve: The Lady's Pictorial* (figure 5), which presents a virtual panorama of what might be called the "passing fashions" of the 1920s. The fashion spread in *Eve* offers a first indication of why it would have been unlikely for the press to conjoin Barker and Hall or masculine dress and female homosexuality, for it depicts active women moving into the once exclusively masculine preserve of motorboat racing and yachting, rakishly boyish society women, a cross-dressed artist, and an actor posing as a tomboy. The four women all sport the same fashion accessory, the beret, but there the similarity ends. The clothing obscures rather than reveals gender and sexuality, so that we might well wonder what each of these women "passed" for in the 1920s? A woman passing as—or taken to be—a boy or man? A heterosexual woman passing as a lesbian? A lesbian passing as heterosexual? A woman of any sexual preference dressing boyishly or mannishly to pass as a woman of fashion? A lesbian passing as a lesbian? A challenge to the commonly held belief that the "most pervasive image of lesbianism in these years is of women who appear at first glance to be male: Radclyffe Hall, Romaine Brooks, or the Marquise de Belbeuf—monocled, tuxedoed, hair cropped short, cigarette in hand" is long overdue.[4] This "image" to which literary critic Shari Benstock refers was indisputably "most pervasive" but did not always signify "lesbianism," as we will see. Moreover, some English lesbians who embraced such a style

did not "appear at first glance to be male." In a culture where cross-dressing was not the exception but the norm, these women would have been positioned by observers at different points along a wide spectrum of female masculinity.[5] Thus we should be cautious in pinning down the cultural
significance of monocles, short hair, and cigarettes to any one effect for, as
Garber reminds us:

> Cross-dressing is about gender confusion. Cross-dressing is about the
> phallus as constitutively veiled. Cross-dressing is about the power of
> women. Cross-dressing is about the emergence of gay identity. Cross-
> dressing is about the anxiety of economic or cultural dislocation, the
> anticipation or recognition of "otherness" as loss. All true, all partial
> truths, all powerful metaphors.[6]

Since in England in the 1920s fashion-conscious women of all sexual per-
suasions were obliged to "cross-dress" by donning boyish or mannish attire
and by cutting their hair short, we must be receptive to the multiple interpretive possibilities of the performance of female masculinity.[7]

If critical assessment of the significance of fashionable cross-dressing for
women and the formation of a lesbian subcultural style is not grounded in
chronological or national specificity, we may err in several ways. Sandra
Gilbert and Susan Gubar, for example, gloss over national differences among
a diverse group of lesbian writers to speculate on the political motivations
underlying some female modernists' fascination with gender and costume:
"from Renée Vivien to Radclyffe Hall and Djuna Barnes, from Vita Sackville-
West to Willa Cather and Gertrude Stein, a number of other women trans-
gressively appropriated male costumes or oscillated between parodically
female and male costumes as if to declare that, as Woolf said, we are what
we wear, and therefore, since we can wear anything, we can be anyone."[8]
For the most pragmatic of these female modernists, gender fluidity was the
name of the game and masculine dress was one way to "usurp male privilege." Gilbert and Gubar rightly posit a connection between women's agency
and the appropriation of male clothing, but their reading clarifies neither
how individual wearers might have assumed different "male costumes" for
various reasons nor how onlookers might have seen in each wearer something completely different. Even the nature of transgression is culturally
inscribed. Thus scholars who focus exclusively on Paris-Lesbos place an
unusual emphasis on the transgressive thrill women in Paris may have experienced in wearing trousers, because they were indeed breaking the law.[9] But
such exhilaration in violating patriarchal law might have been different in

England, where such apparel for women was not subject to regulatory leg-islation. Valentine Ackland (the lifelong partner of novelist Sylvia Townsend Warner) thoroughly relished the shock value of wearing trousers in public in 1926 London, but she did not risk arrest; she writes that "for a short time I took pleasure in thinking I was flouting Society [in her lesbianism], it was exactly the same degree of pleasure that I felt when I . . . first wore trousers and walked in Mecklenburgh Square (in 1926 this was a startling thing to do)."[10] In England, cross-dressing was just as likely to be playful or eroti-cally pleasurable as it was political.

In *Women of the Left Bank: Paris, 1900–1940*, an incisive examination of women artists and writers living in Paris before and after the First World War, Benstock, like Gilbert and Gubar, reads cross-dressing as a serious political strategy that enabled some lesbians to make a "public announce-ment" of their sexuality "in a code that specifically denied an allegiance to womanhood as societally defined (e.g., the feminine)."[11] Benstock's study, carefully grounded in cultural and chronological specificity, successfully chal-lenges Harris's notion of a "more profound nationality of their lesbianism" but surprisingly positions Radclyffe Hall as part of this hub of lesbian intel-lectual and artistic activity.[12] Hall's mythic presence in Paris is so com-monplace that few scholars realize how little time she actually spent there in the 1920s, certainly less than most women of her (upper-middle) social class. Elizabeth Wilson's characterization of Hall's involvement with the les-bian subculture in Paris is typical: "In the 1920s the members of the famous Paris coterie of lesbians . . . included Radclyffe Hall, Romaine Brooks and Natalie Clifford Barney, as well as a number of other artists and writers."[13] Alkarim Jivani writes in the same vein: "The most prominent exponent of the Paris style in Britain was Radclyffe Hall. . . . Along with her lover Una Troubridge, Radclyffe Hall was a frequent visitor to the Parisian salons of Romaine Brooks."[14] In fact, between 1921 and 1925 Hall and Troubridge spent barely three weeks in the French capital.[15] If Hall had been as famil-iar with lesbian life in Paris as critics claim, it is unlikely that she would have conducted a research expedition in 1926 to "[gather] material in the Left Bank homosexual bars and clubs" in preparation for writing *The Well of Loneliness*.[16] This three-week trip practically doubled the time Hall had spent in Paris since 1921, and during the visit the pair were as likely to social-ize with other visiting London lesbians as with women who actually lived in Paris.[17] The myth about Hall's participation in 1920s Paris may have orig-inated in the fact that the couple retreated there after the obscenity trial, on February 5, 1929, and stayed well away from England until November 1,

1929—a period biographer Sally Cline refers to as their "literary exile."[18] Whatever its origin, this exaggeration of Hall's relatively modest role in Paris-Lesbos obscures her involvement in a modern English lesbian subculture and shows why we must be cautious in assigning Hall to a cultural milieu other than her own.

Hall's distinctive appearance was as much a part of her public persona as her literary production, but in England in the 1920s her look was not, as has been claimed, regarded as eccentric, unusual, or bizarre.[19] After the obscenity trial, newspaper photographs of her (short hair, bow tie, cigarette protruding from her mouth or even clenched between her teeth, and hand tucked nonchalantly into a jacket pocket) would haunt the cultural imagination for decades both within and outside the subculture. And plenty of photographic evidence seems to verify that women known to be homosexual, such as Hall and the artist who wished to be known simply as Gluck, subscribed to this one visual formula. But we will see how these alleged visual icons of lesbianism had more to do with the fashionable boyish or mannish female or indeed with twenties fashion in general. Careful scrutiny of the style system and its female masculinities in the years prior to the publication of *The Well* will demonstrate how English fashion of the twenties, in providing space for experimentation, called attention to itself as a "look"—and one quite unsettling in the cultural domain. In the following sections I will turn to the pervasive phenomenon of masculine fashion for women, with its concomitant openness and fluidity, to explore the ways in which some women, primarily of the upper middle and upper classes, exploit the ambiguity that tolerated, even encouraged, the crossing over of fixed labels and assigned categories, such as female boy, woman of fashion in the masculine mode, lesbian boy, mannish lesbian, and female cross-dresser.

II

THE "LOOK" CULTURAL critics such as Benstock now regard as the "most pervasive image of lesbianism" closely resembles that of the 1920s Modern Girl and Masculine Woman. None of these "looks" was carved in stone; rather, they were immanently fluid and can be traced back, though with key differences as I will suggest below, to the codes associated with the New Woman of the late nineteenth century.[20] The iconography of the New Woman, complete with a characteristic manner of dress and even body type, was transmitted so effectively throughout Victorian culture in a range of texts (fiction, drama, and print journalism) that all her salient features could be accommodated in a single verse, awarded a prize for the best definition:

> She flouts love's caresses
> Reforms ladies' dresses
> And scorns the Man-Monster's tirade;
> She seems scarcely human
> This *mannish* New Woman
> This Queen of the Blushless Brigade.[21]

This unflattering caricature so pervaded the popular press that the phrase "New Woman" often worked as a "catch-all for a variety of distinct but overlapping types": "The liberated bachelor girl, unmanageable wife, frustrated spinster, and street-corner demagogue were not so much life studies as embodiments of male fears and fantasies spun about the prospect of female emancipation."[22] Particular items of clothing constituted a kind of uniform, as delineated in a sensational article of 1868: "unmistakable shirt-fronts, linen collars, vests and plain ties, like a man."[23] Such clothing, in turn, prescribed bodily demeanor, and thus a woman so clad "folds her arms or sets them akimbo, like a man" (81). Before the First World War, Troubridge experimented briefly with this look: "like an early suffragette, Una appeared in a stiff collar 'attached to a flannel shirt with cuffs and cuff links,' severely cut coat and skirt and low-heeled patent leather Oxford shoes."[24] Hall too sported the New Woman's highly tailored look (a style popular among the set of her first long-term lover, Mabel Batten) until fashions changed after the war.

Cline argues that Hall's prewar "outré masculine outfits stylistically signified her sense of social dislocation. It allowed her to distance herself from women who desired men, whilst signalling her own desire for other women" (76). Such a reading may owe something to the descriptions of individual female sexual inverts in the work of the sexologists. In 1886 Richard von Krafft-Ebing, for instance, linked lesbianism with "masculine" traits and cross-dressing: "[It] may nearly always be suspected in females wearing their hair short [well before it was socially acceptable], or who dress in the fashion of men, or pursue the sports and pastimes of their male acquaintances"; such women exhibit "masculine features . . . manly gait . . . [and] small breasts."[25] Havelock Ellis may have rejected the physiological characteristics of his predecessor, but he nevertheless in 1897 noted "traits of masculine simplicity . . . [and] frequently a pronounced taste for smoking cigarettes . . . also a decided taste and toleration for cigars."[26] Scholars have yet to trace in detail just how sexological discourses were trickling into the public arena, but clearly such medical or "scientific" knowledge about sexual inversion was in circulation among the educated. At the same time it is far from certain that within the culture at large mannish dress signaled sexual inversion so unequivocally, since masculine fashion for women was also associated with educated or so-called advanced women, spinsters and feminists, among other unconventional women.

Other key elements central to the stereotype of mannish women include Englishness and class. After the First World War, "the clumsy, thick-ankled, untidily tweed-clothed hoyden" was thought to be an upper-class creation associated with the countryside:

> The mock hermaphrodite type is peculiar to this country [England], and it is growing, particularly in the moneyed classes. A stroll through London's shops reveals the high percentage of eminently feminine types and the high percentage of good looks. This is becoming less the case among the classes. All over England the countryside is full of genteel maleish women, many of whom are foredoomed to spinsterhood. It is not the poor who are losing their sex differentials, it is the well-to-do.[27]

Wealth and class status enabled the "mock hermaphrodite" to deliberately ignore public opinion and wear any style she desired, as is evident in numerous photographs in *Country Life*, the *Tatler*, or *Eve: The Lady's Pictorial* of the county set engaged in pastimes such as hunting and riding, or attending dog shows (figure 6). The *Daily Mail* noticed too that this type of woman is found "invariably out of doors . . . [and] does not pander to fashion."[28] Such women could be situated vis-à-vis aristocratic eccentricity, especially by onlookers wholly unfamiliar with sexological taxonomies, as Katrina Rolley suggests: "for viewers who were unaware of [Hall and Troubridge's] sexuality, especially those distanced by class, their appearance might be (mis)read as part of the aristocratic tradition of eccentricity."[29] The fashions I describe in this chapter may have crossed class and age boundaries, but women such as Hall, Una Troubridge, and Gluck, who also gained prominence in the twenties, were among a select group who could afford the luxury of dressing as they wished.[30] Their "mannishness" however, as we will see, was of an entirely different quality than that of the tweedy English spinsters already described.

By the 1920s the New Woman had evolved into the Modern Girl and the Masculine Woman. Yet while both groups borrowed stylistic elements from each other, there were key differences that would render the former far less threatening: the Modern Girl resided safely in the sphere of boyishness rather than mannishness. Known by any number of sobriquets (including boy-girl, boyette, hard-boiled flapper, or boyish female), and with varying degrees of affection or derision, the Modern Girl came into being after the First World War, although some fashion historians, such as Valerie Steele, argue that the "look" existed before the war.[31] By the 1920s, the word "flapper," which in the 1890s could refer, among other things, to a very young prostitute or a young woman inclined to flightiness, came to signify a young woman with a "boyish figure."[32] Because this fashion of female boyishness dictated a particular body type to carry the new clothes, the ideal became youthful and ultraslim, with small breasts, narrow hips, and hair bobbed, shingled, or Eton-cropped.[33] Incidentally, there were significant distinctions between these short haircuts: "To have ones [sic] hair *bobbed* was to have it cut. The *shingle* was an exceptionally short cut in which the back hair was cut and tapered like that of a man. Although the most fashionable cut was short with the hair tapering off to the nape of the neck, many variations were seen. . . . Others followed the extreme *Eton crop*, a style in which hair was exceptionally closely-cropped and dressed like that of a man."[34] Unlike the Eton collar and jacket, with direct links to the uniform of the elite boys' public school, the "Eton" in Eton crop evidently connoted a generalized notion of boyishness rather than the institution as such. Defined by the *OED* simply as "a style of cutting women's hair close to the head all over," the etymology is obscure, although the usage examples reinforce the view that class connotations arising from "Eton" were more distant than overt. Along with the "look" came an attitude of rebelliousness and pleasure seeking— flaunted by the smoking of cigarettes—a new athleticism and an apparent sexual freedom.

The boyish fashion caught on and spread across social classes, helped by the changes in the clothing industry that popularized ready-made clothes. The dictates of fashion became absolutely de riguer, blurring class and age dichotomies; as Mary Agnes Hamilton lamented: "Clothes, hats, shoes, stockings, furs, bag, scarf—all are standardized; everybody wears the same. Face and figure are obediently conventional, too. As a result one cannot guess age and is quite uncertain as to class."[35] This sense of transcending class boundaries is underscored in a 1921 letter to *The Times*, in which an "octogenarian" complained that the "modern girl, half dressed, loud voiced, cigarette smoking, and bumptious mannered, is at present an unlovely object, to whatever social rank she belongs; and at present I am sorry to say, she is found in all grades of society."[36] By 1927 the boyish female had become such a familiar sight on the cultural landscape that, unlike the letter of the "octo-genarian" six years earlier, no angry, shocked, or indignant letters were sent to the editor over this *Daily Mail* report on the seaside phenomenon of the "boyette" (figure 7):

> The "Boyette" has been increasingly prevalent. . . . A year ago one saw only occasional specimens of this very latest type of the young eman-cipated female. . . . The Boyette not only crops her hair close like a boy but she dresses in every way as a boy. Sometimes she wears a sports jacket and flannel "bags" [trousers]; more generally she favors a kind of Norfolk suit. Nearly always she goes hatless. In age she appears to be in the last years of flapperdom and her ambition is to look as much like a boy as possible; but *little feminine mannerisms* disclose her sex and show her . . . amusing herself by masquerade that is harmless enough, though some people may disapprove of it as ultra-tomboyish. What they think does not trouble the Boyette; she wears her boy's suit with a jaunty unself-consciousness and revels in the freedom of move-ment. . . . A point of interest to eugenists is that the Boyette has a finer physique than the average boy of her age. One thing that betrays her is that she cannot manage her cigarette like a boy.[37]

To aid readers in making a positive identification of the boyette, and to make sense of what for some might otherwise register as unintelligible, the text is accompanied by two separate photographs (captioned "Types of the Boyette") depicting fun-loving women both with close-cropped hair and one in a tailored jacket. The photographs are cropped just below the waist, so it is unclear whether or not these particular specimens actually wear flannel trousers or not. Women who wear "bags" on seaside holidays might have chosen the safer option, for just below this article a headline reports the near drowning of a woman whose dress became entangled with the gears of a boat: "Trapped by Dress: Men Hold Girl on Capsized Boat."

As the article on the boyette astutely observes, the Modern Girl's objective is not to pass as a boy but to "look as much like a boy as possible." The "lit-tle feminine mannerisms" that demonstrate how the boyette amuses herself "by masquerade" deliberately expose her true gender. If she is mistaken for an actual boy, the "look" has somehow gone wrong—she has, in effect, sur-passed herself. Commentators in the 1920s who pondered whether or not a girl was actually a boy might then have wondered—though seldom aloud or in print—if the girl was a "boy" who liked girls. By the 1920s, according to fashion historian James Laver, "all young women cut off their hair," so that "there was now nothing to distinguish a young woman from a schoolboy *except* perhaps her rouged lips and pencilled eyebrows."[38] The "except" is exceptionally critical because these traces of make-up mark the all-important dividing line that separates boyish women from boys; as Quentin Crisp notes, "The short skirts, bobbed hair, and flat chests that were in fashion were in fact symbols of immaturity. . . . The word 'boyish' was used to describe the girls of that era. This epithet they accepted graciously."[39] Why graciously? No gender confusion here—Crisp replies, "*They* knew that they looked nothing like boys." The fashionably boyish female never pretends to herself or to an outside observer that she is anything other than a boyish female.

Some Modern Girls did pass (in some sense of the word) as boys by becoming, perhaps inadvertently, the object of male homoerotic desire. H. Montgomery Hyde goes so far as to suggest, with logic more convoluted than Barker concocted, that certain women in the upper and upper-middle classes purposefully "flattened their chests and cut their hair short" to pass as boys because they believed it was the only way they could, in his less than politically correct phrasing, "compete with the 'pansies'" because "certain eligible men were more interested in their own sex."[40] Two members of the so-called Brideshead generation, Cyril Connolly and Evelyn Waugh, did indeed shift their sexual allegiances from young men to young women via the boyish female—the latter serving as training wheels to heterosexuality. In 1927–28 Connolly fell in love with one Horatia "Racy" Fisher and confessed in his journal an admiration for her "very lovely and boyish" appearance in her "boy's felt hat."[41] The following year Connolly found himself attracted to another boyish woman, Jean Bakewell, whose "short boy's hair" and "lovely boy's body" he found irresistible.[42] Waugh went even further and actually married his boyish woman, Evelyn Gardner, whom Nancy Mitford characterized as " 'a ravishing boy, a page.' "[43] Waugh's friends, amused by the couple's androgynous first name, adopted nicknames to distinguish the two, "He-Evelyn" and "She-Evelyn," although some thought She-Evelyn the more masculine. If Gardner's first name "Evelyn" had not already been so conveniently androgynous, she may have had to invent another, like so many other young women of the upper classes who invented "bi-sexual (or sexless) names" for themselves, such as "Bobbie, Billie, Jackie, Dickie, Ray or Jo."[44] The practice was fairly common among members of the smart set, as well as in artistic and literary circles, so that lesbians who adopted masculine nicknames privately among their friends, such as Radclyffe Hall (known as "John"), Mary Allen ("Robert"), Naomi Jacob ("Mickie"), or Marion Barbara Carstairs ("Joe"), might not have attracted as much attention as is often assumed, especially in that such names rarely appeared in print.

Although newspapers drummed up cultural anxieties (and happily increased sales) with stories about boyish women and effeminate men, these anxieties focused on questions of gender rather than sexual identity.[45] For example, in 1921, the *Daily Mail* declared, "Healthy Young Girls Are More Boyish than Boys," their new strength and vigor contrasting sharply with the emasculated male.[46] By 1927 *Eve* remarked: "The curious thing is that just at the very time when Eve is simplifying her garments to an almost masculine severity Adam begins adorning and—dare one say—emasculating himself."[47] In much the same way, a 1928 *Punch* cartoon (figure 8) pities the "helpless clinging masculine type" at the mercy of the Modern Girl. As if surrounded by so many sharks, the meek male—with vaguely feminine facial features—sits demurely in the manner of a woman, legs crossed at the knee and hands resting delicately in his lap. The poor fellow may be the only one in trousers, but his clothing lacks authority as he listens quietly to his fiancée towering above him, hands on hips and legs astride in a stance reminiscent of the New Woman or women in wartime uniform.[48] The two women observing the couple manifest the traits of their type of Modern Girl: short hair, hands in pockets, relaxed posture, cigarette either in hand or dangling from the mouth—styles and gestures heretofore associated with the masculine. By implying that masculine fashions encourage the Modern Girl to practice masculine manners, such cartoons exacerbated the confusion circulating around gender and heightened cultural anxieties that the sexes were somehow changing places.

However, for the most part, boyishness denoted a certain fashionable youthfulness that was never threatening. Thus the boyette is only "amusing herself by masquerade that is harmless enough." The *Daily Mail*'s neologism "boyette" doubly diminishes by reducing the fashionable young woman to a mere "boy" without full masculine power and by adding the diminutive to ensure that no one will take her seriously. As one observer put it, "The modern girl has ceased to be a woman but has not yet become a gentleman."[49] Far from bestowing masculine power or authority through imitation, the new "look" denaturalized women by robbing them of their traditional place inside or outside the home. For instance, a 1927 *Punch* cartoon insinuates that the flapper style is incompatible with the maternal. A woman with ultrashort hair stands before her son, cigarette in hand: "You know, Bobby, you're not nearly so obedient as you used to be. I wonder why that is." The young boy answers, "Well, Mother, if you ask me, I think present-day fashions may have something to do with it."[50] The mother's acquiescence to the "look" results in the loss of maternal authority—and, ironically, the individual who challenges her is a "real" boy. Another cartoon portrays a bobbed Lady Godiva who can no longer influence, or participate in, the political arena. The cutting of one's hair cuts two ways: the short-haired woman possesses a fashionable boyish appearance but without masculine power—she is a mere imitation.[51]

The codes of the boyish Modern Girl (such as short hair, nicknames, or stance) thus became well-established in the fashion and society pages, with the apparent aim of suggesting "immaturity [so that] a young woman would model herself on the equivocal outline of the child of twelve . . . a girl or boy."[52] Many modern emancipated women adopted these codes but were of an age that put boyishness out of reach. Fashion magazines depicted these older women in elegant tailor-made suits and hair bobbed, shingled, and Eton-cropped, but such women contrasted sharply with the "bumptious" and "unlovely object" ridiculed in the octogenarian's letter to *The Times*. In acquiring the look of the Modern Girl the older woman comes even closer to the stereotype of the mannish lesbian that Benstock and others describe. The Masculine Woman, older in age than the Modern Girl, seemed ominously poised to disturb sexuality as well as gender. If codes such as short hair, androgynous nicknames, and hands in pockets denoted trends in fashion rather than sexual identity in the decade of "anything goes," what were the sure-fire signs of an emerging homosexual subcultural style that would distinguish lesbians from boyish girls and mannish women? Were they, as Benstock suggests, the "cigarette in hand," a gent's tie, trousers, or the infamous monocle worn by Troubridge?

In *Young in the Twenties* Ethel Mannin recalls how all the "ladies" who attended her parties "smoked, conscientiously, as the outward and visible sign of sex equality. Long cigarette holders became fashionable."[53] By the late 1920s newspapers and magazines frequently featured images of women smoking, including, on rare occasions, a pipe. In a *Punch* cartoon that portrays a flapper meeting the New Woman, the two women pause during a round of golf to measure their respective pipes as two lads might compare anatomical parts. The formidable-looking New Woman, in her tailored jacket and tie, her felt hat, with legs apart and hand on hip, brandishes a very large pipe, while the flapper's pipe is quite petite. To the latter's query, "I say, isn't your pipe a bit large?" the other woman responds, "Not a bit. I wouldn't be seen dead with an effeminate little thing like yours."[54] This most manly form of smoking inspires women to reach ever loftier heights of machismo and engage in the stereotypically male preoccupation with size—but it does not, apparently, automatically turn them into lesbians. As critic

Richard Klein maintains, "A woman smoking may be thought to be less 'feminine' because more active, aggressive, masterful, but she is not therefore more 'masculine'—in her own eyes or in those of many men."[55] No manner of smoking (the cigarette in its holder, a pipe or cigar) signaled sexual preference, for all such signs were up for grabs.

The First World War gave women the first opportunity to wear trousers with a degree of impunity and, as we have seen, women such as Sackville-West experienced exhilaration. In 1918 the artist Gluck invented her own version of trousers and, in a letter to her brother, exclaimed: "I am flourishing in a new garb. Intensely exciting. . . . It was an experiment [and] I am glad it turned out so well."[56] Women abandoned trousers after the war, but by 1927 some returned to wearing them in public again, though only for specified occasions.[57] *Punch* carefully stipulates in a satiric "guide" the conditions under which trousers might be worn and not deemed "unattractive": "in the form of a smoking suit—and for sports wear they are not unreasonable; but should they be adopted in the city—in the domestic circle—at Ascot—for dinner-parties—or in the ballroom—old-fashioned people may regret [it]."[58] Radclyffe Hall rarely wore trousers in public; the one photograph I have seen is one taken in 1923 at Crufts, the prestigious dog show. And women such as Sackville-West would normally only wear them in private. Only Gluck continued to wear trousers publicly throughout the decade, suggesting less a lesbian persona than an artistic one, as we shall see later in this chapter. Lesbians seem generally to have followed the fashion trends during the 1920s and did not single out trousers as a sign of sexual identity.

In 1952 C. Willett Cunnington, the fashion historian, surveyed fashion trends in the 1920s and concluded that "in order to avoid offending the normal instincts by a too obviously homo-sexual appearance, there was no attempt to . . . assume trousers—the symbol of the adult male."[59] I suspect his observation tells us a good deal more about the homophobic climate of the early 1950s than the 1920s because I have not uncovered any evidence that endorses the claim that women avoided trousers for fear of being supposed "homo-sexual." For example, in a *Punch* cartoon of 1927 (figure 9), trouser-wearing is associated not with lesbianism or the lesbian's attempt to assume masculine power but, rather, with fashion, youth, and the sporting venues of high society. In this depiction of an encounter between an aunt in skirt and hat and a niece with an extremely short haircut, in trousers and holding a tennis racket, the aunt remarks, "Well, I daresay they're comfortable, but—I suppose I'm old-fashioned—I don't much like them. Why, you would think you were a boy." The niece protests, "Oh, come, dear old thing, that's absurd. Who ever saw a boy wear earrings?" The precious, miniscule emblems of femininity can hardly compensate for the overall impression of boyishness; few, *Punch* wryly implies, would take the trouble to hunt for small signs of gender difference, and even fewer would hunt for signs of female sexual inversion. (The *Tatler* observed in 1926, "Earrings are more fashionable than ever, which is only natural, as they take away that naked look from an Eton-cropped head."[60])

And what about that monocle? Garber astutely advises that we read "vestimentary codes" as an elaborate "system of signification."[61] Emphasizing the openness and fluidity of such codes, she explains that they "speak in a number of registers: class, gender, sexuality, erotic style. Part of the problem—and part of the pleasure and danger of decoding—is in determining which set of referents is in play in each scenario. For decoding itself is an erotics—in fact, one of the most powerful we know." Yet her contention that "the monocle, and the cigarette, cigarette holder, or cigar" are "accessories both before and after the 'fact' of lesbianism," forecloses interpretive possibilities and rigidly conjoins accessory and identity (152). Garber, of course, reiterates a widely held belief that the monocle unequivocally signals a particular sexual preference. Cline asserts that Mary Allen's "lesbianism was flamboyantly indicated by her monocle."[62] Allen was certainly flamboyant, and when she toured New York City in the spring of 1924 her monocle generated tremendous excitement, even taking on a life of its own. Allen writes:

> What intrigued them most of all was my eyeglass. They were quite convinced—and so was the whole of America within twenty-four hours—that [the monocle] was a sign of office, like the crozier or the Black Rod! They simply refused to believe I wore it for use. To them, my uniform was incomplete without the eyeglass, and I believe they were firmly convinced that I could not make an arrest until I had screwed it into place.[63]

Allen, monocled and uniformed, was the personification of English chic. If the instrument had any association with lesbianism it would hardly have been a topic for open discussion.

Early in the nineteenth century the monocle became a favorite device among cartoonists to depict the quintessential English aristocrat, but by the early twentieth century one newspaper noted:

> The single eyeglass is no longer the sign of the Englishman of fashion, for the belles of New York and Chicago Society have claimed it for their own. It is the latest craze of the American smart girl, and it has caught on. . . . But it takes a daring woman to use it, not only because it is a

detriment rather than an aid to beauty. . . . She wishes to be original and a bit English and eccentric too, but not for a minute does she wish to look less charming.[64]

Into this swirling jumble of connotations, we should add that the eyewear became associated with another loaded concept, "decadence," which, as Elaine Showalter explains, is "notoriously difficult . . . to define. . . . It was the pejorative label applied by the bourgeoisie to everything that seemed unnatural, artificial, and perverse, from Art Nouveau to homosexuality, a sickness with symptoms associated with cultural degeneration and decay."[65] This small, circular piece of glass clearly possessed a cultural significance several times larger than its size. Michael Baker assumes that Una Troubridge acquired a monocle in order to publicize her lesbianism: "As if to proclaim her allegiance to her regiment of women, Una bought herself a tortoise-shell monocle and . . . began publicly to sport it in her eye."[66] Yet a 1925 *Sketch* photographic layout of the actor Edna Best (figure 10) bills her "the Best ingénue as a bad garçonne": a boyish femme fatale who, from top to bottom, exhibits the tell-tale "accessories," extremely short hair, cigarette, *and* monocle. Is it the sexually suggestive, slinky dress alone that saves her from from the unsavory association with female homosexuality?

The publicity shot of Edna Best—saturated with the codes of an "unpleasantly mannish girl who is one of the members of the fast, decadent set," as the copy underneath explains—is quite intriguing in its complex layout: the "dainty, fluffy, innocent" ingénue floats in an old-fashioned oval shape, softening a corner of the framed femme fatale: "Our photographs make an amusing contrast, as at first sight it seems incredible that they should be portraits of the same lady." The "amusing" juxtaposition demands closer inspection to determine what facilitates the bizarre transformation. The slight tilt of the head is sustained, if in different directions, and the actor's face remains virtually unchanged, although the expression shifts from ironic seriousness to cheerful wholesomeness. The visual pleasure in which the *Sketch* layout invites the reader to participate is precisely that which Garber describes above as the erotics of decoding. There is no guarantee of a stable meaning, however, for just as Showalter reminds us how decadence is "notoriously difficult . . . to define," the monocle itself at once resists and teases. Like the wearing of trousers, the monocle never conveys a single meaning. The innocent "Best ingénue" metamorphoses into a sultry "bad garçonne" via her overdetermined, fashion accoutrements, and especially through the looming monocle which peers intensely at the viewer. But the instrument designed to aid vision *only* in a single eye carries multiple symbolic meanings, denoting class, Englishness, daring, decay, rebellion, affectation, eccentricity—and possibly, but not necessarily, sexual identity.

General commentary about Hall's appearance inevitably included a reference to her monocle, even to remark when she was not wearing it. After the results of the 1927 Femina Prize were announced, *Eve* featured a sketch of the author on the book page with the following description: "Winner of the 'Femina' Prize with 'Adam's Breed,' Miss Radclyffe Hall is in the front rank of . . . modern fashions in dress. The caricaturist . . . has however not thought it necessary to introduce her monocle."[67] In August 1928, when *Eve* informed readers about the library ban of *The Well,* the three-line blurb beneath another sketch of the writer stated: "She patronises a severely tailor-made style of outfit, and usually wears a monocle."[68] Indeed, as Cline puts it, the eyewear had become Hall's most important "media trademark" for "you cannot wear a monocle and hope to be overlooked"—this despite the fact that "not one photograph showed her with the monocle in her eye."[69] Cline tells us that an enterprising journalist from the *Lancashire Daily Post,* who had been acquainted with Hall "for years," maintained that "Hall rarely if ever wore a monocle, but her 'close friend' Una Troubridge did. 'Possibly she has been confused with her very close friend'" (219). Cline completes her discussion about the case of Hall's disappearing monocle with the observation: "Perceptive though this was intended to be, the remark did smack of the notion that once you have seen one lesbian you have seen them all." The biographer reaches this conclusion because she cannot disengage her analysis from the erroneous preconception that the monocle unequivocally signals lesbian sexuality.

III

WHAT WE HAVE become accustomed to reading as distinctively lesbian, I would argue, might represent something else, perhaps something Modern. And if this is the case, all of the ostensibly determinant signifiers of lesbianism—smoking, trousers, monocle—suggested any number of interpretive possibilities in the 1920s. How else can we account for some of the striking photographs published in the newspaper *People* (figure 11)? None of these women, the lighthearted copy informs us, look like girls, and two might even "be mistaken for League goalkeepers." "It's a hard life telling which are men and which are women nowadays." What confirms gender—what "gives the show away"—are vital signs of their sexuality: wedding rings. In the same way, a 1928 *Punch* cartoon (figure 12) features a mannish woman utterly determined in her heterosexuality. In a masterful manipulation of stereotype, a very "feminine" woman congratulates her severely "masculine" friend on her impending marriage: "He certainly looks twice the man you are." How manly might that be? Every aspect of this mannish woman would militate against her marriageability: her monocle, hands in pockets, cigarette holder, slouched posture, very short hair, tie, and jacket. Women such as Hall, Troubridge, and Gluck are today easy for us to identify as lesbians, but it is important to remember that they appeared quite differently to the press and the public in the 1920s. For example, on August 22, 1928, two days before the banning of *The Well of Loneliness*, the *Newcastle Daily Journal and North Star* commented that Hall was "a most arresting personality, she may frequently be seen at West End theatres dressed in what is, save for a tight skirt, a gentleman's evening dress suit, with white waistcoat complete. She wears her Titian hair in a close Eton crop, and looks the strong silent woman to the life. With her notably fine forehead and beautiful hands, her whole aura is high-brow modernism" (figure 13).[70]

And here is how the *Birmingham Post*'s regular column entitled "London Letter for Women" anatomized Hall upon her winning the Femina Prize for *Adam's Breed* in April of 1927: Miss Hall "is a well-known figure at all the interesting parties and public occasions and is easily recognizable by her distinctive appearance, tall, slim, and very well groomed. Miss Hall affects a mannish mode of dress, and has what many people consider the best shingle in London. Her hair is of gold, and cropped as closely as a man's, a natural ripple in it being the only break in its sleek perfection."[71] Mannin, writing in 1930, also found Hall "masculine" but qualifies her word choice:

Usually when people describe a woman as "masculine" they imply . . . the clumsy, thick-ankled, untidily tweed-clothed hoyden. . . . [Hall] is the definitely masculine type of woman, but not by any means in that tiresome and unattractive sense suggestive of police-women or tomboyish daughters of county families. Her masculinity, sartorially, is of the exquisitely tailor-made kind, and she is one of the handsomest women I have ever met. . . . She has a beautiful head, and sleek, close-cropped fair hair with a slight wave; keen, steel-grey eyes, a small, sensitive mouth, a delicately strong aquiline nose, and a charming boyish smile.[72]

Mannin aggressively redefines female masculinity to present Hall as the very model of tailored fashions rather than as a mannish lesbian. Within this context, Benstock's reading of Hall against Stein becomes increasingly untenable: "Stein remained recognizably a woman, something that Radclyffe Hall—in her guise as 'John,' in man's suit and haircut—did not."[73]

When we compare the 1926 photograph of Hall in her "exquisitely tailor-made" suit (figure 14) with the 1926 advertisements for Bernard Weatherill, the exclusive ladies' and gentlemen's tailors (figure 15), and Harrods (figure 16), it soon becomes apparent that she no longer appears *necessarily* as the prototype of the mannish lesbian but as an elegant, modern woman in the height of fashion. This is how the copy for Weatherill's introduces a new evening dress for women: "The present tendency towards the severely masculine mode is admirably demonstrated in this smart evening suit for women." Note too that the model holds a monocle.[74] The Harrods ad announces two new tailor-mades, "with a hint of mannish severity in their trim lines—Two-piece modes of feminine grace! . . . A smart little waistcoat sounds the chic mannish note in this trim tailor-made."[75] What are we to make of these typical examples of mannish modernity? Reading Hall against these ads proves definitively that Hall did not, as Gilbert and Gubar assert, wear "elegant men's jackets and ties" nor was Hall's "masculine garb . . . a clear indication in a woman of a preference for her own sex."[76] Terry Castle's imaginative hypothesis that Hall may have been one of Noël Coward's "many imitators" also fails to credit Hall as a pioneer of a new look of female masculinity and instead perpetuates the myth that Hall wore men's clothing.[77] The sartorial distinction between the mannish woman and the lesbian was by no means "clear." In fact, as one fashion observer affirms: "In the winter of 1925–26, there was a vogue for women—not just the 'man-woman'—to wear dinner jackets."[78] Hall cannot, as Rolley insists, be situated within modernity because of her linkage of " 'masculine' dress and appearance."[79] Hall's version of the masculine mode in the mid-1920s signaled not a loss of femininity but, rather, its redefinition within modernity. Certainly an observer most qualified to comment authoritatively on Hall's appearance would be the sexologist responsible for setting the record straight, Havelock Ellis. Upon meeting Hall in April of 1928, he observed that she was "terribly Modern & shingled & monocled."[80]

Hall and Troubridge shopped prodigiously, and Troubridge kept a meticulous record of the shops they patronized, the particular items they purchased, and when they returned for fittings and refittings. Tracking this shopping record over the decade reveals that the couple's sartorial progress was not only on the forefront of fashion but was also on an upward spiral, from respectable middle-class shops, such as Gamages and Barkers, in the early twenties on to more elite and expensive shops by the middle of the decade. Harrods, for instance, recurs frequently in the diary from 1926 onward, as does Weatherill's. The couple's wardrobe was noticed by journalists because it was distinctively splendid—the clothing put them among the in crowd. In February 1924 Hall appeared in a photograph in the *People* in a tailor-made suit.[81] In the same month the *Tatler* reported: "A few weeks ago and women were looking askance at the tailor-made [suit]—today it is on the crest of the wave. . . . [Some] coats are cut on the lines of a man's dinner-jacket, and they are accompanied with fitted waistcoats of piqué or crêpe de chine enriched with embroidery. . . . Capes take the place of the coat in some of the tailor-mades."[82] When cape coats were fashionable, Hall wore cape coats; when the Spanish hat came into vogue, Hall could be seen in one—again both items were not part of the mainstream but aligned Hall with the far edge of a style favored by the most daring or artistic. Even so, a 1926 Harrods advertisement featured a "dashing military cape," an item characterized by another fashion observer as "absolutely indispensable to the woman of fashion today."[83] The cape and Spanish bolero together became a popular combination in 1926: "The bolero in some form or other is as often present on race frocks as it is on evening gowns, and is frequently reinforced with a cape."[84] Hall was seen in this hat at the obscenity trial and thus in many newspapers at the time, but a random sampling of newspapers and magazines from the autumn of 1928 indicates that the hat would have been regarded as striking but not unusual. A photograph of the artist Laura Knight in the Spanish hat, for instance, suggests that the headwear was the choice of the artistic.[85]

Far from being perceived as the inventor and embodiment of a deviant mannish lesbian style, Hall was seen as a thoroughly modern woman. In fact Evelyn Irons recalls that Hall's dramatic appearance at first nights was the antithesis of mannish: Hall "always wore dinner jackets and skirts with striped braid down the side, not trousers. . . . I had a boiled shirt and black bow tie and she always had sort of jabots and ruffles which I thought was rather effeminate."[86] Observers repeatedly drew attention to Hall's striking "shingle," dubbed the best in London. Although her shingle may look masculine to us, in the 1920s it was considered the most feminine of short haircuts (the Eton crop being the most severely masculine). Hall's hair was cut and styled at Harrods, not at a barber shop, and her side curls added a highly feminine touch to her famous shingle rather than being "an exotic imitation" of masculine "sideburns."[87] Yet when Troubridge cut Hall's long hair off for the first time in late 1920, Cline reports, the new cut gave the budding artist a "muted but powerful lesbian look" (148). Elsewhere the biographer casts Hall anachronistically as "conspicuously butch": "Dressed in riding breeches, capes, big boots and fedoras, [the couple] were a formidable sight. [Hall's] appearance at dog shows was defiantly masculine rather than merely countrified" (151). Such a strange laundry list of exotic clothing and accessories would indeed render the couple comical, to say the least. Of course, the women never donned all of these items at once for each had its venue and occasion. Big boots were the order of the day for a dog show, but if the pair wore riding breeches at Crufts, it was a rare event. A review of about one hundred photo spreads of "The Doggy World," a regular feature in *Eve*, indicates that rather than looking "defiantly masculine" the two women appeared considerably more chic in their countrified look than many of the "formidable" (often dowdy) women posing before the camera with their beloved canines (figure 6).

Biographers who neglect to situate their lesbian subjects against the fashion and culture of the 1920s in England inevitably misinterpret their subjects, as seen in Cline's description of Hall and Troubridge's appearance at Crufts. This misinterpretation is again evident in Cline's analysis of the couple's party to celebrate Hall's winning the Femina Prize in July 1927; the guest list included "half of London's literary establishment."[88] Cline strives to set her biographical subject apart from other guests by highlighting the fact that Hall "wore a man's dinner jacket," while Mrs. Galsworthy, a distinguished guest, "favored a crinoline skirt" (221). Hall's outfit could not have appeared in the least as an aberration or indicative of eccentric lesbian behavior if, as one newspaper reported, "*half* the ladies present favored the masculine mode and *half* the latest Victorian effect."[89] Here we can gauge just how fashionable the "masculine mode" had become and also how popular. In a sense, then, Cline's emphasis on Hall's masculine jacket works against the evidence of the gossip column, which positions her not as unique but simply as on one side of a struggle between the old and the new, as this article entitled "Masculine Modes" demonstrates:

> Let the dead past bury its dead and let us who are living be glad that the long skirts and the crinolines are buried with them. In the meantime, we have gone to the other extreme . . . [to] embrace such things as dinner jackets with waistcoats . . . coats and skirts of mannish cut, with breeches under the slit skirt, hats with hard crown and curly brims, hunting ties and pins, and leather coats with hats to match of such a masculine appearance that any man might be excused for not observing the usual little politenesses due to the opposite sex when he meets its members thus equipped.[90]

The split the author here identifies is, of course, generational. Mrs. Galsworthy and her crinolined companions seem hopelessly old-fashioned against the other half of the literary gathering, whose choice of chic men's dinner jackets may be of "a masculine appearance" but nevertheless represent the pinnacle of modern fashion.

During the heyday of the "severely masculine mode" (that is, the mid- to late 1920s), society women who "embrace[d] such things as dinner jackets with waistcoats" had not, as Benstock asserts, "adopted male clothing as their daily costume" but, rather, outfits specifically designed for women though inspired by men's clothing.[91] Obviously, there was a world of difference between women who adopted the "mannish cut" of female garb and women who actually cross-dressed in men's clothing. Barker, for example, knew she wanted to look in every way a man and seems to have succeeded even before she changed her name and identity. One "informant" reflected with hindsight how even as Mrs. Pearce-Crouch (her then married name), "People often used to bet as to whether [Barker] was a man or a woman. . . . She wore men's breeches, a long white coat, collar and tie and men's boots. She walked like a man and seemed flattered when people addressed her as 'Mr.' "[92] Although at this early stage in Barker's cross-dressing, male clothing did not disguise her true sex, it became in effect the mechanism to expose her psychic self-identification with masculinity. As the headline proclaimed when her sensational life story was serialized for over two months in the *Empire News and Sunday Chronicle* ("I Posed as a Man for Thirty Years!"), Barker's investment in clothing empowered her to become a fully functional male who could move about freely in society. Unlike Barker, the woman who adopted the "mannish cut" did not seek to transform a female body into that of male; rather, she sought simply to assume the "mannish cut" of feminine fashion: "The 'smoking' and waist-coat for women might, if one had not seen Miss Bannerman wearing them, be dubbed masculine, but when one of our betters shows us just how decoratively they can be adapted to feminine uses, they may be said to have their degree in the University of Fashion."[93] Bannerman is held up to readers as exemplary in that she "raises fashion of masculine inspiration to the heights of femininity" (511).

Cline and Hall's earlier biographer, Baker, also misinterpret Hall and Troubridge's excursions to the costume shop Nathan's. Baker contends that Hall and her partner "loved clothes such as capes and tricorn hats which recalled a more romantic era and they had taken to buying garments at Nathan's, the theatrical costumiers."[94] Cline's interpretation is even more elaborate: "It was perhaps the desire for masks, that very theatricality, that led [Hall] towards Nathan's the stage costumiers for tricorn hats and swishing velvet capes. Add a monocle and the performance is unforgettable" (151). As I have already indicated, capes were an acceptable fashion accessory and would have been available at any reputable ladies' clothing shop. At the same time Cline admits this reading of Hall's sartorial style was at odds with her shy personality. A writer of Hall's stature in the mid-1920s may have hoped to capture the public eye by dressing in the current fashion, or even to position herself at the extreme edge of that fashion, but it is highly implausible that a woman as shy and conservative as biographers suggest Hall to have been would court an outrageous, even bizarre, style. Further, Hall and Troubridge, so famous for their taste and style, would hardly have shopped for clothing at a theatrical costumier. Nevertheless, Nathan's is indeed mentioned in the diaries in 1921 and 1923. But like so many others of their class and circle, the pair visited the costume shop in the early 1920s not for everyday clothing but in preparation for fancy dress parties. For example, in April 1923 Hall was fitted at Nathan's for breeches and drove elsewhere to acquire a wig. A few months later Hall, Troubridge, and the lesbian artist Romaine Brooks returned to Nathan's where Troubridge emerged with the garb of a harlequin and Hall that of an Indian chief.[95]

One final example of how biographers who do not understand fashions of the twenties misread their subjects is evident in Richard Ormrod's analysis of the famous portrait of Troubridge (figure 17) by Brooks: "Why Una chose to pose in such a very masculine 'get-up' (black jacket, white starched shirt, monocle) is debatable, and it certainly leaves the viewer in little doubt as to her proclivities. Perhaps that was the point, a public statement of commitment to a cause."[96] Baker too describes the outfit as a "long dark severely cut jacket and pinstripe skirt over a white shirt with stiff wing collar and stock" and continues, "Whatever her original intentions Romaine finished by creating a brilliant caricature of Una, one that caught both her eccentricity and that element of class arrogance."[97] Brooks's biographer calls the portrait a "tour de force of ironic commentary."[98] Such readings are only partially accurate: the element of class is undeniable (Troubridge adopted the title of "Lady" even though her marriage with Admiral Troubridge had broken up), but the myth that Troubridge was Brooks's naive dupe is far-fetched and untenable if one reads the sitter's garb from the perspective of high fashion. Far from being the object of ridicule or the butt of a joke, Troubridge exerted considerable control over her own self-fashioning. The portrait is saturated with codes of Troubridge's devising, for she had a keen fashion sense and an eye for sartorial detail. In April 1924, a month before this portrait was painted, the *Daily Express* announced the "Masculine Note in Fashion" for women: "The most interesting feature of the new spring suits is the return to the ultra-masculine [in cut and fabric]. . . . The waistcoat . . . the collar, the cuff, the pockets, and the stock of sporting proclivities are all there in the region of the latest tailor-made."[99] The piece mentions that "masculine close-cropped" haircuts " 'came, conquered, and stayed,' " and it concludes: "Nothing at the moment is smarter wear than a varnished coat in black satin, loose and three-quarter length, with no trimming beyond either rows of heavy stitchery or a narrow band of military braid." A month earlier (March 25, 1924) the same newspaper had celebrated the "mannish high white collar of stiff but exquisitely fine white linen [as] the latest candidate for honors in the spring collar range. It is shaped in the pattern of a man's double collar."[100] The *Tatler* notes that "fobs, once the prerogative of mere man, have been commandeered by women, and the various forms that they have assumed is quite amusing."[101] Careful scrutiny of the portrait shows that Troubridge has not neglected this playful detail either. She arrived for the sitting not in a "get-up," as Brooks put it, but in clothing that captures the very latest fashion trend: high, stiff collar, tailored jacket, which appears to be of black satin, fob, and monocle—the very picture of "exclusive smartness," to quote the advertisement of a London firm that specializes in the "severely masculine mode" of women's fashion (figure 15).[102] Troubridge was among the first to adopt the bob and the monocle as signs of the "emancipated woman," signs also simultaneously the distinctive marks of a certain social set connoting at once class status and Modern chic. In the spring of 1924 Hall and Troubridge socialized almost exclusively with a group of lesbians in the theater and the arts. Presumably this smart set would have recognized and appreciated the way in which Troubridge manipulated and controlled the masculine mode to pass as a woman in the height of fashion, and at the same time "provided a visual code by which middle- and upper-class lesbians . . . could recognize each other."[103]

Hall and Troubridge courted the public gaze at first nights and other public events dressed, as the society pages suggest, as women with the utmost fashion sense. The artist Gluck's self-presentation, on the other hand (figure 18), may at first suggest the mannish lesbian, especially since she pushed female masculinity even further than Hall by wearing trousers in public. One of the earliest press commentaries points out that the "new and much-discussed artist . . . wears her hair brushed back from her forehead just like a boy, and when in Cornwall goes about in shorts. At her show . . . she had a long black cloak covering a masculine attire."[104] Dressed in men's rather than masculine clothing—never to pass but to violate the rules of fashion as well as social etiquette—Gluck's unique appearance precipitated sharp media dissent concerning her motivations for dressing the way she did, for changing her name from Hannah Gluckstein, and for flaunting her smoking habits. The *Westminster Gazette* refrained from the title "Miss," not in deference to Gluck's own wishes but because "one could hardly call a slim young creature in plus fours, overcoat, and man's shirt and collar Miss Gluck."[105] The *Tatler* bluntly dismissed Gluck as a "young woman who affects pipes and plus-fours and scorns prefixes," while the *Daily Graphic* saw her appearance as a "guess the gender game," reporting that "the young artist . . . might be a boy or a girl."[106] The paper positioned Gluck within the acceptable framework of 1920s boyishness, yet her appearance came dangerously close to violating the cardinal rule of the boyish female who always avoided crossing the line from acting to passing.

Gluck's daring tactic of using her own clothing to emblematize the theme of her 1926 "one-man" show, "Stage and Country," left her vulnerable to more snide remarks. The *Sketch*, for one, commented ironically on Gluck's "performance" by inserting a photograph and a brief mention of her exhibit on the golf page: "Miss Gluck [who] . . . has been rousing a good deal of interest, is very unconventional in regard to dress, and usually wears 'plus-fours.' . . . She is, of course, Eton-cropped."[107] Press attention fixated on Gluck's unquestionably outrageous dress choice, which doubly violated gendered clothing and social protocol; plus-fours, "long wide *men's* knicker-bockers . . . so named because the overhang at the knee requires an extra four inches of material," are by their very definition "usu[ally] worn for golf etc."[108] In an irreverent *Punch* cartoon a mannish female walker on the moors remarks to her male partner, "I say, John, I do hate your plus-fours—rotten cut! Give you an introduction to my tailor if you like."[109] Every familiar code is imposed on the figure of this mannish woman—a glimmer of a monocle, walking stick, tailored suit and tie, hand on hip, and cigarette protruding from the mouth—yet unlike Gluck, the walker does not wear plus-fours herself. As strictly masculine attire, plus-fours are reserved for the country gentleman's occupations of hunting or fishing and are not to be worn in town, let alone at the Fine Art Society in Bond Street.[110]

Gluck's own plain-spoken explanation about "why she feels better in men's clothes" defuses any suspicions about female homosexuality: "I just don't like women's clothes. I don't object to them on other women . . . but for myself, I won't have them. . . . I've experienced the freedom of men's attire, and now it would be impossible for me to live in skirts."[111] For this woman artist, male clothing feels more comfortable and, more crucially, "Gluck's manly equipment did not disguise her sex."[112] In the context of twenties fashion, the viewer sees Gluck as a woman in men's clothing—never a woman passing as a man, even though she "has all her clothes made by man's tailors, wears men's shirts, cravats and hats, [and] carries a cane just like a man."[113] Gluck took exceptional offense to the fact that some of the double takes she received on the street came from so-called Modern Girls—the artist believed that because she did not object to their short skirts, they should not object to her outfit; she saw her own project as continuous with that of the Modern Girls. Gluck's style did seem to enhance rather than inhibit media interest: for an "artist" it is permissible, if not preferable, to capitalize—or cash in—on eccentricity. As a reviewer for the *Daily Graphic* wrote:

> I do not know that I should altogether like my own wife or my own daughters to adopt Miss Gluck's style of dressing her hair or clothing her limbs, but I do know that I should be proud of them if they could paint as well as Miss Gluck paints. . . . This imitation of masculine habits is no more than an outward and visible sign of an inward and spiritual grace, for it is a grace on the part of modern woman to find masculine virtues worthy of emulation.[114]

The wording here is intriguing, for the reviewer makes sense of Gluck's self-presentation by claiming the visible (her "imitation of masculine habits") as an attribute of what is invisible ("inward . . . grace"). He edges toward the brink of acknowledging the complex relationship between (male) clothing and (homo)sexuality, only to retreat by reaffirming more traditional values, those "masculine virtues worthy of emulation."

If, in the 1920s, mannishness in women's fashion meant passing neither as a man nor as a lesbian, then we need to be careful in reading "masculine" as synonymous with lesbian. For this reason we must be cautious when biographers such as Ormrod assert that Troubridge's mode of self-presentation "certainly leaves the viewer in little doubt as to her proclivities"—the whole point of twenties fashion was that no one knew for sure. The writer Ronald Blythe observed how Hall "was seen at the best restaurants and at first nights dressed in an immaculate black tie, starched shirt, monocle, dinner-jacket—and skirt."[115] Although Blythe misattributed Hall's manner of dress to the fact that there was "no law against female transvestism," he went on to comment that "her hair was cut like a boy's, but as a great many heterosexual girls' heads were cropped as severely, this did not seem exceptional." If all the "girls' heads" are cropped, how do we pick out the "real" lesbians? We don't: lesbians might be mistaken for flappers and flappers might be lesbians. In the early 1920s the Labour M.P. Susan Lawrence would hardly have appeared before her East Ham constituents with a "look" firmly associated with lesbianism: "Very tall, with short, cropped hair, severe dress and a monocle, her appearance had stunned her first working-class audiences, while her upper-class accent reduced them to laughter."[116] The playfulness these fashions promoted worked in all directions, and any woman who embraced the trend could revel in sexual ambiguity. For lesbians discovered a space for experimentation that enabled them to break away from the sexologists' model of the mannish lesbian and begin to develop, under the cover of a dominant fashion trend, a unique and uniquely ambivalent lesbian style. Some, such as Gluck, pushed these boundaries further than others. In this way, one woman's risk was another woman's opportunity, for *within* a discrete, perhaps miniscule, subculture, lesbians passed as stylishly recognizable lesbians as well as women of fashion.

The very difficulty within the larger culture, in discerning who was passing for what, was part of the pleasure in this sartorial playground. Even the uniformed Mary Allen was thought chic by some "readers" who attended her speech at the English-Speaking Union in New York City. Members reportedly "enjoye[d] her breezy speeches, her sense of humor, her large-heartedness and not least, her eye-glass, her top-boots and her chic uniform."[117] Cultural critics who now read Hall's appearance as *the* visual representation of lesbian culture in the 1920s fail to recognize how some lesbians, including Allen and Hall herself, could pass in different ways because the blurring of gender lines in the sphere of fashion was not an isolated phenomenon. Misreading is an inescapable part of the risk and pleasure of the game. A good example of the danger of misreading emerges with greater clarity when a figure such as Hall is extracted from her milieu. After winning the Femina Prize Hall's name became known in parts of North America unaccustomed to her masculine look, where her image was unintelligible. The *Houston Chronicle*, for instance, informed its readers: "You Are Wrong—It's Not A Man," and another newspaper (unidentified) queried: "Male or Female?"[118] These sorts of headlines were not uncommon by any means in England, but were made in reference to a figure such as Colonel Barker. Cline accounts for the difference between the American and English press by asserting that the "English press were slightly more discreet." I would argue instead that the difference had less to do with English reserve than with the fact that English journalists were much more familiar with Hall's style. By the late 1920s the English press had witnessed every permutation of the continuum of female masculinities, from boyish to mannish. Hall was more likely to be regarded as artistic, distinctive, or interesting than as a gender puzzle.[119] Even as far north as Newcastle the novelist was thought to radiate an "aura . . . [of] high-brow modernism," a sophisticated reading obviously absent in Texas.

All this open-endedness of the 1920s began to wane slowly with the introduction of the "new feminine look" in 1928 that coincided with the obscenity trial of *The Well of Loneliness*. No one said it better than the lady's magazine *Eve* during that very August: "It looks as if everyone will dress . . . with just an added touch of femininity. The masculine woman is as dead as the dodo in the streets of fashion."[120] A collective sigh of relief could be heard across the country, as the *Sunday Times* asked readers, "What will another generation show?": "Crinolines and simpers; shorts and Eton crops. . . . A generation . . . is going back to long hair, judging by many pretty young schoolgirls one sees, and may make modesty and shyness, feminine frills, and the shade instead of the blaze of the limelight, the fashion."[121] *Punch* depicts a woman who has not yet learned that the new feminine look demands a more feminine posture (figure 19). The young woman on the right has simply thrown on a gracefully elegant evening frock, without a thought as to how she must relearn the feminine role. Any alluring sensuousness that might have been conveyed by her transparent low-cut gown is offset by her Eton crop (with the kiss curls seen earlier on Hall), the long cigarette holder between her teeth, as well as the unfeminine positioning of her arms and legs. The incongruity of stance and garment startles, and apparently no reconciliation between the two fashions is possible, as her friend remarks: "I'll tell you what, old thing, this new feminine touch is all right, but you'll have to adopt a new stance."

After a decade of growth, the fashion of boyish or mannish dress declined and gave way to its opposite. The shift to the feminine had begun gradually in 1927, but no fashion disappears from the scene overnight. In fact, for a year or so after the obscenity trial the "masculine mode" and the "new feminine look" jostled uneasily beside one another in the fashion magazines, so that any outside viewer would think the culture had gone slightly schizophrenic. *Britannia*, for instance, carried a spread in March 1929 where a model in one style is counterbalanced against another on a single page. The accompanying article characterizes the new silk neckties as "another feminine invasion!" and accounts for the "evening gowns of the moment" as "a reaction against the severity of the tailored styles."[122] The ultrafeminine look might have been slowly displacing the tailor-made, but the copy beneath a woman attired in the latter describes the masculine outfit as "amusingly masculine in cut and completed by a waistcoat of the material made on exactly the same lines as a man's. Note the single carnation button-hole." Two months later we witness a similar failure of nerve to banish the old-style forever: "As in other phases of social intercourse, we find in dress evidence of a meeting of masculine and feminine styles. Woman has become 'mannish' in so far as she has put on man-tailored tweeds, [and] walks in low-heels (as she must for golf, for instance)."[123] In the same issue an article entitled "Ladies Prefer Curls" declares that "back to femininity is the cry of the moment. . . . Coiffures, like frocks, must follow fashion's trend" (106). *Bri-*

tannia's attempt to mediate between the two styles reveals that, in the end, no mediation was possible: the masculine style for women now had a specific time and a place, that is, for traveling, motoring, or golf.

The trial of *The Well of Loneliness* no doubt hastened the demise of the Modern Girl and the "severely masculine" look. After the trial and the numerous photographs of Hall that circulated in the context of the trial, sexual inversion became endowed with a human face. As Blythe put it, "Gradually it dawned on the Bright Young Things [flappers and socialites] that many a jolly aunt and her 'companion' who bred dogs in Gloucestershire or helped the vicar at Little Tilling were lovers."[124] Hall's fashionably masculine appearance became inextricably connected with female homosexuality—a development Hall seems to have encouraged. The *Manchester Daily Dispatch* specified that Hall's controversial novel dealt with "sex problems not usually discussed unless in medical works and sociological works not easy of access by the public," and then mentioned that "Miss Hall wears a sober-colored costume cut on straight masculine lines, which, with her blue wide-brimmed Montmatre [sic] hat, gives her the reputation of being the most easily-recognized artistic celebrity in London. She was accompanied by her secretary. Both smoked."[125] Henceforth, both Hall and her partner's manner of dress and even personal habits, such as smoking, would become the distinctive marks of a lesbian subculture. The photographs of Hall, a woman the public associated with the demand for social acceptance of sexual inversion, forced a rethinking of how to interpret women previously thought simply fashionable or artistic, especially women in the arts—actors, artists, and writers—whose appearance would begin gradually to trigger associations of sexual inversion. Moreover, images in circulation prior to 1928 would eventually be subject to reexamination. Women such as Gluck, who reveled in the openness of twenties fashions, became more vulnerable because post-1928 readers, now exposed to the codes by which to identify female homosexuality, would obviously have lost the "innocence" of the pre-1928 context.

The very fashions that facilitated "passing" in an earlier era would thus thrust some lesbians out into the open. If we view the spread in *Eve* (figure 5), for example, from a post-*Well* perspective, our reading shifts somewhat. The editor who decided that berets were chic and assembled a group of active women to illustrate this trend was Sybil Cookson, Gluck's lover at the time, which explains the choice of the artist's "Self-portrait with Cigarette." In the oval-shaped frame to the right, another well-known lesbian, Joe Carstairs, "literally, a leader in the motor world," is shown at the wheel of her speedboat. Women in same-sex relations seem to have been the arbiters of this style. Lesbians were of course everywhere present throughout the decade of fashionable playfulness, but in the "shade instead of the blaze of the lime-light," as the *Sunday Times* put it. Consequently, some lesbians were less than thrilled with the public exposure of Hall. Evelyn Irons, a lesbian and a journalist who worked on the women's page of the *Daily Mail*, complained that "the minute [*The Well*] came out if you wore a collar and tie, 'Oh, you're Miss Radclyffe Hall, Miss,' the truck drivers used to call on the street. And it wasn't at all happy."[126] The presence of Hall's novel and photograph in newspaper reports encouraged the reading public to associate a particular clothing style with a particular sexual preference, hitherto the knowledge of a discreet, private circle. Yet at the height of Hall's trial, Iron recalls that on a visit to her mother in Scotland, "We were making a bed and my mother stopped and said: 'You're a friend of Radclyffe Hall's, aren't you?' and I said 'yes' and she said: 'Well that sort of thing can carry on in Paris but certainly not here,' and we went on making the bed. And there I was in collar and tie and everything—dressed in the uniform—and she didn't realize what the hell it was about."[127]

For the general public, and specifically for women keen to claim membership in a newly emerging lesbian subculture, the visage of female sexual inversion could for the first time be studied at one's breakfast table. In countless newspaper articles for the better part of four months in late 1928 the public was treated to photographic evidence of a specimen invert: Hall alone or accompanied sometimes by her partner. As the visual exemplum of "scientific knowledge," Hall and Troubridge were undoubtedly aware that their self-fashioning was becoming inextricably linked with lesbianism. Troubridge, for example, upbraided one lesbian friend, Toupie Lowther, for abandoning the cause shortly after the trial—specifically, for "letting the side down" through sartorial dishonesty. In Troubridge's view, Lowther turned her back on those of "her own ilk" and deliberately hid her lesbianism by opting for the new feminine look, wearing, as Troubridge phrased it, "scarlet silk 'confections' in the evenings with accordion pleated skirts and low necks."[128] Other lesbians, of course, craved an unambiguous lesbian subcultural style that would humanize the dry clinical discourse of sexology. In examining the diary of the lesbian artist Dorothy Hepworth, for example, I discovered on the back page a full-length sketch of Hall, in a wide-brimmed hat, monocle, short hair with a sharp twist of a curl, tailored jacket, walking stick, and skirt (figure 1). Because there is nothing remotely similar in any of Hepworth's other sketchbooks or diaries, Hepworth and Preece were obviously captivated by the physical appearance of Radclyffe Hall.[129] Such a representation demonstrates the ways in which the author of *The Well of Loneliness* became literally the embodiment of lesbianism. Hall's "martyrdom" to the cause imposed a unified and standardized dress code (such as monocles, collars, and ties) on her followers who would soon create a self-conscious subculture. At the same time, in the massive publicity of the trial, for the public at large the meaning of female masculinity would narrow drastically as the subject of lesbianism exploded like a bombshell.

So, is Hall fashionably Modern or a mannish lesbian? The answer—and the point—is that she is both. Just as boyishness allowed young women and girls to pass or play-pass as boys, twenties fashions allowed older women— past the age to be taken as boys—to pass as the masculine "look." Older women who flirted with this "look" would have been more likely to be taken for fashionable than lesbian, even when they were in fact lesbian.[130] The Modern look and the Lesbian look would not begin to converge until the trial of *The Well* when, at about the time the popularity of the "severely masculine mode" as *fashion* began to decline, Hall's "look" became fixed in the public's mind as *lesbian*. Hall's "look" was not the same as Barker's, which explains why newspapers did not speculate in print about the latter's possible lesbianism, and by 1929 the most extreme version of the mannish lesbian had not yet permeated within the culture.[131] In the 1920s Hall was always recognizably female; she preferred the chic fashion of the masculine cut designed for women worn by women of all sexual preferences. Barker, on the other hand, wore men's clothing to erase her femininity completely. As the living embodiment of film critic Annette Kuhn's dictum, "Change your clothes and change your sex," Barker's male clothing facilitated her gender metamorphosis at a time when such medical technologies were uncommon: "I have undergone no surgical operation to turn me from woman into man, and physically I am, as I started out in life to be, 100 per cent woman. But for so long have I lived as a man, that I have come to think as one, behave as one, and be accepted as one."[132] For Hall, Barker's male clothing disguised her biological sex and allowed her to pass authentically, which is to say invisibly, as a man. But Hall, long assumed to wear her homosexuality on her sleeve, was the invisible finally made visible: she was not trying to pass as anything—she was a sexual invert.

With the lesbian's increased public visibility, the issue of sexuality could no longer be glossed over: fashion worked to reconsolidate gender lines and eliminate sexual ambiguity. Lesbians such as Hall and Troubridge undoubtedly welcomed the change for, although there was an intense narrowing in the range of subcultural styles for lesbians, women could no longer sit on the fence: the link between clothing and sexual identity was becoming established. In 1932 Hall addressed the Foyle's Luncheon at Grosvenor House before an audience of "kindred spirits," comprised of "close cropped feminine heads, some stiff collars and monocles."[133] Women desirous of claiming an unambiguous lesbian identity could now emulate the sartorial style of the author transformed from a woman of fashion to the unofficial spokeswoman on behalf of female sexual inverts. Certainly by the early 1930s the new feminine look was so firmly established that Hall's masculine style was "by no means fashionable."[134] The fashions of a boyish and mannish aesthetic passed out of style, and Hall's profoundly influential construction of the "mannish lesbian" superseded them. In the 1920s there was every sort of passing imaginable, but who knew for certain who or what was passing for who or what. If our scrutiny of Hall's response to Barker reveals anything, it is that a cross-cultural and transhistorical approach to cross-dressing is a risky venture. Without a nuanced and historically detailed reading of the wide spectrum of female masculinities available in the 1920s, we are in danger of collapsing into narrow and limited labels and categories a rich terrain of sartorial and sexual possibilities.

Five

Lesbian Writers and Sexual Science: A Passage to Modernity?

I

To speak of sexology is surely to invoke an obsolete science and a vanished world. The term brings to mind sepia-tinted images of earnest Victorian scholars laboring over lists of sexual perversions with the taxonomical zeal of an entomologist examining insects. Who would claim to be a sexologist nowadays?
—Rita Felski[1]

IN THE SPRING of 1928 Radclyffe Hall and Una Troubridge hand-delivered the typescript of *The Well of Loneliness* to the Brixton home of the famous British sexologist Havelock Ellis, a man they admired as the "greatest living authority on the tragical problem of sexual inversion."[2] Ellis had agreed, if the novel met with his approval, to provide an "opinion" of *The Well* "that could be 'used' by [the] publisher."[3] Hall told Ellis, "I am only sustained in my determination to set forth for the general public the tragedy of such lives by the knowledge of the courage with which men of science, chief among them yourself, have of recent years tried to elucidate the facts of inversion for the benefit of serious students."[4] In a near paraphrase of Hall's letter to Ellis, Troubridge later reiterated Hall's long-standing desire "to write a book on sexual inversion, a novel that would be accessible to the general public who did not have access to technical treatises."[5] The author's primary design then was to achieve in fiction what Marie Stopes a decade earlier had accomplished in prose: to educate the public by popularizing aspects of sexology. (Stopes's 1918 best-seller, *Married Love*, did not, of course, tackle the slender body of sexological work on female sexual inversion.) To ensure the success of her novel Hall thought it imperative to solicit "the support of [Ellis's] unassailable knowledge and reputation," for his name alone, imbued with talismanic effects, would lend the novel legitimacy.[6]

When in June the publisher Jonathan Cape finally accepted the novel, he astutely recognized that an endorsement of some sort from the expert man of science might interest and tantalize readers as yet unfamiliar with Hall's oeuvre, and in at least one instance Cape appears to have been correct. In a review of *The Well* for the *Evening Standard*, novelist Arnold Bennett confessed that he "knew nothing of the author's previous work": "It certainly would not have occurred to me to read Radclyffe Hall's [novel] had I not been attracted by a line in the publisher's advertisement: 'With a commentary by Havelock Ellis.'"[7] Bennett spends nearly half his review reflecting on the significance of Ellis's name and praises the sexologist in one full paragraph as "a very valuable philosophical essayist, [who] counts among the greatest European authorities upon the vagaries or aberrations of nature in the matter of sexual characteristics." Bennett further comments on his indebtedness to Ellis "for the enlargement of my outlook [on the subject of lesbianism]." So, as Hall and her publisher had anticipated, Ellis's participation seemed sufficient to ensure the novel would be noticed *and* taken seriously. Still, it seems odd that a novelist working in 1928 would so value a prefatory statement by a sexologist whose major work on the subject of inversion had appeared over three decades earlier; after all, weren't, as some have claimed, the " 'scientific' categories" reified in *The Well* "already in disrepute by the 1920s"?[8] To understand how and why modern lesbian writers, such as Hall, Bryher (born Winifred Ellerman), and Rose Laure Allatini (who published under the pseudonym "A. T. Fitzroy"), acquired and studied sexological volumes of the most esoteric nature, we need to know far more about sexology's cultural status and significance at the time—a task made all the more complex in that sexology was continually in flux in the 1920s. My purpose here is not to judge the merits or drawbacks of particular sexological theories, some of which would have been regarded as more "modern" than others, but to suggest that we have been operating for too long on insufficient and contradictory information about sexology's importance in this period. In this chapter I explore the ways in which these writers sought out what some contemporary observers now regard as scientifically dubious and outdated sexological material on sexual inversion in order to appreciate why sexology and many of its practitioners were held in such high esteem by those who would characterize themselves as wholly modern.

In the decades since the publication of Hall's novel, the reputation of early sexological writings has so declined that the generous expressions of gratitude to and profound respect for men such as Ellis, reflected in the responses by Hall and Bennett, seem remote. In her memoirs, published in 1963, Bryher offers a warm and affectionate tribute to the avuncular Ellis, a man whose "campaign against ignorance" contributed significantly to "the different world we live in now," but her tone registers as defensive.[9] Despite observing that Ellis's work "seems old fashioned today," Bryher chides those who allowed his reputation to decline irretrievably:

> The pioneers always get the knocks and never the crowns. I had a sharp lesson in human snobbery and neglect when in some studies that appeared about [Ellis] some years ago, his lifework was dismissed as of no importance. . . . Not one of the many thousands whom he had helped had the courage to say a word in his defence.

With the rise of Freudian psychoanalysis between the wars we have lost touch with a sense of sexology as a dynamic new field of inquiry that provided women such as Bryher with models of sexual identity and a language for their desires. As Felski explains:

> One of the effects of the Freudian revolution was to erect a seemingly impenetrable barrier between the modern view of sexuality as an enigmatic and often labile psychic field rooted in unconscious desires, and the work of nineteenth-century sexologists such as Richard von Krafft-Ebing and Havelock Ellis, with its emphasis on the physiological and congenital roots of human erotic preferences.[10]

By the 1960s, perhaps earlier, its practitioners discredited or forgotten, sexology was no longer on the cutting edge of investigations into sexuality. As a result, sexology (especially in its incipient phase from the 1880s to the 1940s) has been far more likely to "get the knocks and never the crowns" at the hands of some contemporary feminist literary critics and historians of lesbian culture. Lillian Faderman, for instance, characterizes early sexology as "a worm in the bud," that is, the means by which the beauty of love between women was spoiled by the damaging pathologizing of medical men.[11] Esther Newton, in her ground-breaking essay, decries Ellis for his purported "antifeminism" and cites a lengthy passage from his study on female inversion only to dismiss it as an "extraordinary mix of fantasy, conjecture and insight."[12] Ironically, the same name and work that several decades earlier piqued Bennett's interest in Hall's novel now dissuades many contemporary feminist readers from picking up the book out of embarrassment over "all those outmoded quasi-scientific theories about lesbians."[13]

More recently, signs of renewed scholarly interest in the early phase of sexual science suggest a move toward a more nuanced and sophisticated understanding of the field as a body of knowledge constantly in flux, with dramatic shifts and theoretical reversals, rather than as an inflexible monolith of dubious, outdated scientific categories. Many of the essays in *Science and Homosexualities*, a collection that reassesses the achievements of, among others, Karl Heinrich Ulrichs, Krafft-Ebing, Ellis, and Magnus Hirschfeld, illustrate some of the key differences in the theoretical perspectives of individual sexologists, such as historian Harry Oosterhuis's persuasive argument that "Krafft-Ebing's views were far from static or coherent, and in several ways his scientific approach to sexuality was ambivalent."[14] Elsewhere, in innovative work on transsexuality, cultural critic Jay Prosser argues that nineteenth-century sexology "can be seen to have been powerfully enabling and productive."[15] New work by feminist critics has also enhanced our appreciation of sexology's role in, for instance, the formulation of lesbian self-identity or self-creation, or in literary representation in the first half of the twentieth century. Martha Vicinus, for example, challenges scholars stymied by "early sexologists and their embarrassingly crude classifications of sexual behavior" to consider how "rather than labeling the sexologists' descriptions benighted misogyny, we might learn more from them about both contemporary lesbian mores and masculine attitudes."[16] In a recent collection of essays considering the impact of early sexology on Anglophone culture, Suzanne Raitt concludes her examination of the handling of emotions in both psychiatric and sexological circles in relation to the writing of Vita Sackville-West with new insight on sexology in relation to Freud: "Ellis and Carpenter looked to love to redeem the fallen nature of their homosexual patients and subjects; but for Freud . . . love—and women—were part of the problem."[17] These sexologists may have invested in an overly idealized conception of love but, unlike Freud, they never lost sight of its role in sexuality.

In this chapter I want to build on this growing body of work by recuperating for present-day cultural critics a sense of how cutting edge was the use of these early sexological writings on sexual inversion in literary representation in the decade after the First World War. Obviously, sexology was not the only influence on these novelists (Hall, for instance, was equally immersed in the " 'spicier' French sapphic tradition"[18]), but unlike other literary sources, sexology held the allure and status of "science." I investigate why some modern lesbian writers were drawn to sexological explanations of homosexuality and, more particularly, how these writers, in seeking to popularize the "science" for their readers, negotiated sexology's key concepts and theories in literary representation. Like much of the ongoing work on this topic, I focus primarily on Hall's *The Well of Loneliness*, though Bryher's first two novels, *Development* (1920) and *Two Selves* (1923), and Allatini's *Despised and Rejected* (1918) enter the discussion because they exemplify vividly the usefulness of sexology for the modern lesbian writer. In the first of two sections I reexamine the question: Who knew what when? In other words, which constituencies were familiar with sexological models of female sexual inversion in the immediate postwar period? I cautiously retrace sexology's gradual emergence and circulation among a certain small group of writers, artists, and other professionals, probably quite unrepresentative of public culture, to gauge something of the status of sexology as a "science," with its potentially illuminating explanatory models of sexuality and identity. For such readers sexology may not have been a "worm in the bud," a powerful force inhibiting sexual expression and stigmatizing relations between women, but an innovative new science offering modern conceptualizations of sexual relations between women that they could in turn accept or reject. In the final section I explore how some lesbian writers found in sexual science a utilitarian value and introduced its key concepts to their readers, filtered through personal experience, so that various identities, categories, and theories jostle beside one another, sometimes uncomfortably. Hall, as mentioned, understood that sexual science could lend scientific or medical legitimacy to her cause on behalf of the female sexual invert, yet she was just as likely to incorporate non-sexological notions strongly rejected by sexologists. Moreover, Hall grasped that sexology itself was not a unified and coherent body of knowledge but was comprised of diverse and at times awkwardly conflicting theoretical positions. Writers such as Hall, Allatini, and Bryher were thus far more sophisticated and astute in their literary deployment of sexual science than critics have yet suggested.

Sexology, as practiced by men such as the highly respected Ellis, *seems* out of date and out of touch to us now, but its cultural status after 1918—its distinctive modernity before its gradual displacement by Freudian psychoanalytic theory in about the 1940s and 1950s—was rather different. A handful of women writers, as documented through their diaries and letters, read an enormous amount of sexological material and were in close contact with men such as Ellis. Sexology for these women was distinctively modern and "appeals to the modern and the new could . . . be appropriated and articulated anew by dissident or disenfranchised groups to formulate their own resistance to the status quo."[19] If we situate sexology within the historical particularity of a ten-year period after the war, and suspend our own discomfort with an "obsolete science" of "a vanished world," as Felski puts it, we might gain a fuller understanding of its appeal for these writers, its cultural status and impact, and how it may have facilitated their passage to modernity.

II

IN 1896 AN editorial on "The Question of Indecent Literature" in the medical journal the *Lancet* harshly chastised Havelock Ellis for the method of publication of *Sexual Inversion*: "Why was it not published," the editor demanded, "through a house able to take proper measures for introducing it as a scientific book to a scientific audience?"[20] *Sexual Inversion* should have been available only to "persons of particular attainments," since lay readers "totally unable to derive benefit from [the book] as a work of science" were likely to "draw evil lessons from its necessarily disgusting passages." (In fact, some of the actual case histories in Ellis's study illustrate how nonprofessional readers tended to be rather more sophisticated in their reading of medical texts than this suggests.) The *Lancet* was committed to the diligent policing of sexology's readership, as evident in the editor's adamant assertion that under no circumstances should the subject of homosexuality "be discussed by the man in the street, not to mention the boy and girl in the street." Carefully differentiating between appropriate and inappropriate readers, the medical establishment's aim was to ensure that "very few members of the general public had direct access" to such material and that "sales and borrowing from libraries were restricted to people such as doctors, lawyers and scientific researchers."[21] Thus it was with some trepidation and reluctance that Ellis honored the request of the twenty-five year old novelist Bryher and sent her the entire series of his major publication, *Studies in the Psychology of Sex* (1896–1910). Prior to forwarding the package in the spring of 1919 Ellis tactfully informed her that normally such books were sold only "to professional people or the like."[22] Although not a "professional" in Ellis's sense of the word, that is, of the medical or legal professions, Bryher succeeded in persuading Ellis that his "Studies" were necessary for her own creative work—and even brazenly announced that the vast information contained in the "Studies" on every aspect of human sexuality was too valuable to be limited to a select few: "Everybody," Bryher insisted, "ought to read them."[23] Ellis was fully cognizant that his actions would in the eyes of his colleagues be regarded as inappropriate and issued her a stern proviso: "The books should not be left lying about but kept locked up."[24]

Bryher was presumably not the only reader of such material exhorted to be discreet, but if a young novelist could order a set of the "Studies" from its author with relative ease, how successful were the medicolegal community's prodigious efforts in containing the medical exploration of "normal" and "abnormal" sexual behaviors and identities after the First World War? Due to public reticence over the explicit nature of the science of sex, scholars have found it difficult to determine the extent of sexology's dissemination into public culture by the 1920s, especially with regard to so-called deviant sexual practices, but the dominant view is that few had access to the information. Such a position finds support in the 1921 parliamentary debate on the antilesbian clause when the Lord Chancellor declared that "the overwhelming majority of the women of this country have never heard of this thing [lesbianism] at all. . . . I would be bold enough to say that of every thousand women, taken as a whole, 999 have never even heard a whisper of these practices."[25] The one woman to stand apart from 999 others must have been a physician or nurse since the feminist Stella Browne, one of the very few women to enter into the scientific discussions on female inversion in the early twentieth century, assumes in her 1923 paper "Studies in Feminine Inversion" that Case D's "medical training" indicated that she must not be "ignorant on the subject of her own sex nature."[26] Browne thus reaffirms that the knowledge did not generally circulate to a wider nonspecialist readership. The writer Vera Brittain suggests that as late as 1928 "the psychological variation known . . . as homosexuality" would only have been familiar to a "scientific few."[27] Most recent scholars concur with Browne and Brittain, as seen in Sonja Ruehl's assertion that female " 'congenital inversion' remained a definition restricted to scientific discourse until given wide publicity through *The Well of Loneliness*."[28] Occasionally, however, scholars swing too widely in the other direction and presume that such information was pervasive. For example, George Piggford writes: "By the time of Virginia Woolf's composition of *Orlando* (1927–28), theories of sexuality developed by sexologists such as Havelock Ellis and Richard von Krafft-Ebing and through the psychoanalytic method of Sigmund Freud had *saturated* the cultural consciousness of England."[29] Such a sweeping generalization—like the proposition that knowledge of sexual inversion was restricted to an elite few—cannot be sustained in the absence of detailed research demonstrating convincingly that this was in fact the case—a predicament all the more slippery because sexological discourse was, throughout the 1920s, in the very process of dissemination from the few to the many. To address the tricky question of who was in the know and when, I will examine in this section how writings on sexuality became accessible to a handful of women writers and artists puzzled by aspects of their own sexual nature.

If, after the First World War, "for many women of Radclyffe Hall's generation, sexuality—for itself and as a symbol of female autonomy—became a preoccupation," this interest sometimes translated into a scholarly pursuit via the primary works of sexology, even though some of its theories were antithetical to female liberation and autonomy.[30] As I discussed in chapter 2, the first women to have easy access to sexology were those in the immediate prewar period who drew on the resources of the Cavendish-Bentinck Library, an institution that "was at that time supplying all the young women in the suffrage movement with the books they could not procure in the ordinary way."[31] Margaret Haig Mackworth (later Vicountess Rhondda) borrowed Ellis's "Studies": "It was the first thing of its kind I had found. Though I was far from accepting it all, it opened up a whole new world of thought to me" (126). Mackworth recalls how after discussing some of Ellis's theories with her father (a Liberal Member of Parliament), he became extremely interested and decided to "buy the set of volumes for himself"; however, "in those days one could not walk into a shop and buy 'The Psychology of Sex'; one had to produce some kind of signed certificate from a doctor or lawyer to the effect that one was a suitable person to read it. To his surprise he could not at first obtain it" (127). In discussing the difficulties in obtaining books that readers "could not procure in the ordinary way," Mackworth notes with pleasure the unusual reversal in terms of both gender and generation; unlike Stephen Gordon in *The Well*, Mackworth had already read what her own father could not.

While we probably cannot gauge precisely how many readers in the 1920s had general access either to primary sexological texts or works by its popularizers, it is clear that the numbers were increasing. Stopes's *Married Love*, for example, a basic introduction to human physiology and the (heterosexual) facts of life, "sold over 400,000 copies in hardback between 1918 and 1923."[32] This handy volume satisfied readers' demands for information on what Brittain characterizes as the "nice"—as opposed to the "nasty"—sexual phenomena.[33] But what was available for readers interested in the "nasty," that is, the deviant rather than normative? An examination of the personal papers or libraries of three lesbian writers in the 1920s—Bryher, Sackville-West, and Hall—suggests that sexological works were not especially difficult to obtain for wealthy and well-educated women of the upper or upper-middle classes. As the daughter of the successful shipping magnate Sir John Ellerman, Bryher could well afford the monumental cost of the multivolume set of Ellis's "Studies." She and her then lover, the poet H.D., subsequently devoured books they obtained with Ellis's assistance and circulated the volumes among their close circle. Bryher also discusses how she had either read or was interested in work by Edward Westermarck (*The History of Human Marriage* [1891]), Hirschfeld (*Die Homosexualität des Mannes und des Weibes* [1914]), Otto Weininger, Norman Haire, Stella Browne, and "East" (probably William Norwood East). The bookshelves in Sackville-West's turret room also contained the six volumes of Ellis's "Studies," as well as Carpenter's *The Intermediate Sex* (1908) and Weininger's *Sex and Character* (1903).[34] Sackville-West apparently immersed herself in the literature at about the time she became sexually involved with Violet Trefusis (the spring of 1918) to the extent that she felt "qualified to speak with the intimacy a professional scientist could acquire only after years of study and indirect information."[35] Like Bryher, Sackville-West shared her books on the psychology of sex with her lover, Trefusis, and her husband, Harold Nicolson. Finally, Troubridge kept a careful record of books purchased and read, and from the relatively early year of 1913, she and Hall, although primarily interested in works on hypnotism and psychology, pored over the relevant work of Albert Moll and August Forel. Near the end of the war Troubridge and Hall also borrowed books by Freud and his early disciple, the Austro-Hungarian Sándor Ferenczi, from Miss Newton at the Society for Psychical Research.[36] Later, in 1926, in preparation for writing *The Well*, the couple read Ellis, Dr. Jacobus X, and Hirschfeld's *A Manual of Sexual Science* (1926).[37]

Although passed from reader to reader, the acquisition and study of these books became a closeted affair. Just as Ellis had advised Bryher to keep the books "locked up," H.D. urged Bryher, "Will you be *sure* [underlined heavily three times] to keep the books well shut away. Remember they are reference books of a very special order."[38] Like a guilty secret or pleasure, treatises on the science of sex were placed discreetly in a locked cupboard, or in a room forbidden to the rest of the household, or in the voluminous recesses of a desk. The British Library's collection of the central texts of sexual science, for instance, were reputedly stored among the "pornographic" materials in the infamous "little cupboard."[39] Sackville-West likewise sequestered her collection of such books in her study, a turret room with its own separate staircase: "No-one ever entered this room except Sackville-West. Even when she was wanted on the telephone, or for meals, family members would merely come to the foot of the turret staircase and call up to her."[40] In fiction, too, such dangerous material is not left lying around. In *The Well* Hall relates how Sir Philip, father of protagonist, Stephen Gordon, and owner of "one of the finest libraries in England," unlocks a drawer in his "ample desk" to withdraw a well-marked treatise by the German lawyer Karl Heinrich Ulrichs, the "first theorist of homosexuality."[41] Later in the novel the books have been mysteriously "locked" away in a "special book-case" (204).

That a small group of financially comfortable, upper or upper middle class lesbian writers—Bryher, Sackville-West, and Hall—owned and shared among their respective circles books on sexology may not be especially surprising, but these medical and scientific materials also seem to have found a way into circulation in the 1920s among the less well-off and well-connected, as illustrated by an annotated reading list found in the artist Dorothy Hepworth's 1927 diary.[42] The list includes full publication details of the major sexological texts on sexual inversion, including: Krafft-Ebing's *Psychopathia Sexualis* (1886), Iwan Bloch's *The Sexual Life of Our Time* (1908), thirteen titles by Ellis, and several by Freud. In addition, the diary contains information on the obscure study *The Intersexes* (1909) by "Xavier Mayne" (the pseudonym of Edward Irenaeus Prime Stevenson), of which only 125 copies were privately printed, and the sixth pamphlet of the British Society for the Study of Sex Psychology on *The Social Problem of Sexual Inversion* (1914). The detailing of titles is thorough and wide-ranging, and all the more amazing because Hepworth, a fairly isolated and shy woman, lived quietly with the artist Patricia Preece in the small village of Cookham. If sexological works circulated only among a very few, it is puzzling that artists of such modest means, who lived on the fringes of any leading intellectual or artistic circle, would have known about so many books either familiar or rare on sexual science. The possession of such a reading list points to the existence of an incipient community of female and male inverts—largely with connections, however tenuous, to literary and artistic production—who eagerly exchanged relevant information on the "problem" of homosexuality as well as on other aspects of sexual science. Familiarity, among some members of this constituency, bred not contempt but ennui, as seen in the homosexual writer Norman Douglas's remarks to Bryher: "I know Westermarck's book; that is, I read it ages ago. Don't dream of sending it here. I am sick of marriage, and sex, and homosexuality, and fornication, and pederasty, and all the rest of that damned tribe. They only use up one's nerves and time—whether one does them, or merely reads about them. To hell with the whole lot!"[43] One supposes that Douglas would have approved of the way early sexology had become the butt of humor among the cognoscenti in private and in the London Soho and Fitzrovia club scene soon after the war.

By the early 1920s a substantial number of the so-called Bright Young People (the upper-class fast set) were familiar enough with sexology to find it a source of "cynical amusement": "At a party given by Bright Young People in the early twenties, [the novelist Douglas Goldring] heard a Mayfair lovely read aloud, amid shouts of girlish laughter, passages from the works of Krafft-Ebbing [sic] and Havelock Ellis which she had just unearthed in the library of her grandfather, a retired major-general of extreme respectability."[44] The intellectual avant-garde too were sufficiently sophisticated to appreciate the actor Elsa Lanchester's naughty cabaret act at the Cave of Harmony which lampooned Krafft-Ebing's modus operandi. Lanchester captured perfectly the quirky kinkiness of one of Krafft-Ebing's case histories in a clever sketch called "Krafft-Ebing, Case #74B of Zurich," in which she played "a nun called Blankebin [who] spent her time looking for the foreskin that was cut from Christ when he was circumcised."[45] The Cave of Harmony, and other nightclubs such as the Orange Tree and the Ham Bone, attracted a wide spectrum of individuals, as writer Ethel Mannin relates in her description of the Ham Bone; the clientele were "young, artistic, unconventional, and, in general, what we liked to call 'Bohemian.' Writers, artists, theatrical people."[46] Mannin does not, however, mention that these clubs also became the "fashionable haunts" of gay men and "artistic or wealthy lesbians," including Hall and Troubridge.[47]

In his memoirs of 1920s London, Goldring reflects on the odd, very "heterogeneous" crowd that frequented a political society known as the 1917 Club, also in Soho and near the Cave. The chic and fashionable of every political and religious conviction gathered here to pass convivial hours drinking and dining, but also to attend lectures on controversial or frank sexual subjects inconceivable in another public venue, such as a town meeting hall. This "home of political idealism, democratic fervor and serious progressive thinking" consisted of

> Hindus, Parsees, puritans, free lovers, Quakers, teetotallers, heavy drinkers, Morris dancers and Folk Song experts . . . members of the London School of Economics, Trade Union officials, journalists, poets, actors and actresses, Communists, theosophists. In short, every color and creed, every "ism" and "ist" was represented. . . . Apart from the fact that all the members could be labelled "Lefties" and were opposed to the reactionary clique in power, there was no other recognizable nexus and no uniformity of political opinion.[48]

The common denominator at the Club was an interest in politics, ideas, literature, and the arts. Goldring reports how on one occasion he glimpsed an "elderly Quaker company director" fleeing from a meeting room with "flaming cheeks," while the remaining "mixed audience" listened intently to "a

bearded young 'sexologer' in horn-rimmed spectacles . . . delivering a lecture . . . on the subject of masturbation!"[49] Goldring's point was to demonstrate that such an event was not extraordinary but the norm—to be with
the "in" crowd was to be modern, and to be modern was to be knowledgeable about emergent discourses on sexuality.

If some lesbians just before and after the First World War were already
acquiring a range of sexological materials on female inversion, what impact
did their reading have on their self-esteem and self-understanding? When
Ellis forwarded his "Studies" to Bryher, he commented, "Since you ordered
them I have felt rather afraid you might find parts rather repulsive or disturbing."[50] Neither Bryher nor any of her friends found the work repulsive
or upsetting in the least; on the contrary, there was evidently an immense
hunger for more knowledge, even among friends who feigned shock at such
ostensible prurience. H.D. reported to Bryher that while her friend Nora
Joyce, wife of novelist James Joyce, expressed horror "at [H.D.'s] having
read [Ellis's "Studies"]," she nevertheless bombarded the poet "with all kinds
of questions on the subject, which is slightly ironical, is it not?"[51] The physical acquisition of the relevant volumes, as this incident clearly illustrates,
was only one route to the attainment of sexological knowledge. Those too
shy or naive to attain such works on their own obviously turned to friends
so that sexological knowledge was disseminated second-hand, third-hand,
and so on. So-called nonprofessional readers who shared their knowledge
with the wholly uninitiated, from H.D. and Bryher to the homosexuals who
participated in Ellis's study a generation earlier, were supremely capable of
negotiating sexological material intelligently, rejecting the irrelevant, and
embracing what seemed germane.

Of the six case histories of women in *Sexual Inversion*, the two informants
who mention that they "came across" books on sexual inversion are the most
articulate about their reasons for participating in Ellis's project.[52] Both
women emphasize the importance of their discovery of sexological knowledge
and its role in their own self-affirmation, even as they repudiate certain of its
"scientific" conclusions, as in the case of Miss M. (History XXXVII). In contemporary parlance, the women's willingness to work with Ellis became
bound up with the process of their politicization. Miss M. informed Ellis that
had she not stumbled across the work of Krafft-Ebing she would have been
ignorant that her "feelings" were " 'under the ban of society' as he puts it, or
were considered unnatural and depraved."[53] Miss M. credits Krafft-Ebing
only with providing information concerning society's prejudices before she
points out the error of his conclusions. If sexology, as Faderman contends, is
"a worm in the bud," why were women such as Miss M. and Margaret Haig

Mackworth "far from accepting of it all"? Sexology and society may judge Miss M. "unnatural and depraved," but this woman of "good intelligence" nevertheless holds the firm conviction that her feelings are right and natural, and that inverts have a "perfect right to live in freedom and happiness" (228; 229). The confident Miss M. tackles Krafft-Ebing head-on with a piercing dismissal of his text when she argues that only the unenlightened react negatively to inversion; Krafft-Ebing's work, Miss M. implies, is ultimately unhelpful for it fails to fulfill the primary task of sexual science: to educate society. Any negative impact implicit in Krafft-Ebing's somber phrase ("under the ban of society") is quickly undermined, for what precedes the phrase is Miss M.'s succinct assertion that she "can see nothing wrong in her feelings." Immediately following the reference to Krafft-Ebing, and in reaction to it, Ellis inserts Miss M.'s passionate explanation of her interest in Ellis's study: "She would like to help to bring light on the subject and to lift the shadow from other lives." Thus Miss M. sheds light by exposing the dark side of Krafft-Ebing's meticulous taxonomies of sexual perversions.

The second woman to refer in her case study directly to the literature on sexual inversion is Miss V. (History XXXVIII), who confesses to Ellis that "throughout early life up to adult age she was a mystery to herself, and morbidly conscious of some fundamental difference between herself and other people," but unable to find anyone to talk to about her "peculiarity." Miss V.'s first glimmer of understanding into the nature of her difference occurred when she came across a passage in a book where a character thought "she had a 'boy's soul in a girl's body.' The applicability of this to myself struck me at once, and I read the sentence to my mother who disgusted me by appearing shocked" (232). (The mother was obviously not ignorant of the implications.) Several more years passed until Miss V. "came across" another source, referred to cryptically as "a book on sexual inversion which proved to be a complete revelation to her of her own nature" (229). The unnamed book ameliorated her suffering "by showing her that she was not an anomaly to be regarded with repulsion"; this in turn "brought her comfort and peace." Such a response resonates with Carpenter's energetic arguments on the naturalness of the "intermediate sex," which reassured its many readers: "In a vast number of cases [sexual inversion is] quite instinctive and congenital, mentally and physically, and therefore twined in the very roots of individual life and practically ineradicable."[54] Kathlyn Oliver was one among several whose appreciation of Carpenter's work on "homogenic love" culminated in a letter in which she explained how it finally "dawned" on her that "I myself belong to that class."[55] For both Miss V. and Oliver these early writings on sexuality were both transformative and extremely positive.

Like Miss M., Miss V. agrees to share the intimate details of her psycho-sexual development with Ellis because she believes unreservedly that her story can help "other women who may be suffering as in the past she has suffered."[56] In back-to-back paragraphs, both women open up sexological writing to strenuous scrutiny: Miss M. demonstrates the limited value of Krafft-Ebing's work and thereby queries its status as objective science, while Miss V. points to the potential good of other writings on sexuality. The reader of *Sexual Inversion* learns that inverts should pass over Krafft-Ebing's delineation of the perversities of sexual abnormality and instead consult other works that advance a more progressive, indeed radical, view. Ellis's incorporation of his female invert-informants' often lengthy narratives allows their voices to be heard without intrusive commentary, but more important, it enables these women to become participants in the larger project of challenging and even overturning certain widely held beliefs about inversion that Ellis thought no longer tenable. Jay Prosser explains: "For a sexual historiography intent on reconstituting the invert as subject, the case histories are key; for it is here that inverts make their most sustained appearance as subjects."[57] No wonder the *Lancet* jumped quickly to Krafft-Ebing's defense: "such matters are far better treated from the psycho-pathological standpoint of Kraft-Ebbing [sic] than from that of Ulrichs, with whose theory as to the naturalness of homo-sexuality Mr. Havelock Ellis seems in agreement."[58]

This bold new use of the case history as critique was unprecedented in the literature, and no doubt further provoked the *Lancet* to assert that Ellis's compilation of "historical references and . . . 'human documents' " would fail "to convince medical men that homo-sexuality is anything else than an acquired and depraved manifestation of the sexual passion." The inclusion of the Misses M. and V.'s negotiation of sexology reveals the subtlety of Ellis's challenge to sexological pronouncements he regarded as outmoded, but elsewhere in his study his attack could be forceful and forthright. Ellis sharply refuted Krafft-Ebing's long-held view that homosexuality signaled degeneration or disease (a position Krafft-Ebing advocated during most of his career), and also his formulations of a typology of inversion: "The early attempts of Krafft-Ebing and others at elaborate classification are no longer acceptable. Even the most elementary groupings become doubtful when we have definitely to fit our cases into them."[59] Ellis recognized Krafft-Ebing's unique contribution to the etiology of sexual perversions, but argued that he should best be remembered "as a clinician, rather than as a psychologist" (70). Ellis's serious reservations about Krafft-Ebing's theories and his "rather fine-spun classification" system suggests that *Psychopathia Sexualis* would hardly have been the former's first choice as a useful introduction for the novice-invert. Scientifically dubious, the handbook "for lawyers and doctors discussing sexual crimes in court" could prove more damaging than illuminating for those inverts unable to subject its findings to thoughtful critique.[60] Thus it is strange that in the novel Ellis sanctioned, the first volume Stephen Gordon extracts from her father's cache of sexology books is a "battered old" copy of Krafft-Ebing's unnamed but undoubtedly *Psychopathia Sexualis* (204). Critics often point to this important scene in the narrative as *the* moment of self-discovery, but few speculate on what it is Stephen actually finds.[61]

After prolonged scrutiny of Krafft-Ebing, Stephen returns to the bookcase for "another of those volumes, and another," until the study—a repository of sexological knowledge—grows dim; "there was little light left to read by, so that she must take her book to the window and must bend her face closer over the page; but still she read on and on in the dusk" (204). Sexology, the narrator implies, provides insufficient light, and Stephen unconsciously shifts her body more closely and instinctively toward nature, emblematized by the garden outside. When Stephen finally utters her first response several hours later, she does not declare like Miss V. that the material offers "a complete revelation of her own nature." Instead, she issues a reprimand to her father: "You knew!" Inexplicably drawn to the books that hold the secret of her nature, Stephen recognizes her "self" not in the sexologist's text—which initially means nothing to her—but in the book's margins, where her father had written her name. Stephen therefore enters into a scholarly investigation of her sexual nature only via the mediation or intervention of her deceased father, whose knowledge of "this thing" is evidenced by the "little notes all along the immaculate margins" (204, 26). Philip's command of the relevant sexological literature on inversion becomes, in effect, his sexual secret as he withholds vital information concerning his daughter's sexual nature from her and from his wife. Even when he "would get out a slim volume recently acquired, and would read and reread it in the silence," Philip only cryptically told his daughter that these same materials would someday provide answers: "I want you to be wise for your own sake, Stephen, because at the best life requires great wisdom. I want you to learn to make friends of your books; some day you may need them, because . . . you mayn't find life at all easy . . . books are good friends" (26, 61) Yet Philip refrains from disseminating his knowledge; sexology is an invisible presence in the novel that influences and guides readers as a *silent* internalized process. Thus Stephen's first sustained encounter with sexology is as knowledge *qua* paternal knowledge, and her initial response of anger arises in response to the damaging repercussions of its sequestering.

Stephen's early progression in the narrative is to the place of her father, his study and books—a rite of passage that promises to alleviate the suffering caused by her own lack of knowledge as well as her mother's. Yet after reproaching her father, and discerning from her reading that she is not alone in the world ("there are so many of us—thousands" [204]), Stephen becomes obsessively preoccupied with the notion of inversion as bodily or psychical affliction: inverts, she agonizes, "have no right to love, no right to compassion because they're maimed, hideously maimed and ugly—God's cruel; He let us get flawed in the making." The reading of sexology, this passage implies, inevitably puts the reader at risk, since knowledge produces unhappiness and self-hatred: to be inverted, for Stephen, is to be maimed. Yet this troubling equation is at odds with the conclusions of the major sexologists, including Ellis and even Krafft-Ebing in his final verdict. Oosterhuis notes that by 1901 Krafft-Ebing's views had shifted remarkably so that he no longer believed homosexuality was "incompatible with mental health or even with intellectual superiority. It was not a pathological phenomenon, but a biological and psychological condition that had to be accepted as a more or less deplorable but natural fate."[62] Carpenter too, in taking stock of the changes within sexology, distinguishes between old and new:

> Formerly it was assumed as a matter of course, that the type [the inverted or "intermediate sex"] was merely a result of disease and degeneration; but now with the examination of the actual facts it appears that, on the contrary, many are fine, healthy specimens of their sex, muscular and well-developed in body, of powerful brain, high standard of conduct, and with nothing abnormal or morbid of any kind observable in their physical structure or constitution.[63]

Hall's characterization of Stephen in body and mind is more congruent with this 1908 description of the intermediate type by Carpenter than with Krafft-Ebing's study of 1886, with its outmoded emphasis on degeneration and pathology.[64] Hall, in fact, scrupulously ascribes to her protagonist the same qualities Carpenter outlines: a well-developed body, powerful brain, and high standard of conduct. If Stephen had opened volumes by Carpenter or Ellis, she would have been more likely to proclaim the naturalness of her inversion as well as her perfect right to love, instead of insisting on a reading incompatible with most contemporaneous sexology.

In an interesting twist on the biblical expulsion from Eden, in which Eve's hunger for knowledge triggers her fall from paradise, Stephen's downfall stems from what is buried in her genes—only after her fall or banishment does she obtain a (flawed) version of that knowledge that in turn leads to her distressed exclamation that God allowed her to be "flawed in the making." There is a profound chasm between Stephen's negative moral phraseology ("flawed in the making") and Ellis's objective, scientific notion of biological anomaly or "predisposition."[65] Stephen, apparently unable to assimilate the cold neutrality of sexological discourse, turns elsewhere for answers and explanations: "before she knew what she was doing" Stephen opens another of her father's "well-worn" volumes, the Bible: " 'And the Lord set a mark upon Cain' " (204; 205). Gillian Whitlock argues that this juxtaposition of the Bible with sexological texts constitutes an equivalency of labeling within patriarchal discourse through which the sexological category of invert becomes, in biblical terms, "the mark of Cain," and thereby emphasizes the " 'constructed,' rather than the innate."[66] However, the equivalency she posits is misleading because the medical label "invert" describes not a visible and damnable perversion but an invisible and innate—as opposed to culturally constructed—"biological variation," considered by Ellis to be "a 'sport,' . . . one of those organic aberrations which we see throughout living nature, in plants and in animals."[67] (Later in the narrative Hall describes inversion as "Nature's most inexplicable whim" [334].)

Stephen's initial internalization of negative readings of her sexual abnormality causes her acute suffering, until she is interrupted by her tutor Miss Puddleton (Puddle), who neutralizes the damaging linkage of homosexuality with morbidity.[68] Puddle arrives on the scene at just the right moment to correct Stephen's flawed reading, and together the women form an incipient interpretive community, with the older instructing the younger in the ways sexological systems of knowledge must be negotiated. This lack of a discourse community, due to Sir Philip's reluctance to share his knowledge with his daughter, had contributed to Stephen's first pained response upon her discovery. In this way Hall disrupts Stephen's orgy of self-pity with the assurances of a fellow intermediate, whose voice echoes the mysticism of Carpenter and supersedes both Krafft-Ebing and the Bible: "We're all part of nature" (205). Puddle's Oxford education has apparently included *The Intermediate Sex*, as she tells her pupil: "Because you are what you are, you may actually find that you've got an advantage. You may write with a curious double insight—write both men and women from a personal knowledge."[69] Carpenter's very term for homosexuals, the "intermediate sex," highlights the advantage of a (superior) vantage point between the two sexes: intermediate types possess an "extraordinary gift" in their "double point of view, both of the man and of the woman," and their "double nature" enables them to open "the secrets of the two sexes."[70] Puddle's minisermon—a swift riposte to Krafft-Ebing's negative discourse of "taint" and "morbidity"—sensibly iterates the more positive and idealistic approach to homosexuality advanced by Carpenter, although the lingering effects of Stephen's initial encounter with the discourse of sexual abnormality never dissipate completely.

If, as I suggest, Carpenter's theories on the "intermediate sex" displace all others in this scene, why is it so few have noticed?[71] By the early 1920s Carpenter's once huge reputation had gone into eclipse, whereas Ellis's "Commentary" serves as a highly visible and constant reminder of how his theories of inversion helped shape Hall's understanding. Still, critical neglect of Carpenter is surprising since, as Lucy Bland explains, his "writings on homosexuality . . . were at least as influential as those of Ellis."[72] Of all the treatises on sexuality in the early twentieth century, Carpenter's were by far the easiest to obtain and quite accessible to a nonspecialist reader, a fact that the medical establishment held against him. In a vicious and disparaging review of *The Intermediate Sex*, the *British Medical Journal* complained that the volume's affordability called into question its scientific value and warned that "serious people in England might be spared the waste of time consumed in reading a low-priced book of no scientific or literary merit advocating the culture of unnatural and criminal practices."[73] Despite such hostility from the professionals, Carpenter's work sold extremely well; the volume containing his essay on "The Homogenic Attachment" enjoyed "phenomenal" sales and was reprinted three times in 1915 alone.[74] In 1915 and 1916 nearly ten of Carpenter's books were in circulation, along with important new assessments of his oeuvre (20). If figures such as E. M. Forster, D. H. Lawrence, and Siegfried Sassoon, among others, acknowledged Carpenter's influence, it is unlikely that his work did *not* have an impact on Hall, as well as on Bryher and Allatini, since as scholar Keith Nield points out, Carpenter's "*mass* appeal . . . was very large over a period of twenty or thirty years."[75]

The more experienced and well-read Puddle discovers in Carpenter's writings the mechanism to dispel strategically the negative effect of Krafft-Ebing and to guide Stephen—and the reader—through the intricate processes of resistance and acceptance. This turning point dramatizes how reading (or, in Stephen's case, browsing) is no guarantee of comprehension, especially for young and inexperienced inverts who attempt negotiation in the absence of a larger intellectual context or historical perspective on the critical shifts on inversion within sexology itself, traced scrupulously by Ellis in *Sexual Inversion*. Hall, well-informed about sexology's competing and often conflicting theories on a range of topics, inscribed in representation warnings of the dangers of passive or uncritical consumption of sexological knowledge and of the need to balance sexological opinion against experience and personal knowledge. Sexology should be read with extreme care, but so too should the novels of Hall, Bryher, and Allatini for they represent, as we will see, an uneasy mixture of the pure and impure, medical and mythic, scientific and utopian—hardly sexology in the "completely faithful and uncompromising form" Ellis inexplicably claimed in his commentary on *The Well*. Literary negotiation of the dominant writings on sexuality and intersecting theories became the site of a sophisticated and complex refashioning, in effect, a wildly eclectic free-for-all.

III

ON JULY 19, 1928, Radclyffe Hall wrote to Havelock Ellis concerning his brief statement on *The Well of Loneliness*: "I was so overjoyed and proud at winning your good opinion for my book that I should have liked to walk up and down Piccadilly with it on a sandwich board. . . . [There is] nothing I prize so highly or consider so vitally important for my book as your friendship and approval."[76] Hall paid a high price for the sexologist's "good opinion," if Adam Parkes is correct in his assessment of the stakes: "Granting priority to Ellis's commentary, Hall effectively asked him to authorize her novel so that it could be seen to perform his theory of female inversion. The 'sincerity' exuded by the novel would simply reflect the degree to which Hall succeeded in mimicking Ellis's voice."[77] Critics who overstate the sexologist's influence on the novelist regard Ellis's commentary as only the tip of the iceberg. Beneath the glaringly obtrusive imprimatur lies a theoretical foundation slavishly faithful to the master because, this critical perspective argues, Hall effectually relinquished authorial control "so that ultimately Ellis's word would count for more than her own" (441). Sandra Gilbert and Susan Gubar, for example, contend that Hall advanced a theory of the origins of inversion essentially lifted from the pages of Ellis's *Sexual Inversion*: Stephen is "a congenitally masculine girl born to a father who confirmed her inversion by treating her as the son he wanted."[78] Such a "myth of origins," these critics confidently assert, "accords with the etiology of homosexuality Havelock Ellis had developed and therefore explains his defense of the novel in the famous court case brought against it." Leaving aside the historical inaccuracy (Ellis refused to help Hall with her court case),[79] this reading interestingly draws our attention to the way in which Hall actually pulls away from the congenitalist position advocated by medical men such as Ellis and thus inadvertently reveals that Hall was far from "mimicking Ellis's voice."

That *The Well* both conformed to and deviated from Ellis's congenitalist view was first discerned as early as 1928 by the *Lancet*, which praises Hall's "considerable dramatic skill" but finds her "emphasis . . . sometimes misplaced": "The implication that the parents' desire to produce a son may alter the emotional affinities of the daughter born to them is difficult to accept; the origin of abnormal sex attractions cannot be so simply explained."[80] To suggest that Sir Philip's intense desire for a son, compounded by his unorthodox form of childrearing (from naming his daughter Stephen to treating her like a boy), contributes to Stephen's inversion, is to subscribe to a "nurture over nature" etiology antithetical to the congenitalists, whose major proponent was, of course, Ellis. As critic Alison Hennegan, in her perceptive introduction to *The Well*, notes: "For much of the book Hall seems to be allowing two different theories of sexuality to run in tandem. Explicitly she argues that sexual orientation is inborn. Yet often explanations based on environment and psychology seem to hover in the background, especially in her account of Stephen's childhood and adolescence."[81] Thus Hall both keenly accepted "the parameters set up by Ellis" and veered off in multiple directions, so that her novel "is not simply an exemplification of Ellis's views in literary form."[82] Hall replicates the disjunctions and ruptures within the early theorizing of homosexuality and thereby exposes her curious and sympathetic middle-class readers to a wide spectrum of explanations, from notions wholly incompatible with sexual science to notions culled from Ellis and other theorists, including Ulrichs, Krafft-Ebing, and Carpenter.[83]

Hall's refusal to present sexology as a coherent and unitary body of knowledge accounts in part for the troubling paradox at the heart of *The Well*'s panoply of medical arguments and (pseudo)scientific theories of sex and sexuality: the novel vividly represents the physical acquisition of books on sexual science but not, with any clarity, its pronouncements. As a result, Stephen's confused response to her reading of sexology in turn confuses critics who wonder—understandably—what Hall was up to when she reproduced three distinct and opposing positions on homosexuality in a single episode: as degeneration, as sin, and as advantage. The only consistency in the novel is, as critic Bonnie Kime Scott observes, its "inconsistent view of lesbianism."[84] But what seems contradictory—indeed what is contradictory—is purposeful, part and parcel of "a deliberate political intervention."[85] We know all too little, however, about *how* Hall concocted her own sexological "stew" for her readers' consumption, perhaps because our critical frameworks have been too narrowly focused on sexological constructions of sexuality, obscuring our understanding of how Hall and other lesbian novelists may have been influenced by—and exploited—other of sexology's equally important ideas and "discoveries."

In this section I propose to map out a wider area of investigation by tracing in greater detail how Hall, Bryher, and Allatini relied on or flatly cannibalized for their own narrative purposes diverse writings on sexuality drawn from sometimes irreconcilable sources—science and myth, experience and theory. All three writers freely exploited anything deemed useful to their projects and, as a result, the end product was as likely to be suffused with Ellis's crisp and "scientific" precision as with Carpenter's metaphysical vagueness. Ellis's conceptualization of inversion was undeniably central, but, as we will see, Carpenter's powerful models of intermediate types may have proven the more useful and provocative for the lesbian writer's ambitious political agenda, untroubled that such traits and qualities were often reserved for males. Thus Ellis and Carpenter may not have provided a blueprint so much as a theoretical starting point for the lesbian literary imagination. But it is Carpenter's radical proposal that the homosexual constitution and sensibility signaled a new stage in evolutionary development that may have been ultimately the more provocative for these lesbian novelists, especially Hall. Lesbian literary production at this time was far more sophisticated than we have hitherto recognized: the inscription in representation of a patchwork of sexological and related theories, including the controversial argument on behalf of homosexual "superiority" and evolution, marked the lesbian's entry into a distinctively modern age.

Shortly after the First World War Bryher began to compose the first of two autobiographical novels, *Development* (1920), followed in 1923 by a sequel, *Two Selves*. During this time she entered into regular correspondence with Ellis, who H.D. wryly dubbed "the good doctor and father-confessor."[86] Bryher initially contacted the sexologist because she required more information on the subject of "transvestism or cross-dressing in women" for her novel, or so she claimed.[87] In the spring of 1919 the two met at Ellis's Brixton home where they discussed—apparently in this order—"color-hearing," "cross-dressing," and "the question of whether [Bryher] was a boy sort of escaped into the wrong body."[88] In this intriguing sequence of topics Bryher twice invokes scientifically correct terminology but lapses into a common euphemistic phrase for female sexual inversion. At this stage she was either not yet willing to accept the label "female invert" or to acknowledge a notion held by several major sexologists: that the desire to be a boy in a young woman could signal a tendency toward inversion. Ellis for one observes that "the commonest characteristic of the sexually inverted woman is a certain degree of masculinity or boyishness."[89] He reports how Miss V. "used to pretend [she] was a boy" and Miss M. exhibited an instinctive boyishness in her "many boyish tricks of manner and speech" (230, 229). Likewise Miss D. recounted, "I always surveyed [everything] from the point of view of a boy" (239). All these case histories exhibit the boyishness Ellis indicated occurred "frequently, though not always" among "inverted women."[90] In "Studies in Feminine Inversion," Browne's Case E, described as "an invert of the most pronounced physical type," also manifests distinctly boyish characteristics: "Her tall, stiff, rather heavily muscular figure, her voice, and her chubby, fresh-colored face . . . were so like those of a young and very well-groomed youth, that all the staff of the school nicknamed her 'Boy.' "[91] In fact, Browne expresses surprise that none of the fellow staff-members "clearly realized what this epithet—and her intimacy with a woman of such strongly contrasted type, implied" (55-6). Regardless of whether Bryher knew or accepted the connection between boyishness and inversion, she expressed relief when writing afterwards to H.D. about the meeting with Ellis that the sexologist had assured her she was "quite justified in pleading [she] ought to be a boy—I am just a girl by accident." Bryher would recycle this last phrase in *Development* ("this accident of being a girl"), as it reaffirmed her sense, if not of inversion, of the naturalness of "boy-ness."

Boyishness—rather than boy-ness—in young women surfaces repeatedly in the novels of Bryher, Hall, and Allatini.[92] Bryher continually links her protagonist's dreams and her infatuation not with actual boys—none appear at any point in either of the two novels—but with her own imaginative, idealistic construction of the boy: Nancy's "one regret was that she was a girl. Never having played with any boys, she imagined them wonderful creatures, welded of her favorite heroes and her own fancy, ever seeking adventures, making them, if they were not ready to their hand, and, of course, wiser than any grown-up people."[93] Young Stephen too constructs for herself an imaginary boyhood based upon literary representations of male heroism: "such stories [about heroes] so stirred her ambition, that she longed intensely to live them. She . . . now longed to be William Tell, or Nelson" (19). Both labeled "queer" by others, Nancy and Stephen experience what critic Leigh Gilmore calls "embodiment as alienation"[94]; that is, a profound discomfort in their young female bodies emblematized by cumbersome feminine clothing: Nancy's "draggling skirt made impediment at each step. Would she were out in a boy's suit, free and joyous and careless as a boy is" (141). Stephen also hates the soft femininity of her female garments: "Her legs felt so free and comfortable in breeches" (20). Stephen daringly envisions a gender change enacted through will power alone, "I must be a boy," Stephen declares, "'cause I feel exactly like one" (20), while Nancy "was sure if she hoped enough she would turn into a boy" (7). Allatini's Antoinette also possesses boyish traits, such as a "supple boyish figure" and a "short mass of hair."[95] When she falls in love with the dark Hester, Antoinette "quite unconsciously . . . [pleads] as a very young boy might plead with his lady-love" (46). Boyishness is natural for Stephen, Nancy, and Antoinette, but girlishness must be acquired: Nancy's knowledge of performing "girlishness," for instance, was "confined to one book read by accident, an impression they liked clothes and were afraid of getting dirty" (7).

Yet none of the numerous reviews of *Development* commented on whether Nancy's persistent desire to be a boy signified abnormal sexuality, despite the protagonist's complete lack of interest in the opposite sex; a typical review states matter-of-factly that Nancy "desires adventure and to be a boy."[96] Still, Nancy strikes many reviewers as distinctly odd, though most cannot figure out why. The *Athenaeum* perceptively locates this strangeness in Nancy's "strange lament . . . that she is not a boy," but reads the lament as a sign not of sexuality but of Nancy's naïveté about newly emancipated young women: "There is no longer any need for girls to wear draggled skirts or to sit at narrow windows or to scream and twitter."[97] Another reviewer compendiously lists the qualities connoting modernity: Nancy's "restlessnesses, her dissatisfactions, her habits of introspection, her curiosity about life, her impatience of restraints, her independent judgments of people and things, are all characteristic of *one variety* of the very modern girl."[98] The phrase "one variety" is sufficiently and tactfully ambiguous, unlike that of the rabid fomenter James Douglas who is rather more blunt; in his characteristically adroit handling of language, he asserts, "Nancy is a freak."[99] The *Daily Telegraph* also hints that Bryher's "depressing study" is "even morbid in certain of its tendencies."[100] The nature of these "tendencies" is not spelled out, but the fact that "the male is wholly absent" and the young heroine "desire[s] to be a boy" suggests the applicability of the terms "abnormal" and "morbid" tossed around in some of the reviews, obviously without Ellis's crucial differentiation: "Many people imagine that what is abnormal is necessarily diseased. That is not the case. . . . The study of the abnormal is perfectly distinct from the study of the morbid."[101]

"Mr. Polygon Amor" of *The Literary Review* offers a more astute assessment of Nancy's unique qualities, in particular her rare ability to connect words, spoken or read, to color—the phenomenon known as color-hearing—

when he writes: "For there are some few who are genuinely abnormal, genuinely 'different,' not because of what they lack but because of *what they have*."[102] This fascinating comment succinctly encapsulates Ellis's strategic revision of the terms of comparison proffered by his early collaborator John Addington Symonds, one of the first to advocate the view of inversion as a quirk of nature, a "biological variation" comparable to, say, color-blindness.[103] Ellis summarized Symonds's explanation as follows: "Just as the ordinary color-blind person is congenitally insensitive to those red-green rays which are precisely the most impressive to the normal eye . . . so the invert fails to see emotional values patent to normal persons, transferring those values to emotional associations which, for the rest of the world, are utterly distinct." While Ellis agreed that "such a comparison [was] reasonable" and conveniently emphasized a condition both innate and harmless, "color-blindness" still held a negative value in denoting loss or defect. Ellis understood that in order to destigmatize this sexual anomaly—a top priority—and thereby break down social prejudice and eliminate current regulatory legislation, it was imperative to characterize genuine abnormality, in Mr. Amor's terms, not as "lack" but as "what they have." Ellis achieved this shift by swapping color-blindness for another condition, namely "the phenomenon [known] as color-hearing, in which there is not so much defect as an abnormality of nervous tracks producing new and involuntary combinations." This revision constituted a marked improvement in that neither inversion nor color-hearing could be regarded as disease.[104] Bryher eagerly seized on Ellis's simile (inversion is like color-hearing), but refashioned the figure of speech into a metaphor (color-hearing is inversion). The two conditions become so intertwined that one might be substituted for the other and still retain intelligibility, as seen in a passage where the narrator ponders the nurture/nature question, ostensibly in relation to color-hearing: "Environment, heredity? A thing [Nancy] was not responsible for, yet desired."[105] Nancy recalls: "From earliest remembrance certain phrases, names especially of places or of persons, were never free from an association of color, fashioned of a tone, written in it; and as [Nancy] grew, this feeling developed, unconsciously expanding until her whole vocabulary became a palette of colors."[106] But Bryher—subversively—takes the metaphor one step further and, in a clear break from Ellis, represents color-hearing not merely as variation, but as a superior sensibility, an added extra that raises Nancy above her ordinary peers: "[I]t was only by accident she discovered, at fifteen, [words] were printed symbols to the *multitude*."[107] *Development* and *Two Selves* thus become the site for a selective appropriation and strategic revision of Ellis and, as we will see, for positing a bold convergence of Ellis and Carpenter.

Both Ellis and Carpenter believed that inversion, while not pervasive, occurred with far greater frequency than had been hitherto appreciated.[108] According to Ellis's research findings, in "the *professional and most cultured* element of the middle class in England there must be a distinct percentage of inverts, which may sometimes be as much as five per cent. . . . Among women of the same class the percentage seems to be at least double."[109] Ellis's phrase "the professional and most cultured" signals his political sympathies and efforts to counter social hostility and challenge the view still prevalent in medical circles that homosexuality is unnatural and depraved; as Weeks explains, Ellis "went to great lengths . . . to demonstrate that homosexuality was frequently associated with intellectual and artistic distinction. . . . The case-histories . . . very effectively [demonstrated] . . . the moral, personal and intellectual quality of homosexual people."[110] For example, Ellis points to the extraordinarily high number of his cases ("68 per cent") that showed "artistic aptitude in varying degree" as opposed to the normal population, where the figure is a paltry thirty per cent.[111] In his chapter "The Nature of Sexual Inversion" Ellis reviews the employment of his subjects and concludes: "At least half a dozen of my subjects are successful men of letters, and I could easily add others by going outside the group of [Case] Histories included in this study" (293–4). Ellis's apparent exemption of women in this list poses no stumbling block for Bryher or Hall who, despite Ellis's less thorough treatment of inverted women, transfer to their lesbian protagonists the artistic qualities and professions Ellis observes in inverted men.

There is, however, an immense leap from Ellis's recognition that *some* homosexuals exhibit exemplary moral qualities or artistic talent to Carpenter's assertion that *many* homosexuals are by their nature superior. Carpenter was the most influential and resolute advocate in England of the superiority of what he termed the Uranian or "intermediate type" and asserted emphatically, "Uranian men are superior to the normal men."[112] Carpenter drew upon the language of an earlier campaigner for homosexual rights, Ulrichs, whose term "Uranian" designated a love "of a higher order than the ordinary [heterosexual] attachment" (20n.). Carpenter, and a handful of (inverted) men who wrote on sexuality, such as Symonds and Hirschfeld, embraced the superiority argument wholeheartedly and maintained that inversion was an advantage for the individual invert and advantageous for society at large, but acceptance of this position was not always enthusiastic. The writer Cyril Connolly, in his review of *The Well of Loneliness*, complained: "Most of us are resigned to the doctrine of homosexuals, that they alone possess all the greatest heroes and all the finer feelings."[113] The "superiority" doctrine, however, was not universally accepted by sexologists, so it is misleading to suggest that "sexology's attribution of a tendency to moral and intellectual superiority in homosexuals is well known."[114] The collapsing of multiple and often divergent positions into the monolithic construction "sexology" glosses over key differences; many medical practitioners, sexologists, and physicians spoke against the notion that the invert might be a higher type. Forel, for instance, patently dismissed the invert's claim to superiority: "Ulrichs and his disciples endeavored to prove an absurdity by maintaining that homosexuals are a special kind of normal men."[115] The journal of the British Medical Association severely criticized Carpenter's *The Intermediate Sex* for "reiterat[ing] *ad nauseam* praise and laudation for creatures and customs which are generally regarded as odious."[116] Feminists too were quick to attack the "superiority" argument. In her BSSSP paper Browne argues: "I think it is perhaps not wholly uncalled-for, to underline very strongly my opinion that the homo-sexual impulse is *not in any way superior* to the normal; it has a fully equal right to existence and expression, it is no worse, no lower; *but no better*."[117] In 1929 Rebecca West speaks scornfully of "this army of young prigs who are as self-righteous about their abnormalities as missionaries who volunteer for Africa in pious mid-Victorian novels."[118]

The literary adaptation of the "superiority" doctrine could backfire as well, as is evident in the legal deliberations over the banning of *The Well*. Stephen's very worthiness—her moral superiority—was cited as particularly disturbing by Sir Chartres Biron, the chief magistrate who presided over the prosecution of *The Well*: not only is Stephen "presented . . . as a very fine character" but "everybody, all the characters in this book, who indulge in these horrible vices are presented to us as attractive people and put forward for our admiration; and those who object to these vices are sneered at in the book as prejudiced, foolish and cruel."[119] Baker accounts for Hall's creation of "a heroine of the highest moral character, superior in some ways to the 'normal' people around her" as being part of an effort "to drive home the injustice" done to inverts by society; certainly Hall's argument at the end of *The Well* would seem to reinforce such a position: "The sooner the world came to realize that fine brains very frequently went with inversion, the sooner it would have to withdraw its ban, and the sooner would cease this persecution."[120] The artistic superiority of Bryher's Nancy—and the incessant dithering about it—also struck some reviewers as unpleasantly arrogant; the *Glasgow Herald* for one found Nancy a "precocious . . . thoroughly unpleasant prig."[121] However, the external signifiers of the invert's superiority that proved so seductive for Hall and Bryher (social class, a keen moral sense, or artistic nature) represent only the outward manifestations of the invisible, not mere *compensation* for congenital taint or morbidity, or just part of a potent challenge to homophobia.[122] Stephen and Nancy are by their (sexual) *nature* superior.

Some feminist literary critics also find Stephen's class superiority insufferable and complain that "the appeal to moral excellence is made in specifically class terms, feeding into current ideas of lesbianism as an aristocratic aberration."[123] Stephen's masculinity, Ruehl argues, is "saturated with class. What she grows up to be is a 'perfect gentleman.' " (25). Yet if we position Stephen's roots in the landed gentry against the ideas about biological inheritance prevalent in the late nineteenth century, Hall's rationale becomes somewhat clearer. As critic Carolyn Burdett points out, "Sexual science took the population *en masse* as its object of enquiry. . . . Biological heredity made sex the court at which the future would be decided, a future which would be one of improvement and progress or one of degeneration and decay."[124] Burdett explains that Francis Galton, the first to formulate the science of eugenics, strongly believed that "progress and improvement lay neither with a decaying landed gentry, nor with a vulgar and self-interested entrepreneuralism, but with the aristocracy of intellect found in the professional classes. Inheritance, in the modern world, meant the passing on of a *healthy physique* and a *good brain*, rather than property and land" (46, emphasis mine). Stephen's expulsion from the land of her ancestors, the "decaying landed gentry," inaugurates her transition to the "aristocracy of intellect," and no being is better prepared for the role in body and mind than this female intermediate, who possesses a "splendid young body," "splendid physique," and the extraordinary intelligence and "intuition of those who stand midway between the sexes" (82, 301, 83).

Hall's phrase echoes Carpenter's words about those "who stand mid-way between the extremes of the two sexes" and links Stephen directly with Carpenter's construction of the intermediate type, a being singularly poised to undertake a unique and special role in the larger scheme of creation.[125] In Carpenter's parlance, Uranians were a "respectable and valuable class," with an "extraordinary gift for, and experience in, affairs of the heart. . . . It is not difficult to see that these people have a special work to do as reconcilers and interpreters of the two sexes to each other."[126] An intermediate on the far edge of her "type" and "altogether different from other people," Stephen combines "the strength of a man with the gentler and more subtle strength of a woman" (144, 177). Bryher's Nancy, as the *Athenaeum* notes, also combines traits associated with both genders, which underlines her modernity: "Although we are told she possesses 'the intellect, the hopes, the ambitions of a man, unsoftened by any feminine attribute,' " she also embodies something more feminine, for "what could be more 'female' than her passion for rummaging in, tumbling over, eyeing this great basket of colored words?"[127] Carpenter's vision of the Uranian also appears throughout Allatini's *Despised and Rejected*, even paraphrased as those "who stand mid-way between the extremes of the two sexes . . . perfectly balanced, not limited by the psychological bounds of one sex, but combining the power and the intellect of the one with the subtlety and intuition of the other; a dual nature, possessing the extended range, the attributes of both sides, and therefore loving and beloved of both alike."[128]

For all three writers the superiority of the invert could be inscribed in literary representation in any number of ways: color-hearing, high morals, class position, superb physique, an artistic sensibility, and the dual vision of both sexes. These lesbian writers found in Carpenter's "intermediate" a powerful model of a superior specimen. Yet not all Uranians are created equal: Carpenter established important distinctions between the male Uranian's "instinctive artistic nature . . . sensitive spirit, his wavelike emotional temperament, combined with hardihood of intellect and body," and the female's "frank, free nature . . . her masculine independence and strength wedded to thoroughly feminine grace of form and manner."[129] This distinction does not seem at first glance particularly depreciatory; however, from an evolutionary perspective the homogenic woman represents not a step forward but several backward, as critic Beverly Thiele explains: "The characteristics of the homosexual male (tender, emotional, intuitive and caring) pointed to an advance in human evolution: a new sexual type," while lesbians, on the other hand, just "did not measure up. . . . For all they might be an intermediate type, [they] were closer to the undesirable model of conventional male sexuality."[130] If we accept Thiele's claim that Carpenter thought Uranian women "were not part of the social dialogue which [he] hoped would transform contemporary sexual relations," then how can we account for Carpenter's strong appeal for Bryher, Hall, and Allatini? The answer is that these writers incorporated into their narratives an even more radical concept of homosexual superiority by producing highly intelligent and sensitive female as well as male characters. In different ways each writer undertook a selective reading of the literature on homosexuality, ignoring or conflating the gender differences propounded by men such as Carpenter and Ellis. Hall and Bryher, as they had done with Ellis, disregarded Carpenter's assertion that it was the male Uranian who was especially well-suited for a career in writing because of his "exceedingly sensitive and emotional" temperament.[131] The young Stephen, for instance, expresses an early interest in language and writing and shares "her queer compositions" with her father (79). Her "secret ambition" to become a writer is depicted as a manly avocation that draws the daughter closer to her father in a kind of male camaraderie.

In *Despised and Rejected* Allatini launches a different sort of challenge to Carpenter's notion of the superior male Uranian by calling into question the psychological or emotional characteristics that distinguish him from all others. The character of Dennis appears initially as an excellent specimen of his type and, as a composer, he sits comfortably among the "large number of the artist class, musical, literary or pictorial [who] belong to this description. That delicate and subtle sympathy with every wave and phase of feeling which makes the artist possible is also very characteristic of the Uranian (the male type), and makes it easy or natural for the Uranian man to become an artist."[132]

But what Carpenter depicts as an incredible gift Allatini represents as a drawback. Dennis's Uranian temperament may be ideal for his chosen profession, but it also drastically inhibits his potential for self-acceptance—the hypersensitive Dennis is virtually debilitated by self-revulsion: "Abnormal—perverted—against nature—he could hear the epithets that would be hurled against him, and that he would deserve. . . . What had nature been about, in giving him the soul of a woman in the body of a man?" (107). Dennis, overwhelmed with "fear . . . horror, and . . . loathing," whiles away much of the novel agonizing about the condition that will leave him lonely and miserable throughout life. Antoinette, on the other hand, while without a profession as such, is glimpsed in the opening pages of the novel dabbling in an amateur stage production—another "typical" profession of male inverts.[133] Antoinette feels "not in the least unnatural, that all her passionate longings should have been awakened by women, instead of by members of the opposite sex."[134] In Antoinette Allatini thus creates a well-adjusted female Uranian who is more capable than her fellow Uranian Dennis in coping with a life on the margins of so-called normal society: "Antoinette was free from the least taint of morbidity; unaware that there was aught of unusual about her attitude . . . she merely felt that she was coming into her own . . . and was healthy-minded and joyous in her unquestioning obedience to the dictates of her inmost nature" (69). Antoinette's embodiment of the best traits of Carpenter's so-called normal homogenic woman renders her especially well equipped to deal with Dennis's revelation, "There's a certain amount of the masculine element in you, and of the feminine element in me" (220). Her "abnormality" never causes her the slightest unease—"she had gone scot-free"—while Dennis "had always suffered, as a boy, as a man." (218).

Even more radically, Allatini and Hall claim for the female intermediate the "important role . . . in the evolution of the race" Carpenter designates for the male.[135] Weeks characterizes Carpenter's philosophy as a "sort of sexual millenarianism" that "gave Carpenter a special aura among nineteenth-century sexual radicals. The utopian belief in a new era of sexual freedom was not unique . . . but Carpenter was almost alone, after Symonds's death, in publicly asserting the possibly higher moral possibilities of homosexuality."[136] But where is the lesbian's place in the evolution of the "new humanity"?[137] Not on the periphery but at the center: the female Uranian is crucial for she alone can reproduce a race of the highest caliber in her unique capacity to love her male counterpart and in her potential to create pure-bred intermediates. Allatini literally fleshes out Carpenter's idealized vision of the future and positions Antoinette in the forefront of "the advance-guard of a more enlightened civilization":

> The time is not so far distant when we shall recognize in the best of our intermediate types the leaders and masters of the race. . . . From ["those who stand mid-way"] a new humanity is being evolved. . . . They're necessary to the production of the higher type, though. . . . Bad specimens—and yet forerunners! For out of their suffering, out of pain and confusion and darkness, will arise something great. (348, 349)

Antoinette is an intermediate in the fullest sense of the word since, unlike Dennis, she has the capacity to love an intermediate of the opposite sex and thus contribute to the biological reproduction of a new race.[138]

Yet what role can a female intermediate such as Stephen play in a revised evolutionary plan if she is "sterile" (187)? Hall writes that "had nature been *less daring* with [Stephen], she might well have become . . . a breeder of children, an upholder of home, a careful and diligent steward of pastures" (108, emphasis mine). In *The Well* the lesbian sage Valérie Seymour outlines the contours of Stephen's dilemma by pointing out the inherent contradiction embodied in her physical and psychical constitution: "You've the nerves of the abnormal with all that they stand for—you're appallingly over-sensitive . . . [*and*] you've all the respectable county instincts of the man who cultivates children and acres" (407). The problem is how to "bring the two sides of [Stephen's] nature into some sort of friendly amalgamation," but while Valérie admits she cannot "see [Stephen's] future," the novelist does. Hall's solution is to cast Stephen as a progenitive facilitator who drives her lover Mary Llewellyn into the arms of Martin Hallam, an old friend of Stephen's; in this way, Hall's protagonist fulfills, albeit indirectly, the dictates of her biological destiny to "produce," as Allatini puts it, "the advance-guard."[139] This is what Puddle prophesied early in the narrative: "You're neither unnatural, nor abominable, nor mad; you're as much a part of what people call nature as anyone else; only you're unexplained as yet—you've not got your niche in creation. But some day that will come" (154). That "some day" arrives near the end of the narrative, not in what is commonly regarded as a conventional heterosexual plot, and not in the manner of Carpenter, but in Stephen's successful pairing of a female normal intermediate type with her male counterpart, a man cast abruptly in the novel's final pages as "thoroughly normal."[140]

To understand how Hall accomplishes this we need to examine her handling of characterization in *The Well* vis-à-vis Carpenter's delineation of the intermediate type—a task all the more difficult because of Hall's own inconsistencies. Although, as I mentioned in the previous section, Ellis expressed considerable skepticism over attempts to classify various inverted types into groups, Hall persistently makes such distinctions, even while admitting it was problematic: "Why, the grades were so numerous and so fine that they often defied the most careful observation. The timbre of a voice, the build of an ankle, the texture of a hand, a movement, a gesture—since few were as pronounced as Stephen Gordon" (352–3). Hall's curious investment in the somatic constitutes a rupture with most post-Krafft-Ebing sexology. Carpenter was adamant that "in bodily structure there is, as a rule, nothing to distinguish the subjects of our discussion from ordinary men and women."[141] Within the "intermediate race," however, Carpenter identified two broad types, conceptualized not as a wide spectrum but as a strict binary: first, "the extreme and exaggerated types of the race, and then the more normal and perfect types."[142] In the former we easily recognize Stephen in her "strong passions, masculine manners and movements . . . and *outré* in attire; her figure muscular . . . and not without a suspicion of the fragrant weed in the atmosphere" (30–1). This is the type, as Carpenter and Hall both suggest, that attracts attention in public spaces—Stephen is frequently stared at wherever she goes. On the other side of Carpenter's binary is "the more normal type," exemplified by the characters of Mary and Martin (32). Ellis would have most certainly rejected the rigidity of Carpenter's binarism, though we can see that Hall's characters owe something as well to the descriptions in *Sexual Inversion*.

Mary's description in the novel as a "perfect woman" has often led critics to view her as the feminine complement to Stephen's masculinity, but Mary is in fact rather more complicated (314). For one thing her traits and qualities do not conform to any of Ellis's categories of female inversion. The woman of this type is usually "not very robust," whereas Mary, "ardent, courageous, [and] impulsive," speaks of her intense desire for personal freedom.[143] In her extreme youthfulness, Mary appears boyish with her "recently . . . bobbed" hair and "pluck" (286; 278). Short hair separates the "less orthodox sisters" on the Western Front from the "women with hairpins," and is often a sign of boyishness (271). Dismissed by Newton as "forgettable and inconsistent," Mary is shorter, younger, and poorer than Stephen, who is quick to coddle the new recruit in the ambulance unit, even after Mary has proven her abilities.[144] Stephen's insistence on referring to Mary as a child, and on assigning her the more stereotypically feminine tasks in the early months of their relationship, suggests that Mary regresses to a passive feminine role in compliance with her lover. But Stephen's attempt to make Mary conform to the "womanly" type of invert fails as the more feminine Mary rejects the sexual passivity Ellis attributed to this category. During the women's courtship Mary is consistently the sexual aggressor ("kiss me good night . . . do you know that you've never kissed me?"), and actively pursues the now passive Stephen: "Mary imprisoned [Stephen's] nervous fingers in her own, and Stephen made no resistance."[145] Mary Llewellyn, Hall writes, "was no coward and no weakling," and neither was she drawn unwillingly into a lesbian relationship with Stephen: "All my life I've been waiting for something," Mary confesses to Stephen, "I've been waiting for you" (311, 294).

In the spectrum of types presented in *The Well*, Mary clearly falls somewhere within the range of Carpenter's "more normal" intermediate in "her frankness" and in her "great longing to be independent" (429, 285). As Carpenter writes: "The frank, free nature of the [intermediate] female, her masculine independence and strength [is] wedded to thoroughly feminine grace of form and manner."[146] Stephen's previous lover, Angela Crossby, who indulges in "a few rather schoolgirlish kisses," is representative of what Ellis termed the "spurious kind of homosexuality, the often precocious play of the normal instinct"—this is not "true sexual inversion"; rather, it is the playful exploitation of opportunity.[147] The boyish Mary, sexually attracted to the manly Stephen, also seems to have a capacity for attraction to the rare intermediate type of man, as did Antoinette.[148] In a complicated passage Hall writes: "In her very normality lay her danger. Mary, all woman, was less of a match for life than if she had been as was Stephen. Oh, most pitiful bond so strong yet so helpless; so fruitful of passion yet so bitterly sterile" (423). Newton argues that in calling Mary "normal" here Hall means "heterosexual," but if we turn instead to the language of Carpenter that so pervades this novel, we see that Mary is a perfect fit: "To come now to the more normal and perfect specimens of the homogenic *woman*, we find a type in which the body is thoroughly feminine and gracious."[149] Mary, feminine without being one of "those purely feminine women," as Hall refers to them, is the quintessential female Uranian prepared, as was Antoinette, to propagate the "new humanity," since she occupies the "median" of the human spectrum

(271). For Carpenter, as Jeffrey Weeks explains, "felt that there were many signs of an evolution of a new human type which would be *median* in character, neither excessively male nor excessively female."[150]

Likewise Martin, with his "strong, young body" yet so "sensitive" and "restrained"—hardly what Whitlock calls a "real" man—compares favorably with Carpenter's description of "the more normal type of the Uranian man" who, "while possessing thoroughly masculine powers of mind and body, combines with them the tenderer and more emotional soul-nature of the woman. . . . Such men . . . are often muscular and well-built . . . but emotionally they are extremely complex, tender, sensitive, pitiful and loving."[151] Martin is not an artist but "a dreamer, of brooding, reserved habits," as Carpenter puts it (32). Stephen is drawn to Martin's sensitivity and intense responsiveness to beauty and declares to him, "We're like brothers, we enjoy all the same sort of things" (95). Martin's "primitive instinct," especially his "almost reverential" passion for nature, especially—curiously—trees, is portrayed as a positive attribute against the exaggerated machismo of Stephen's neighbor Roger Antrim's "masculine instinct" (92, 183). Martin's sense of unity with trees demonstrates his separation from civilization and connection with nature. Carpenter, as critic Christopher E. Shaw explains, viewed "the cosmos as an integrated and organic unity striving teleologically toward an as-yet undiscovered end state."[152] Hall's characterization of Martin's "strange love of trees and primitive forests" renders him a suitable candidate for the new society where, as Shaw notes, "rocks and stones and trees, plants and insects and animals all had their individuality and were made of the same mind stuff, the underlying vivifying principle of the universe."[153]

Initially, the relationship between the two "brothers," Stephen and Martin, is tinged with the homoeroticism of comrade-love in the mode of Carpenter, who in turn was inspired by Walt Whitman: Stephen "had felt so contented, so natural with [Martin]; but that was because they had been like two men, companions" (100). Stephen's interactions with this "queer, sensitive fellow" become inextricably bound up with her keen longing "for the companionship of men, for their friendship, their good-will, their toleration" (94, 96). Martin, who discovers in Stephen "the perfect companion," addresses Stephen "as one man will speak to another"—Stephen in turn asks "thoughtful questions . . . such as one man will ask of another" (94, 92, 93). When riding and hunting, "these two would keep close to each other" (94). The sexual frisson of this relationship is not that of man and woman but of comrade-love "ten times superior to the intimacy that men and women normally share"; the sort described in an 1894 essay by Charles Kains Jackson: "of the river, of the hunt and the moor . . . and the exhilaration of the early morning swim."[154] Stephen marvels that she has become "fond of Martin—isn't that queer after only a couple of months of friendship?" (96). For a short time in the narrative Hall explores the potential for such a relationship between an "extreme" female intermediate (Stephen) and a "normal" male intermediate (Martin); however, on a day in early spring, the fecundity of new buds and blossoms arouses another side of Martin, who turns away from what Carpenter termed the homogenic attachment between men: "Martin looked into his heart and saw Stephen—saw her suddenly there as a woman" (97). Stephen's response of "outrage" and horror over Martin's advances stems less from her realization that Martin recognizes her "as a woman" than that he is attracted to her as a fellow "normal" intermediate (98).

Martin is indisputably "different somehow" until, near the end of the novel, Hall transforms him into a "thoroughly normal" man to allow Stephen to execute the final act of engineering the production of a "new humanity" by pushing Mary toward eventual procreation with Martin (96, 417). All the sexual ambiguity that hovered throughout the narrative, suggesting that Martin was somewhere on the borders of the intermediate, evaporates; Martin's masculinity hardens in his competitive struggle with Stephen for Mary, and he becomes unequivocally (and unrecognizably) heterosexualized. In a dream-vision near the end of the narrative, Hall writes:

> Suddenly Martin appeared to Stephen as a creature endowed with incalculable bounty. . . . In a kind of dream she perceived these things. In a dream she now moved and had her being; scarcely conscious of whither this dream would lead. . . . And this dream of hers was immensely compelling. (430)

Such unusually poetic language in an otherwise quite conventional realist novel sets this strange passage apart, especially because Hall has already informed her reader that dreaming holds the "only truth" (331). Against the metaphysical discourse of the seer Carpenter, the passage intriguingly foreshadows how an "extreme" intermediate might engender the new race and at the same time subversively transform Carpenter's ideal union. For Carpenter, "the real alliance to be forged was between homosexual men and heterosexual women who most closely approximated the type of sexuality which a free society needed and which evolution favored."[155] Hall, on the other hand, proposes an alternative configuration between a recently heterosexualized man and a "normal" intermediate woman at an unspecified moment in the future, beyond the boundaries of the narrative. In this way Hall's novel envisions the eugenist's worst nightmare: the alarming and threatening prospect of a tainted gene pool. The Swiss sexologist August Forel, for example, issued dire warnings to physicians to desist from recommending marriage as a suitable "cure" for inversion, calling the tactic "a social monstrosity"—the last thing society needed was "to breed young inverts!"[156] Is it any wonder that Hall countered such pronouncements with a "sexology" or a "eugenics" of her own?

The probable union between Mary and Martin marks for Stephen an exchange of barrenness for fruitfulness (Stephen's "barren womb became fruitful"), even as Stephen's loss of Mary fetishizes sacrifice and suffering— the extreme invert's superior intuition is "so ruthless, so poignant, so accurate, so deadly, as to be in the nature of an added scourge."[157] Stephen stoically embraces her task with all the dedicated fervor of a masochistic saint ("and the pain would be sweetness" [300]), although she, like Mary, has little choice in the matter: "predestined; she could not have acted otherwise. . . . Stephen walked on the brink of her fate . . . in obedience to the mighty but unseen" (430). The rhythmic repetition in the subsequent series of (Blakean) phrases, in which Stephen terminates her relationship with Mary, simulates the painful contractions of a birthing process with a difference ("with each fresh blow . . . with every fibre . . . with every memory . . . with every passion . . . with every instinct").[158] In this depiction of Stephen's pain Hall extends Olive Schreiner's "parable" of the suffering woman of genius to the extreme intermediate woman:

> Once God Almighty said: "I will produce a self-working automatic machine for enduring suffering, . . . capable of the largest amount of suffering in a given space"; and he made woman. But he wasn't satisfied that he [had] reached the highest point of perfection; so he made a man of genius. He was [not] satisfied yet. So he combined the two— and made a woman of genius—and he was satisfied![159]

The final paragraphs of the novel blend Carpenter's mysticism with Christian imagery to situate Stephen at the top of the evolutionary scale as, in the phrase of Schreiner, "a self-working automatic machine for enduring suffering": "Rockets of pain, burning rockets of pain—their pain, her pain, all welded together into one great consuming agony" (437). Appointed by her literary creator to bear the suffering of the other millions like her, the exemplary Stephen accepts the "appalling burden" to become the designated spokeswoman of her race.

The first critic to assess the interesting ways in which sexology *and* evolutionary theory converge in Hall's work is Claire Buck who examines, among other works, Hall's 1926 short story, "Miss Ogilvy Finds Herself." Buck speculates that if the primitive man "on the verge of extinction" in Miss Ogilvy's dream "is Miss Ogilvy's earlier self, what implications does the story have for a vision of a future in which the invert can be accepted by her society as a full sexual being? What kind of forerunner is he? In part, the answer lies . . . within evolutionary theory and in its intersections with sexology."[160] More specifically, I would argue, the answer lies in *Carpenter*'s evolutionary theory, what Weeks terms "moral evolutionism": "a concept of internal growth, of spiritual development towards a higher form of consciousness. . . . There was in man, even under the toils of civilization, the growth of a higher awareness, of love and comradeship. In this Carpenter saw the hope for a better society which would transcend 'civilization.' "[161] Influenced by Hegel, Marx, and Rousseau, Carpenter traces evolutionary progress from the primitive to the modern industrial age to the third and final destiny of the universe. The primitive stage offers an appealing unity of man and nature ("the natural life of the people was in a kind of unconscious way artistic and beautiful. . . . Nature and man lived friendly together"), but is only the first step to what Carpenter termed the "third state," that is, "where every object . . . is united to every other object . . . by infinite threads of relation."[162] Martin embodies both the positive and negative aspects of the *primitive* stage in that he is wholly interconnected with nature ("this young man loved trees with a primitive instinct, with a strange and inexplicable devotion"), yet he finds social interaction and interpersonal relations exceedingly difficult ("had you asked Martin . . . to explain why it was that he accepted [Stephen] . . . he would surely have been unable to tell you").[163] Intermediates such as Mary and Stephen reside in what Carpenter described as the "strange condition of illusion which belongs to the second stage," among the "exiles from the Eden-garden."[164] Of the two, Mary, a normal Uranian, most closely resembles Carpenter's ideal; the extreme types, however, were ascribed a lesser function: they "are of the greatest value from a scientific point of view as marking tendencies and limits of development in certain directions." It would, however, "be a serious mistake to look upon them as representative cases of the whole phases of human evolution."[165] Hall's first tactic—to advocate an active and significant role for the "normal" female in the propagation of the new humanity—suggests a slight modification of Carpenter, but her designation of the extreme homogenic female as the facilitator in the progression to a "third state of consciousness" signals a complete ideological break: Stephen stands apart from—and above—normal intermediates as a new-age savior who demands on behalf of the entire race "the right to our existence!"[166]

In Carpenter's utopian evolutionary theory Hall discovers how the lesbian might become, as Felski claims for the New Woman, "a resonant symbol of emancipation, whose modernity signaled not an endorsement of an existing present but rather a bold imagining of an alternative future."[167] Hall rewrites Carpenter's evolutionary theory to claim such a "bold imagining" for her extreme type: "It certainly does not seem impossible to suppose that as the ordinary love has a special function in the propagation of the race, so the other has its special function in social and heroic work, and in the generation—not of bodily children—but of those children of the mind, the philosophical conceptions and ideals which transform our lives and those of society."[168] In severing the cord that binds the extreme to the normal intermediate, and in launching Mary toward Martin's "incalculable bounty," Stephen surpasses "ordinary love" to assume the more heroic and awesome task of enabler. In this respect, Stephen's rise is at Martin's expense: the virility or "bounty" of the heterosexual male is, if not a backward slide in Hall's evolutionary schema, less central. Stephen's productivity is thus twofold: she is the force underlying the reproduction of the new humanity and, as a writer, she creates "those children of the mind" with the potential to "transform our lives and those of society."

In the novels of Bryher, Allatini, and Hall we observe a daring new direction in twentieth-century lesbian literary representation because in their queer protagonists—Nancy, Antoinette, and Stephen—we find not tragic or pathetic invert-victims debilitated by self-loathing, frogmarched into heterosexual marriage, or doomed to a lonely outcast existence (unless rescued by an early death) but an exceptional group of women in possession of an array of rare and extraordinary gifts: color-hearing, a "healthy-minded and joyous" self-acceptance of sexual difference, high intellect, artistic sensitivity, intuition, or the fabulous vantage point of those lucky few who stand between the sexes.[169] None of these women has *achieved* such greatness— in accordance with the "dictates of [their] inmost nature," their superior sensibilities and temperaments are congenital, the result of a quirk of nature and therefore ineradicable (69). These qualities distinguish intermediates from ordinary folk and single them out for a major part in the evolutionary process. Bryher, Allatini, and Hall are not the inventors of these ideas, but neither are they the slavish disciples of others. The pioneers of a new lesbian literary tradition, these women's narratives represent a strategic negotiation of the most radical writings on sexuality of their time by men who were criticized and even ridiculed by a hegemonic medical establishment. While Bryher appropriated as a metaphor for inversion Ellis's terms of comparison, Allatini snatched for the female intermediate traits Carpenter reserved for the male. Hall's novel too—idealistic, hopeful, and, it must be said, supremely arrogant—is not a literary realization of either Ellis or Carpenter but a fusion of various sexologies, myths, utopian evolutionary theory, and religion. In a twisted and almost encyclopedic account of same-sex desire between women and of the lesbian's pivotal role in society's future, Hall probes, as part of a political project, some of the contradictions within sexology, even as she appropriates its scientific status. All these writers sought in some way "the domestication of scientific, medical knowledge, placing it on the agenda of household conversation in an unprecedented way," because they recognized, as Hall puts it in *The Well*, that most people would "not read medical books; what do such people care for the doctors? And what doctor can know the entire truth? . . . The doctors cannot make the ignorant think, cannot hope to bring home the sufferings of millions; only one of ourselves can some day do that."[170]

For these lesbian novelists the literature on female inversion and Uranism was not an outmoded pseudoscience but a dynamic and ground-breaking body of knowledge, brimming with useful "scientific" information, "medical" explanations, actual case histories, and philosophical rationales. The material was eagerly sought out and examined thoroughly, not with an eye toward replication but toward refashioning, sometimes beyond recognition. The treatises of sexual science emboldened these women novelists to demand and expect the impossible: acceptance, and indeed, ascendance. In this chapter I have sought to contextualize sexology and recuperate more fully something of its diversity and daring in its early phase. We cannot hope to understand sexology's cultural status and appeal among writers in this period if we dismiss its construction of inversion or homosexuality, minimize its influence and accomplishments, or simply label it antifeminist, misogynist, or a "worm in the bud." We need also to expand our critical framework to include other influential writings on sexuality and to ascertain how sexology intersects with other key theories, such as evolution. Sexologists, for better or worse, shaped our discourse on sexuality through coining neologisms and inventing categories, and lesbian writers in turn subversively reshaped that sexology to create, out of the very texts that had marginalized and even excluded them, innovative reconceptualizations of the lesbian subject and her place within modernity.

Six

Portrait of a Sapphist?
Fixing the Frame of Reference

I

IN A 1926 *Punch* cartoon, entitled ironically "The New Feminine Photography," an austerely Eton-cropped flapper, with cigarette in hand, elbow on knee, and an aggressive attitude to match, poses before the camera of a nonplussed elderly studio photographer (figure 20).[1] With legs spread wide apart in an arrogant and most unladylike manner, the slim sitter with fine angular facial features, wearing a short, slinky frock and high-heeled shoes, leans in toward the lens and demands bluntly: "I don't want one of those sloppy pictures. Just get the character and let it go at that." The joke from *Punch*'s point of view, of course, is that no one—and in particular, an older gentleman—would ever accuse this sitter of looking "sloppy," or sentimental. The bewildered photographer is obviously daunted by the complicated task of reconciling the apparent incongruities of her appearance. True enough, for some viewers she possesses boyish good looks, but her severe haircut and determined stance present a puzzling combination of masculinity and femininity, what the caption wryly calls the "new feminine" or, from *Punch*'s perspective, distinctly *un*feminine. Above all, the sitter, although technically the object of the photographic gaze, assumes a proactive role in the creative process and refuses passivity. Her insistence that the photographer capture only her "character and let it go at that" further complicates the portraitist's dilemma, since, as critic Graham Clarke reminds us, "the portrait photograph exists within a series of seemingly endless paradoxes. Indeed, as the formal representation of a face or body it is, by its very nature, enigmatic. And part of this enigma is embedded in the nature of identity as itself ambiguous, for the portrait advertises an individual who endlessly eludes the single, static and fixed frame of a public portrait."[2] What the *Punch* cartoon encapsulates so effectively are these "endless paradoxes" of a visual form that, while in possession of what Roland Barthes calls "evidential force," must also contend with the multiple demands and expectations of the photographer, the sitter, and the viewer.[3] In this chapter I examine how this one particular visual medium—photography, and especially portraiture—became, for women with the resources, acumen, and know-how, the premier site for self-promotion; that is, until late 1928, when the "enigmatic . . . nature of identity" became fixed in a single frame.

In the 1920s Radclyffe Hall, Una Troubridge, Mary Allen, and the artist Gluck, among others, strategically harnessed photographic imaging—as portraiture, documentary evidence, or narrative sequence—for the purposes of public relations to further any number of agendas, personal, professional, or political. For example, Hall and Gluck were prominently in the vanguard of fashioning their own self-images to enhance their aura of glamour and success, while Allen, as former commandant of the Women Police Service, staged, along with her WPS cohorts, daring illustrations of their capabilities. Yet when some historians scrutinize these same photographs, this range of motivations quickly narrows, as the images are reduced to representations—pure and simple—of mannish lesbians. For instance, when historian Emily Hamer surveys these images, she describes Hall and Troubridge as "both butchish"; similarly, early portraits of WPS leaders "appear equally butch."[4] Esther Newton too, one of the first to invite contemporary readers to take a second look at such photos, regards them as mirrors reflecting the mannish lesbian of the past: "You see [a figure] in old photographs or paintings with legs solidly planted, wearing a top hat and a man's jacket, staring defiantly out of the frame, her hair slicked back or clipped over her ears."[5] Writing almost a decade later, critic Mandy Merck correctly challenges what she terms Newton's "ontology of the photograph," which, by presuming a "relation to a 'real' referent," is based on the problematic assumption that "the photograph . . . [constitutes] visible proof of the subject's existence."[6] Merck urges caution in approaching the photographic portrait as a transparent record of "lesbian identities," and her reminder that the photograph is at once "the simultaneous assertion and deconstruction of identity" complicates Newton's reading of the image's "face value" (100). Even so, all these examples of the critical analysis of lesbian visibility and identities in the early twentieth century inevitably focus on what we—as contemporary viewers—see when we look at such photographs. And, as a result, contextual specificity—whether in terms of history or visuality—is conspicuous by its absence.

The fact that some photographs commissioned and circulated by women of this era now seem among the most extraordinary and provocative images of mannish lesbians suggests that our viewing contexts have shifted and perhaps narrowed in ways we have yet to understand fully. When we invoke current standards to assess how women of this era—in terms of manner of dress, stance, and expression—appear as exemplary specimens of mannish lesbians or "butches" of the no-nonsense variety, not only do we close down the opportunity for competing readings of these images, we also enter a realm rarely mentioned before 1928 in public discourse, let alone by the photographic subjects, photographers, or critical commentators of the time. As cultural critic Judith Halberstam aptly observes, "neither . . . John (Radclyffe) Hall, Colonel Barker, Robert (Mary) Allen, the women in Havelock Ellis's case histories nor their lovers would have identified as lesbians."[7] When contemporary critics "describe them unproblematically as such . . . [there is a tendency to] stabilize contemporary definitions of lesbianism." As with the sexual categorizing of some women earlier in the century, how tempting it is for the "photographic audience" to reconstruct "the image by an act of imagination which is stimulated by the photograph."[8] In reading Hall or Allen as "butch," Hamer's imagination—like Newton's—has obviously been stimulated by an event in late 1928 that changed resolutely and irrevocably the way in which such images of "mannish lesbians" have been perceived. My aim here is to complicate our reading of these women's self-presentation, not to argue that the mannish lesbian was absent from culture at this time, nor to assert that the mannish lesbian was not intelligible to some viewers as such, but to suggest that such images were far more multivalent in cultural consciousness than we have hitherto imagined. What was happening before that moment when the frame of reference was fixed so indelibly is the subject of this chapter, which attempts to recuperate the context of the handling of visuality generally and, in particular, the role of the portrait in lesbian self-imaging, since: "more than any other kind of photographic image, the portrait achieves meaning through the context in which it is seen."[9]

I begin with an examination of the ways in which photography became an essential component of the WPS leadership's propaganda apparatus in an attempt to ensure their long-term survival in the 1910s and early 1920s. Through the use of official portraits and narrative sequences the WPS leaders, and Allen in particular, painstakingly perfected an imaging strategy to reinforce their campaign for official recognition by the London Metropolitan Police. I then look at how Hall and Gluck positioned themselves among the avant-garde of fashion and modern life through visual representation to secure their status as women writers and artists who mattered. Self-imaging, among the financially comfortable and artistically successful, was an intensely serious and empowering affair, involving careful negotiations between the photographer and the sitter who activated and animated the creative process. In the 1920s studio portraiture became the preeminent site of self-imaging for the status-hungry upper-middle classes, and women such as Hall and Gluck, who could well afford to engage the most sought-after photographers in the profession, regularly commissioned work to mark an occasion such as the completion of a novel or a successful gallery exhibition. The subsequent circulation of the photographic portraits in the press assisted Hall and Gluck in their quest for greater artistic fame and even contributed, in varying degrees, to their becoming cultural icons, but not without significant risk, as we will see. In the final section I discuss the ways in which the cost of fame ultimately culminates in a loss of the frame. As the image filters into public culture, its message, formerly at the service of the photographic subject, is resituated in a different context, one that effectively steals away the earlier frame. The portrait thus becomes a "frame" entrapping the would-be framers, so that, by the late twenties and early thirties, due in great part to the intense media exposure of Hall, one particular "look" we now recognize as "butch" would begin to evolve in the aftermath of the obscenity trial and become inextricably connected with an entity known as the mannish lesbian—a cultural icon fixed for decades in the public consciousness and perpetuated by contemporary cultural critics.

II

POLICEWOMEN, MARY ALLEN strenuously contended, were at least the equal of policemen. To substantiate this claim, none of her accounts of the WPS was complete without photographic illustration, whether in formal portraits of individuals and groups or in what might be termed "narrative sequences," that is, depictions of women actively engaged in aspects of policing. The visual record of WPS activities, and the group's later incarnation as the Women's Auxiliary Service, is therefore extensive: first, in the numerous photographs that appear in all the WPS Annual Reports (from 1915 to 1919) and again in the reports of the WAS (1920–21); second, in the two histories Allen published (*The Pioneer Policewoman* [1925] and *Lady in Blue* [1936]); and finally, in *The Policewoman's Review*, which Allen launched in May 1927. According to historian Joan Lock, this latter publication "was quite an ambitious creation, printed on glossy paper and liberally sprinkled with well-produced photographs of serving women police."[10] By scrutinizing several of their publications, this section focuses on how the WPS photographic project illustrated their purpose and accomplishments.

Allen's acute understanding of how photography could present the mission and activities of the early women's policing organization almost certainly grew out of her experiences as a militant suffragette in the Women's Social and Political Union, a background she shared with her WPS colleague, Superintendent Isobel "Toto" Goldingham. The women's suffrage campaign made excellent use of diverse visual materials: "posters, postcards and large-scale public spectacle," as art historian Lisa Tickner writes.[11] Tickner credits the women's suffrage movement with being the first to discern how "to exploit new publicity methods" as well as "to develop a pictorial rhetoric which drew on, but also challenged, the terms of bourgeois Edwardian femininity" (xii). Militant suffragism gave women such as Allen and Goldingham their first experience in learning the necessary skills and methods to convey political ideology in the public arena, quite literally, taking their message to the streets. In *Lady in Blue*, for example, Allen acknowledges the ways in which her early training in political activism contributed to her promotional techniques for the WPS: "For just as it is an axiom that the ex-poacher makes the finest gamekeeper in the world, so it is true that Suffragette experience has been invaluable to me over and over again in my police work."[12] A photo entitled "Miss Allen Working as a Suffragette," depicting the young recruit ready to hit the streets with her satchel of copies of the organization's newspaper, *Votes for Women*, presents the earliest indication of the future leader's insight into the potential relationship between photography and politics.

WPS photography, like suffrage imagery, "is political in the very specific sense that it was designed to meet the needs of a particular campaign, with the aim of bringing about short-term political and, in consequence, long-term social change."[13] For example, some WPS photographs arrange WPS officers and constables in configurations suggesting an equivalency with their male counterparts, as seen in a 1918 WPS *Report* photo that depicts two WPS women speaking with a policeman. The simple caption, "Three Sergeants," works in tandem with the image to gloss over the political reality: the organization in which the women in the photograph belonged had only very limited powers, while the Met sergeant was in full possession of the power to execute the law. The WPS image and caption also imply collegiality and equality, conditions that were in fact entirely absent, as the Met was already moving assiduously toward the elimination of independent female policing groups such as the WPS. This attempt to visually connect the WPS with the power of the official police is seen again in a photo of the diminutive Damer Dawson, who converses with an unidentified male officer whose large and towering figure fills the entire frame. Although physically dwarfed by the male figure, Damer Dawson, in her debonair uniform, not only holds her own but, in gazing straight ahead, forces the male officer to turn and lower his head to meet her eyes; again, the impression is of equals deep in discussion. Another portrait of this formidable police officer, tucked into the pages of *The Pioneer Policewoman*, projects an image of a wholly professional woman, with qualities of toughness and resolve. Despite her stern austerity, however, Damer Dawson embodies dash and panache. Nothing else in the photograph distracts, mitigates, or softens: the viewer's attention focuses squarely on this woman in uniform. Damer Dawson, the viewer must conclude, knows what she is about. Several other photos from *Lady in Blue* show Allen and Tagart (the latter often unidentified) with foreign police chiefs in an array of exotic countries, from atop camels at the Egyptian pyramids to a remote outpost in Finland.[14] Time and again, Allen mastered the art of exploiting images capable of lending prestige and respectability to her cause, as seen in a press photo of Allen standing beside Lady Astor, M.P.[15]

The attempt to underscore their professionalism is further seen in the official portraits of the top WPS leadership—the so-called "Council of Three," comprising Damer Dawson, Allen, and Goldingham—who, in poses reminiscent of the officer as gentleman, convey an entirely new ideal of female masculinity. Such portraits provided skeptics and supporters alike, including government agencies, with ample documentation of what these new women would look like and thus represented a breathtaking view of a future in which autonomous women, with the power of the law, would perform a hitherto unimaginable role. Goldingham takes the performance the furthest in her formal portraits: one shows her with arms akimbo, while in another she breaks a taboo for women by slipping her hand halfway into her uniform pocket, thereby appropriating a gesture reserved for men. Goldingham's portrait also violates generic conventions, since "army commanders *are* usually stiffly erect," a posture emulated in one of Damer Dawson and Allen (figure 2).[16] In striving to emulate the look of the officer-gentleman, photos of WPS leaders exude a class-based elitism that firmly separates them as a breed apart, both from the other ranks of their organization and from female officers of similar organizations. In addition to a certain stylish elegance, the official portraits of the Council of Three demonstrate a firm command over the processes of image-*fashioning*, an aspect less evident in portraits of leaders of similar groups. The distinctiveness of the WPS leaders' self-invention, and their talent in assisting the photographer to "get" their character, are especially noticeable when their photographs are juxtaposed with representations of prominent, and sometimes dowdy, women officers of rival policing organizations. Reading the full-body double portrait of Damer

Dawson and Allen (figure 2) against these other portraits reveals significant differences not just in the uniform—although it is clear that the latter wear skirts, while the former disguise what is underneath their greatcoats—but also in the way the WPS women confront the camera. For example, a portrait of Superintendent Sofia Stanley of the Metropolitan Women Police Patrols shows a woman in a proud display of her status and uniform, but the overall effect is far softer and gentler, her stance less bold (figure 3). By comparison, Damer Dawson and Allen, in terms of posture, expression, uniform, and accoutrements, appear in every way as classic, suave officer-gentlemen. In their attempt to shape a new Modern femininity, daringly inflected with masculinity, these WPS portraits offer a partial glimpse into the ways in which masculine power could be appropriated.

Like suffrage imagery, the WPS images were "inextricably bound up in countering other, sometimes heterogeneous but always more dominant and conventional, representations of middle-class femininity."[17] The problem in both movements—suffrage and women policing—was how to reconcile the incongruity of a woman in possession of traditional male power, since "womanliness" itself "was in some respects a less coherent category in the twentieth century than it had been in the 1860s" (226). Yet, although the chasm between material reality and the stereotypical and unrealistic notion of "womanliness" was widening (a destabilization that stemmed in part from the suffragette negotiations with femininity), it did not interfere with the category's continuing cultural significance: "in the symbolic register the meanings accruing to femininity were the embodiment of women's physical possibilities alone—motherhood, nurture, sexual pleasure and comfort." Moreover, this cultural ideal was "encoded . . . through details of physique, expression, costume and accessory." The WPS's predicament was how, in a highly charged political atmosphere, to retain femininity in their bid for masculine power. The challenge such radically undomesticated leaders faced was to align themselves somehow with the maternal role—a seemingly impossible task, in light of the austerity of their uniform, not to mention the stiff and uncompromisingly unfeminine rigidity of body posture seen in the portraits of individuals.

One solution was to rework the image of femininity in public space through propaganda pieces, such as the representation of two officers dealing with a lost child. In the first photograph of a sequence of two (not shown), Allen sits astride her motorcycle in full dress uniform, accompanied by a giddy Damer Dawson, who scrambles out of the sidecar to "rescue" a small child sitting on the curbstone. In the second image (figure 21), depicting a happy resolution for the lost child, Allen is again in full control of the motorcycle, and as she heads off to what is presumably a suitable destination for the youngster, Damer Dawson gazes tenderly at the bewildered foundling, who alone confronts the camera. Unlike the formal portrait (figure 2), in which the direct gaze toward the camera works to efface facial contours, the staged "rescue" shot highlights the women's cheekbones and thus heightens the viewer's awareness of their femininity. This image was apparently designed to reassure the viewer of the child's safety in the hands of its rescuers. Yet if, as Lock claims, the "four motor cycles (three with side-cars) . . . appear to have been largely for the use of the senior officers, mainly for inspection purposes," the "rescue" contrived in the narrative sequence would have been the exception rather than the norm. In that case, why was it given such a prominent place in WPS publicity apparatus?[18] Like some of the other visual images the group coordinated, this sequence—helpless child plucked from danger by two WPS officers and whisked away to a place of refuge—ostensibly projects the message necessary to convince a potentially skeptical viewer of the organization's value, resourcefulness, and special purpose in society. As Allen explains in the text, a young child "would *naturally* run either to its own mother or to another woman for protection. Its actions would not be reasoned, as in the case of an older person, but instinctive. It is questionable whether the intervention of a policeman would not add to a child's confusion and terror."[19] While contemporary viewers might question whether a young child would recognize in such formidable officers of hypermasculine attire any traces of the maternal, Allen's claim on behalf of all women's innate biological capacity for assurance and nurturing care is clearly an attempt to argue for the superiority of policewomen over men: the women's very femaleness allows them to perform certain duties better than their male colleagues.[20]

This attempt at propaganda demonstrates that Allen understood that "what lies 'behind' . . . the image is not reality—the referent—but reference: a subtle web of discourse through which realism is enmeshed in a complex fabric of notions, representations, images, attitudes, gestures and modes of action."[21] This is best seen in a group photograph, included in *The Pioneer Policewoman* with the caption, "Babies at the Damer Dawson Memorial Home with Inspector Saunders" (figure 22). A dozen babies sit at the feet of a lone inspector, a gentle and matronly type rather than a stern officer, who sits calmly sandwiched between nurses at the home. Here the policewoman does not appear incongruous with her surroundings, but then her rank is not equivalent with the WPS officers; her kindliness and slightly hunched-forward posture allow her to settle in with the group rather than stand apart. Portrayed not as a figure of power, her appearance fits more smoothly and harmoniously with the maternal. The setting, a cozy room at the Damer Dawson Memorial Home, exudes a domestic if institutional feel and softens the effect of the woman in inspector's cap and uniform. The tight framing of the image, with its sea of babies literally crammed into the bottom of the photograph, focuses the viewer's attention on the four adult women. The most maternal of the group, her veil gracefully billowing, stands upright on the left and holds a baby on her hip, while the remaining adults crouch successively lower, until finally meeting the babies at their own floor level; the nurse furthest on the right bends over most demurely in her effort to hold up a child for the camera. The group is framed with images associated with warmth and domesticity: the children lie on a rug on the floor and, behind the heads of the adults, one glimpses a large stone fireplace. This image represents the WPS's attempt to break new ground ideologically in advocating a new vision of policing itself, one that inextricably connects social control and social welfare. Hovering in the background, behind the group of babies and their attenders, is a fuzzy image of the official portrait of the home's founder, the late Damer Dawson. Such WPS images sought to meld maternal and masculine protection in a newly invented cultural ideal and thus cleverly advocate their own version of women police by claiming a function exclusive to their gender.

In the hands of the WPS, photography became the mechanism to insert into the social imaginary the idea that women could make a difference; however, photography may have also become a utopic space for imaginative experimentations with gender and self-imaging. An incident (mentioned briefly in chapter 3) involving the production of another propaganda piece, specifically a photographic sequence demonstrating how women police might remove a troublesome drunk from a public street, highlights the dangers of using such manipulated images (figures 23 and 24). In the first photograph, reproduced in one WPS report with the caption "Women Police Picking up a 'Case,'" Allen and Damer Dawson shift a large and ungainly drunk toward the motorcycle sidecar. Allen barely stifles an uncharacteristically broad smile and exposes the constructedness of the jocular incident, more reminiscent of a lark than a serious police incident. In the second photograph ("Women Police Motorcyclists Taking Charge of a 'Case'"), the drunk has been successfully bundled into the sidecar and slumps toward Damer Dawson, who offers support with a firm embrace. At first glance, the two photographic sequences—the child rescue and the incident with the drunk—seem remarkably similar: both present resourceful women seizing the initiative to clear the streets of social problems and take a "case" into protective custody, and both feature the same motorcycle and sidecar, a vehicle embodying the essence of modern urban mobility. In command of the streets and the machine these WPS women appear to patrol the streets with expediency and respond quickly to any unusual circumstance. In effect, the photographic images become the battleground where street skirmishes offer the women an opportunity to prove themselves, yet at the same time, in the act of performing public surveillance, the women officers had—evidentially—themselves become the surveyed.

The WPS's physical handling of the incident (taking charge of a drunken man) was, as with their other photographs, calculated to demonstrate the range of their capabilities in the streets of cities and towns across Britain, but the photograph of this staged action worked against them when it was presented in evidence by the former Commissioner of Police of the Metropolis, General Sir Nevil Macready, to the Baird Committee (the committee formed to consider the future employment of women in policing) in February 1920.[22] Macready produced the photograph as *evidence* to support his claim that the WPS uniform was creating havoc by confusing ordinary citizens who could not tell the difference between official and unofficial policing groups. In this way he transformed the photograph from a propaganda device into what had become one of the most valuable tools of police work to have developed in the nineteenth century.[23] Macready's deployment of the photograph as a different kind of evidence thus challenged the publicity apparatus of the WPS, whose own deployment of photographs had hardly constituted "a direct transcription of the real" (98). As the WPS would soon discover, "photographs are easy targets for scandal because they are what semioticians term 'open signs.' They masquerade as compelling evidence of the real, while obscuring their status as (always already) mediated representations."[24]

During his testimony Macready told the committee, "A man and his wife in Edinburgh, who had a missing son, wrote officially to me and said would I kindly ask my police whether this [the drunk being arrested] was their son. There is a picture of the supposed son. . . . It is not much, but it shows you can mistake the [WPS] uniform [for that of the MWPP]."[25] In Macready's eyes two distinct forms of perversion were on view in the photograph. The first concerns the problematic relationship of the "original" and the "copy." Macready claimed that, because Allen and Damer Dawson's uniform "could reasonably be mistaken for that of the Metropolitan police women," an organization Macready had founded, the public (as represented by the letter he had received from the Edinburgh couple) was likely to mistake the bogus for the authentic. Therefore the WPS uniform was deemed a perversion of *his* original. While Macready refrained from baldly accusing WPS members of wearing uniforms so utterly masculine as to render them masqueraders of police*men*, almost as an afterthought, he neatly slipped into his extended testimony an even more damning accusation: "The 'son' is a woman dressed up as a man." If, to borrow art historian John Tagg's rationale, embedded in the photograph, is "a whole hidden corpus of knowledge, a social knowledge, that is called upon through the mechanism of connotation," Macready's photographic evidence was very damaging indeed to the WPS's reputation.[26] Presuming the women guilty by association, Macready's well-timed, terse statement allowed him to successfully smear the organization as a whole through the appropriation of their own self-imaging. In catching the WPS off guard, Macready revealed the tenuousness of the image-maker's control over the imaging process itself.

In their own testimony several days later, Damer Dawson and Allen ignored the charge that the "man" in the photograph was a cross-dressed woman and instead addressed only the questions relating to the uniform. It was a much simpler affair to aver that they had designed the uniform themselves, and thus could not be accused of wearing a copy of an original, than to unravel the ways in which their construction of female masculinity might itself be seen as a copy of an original. The WPS later claimed they did not seize the opportunity to defend themselves against the charge during the Baird hearings because the "chief officers of the service were in ignorance that such a statement had been made, so could not repudiate it."[27] This seems improbable, however, since the group must have closely monitored government hearings that had such a direct impact on the future of their organization. Whether the WPS leaders were too badly shaken by the cross-dressing charge, or wisely recognized that even a vigorous denial could harm their cause, they postponed confronting Macready's comment. Such an accusation, however, could not be overlooked indefinitely, as Macready's testimony had "been given a good deal of publicity." Choosing their own time and a less public place, the women's group stated matter-of-factly, in their own annual report: "The young man in question is a respected member of a well-known company . . . [willing] in case it should be necessary to testify on oath as to his identity." Fortunately for the WPS, it never became necessary to expose the identity of the young "male" actor, since the individual in question uncannily resembles the WPS's Superintendent Goldingham, whose attempt at impersonating a street drunk may account for Allen's bemused expression in the photograph. The leadership may have reasoned that with such high stakes—the continued existence of their organization and possible official recognition—it was a far better option to fabricate rather than confess.

Still, the question remains, why was Macready so cocksure that the photograph in question did indeed represent a woman cross-dressed as a man?

The emphatic matter-of-factness in his interpretation of the photograph certainly surprised the WPS; their report explained that Macready said, "quite definitely: 'The "son" is a woman dressed up as a man.' "[28] The unseemly prospect of such women holding the power to arrest a drunk was, for Macready, distasteful in the extreme and perhaps accounts for his motive, if not his certainty in leveling such a charge. In a letter to the Home Office, Macready wrote, "I do not think—except once in a blue moon—you will have any snapshot in the illustrated Press of the drunken bargee locked in the arms of the Policewoman!"[29] His own policewomen (the MWPP) would not provide the print media with an arresting image of women legally empowered to manhandle men. While the WPS dismissed Macready's statement as "inaccurate," both sides were aware of its likely effect; such a charge could only bring the organization into "disrepute."

The WPS's ground-breaking effort in engineering self-imaging would seem, from a suffragist perspective, to have gone a step too far, in losing sight of a central tenet of the suffrage campaign that called for "the emancipation of feminine virtues into public life [as] a necessary condition of social reform."[30] Although some photographic images attempted just this, the aims of the WPS were ultimately largely antithetical to those of the suffrage campaign. Damer Dawson and Allen were less interested in inserting feminine virtues into the public sphere than in envisioning a gender within modernity in the form of a less conventionally sexually differentiated being. This accounts for their underlying rationale in constructing the official portraits of WPS leaders and in producing an emotionally charged—and culturally dangerous—image of a (police)woman holding power over a man, even though he was incapacitated and was, in truth, a "man." The WPS officers did not strive simply to replicate an authentic masculinity, however, for in their own portraits and in their deeds there remain a residual femininity. Their project is reminiscent of what critic Jacqueline Rose, in describing a different set of images in another context, refers to as the "curious desexualization, or rather the way that this absorbing of sexuality into the visual field closes off the question of sexual difference."[31] The WPS photographic project marks a break with both the feminist ideals of the suffrage campaign and the received notions of a gendered identity; it produced a female masculinity neither wholly conventionally female nor male, a visual prospect in my view as visionary as it was disruptive.

Because WPS imaging diverged so profoundly from conventional gender constructions, their project courted hostility from other quarters. By the early part of the 1920s the leadership of the Women Police Service recognized the power of the visual image in designing their promotional materials, but the women also learned that they were vulnerable in that such images, once in public circulation, were not subject to their control. Allen and her colleagues may have framed the shot, but once the collaborative process with the photographer ended and the narrative sequence was integrated into their own newsletters and reports, their visual images could be extracted and inserted into another context entirely. Surprised by Macready's introduction of the "drunk" photograph as evidence at an official hearing, the WPS learned a little too late that shifting contexts could be a source of trouble because "cameras can't see."[32] The subject, once photographed, loses command over the context and the frame. Consequently, the WPS's dynamic and, it must be said, protofascist images would have only limited currency as they lost control of their self-imaging and, finally, their bid for official recognition. The WPS may have failed in the wider public realm, as they failed in their short-term political aims for autonomy, but, as I discuss in following section, they may have inspired a small number of equally forceful lesbians, who in turn contributed to a modern English lesbian cultural sensibility. Allen may not have achieved her aspirations, enduring marginalization even by other female policing groups, but her sexual glamour and her daring deeds would be celebrated by Hall, Troubridge, and Naomi Jacob, among others.[33] Although the city streets became, for the WPS, the scene of their crime and the site of their political struggle, their photographic images were the embodiment of "the modern woman, whose presence in the street signals the dawn of modernity."[34]

III

IN THE AUTUMN of 1924, just as Hall's novel *The Unlit Lamp* was published, "Una felt John should be photographed at this critical stage in her career so the writer posed for the elegant Lafayette studio."[35] From the early 1920s on, Hall—and often Troubridge as well—visited the studios of professional portrait photographers to document significant occasions, such as the publication of a new novel or the awarding of a literary prize, constituting, in effect, a photo-biography of crucial junctures in Hall's career. Hall and Gluck actively sought out the most fashionable and famous studio photographers of their day, men such as E. O. Hoppé, Howard Coster, and the man known only as Douglas.[36] With each portraitist, these women entered into a kind of collaboration because, unlike other forms of photography such as the snapshot, the portrait is "never accidental, never something found by accident.

It is arranged, agreed upon. At the heart of the occasion is a contract between the subject and the photographer. . . . The subject *consciously* consents to the occasion."[37] Hall and Gluck entered eagerly into this process in the meticulous selection of striking outfits and objects to situate themselves, and their work, on the cutting edge of fashion, and even of fashionable living. In this section, I focus first on how both women managed the studio portrait as a mode of self-imaging, and how they colluded with the photographer in exploring—and evading—"the nature of identity."[38] I then consider how the photographic portrait—as "a commodity, a luxury, an adornment"—as well as the publicity shot taken by photographic agencies worked to maintain and enhance the public reputation of the celebrity writer and artist, respectively.[39] In this way I attempt to explore more fully the ways in which Hall and Gluck, each of whom were keenly aware of the multiple interpretive possibilities surrounding the image of the "masculine woman," exploited, even as they underestimated, the image's power, as the *Punch* cartoon puts it, to "get the character" (figure 20).

In 1926, to commemorate the publication of *Adam's Breed*, Hall "posed for her now statutory post-publication photograph, this time taken by the fashionable photographer Douglas" (figure 14).[40] The portrait of this supremely Modern woman highlights her cool austerity, with the high collar of the crisp white ruffled shirt and the smooth lines of her Spanish hat. This photograph, when juxtaposed with one Douglas took of Gluck, is quite revealing in terms of illustrating vividly the important differences in the constructions of female masculinity of these two key image-makers of artistic modernity. In Douglas's (undated) study of Gluck (figure 25), in many ways a depiction of the artist as a young man, the stunning planes of her smooth, angular face are lost, virtually swallowed up by her hat and the upturned collar of her coat, while the artist's eyes are partially obscured by the shadows cast by the brim of the hat. The only object breaking up the darkness that surrounds Gluck's face is a delicate boutonniere. Gluck stares intently at the camera and seems almost on the verge of a smile, but her gaze, which remains enigmatic, is not the keyhole to her inner nature. Her male clothing is what is most important about her and, while there is no question that Gluck's fashion choice is inextricably bound up with her artistic temperament, her mysteries remain resolutely mysterious. As I have demonstrated in chapter 4, there is a world of difference between Gluck's unique version of suave, debonair manhood—so obviously a woman dressing as a man, for a gentleman rarely posed formally in fedora and a large, bulky coat, accessories that cloak Gluck's body—and Hall's distinctive cultivation of the elegant, if sartorially severe masculine mode in women's fashion.[41]

Another influential society photographer was Hoppé, who concentrated, until the mid-1920s, on "members of the upper strata of society."[42] Evidently, "everybody who was anybody . . . visited his famous studio" in Kensington, as seen in the collection of luminaries featured in his short essay for *Royal Magazine*, entitled "As Others See Us."[43] These include actor Ellen Terry, playwright Bernard Shaw, political figure Benito Mussolini, cellist Madame Suggia, socialite and model Lady Hazel Lavery (wife of the painter Sir John Lavery), writers Thomas Hardy and John Galsworthy, and Gluck. In Hoppé, Gluck found a supportive benefactor—"the leading photographic portrait maker of the day"—willing to work on behalf of the young artist, by aligning her with a group whose social stature was already well established and thus achieve one major effect of the portrait photograph: "the inscription of social identity."[44] In return, Gluck offered the studio photographer her most impressive natural asset: a singularly remarkable face (figure 26). For Hoppé, the one common denominator among the extraordinary assortment of public figures he includes in his essay is their strong personal beauty, which was "dependent on personality and structural arrangement of features."[45] In Hoppé's view, the face alone exposes the sitter's inner nature and, consistent with his exclusive privileging of the somatic, his critical commentary also focuses intensely on facial features, as seen in his description of Ellen Terry's "sweet personality" that "is written in every line of her face," framed in this photograph only by a white turbanlike head scarf. A lifetime of playing other characters on the stage cannot prevent the photographer from capturing the essence of the actor, which is, as he puts it, a distillation or "emanation of all the parts she has played upon the stage of life." The other female subjects also properly manifest appropriate feminine qualities; the cellist's face, for instance, "can no more help showing in her looks her love for music than a mother can help showing her love for her child," while the "outward beauty" of Lady Lavery's face "is intensified and given soul and charm by the innate artistry of her nature" (111, 114).

The men's features, on the other hand, reflect their involvement in the world, even if that activity is thinking, as seen in the faces of Hardy or Galsworthy: "The wonderful head of Thomas Hardy shows how deeply he has probed into the problems of life," while "Galsworthy's fine face reveals his firm grip on the realities of life" (114). The portraits of Shaw and Mussolini even more aggressively unleash forces of humor or political power into the world. In his brief, albeit lofty, formalist analysis of each photograph, Hoppé argues that the face, every minute line and wrinkle, allows the viewer to glimpse the invisible, the subject's inner nature: "I see in each person something fascinating, something which I must try to seize upon and depict in my finished work. . . . I ask no better gift than to be able to discern and portray the *hidden* beauties of the mind latent in every human being" (112, 114, emphasis mine). In expressing a desire to "portray the hidden beauties of the mind," Hoppé reveals his investment in the "belief that reality is hidden. And, being hidden, is something to be unveiled. Whatever the camera records is a disclosure."[46] So, how does this photographer "see" Gluck? In a trenchant commentary on Gluck's appearance, Hoppé writes: "To look at the face of Gluck is to understand both her success as an artist and the fact that she dresses as a man. Originality, determination, strength of character and artistic insight are expressed in every line. . . . Gluck's facial contour indicates the qualities expressed in her paintings, combining force and decision with the sensitiveness of the visionary."[47] The exquisiteness of Gluck's face accounts both for the underlying rationale for her cross-dressing and for her success as an artist—period. Ignoring his own theory that the photographer "must necessarily be something of a psychologist and be able to seize in a few minutes the essential characteristics of his sitter," Hoppé neatly sidesteps any inferences such mannish dress on the body of a woman might provoke (eccentricity, artistic sensibilities, aberrance, fashionableness, or bohemianism) and instead concentrates primarily on Gluck's face (109). But by drawing attention to what her face expresses—"determination," "force," and "decision"—Hoppé inadvertently or unconsciously aligns her not with others of her sex but with those opposite. Inasmuch as the locus of significance is Gluck's face—one with manly qualities—her impulse to cross-dress is quite literally written on her body. Still, what is most visible to the viewer is not that which exposes something of the subject's inner nature or "beauties of the mind." For all of Hoppé's attempts to invest meaning in the face and to see in the somatic material evidence of what is otherwise hidden, the clothing remains a visible sign that cannot be hidden: Gluck "dresses as a man," a fact that clearly, on one level, disturbs him, since his essay does not mention clothing in connection with any of his other seven subjects.[48]

Gluck's penchant for cross-dressing, as I have mentioned in an earlier chapter, was likewise seen by the print media of the mid-1920s as a sign of artistic temperament or a bohemian lifestyle rather than as perversion or sexual deviance. In the absence of a public discourse of female sexual inversion, the *Evening News*, like Hoppé, associates Gluck's masculine accoutrements with her natural artistic talent: "The young woman artist . . . wears a man's soft hat and breeches, and sometimes smokes a pipe. That effort does not absorb all her talent. She paints landscapes in a curiously effective way."[49] Gluck's appearance—via the photographic image—put the young artist on the cultural map and, in conjunction with a few intriguing details to accentuate her eccentric lifestyle, achieved the necessary objective of enticing the press, as seen in one of the earliest commentaries: this "new and much-discussed artist . . . wears her hair brushed back from her forehead just like a boy, and when in Cornwall goes about in shorts."[50] Buried in the final line of this short article is a mention that some of her work is "very clever." Of course, such eccentricity in dress and manner of self-presentation was a sign of class privilege, but it is clear from these reviews that Gluck's contemporaries were reluctant to tease out or expose insinuations of what *seems* most apparent to us now in examining photographs of Gluck: that lesbianism is tantalizingly suggested in her bold performance of cross-dressing. The availability of other interpretive frameworks meant the reading public in the 1920s, exposed to several formulations of the "masculine woman" in the print media, could opt for alternative readings and thus see in photographs of Gluck precisely what she demanded of the studio portraitists: to get "the character and let it go at that."

If we insist on reading photographs of Gluck and others (see for example, figures 7 and 11) exclusively as "butch," or assume that these images conveyed to the general public the mannish lesbian, then we paint ourselves into a corner, for what then are we to conjecture about the 1925 photograph of a socialite such as Mrs. Tudor Wilkinson (figure 27) or the astonishing engagement portrait—published four months after the obscenity ban—of Miss Elizabeth Ponsonby (daughter of the first Baron Ponsonby of Shulbrede) and her fiancé (figure 28)?[51] Such women occupied the extreme edge of a fashion style called the severely masculine mode, popular among a group dubbed the Bright Young People, but it is highly improbable that they were all mannish lesbians or that anyone would have suspected as much. This was, after all, the era in which the "masculine woman" had become the subject of a 1926 popular song, "Masculine Women and Feminine Men," with its humorous, insistent refrain: "It's hard to tell them apart today." True enough, traditionalists may have been aghast at such portraits. In the eyes of fashion mavens, however, portraits of this kind, published frequently in fashion or society magazines, represented woman who embraced masculine clothing as a fashion statement; anyone who regarded such women as outlandish, aberrant, or disgustingly mannish, would have been dismissed as conventional, old-fashioned, and uninformed. At the same time, such photographs of masculine women may have indicated particular sexual proclivities to others, especially those familiar with "scientific" categories of sexuality or with one meaning of the phrase "masculine woman." The point is, however, that reading strategies were wholly dependent on context because there were multiple interpretive possibilities; Gluck, for instance, may have been regarded as a woman who cross-dressed (whether for fun, personal preference, public attention, or professional reasons) because she was an artist and therefore bohemian, or because she exploited the playfulness of twenties fashion, or because she was a lesbian, or all (or none) of the above (figure 26).

With the availability of a far wider range of interpretive frameworks, viewers in the twenties may have seen the women *we* now read as lesbian or "butch" in any number of ways: as the quintessence of the ultramodern, in congruence with the fashionably boyish or mannish style of dress for women (the interpretive angle of this chapter), *or* as slightly antiquated holdovers from the New Woman (if there were signs of residual dowdiness), *or* as women who were sexually attracted to others of their sex or "close companions," *or* as eccentric. To return to my earlier taxonomy of readers— those in the know, those unknowing, and those who knew-but-didn't-know— the interpretation of images of the "masculine woman" depended on various sorts of "insider" information, drawn from any number of realms, including personal acquaintance, high fashion, sexual science, or newly emerging subcultural codes. Quite simply, female masculinity was not bound up with any particular sexuality, and the differences among female masculinities were many and often quite subtle.

Like Mary Allen, Gluck and Hall understood the power of photographic images in mass culture—photography's ability "to sell, inform, record, delight"[52]—and consciously perfected the art of being public figures. This talent at self-promotion through this visual medium positioned them in the vanguard during "a time when magazines and newspapers were clamoring for picture stories."[53] These media-savvy women knew intuitively how to exploit commissioned and noncommissioned images to fashion an aura around their public personae. At a time when "book publishing" was particularly "encouraged by and driven through the insatiable desires of its public," Hall, along with many others, happily satisfied the reading public's craving for photographs of the most popular writers.[54] Hall even depicts the new world of publishing demands in *The Well of Loneliness*, where fiction seems to imitate life. In 1927, according to one of Troubridge's diary entries, the couple were visited by photographers and a journalist the day after Hall, who had just won the Femina Prize, had been working on *Stephen* (the working title for *The Well*).[55] In *The Well* Hall writes: "It was Puddle [Stephen's tutor] who had forced the embarrassed Stephen to let in the Press photographers, and Puddle it was who had given the details for the captions that were to appear with the pictures. . . . There was old Puddle waiting to waylay the anxious young man who had been commanded to dig up some copy about the new novelist."[56] Just as Hall's Femina Prize generated intense media interest, so too does her protagonist Stephen's literary success invite the limelight; by definition, success meant: "old photographs of Stephen could be seen in the papers, together with very flattering captions" (365).

One of the reasons so many women writers participated wholeheartedly in the "professional world of marketing" was because they were not yet "regarded as professionals": "by 1921 when the Society of Bookmen was founded, exclusion of women was inadmissible, but the society's name is expressive of the masculine aura of literary professionalism. Other institutions maintained older attitudes."[57] As late as 1935, Virginia Woolf, for one, was "enraged" when informed that the London Library Committee had turned down a proposal to accept women "because they found 'ladies impossible' " (36). One way to circumvent such old-fashioned sexism was to achieve success through literary prizes, especially the Femina: "such awards bridged the world of institutional respectability in which women were not natural members, and the world of publicity in which they were much more central" (37). Hall was thrilled with such awards because she, like "most writers of this period," knew full well "the advantages involved in the excitements surrounding book publication . . . in the form of prizes . . . book-promotion tours, and the authority accorded the more regarded reviewers" (38). For this reason, Hall welcomed publicity from newspapers such as the *Daily Mirror*, which had as its slogan, "The Daily Picture Newspaper with the Largest Net Sale." In its April 1927 coverage of the Femina Prize, Hall faces the camera directly in a full-length portrait positioned in the upper left-hand corner of the back page (figure 29). As always, she poses gracefully, exuding sartorial elegance, in a smartly tailored suit of her favored severely masculine mode, with high collar and tie, cigarette poised in one hand, and the other holding the leash of her dog, Colette.[58] After announcing in bold letters, "Award for Novel," the caption notes that the prize recognizes Hall's novel as "the best English imaginative work of the year." Such publicity catapulted Hall into the public eye: "Sales spun. *Adam's Breed* was on show in every London bookshop, John on show in every newspaper and magazine. Her photograph was everywhere."[59] On view in newspaper articles and photographs was the Radclyffe Hall that Rebecca West would later describe as "a personality whom most of us like and admire. She has a kind of austere, workmanly handsomeness. . . . Her character matches her appearance. She has all the virtues of the English aristocratic type, courage, self-restraint, steadfastness, and a very fine intelligence."[60]

In our own cultural age, with its incessant bombardment of the worst abuses of self-promotion, it is tempting to brand Allen, Gluck, or Hall as cynical, opportunist, vain, perhaps even comical or ridiculous, and, alternatively, to admire, for instance, Woolf, who cringed at such awards and shunned the trappings of glamour. For Woolf, whose disinclination to dress well, a fashion statement in itself, was part of her general reluctance to deploy her own self-imaging to promote her literary career, "high society meant dressing up, and so meant fear and self-consciousness."[61] This modernist writer "knew she would never be fashionable. She took refuge in jokes about her clothes being unsuitable for the aristocracy or about her eccentricity and shabbiness. . . . 'Bloomsbury' was not chic" (469, 470). Yet, within the context of the 1920s, receptivity to the press was a sign of a more progressive attitude in tune with the most advanced technologies of the new pictorial journalism. What is somewhat surprising, in fact, is that the older Hall (born in 1880) was—thanks to the influence of Troubridge, it seems—as hip as Gluck, who was fifteen years younger. Hall's own contemporary, the artist Romaine Brooks (born in 1874), was, in contrast, more resistant to the swift pace of change, as art historian Bridget Elliott comments: "When Brooks dismissed Gluck's schoolgirl antics, one senses that she was irritated by the vulgarity of a younger artist who was willing to court the media in endless rounds of sensational interviews and photographs."[62] One such example depicts, according to the copy beneath, the "Ultra-Modern" Gluck, "Eton cropped and trousered," standing at her easel putting the finishing touches to a canvas.[63] The brief caption informs readers that her work is currently on exhibit in Bond Street and that Gluck is a "much-discussed woman artist"—this information is hardly surprising in light of her physical presence in the full-length publicity shot, one leg raised on the easel's platform and cigarette hanging from her mouth. Other press cuttings likewise include snippets of information about the artist, designed as though by a publicist to stimulate public interest and build a sense of the artist as celebrity.

Women's magazines, such as *Eve: The Lady's Pictorial*, were at the forefront of promoting women's artistic achievements and activities, and both Gluck and Hall, as well as Allen, appeared in its pages. One lavishly illustrated column of September 1926—with the alliterative title, "Women in the News: Positive Personal Paragraphs on Pleasantly Pertinent People"—included the Douglas portrait of Hall after the publication of *Adam's Breed*, under the subheading "A Literary Jekyll and Hyde."[64] The reference to Hall's split personality, according to the article, is manifested in the pattern of her literary production, but the dashing adjacent portrait may have been a sly allusion to her stylish manner or even, in light of the lesbian presence on the editorial board at *Eve*, a cryptic reference to gender or sexuality: "After a big serious book, Miss Radclyffe Hall develops a flippant mood and settles down to a light novel, for her two serious books have been followed by two slight ones." Hall shares the page with several other women, also noted for their remarkable accomplishments in arts and letters or in the field of education. The following year, *Eve* celebrated Hall's success upon receiving the Femina Prize with the publication of a sketch of the novelist by the artist Paul Bloomfield.[65] Underneath, a lighthearted caption notes that the artist has failed to include Hall's "monocle, and there is no room in the picture for her parrot or French bulldog. The latter is also a breed that interests this distinguished author." Such non sequiturs work in tandem with the sketch to heighten interest in a fashionable author and, hopefully, to increase sales.

Commandant Mary Allen too had been featured some months earlier for doing her bit during the General Strike. *Eve* assured its upper and upper-middle-class readership that "the women of England of every degree have done magnificent work in defence of constitutional government, and in support of the splendid efforts of all loyal citizens to maintain supplies and minimize the hardships imposed on all by the strike."[66] Looking as imposing as ever in full dress uniform and staring steadily at the viewer, Allen occupies the literal center of the spread, "Society and the Strike." "Society" is well represented with studio portraits of an assortment of primarily aristocratic women, as well as the prime minister's wife, Mrs. Stanley Baldwin. A caption appears underneath each portrait, detailing, with admiration and appreciation, their generous efforts and contribution, primarily in the realm of transport, during a moment of national crisis. Surrounded by so many glamorous women of the upper classes, Allen's image seems to us completely incongruous in its severe formality; for the copywriter at *Eve*, however, Allen's quick response to the emergency represents the pinnacle of efficiency.

Far from being self-serving or representing the egotistical artist, such images highlight not necessarily what was flamboyantly or uniquely lesbian but—more likely for the majority of readers who would not yet possess either a coherent image of the lesbian or a vocabulary—what was new and daring for these modern women entering a male-dominated profession. Hall, Gluck, and other aspiring celebrities of the 1920s understood that a press hungry for copy could be supplied with images and information for captions, but their bid for publicity entailed risk because, once the portrait-cum-publicity shot spilled into the public domain, the individual celebrity no longer determined the frame. As Troubridge recalled, once Hall had published *The Well*, "since John's photograph had been in all the papers and her appearance was the most individual there was no avoiding a continuous publicity."[67] Hall's public image—one hitherto punctiliously cultivated and managed, with only the most discreet hints to a few in the know—would change within public culture radically and irrevocably in the next few months, as the concluding section of this chapter explores. Some of the same stylish studio portraits Hall had produced in collaboration with individual photographers to celebrate her many successes would now be snapped up by the press to present "the single, static and fixed frame of a public portrait" over which she was to have no control.[68]

IV

IN AUGUST 1927 Hall, still the subject of press interest stimulated by the Femina Prize she had won some months earlier, welcomed with Troubridge into their South Kensington home a photographer from Fox Photos, a London agency with a national and international reputation.[69] Fox Photos, known for their photographic excellence since their inception in 1926, supplied photographs that offered "a clear social indication of the style of life at that time" to newspapers such as the *Daily Express* and the *Daily Mirror*.[70] While "the subjects of photographs" often appear to us as "passive" rather than "as actively projecting their sense of self," Hall and Troubridge were highly skilled and practiced in the staging of their own self-image.[71] Here the couple pose before the camera in a glamorous, though relaxed, stance, Troubridge the very picture of a sleek flapper and Hall, true to form, as the ultramodern woman sporting the severely masculine mode, with the familiar clothing and hairstyle (figure 13); in fact, as *Eve* had described her the previous month, Hall was "in the front rank of those active women who really carry off modern fashions in dress."[72] In every way Hall looks the thoughtful and serious writer whose work had now been judged as among the best: confident and unassuming, head turned slightly to one side, and eyes staring pensively to the viewer's left. One hand holds an unlit cigarette and monocle, while the other is tucked casually into her skirt pocket; Hall's straight skirt is in clear view as is a glimpse of her calf behind a sofa covered with an exotic animal skin. Hall dresses formally for the occasion in a "tailor-made" with, as an ad for Harrods puts it, "a hint of mannish severity . . . [and] feminine grace" (figure 16). Troubridge huddles daringly close to Hall, the contours of her arm hugging Hall's skirt; here we have the helpmate, Hall's first reader, editor, supporter, and chief publicist. The third member of the ménage, barely visible in the upper left corner, is Hall's previous partner, Mabel "Ladye" Batten, whose presence, in a painting by John Singer Sargent, completes the family portrait. (Batten was, to the confusion of many readers, the mysterious third party referred to in the dedication in *The Well*: "Our three selves.") From our perspective, decades later, the 1927 Fox photo is unequivocal in its depiction of a quintessential butch-femme couple, with even a touch of sexual danger. But to some viewers at the time, more accustomed to a wide range of styles embraced by "modern" women, the Fox photo may have captured perfectly the Hall-Troubridge household in its entirety and in its exquisite modernity. Aided and abetted by the thoughtful orchestration of detail, this lesbian couple, emboldened by literary success, may have been on the edge of disclosing, with tasteful discretion, a dimension of their union—but strictly on their own terms and in a manner of their own design.

Hall and Troubridge present themselves in the Fox photo in a dignified manner, visually embodying the qualities represented in Hall's prize-winning novel, *Adam's Breed*, which was described as "one of the most discussed novels of the season" and as "an astonishing piece of work."[73] "With every novel she writes," the *Observer* remarked, the author "makes strides as an artist, but nothing in her gathering power and veracity had prepared us for the austere triumph of her new book." Situating Hall's work well within the realist tradition, the reviewer issues praise that matches the careful construction of the Fox photo pose. As with the photograph, the author of *Adam's Breed* "has studied detail with a searching vigor and a materialistic gusto which at first disguise her meaning. . . . It has an uncommon power of construction. It is built up with a massive patience." The meticulous care Hall took in writing her novel ("distinguished by a sympathy, strength and skill in craftsmanship rare in these hurried, novelty-seeking days"[74]) is seen in equal measure in each aspect of the complicated composition of the Fox photo, which, with "searching vigor and . . . materialistic gusto," issues a discreet invitation to the viewing public to peruse the cozy domesticity of the award-winning novelist and her companion, sanctioned by the artist herself. By celebrating a literary artist in the immediate aftermath of her success, the photograph operated in this context as an acknowledgment of Hall's increasing stature and accomplishment in the world of letters; however, no photographic image is exempt from tampering, especially when or if the press wants to tell another, or different, story. Hall and Troubridge, so confident of the camera's ability to convey something of their modernity, can hardly be blamed for failing to predict impending disaster or to forestall the media's appropriation of their own self-imaging to intimate sickness or perversion. As the Fox photograph illustrates so convincingly, "the age of Photography" coincided with "the explosion of the private into the public or rather into the creation of a new social value, which is the publicity of the private"; but Hall's aim to expose "interiority without yielding intimacy" was ultimately to be an abysmal failure.[75]

In August 1928 the whirlwind of publicity generated by the Douglas "prussic acid" editorial meant that journalists from every sort of news apparatus were hustling for copy, and old file photographs of Hall became the raw material for a reframing of the author of *The Well of Loneliness*. The 1927 Fox photograph of the prize-winning novelist was now harshly cropped by the editors of the *Sunday Express* to accompany Douglas's call for the ban (figure 30). The *Express* layout consisted of a large—six inches by three inches—detail taken from the Fox photograph showing only Hall, thus expurgating her partner and elegant home furnishings. The body or upper torso of the author was outlined with a heavy black line—the top of the frame cutting just below and behind the author's head—as if to lend visual emphasis to the fact that this woman had been audacious in her outspokenness on an unpleasant topic. Whether the newspaper sought to avoid litigation by excluding Troubridge, or whether the larger photograph was deemed too unwieldly and complex in purely visual terms to be suitable for the layout, what better way to execute a strategy of containment than to focus readers' attention squarely on an individual specimen through the photographic frame, which

> functions first and foremost as a device for distinguishing or setting off a certain kind of space . . . from the surrounding area. Constituting a limit or boundary between the "inside" and "outside" . . . it demarcates a perceptual field within which what is being looked at signifies differently. Frames are therefore constitutive of visual signs as well as having the potential to carry messages to the viewer about how these signs may be interpreted.[76]

The trick was to customize the image to meet the demands of the story. Subsequent viewers were confronted not with the original Fox photograph but with a detail cleverly excised by the *Sunday Express* to enforce an entirely different context; such a dramatic shift in the cultural frame is possible because photographic "reproduction can put the copy of the original into situations which would be out of reach for the original itself."[77] The success of the *Express* campaign to reframe Hall was achieved by strategically displacing the original context of the Fox photo. Through a process of ruthless cropping, the new frame initiated the cultural processes that would affix Hall's image to that of lesbianism—she would never again recover her reputation as primarily a well-known novelist of middlebrow fiction. Hall's famous image, previously the epitome of chic modernity for readers of magazines such as *Eve*, would gradually become the visual emblem of female sexual inversion because, once the *Express* had assigned Hall her new label and illustrated the "type" for public consumption, the process could not be reversed. Thus by the time feminist Vera Brittain analyzes the *Express* layout in 1968, not only have all traces of the glamorous, Femina Prize winner vanished completely, but the severity of the cropping renders Hall almost unrecognizable: the photograph "showed a monstrous-looking figure with short hair and a bow tie. The heavy jaw (not characteristic of Radclyffe Hall) . . . were all calculated to be prejudicial to the readers of that day."[78]

One of the few biographers of Hall to consider the consequences of the *Express*'s cropping job is Baker, who perceptively observes:

A large photograph of John accompanied the [Douglas] article, showing her in one of her more masculine poses—one hand in the specially-made pocket of her skirt, the other languidly holding a cigarette at waist height—and wearing a gentleman's silk smoking jacket, a high collar and black bow tie. The picture was cut off at the knee, thereby eliminating the stockinged ankles and low heeled shoes which would have softened the severe image.[79]

Hall's other biographers—Cline and Souhami—likewise read this provocative image as a defining moment in the cultural construction of Hall as masculine lesbian, but their speculations suggest that Douglas's damning editorial had already seeped into public discourse, as it inevitably would. Neither explains how the singular cropping of the *Express* illustration of Hall assisted in constructing another Radclyffe Hall (from celebrated writer to the embodiment of a sexual category) or how such a transformation of the image ever occurred. Cline, for instance, calls the image "a startling photograph of the author. One hand . . . held a burning cigarette. Readers knew she would let it burn to the end. She looked languid, elegant—with a hint of the haughty, the decadence of the dandy."[80] More recently, Souhami comments, "There she was with short hair, bow tie, chappish clothes, hand in pocket, lighted cigarette, clearly lesbian."[81] The narrowness of such readings of the *Express*'s imaging of Hall results from an overreliance on the kinds of "falsifications" that occurred in the press coverage of the events in late 1928.[82] As critic Victor Burgin asserts: "The structure of representation—point-of-view and frame—is intimately implicated in the reproduction of ideology (the 'frame of mind' of our 'points-of-view'). More than any other textual system, the photograph presents itself as . . . a 'thing' which we invest with a full identity, a *being*."[83] Hall's image became—quite literally—crudely reduced to an illustration of "a 'thing' which we invest with a full identity"; that is, what we now recognize as a new sexual category called the mannish lesbian.

Of course, such a visual formulation in twenties' journalistic discourse was by no means as articulate or precise.

In the subsequent tug of war conducted by various news organizations, Hall's image, in fact, fares quite differently because some newspapers were intent on destroying the author's reputation as well as the offending novel while others remained sympathetic to Hall's work and political cause. As individual newspapers marshaled photographic images and accompanying captions in order to convey their own message or story about the controversy, each invariably contributed to the "falsifications" of the novelist's image. In unraveling the complexities of reading the "press photograph," Barthes argues persuasively that

> the press photograph is a message. Considered overall this message is formed by a source of emission, a channel of transmission and a point of reception. The source of emission is the staff of the newspaper. . . . The point of reception is the public which reads the paper. As for the channel of transmission, this is the newspaper itself, or, more precisely, a complex of concurrent messages with the photograph as center and surrounds constituted by the text, the title, the caption, the layout and . . . the very name of the paper.[84]

The message the *Express* continued to send its readers was reinforced repeatedly by the same cropped Fox photo of Hall; most later reports on further developments in the case required only a simple modification of title, caption, or layout. For example, a few days after the publication of the Douglas editorial, the *Daily Express* reprinted the same detail, but this time cropped so tightly into the narrow column it is difficult to ascertain whether the novelist is wearing a skirt or trousers, accompanied by the large headline, "Woman's Novel Banned."[85] In December this tightly cropped image was again neatly inserted into one newspaper column below the headline "Scathing Comments on Miss Radclyffe Hall's Novel: 'Subtle and Corrupt.' "[86]

The sensational *Sunday Chronicle*, which conducted an even more aggressive visual campaign against Hall, printed an unusually ungracious photograph of the author with a cigarette protruding between her clenched teeth (figure 31). In its attempt to snatch credit for the ban away from the *Express*, the *Sunday Chronicle* article, with the headline "Wise Decision to Ban Novel," implied that it was responsible for the ban, because it had "urged the Home Secretary to take immediate action" against a novel that "dealt with a hideous form of vice existing between women of perverted instincts."[87] The headline adjacent to Hall's photograph indicates that the paper pitched to a readership unlikely to be regarded seriously by the sensible: "Cannibals in Gipsy Camp. Victims Robbed and Eaten. Hated Chief of Gang." A front-page spread in the paper's November issue, headlined " 'Knocked Flat' by Book Ban: Miss Radclyffe Hall to Sell Assets and Fight On," was accompanied by separate photographs of Troubridge and Hall in their dog-show gear, apparently at their most competitive, as each holds up for the camera a prize-winning pooch.[88] Curiously, this is the only time during the controversy that the couple were pictured side-by-side, and even here each occupies her own photographic space with a firm line setting them apart, as if the union of two such women in a single frame was too dangerous to display graphically after the public disclosure of their relationship. This also may explain why the uncropped Fox photograph of Troubridge and Hall together never appeared in newspapers or magazines in the 1920s, although, from our vantage point, it offers the more compelling illustration of lesbian deviance.

In the press most supportive of Hall and against the ban, which included the *Daily Herald* and the *Evening News*, the captions were more neutral ("Novel Sent to 'Jix' for Judgment") and the photographs, such as the Douglas portrait, presented the author in a more positive light (figure 14).[89] Although the *Bulletin and Scots Pictorial* also used the Douglas portrait in their earlier coverage of Hall's Femina Prize success, the newspaper chose a different photograph for their brief story on August 22, 1928, concerning the "storm over novel." This closely cropped photo of a smiling Hall in what is clearly a jacket and tie hints at masculinity but is considerably more flattering and sympathetic than the other photograph from the same series of poses used by the *Chronicle* and the *Yorkshire Post*; the *Bulletin*'s caption discreetly reports that her "outspoken" novel had been sent to the Home Office "following protests."[90] *Eve: The Lady's Pictorial* entered the fray with more muted support for the now controversial writer. In August the magazine ran a sketch rather than a photo of Hall in its regular column, "Talking about Books," with the cryptic caption: "The author of 'Adam's Breed,' which was awarded the 'Femina' prize, is a distinctive figure in the literary world. She patronizes a severely tailor-made style of outfit, and usually wears a monocle."[91] The article then went on to announce that *The Well* had been banned by libraries. However, by September, the strongest statement *Eve* could muster on the author's behalf was to reprint her poem, "A Simple Psalm." The poem's curious religious celebration of heterosexual reproduction, printed in the center of the page and enclosed by a black box, along with a studio photograph of the condemned author by Peter North, seemed more an obituary than a rigorous defense. Under the portrait the editors inserted an anodyne caption: the "author of the banned novel . . . began her literary career by writing verses, many of which were set to music."[92] Some on the editorial staff of this ladies' magazine evidently felt too exposed to proclaim vociferous support for Hall, which perhaps explains why the lesbian "Evelyn Irons did not use her position as deputy editor of the *Daily Mail* women's page to promote *The Well*'s cause."[93]

Finally, mention must be made of the striking format in *London Calling*, in which the Douglas photographic profile of Hall—embodying so successfully her "aura" and sartorial sensibilities—appears right in the middle of the page, with an angular, fanlike background, giving the portrait almost the cool geometric faceting of a cubist painting (figure 32). Within a space defined by lines almost in the shape of a headstone flowing from the bottom of the portrait, the copy, under the heading "Miss Radclyffe Hall," reads:

> Distinctive people have a queer way of reminding you irresistibly of other distinctive people. . . . The first impression [of the author] is blurred. She continues to remind me of a French aristocrat. I feel she would have graced a tumbril, and defied a whole mob with supreme tranquillity and much secret zest. Perhaps she could *meet* a great moment more adequately than achieve one. I am aware in her, perhaps inaccurately, of an eternal, watchful defiance of life. At the moment, the muck-hounds are on her track, and her latest book . . . has been withdrawn.[94]

Also appearing on this page is an extremely positive review of *The Well* ("an amazingly fine book of a totally different type") by "a famous woman novelist," followed by a sharp condemnation by the magazine's editor of both the government's action and of the less than "edifying" "newspaper campaign of drum-banging and self-boosting."

The framing of Hall—whether by the *Express* or *London Calling*—was, of course, facilitated by the author herself whose willingness to court the press for the sake of her own literary reputation provided the print media with a wealth of visual evidence, as the *Daily Herald* commented in its coverage of the trial: Hall "was wearing [an outfit] . . . made familiar in photographs of her."[95] Self-promotion came back to haunt her, following editor Douglas's condemnation of homosexuals who, he claimed, purposely sought the limelight: "They do not shun publicity. On the contrary, they seek it, and they take a delight in their flamboyant notoriety."[96] Had Hall avoided such publicity, a subcultural style may have evolved in other directions since, as Goldring noted, "unless *purposely paraded*, such friendships [between women] aroused little curiosity or comment."[97] Over a period of months in the autumn of 1928, the *Express*'s relentless deployment of their custom-cropped Fox photograph slowly eroded Hall's own self-construction of the artist-as-fashion-maven. In effect, the *Express* framed—that is, implicated—Hall by stealing the context of "success" (as represented in the Fox photo) and supplanting it with another of the paper's own making. The *Express* layout skillfully underlined the message contained within its editorial: such women "flaunt themselves in public places with increasing effrontery and more insolently provocative bravado."[98] The newspaper "responsibly" alerted readers to this danger by offering an example: *this* is what they look like. The image Hall had cultivated with such care, one conveying panache and muted sexuality, now emblematized instead deviance and, for some observers, social danger. Hall's self-presentation became a visible reminder to readers of a woman's uncompromising appropriation of the masculine, and gradually from the late 1920s and into the early 1930s, this image, in turn, came to be linked unequivocally with sexual abnormality. Consequently, Hall's image became fixed in the public consciousness within a frame not precisely of her own making but one cropped for the convenience of a different spin on the woman author of a now notorious novel.

One wonders if, on some level, Gluck became aware of this predicament. A few years after the obscenity trial of *The Well*, she turned her artistic attention to the actual, physical frame, which she called simply "the Gluck frame," and "of which she was extremely proud."[99] The Gluck Room at the Fine Art Society in Bond Street, London, became an exhibition space both for Gluck's paintings and for her specially designed frame, which, in the 1932 version, was "painted white with three undercoats and one finishing coat" (105). Ideally, this minimalist frame flows into the physical space of the room and thus becomes invisible, a strategy some associate with modernity and the non-representational; moreover, "frame-breaking is yet another way of asserting control over the borders of a visual image."[100] The Gluck frame, according to notes left by the artist herself, inverted the "essence of all frames," so that the "outer edge" prevailed: "it was made to die away into the wall and cease to be a separate feature."[101] Gluck's evolving framing system constitutes a literal assault on the visible frame but also seems a shrewd political response, even if unconscious or inadvertent, which challenges the frame's ability to demarcate "a perceptual field within which what is being looked at signifies differently."[102] Protected perhaps by social expectations of painters as bohemian, Gluck was among the few to escape any negative fallout after the trial of *The Well*; her exhibition of 1932 "could not have had better reviews or received more attention than it did."[103]

The circulation of Hall's "brilliantly concise image" in public culture fixed the frame of reference around the lesbian more vividly and indelibly than the surfeit of vague and euphemistic language reported in the press: "certain relations among women"; "offences beween women"; "immoral instincts"; "tendencies"; "unnatural practices"; "this type of woman"; "this horrible vice"; and, "the masculine woman in all its implications."[104] New public awareness left such women exposed and vulnerable, including the dashing motorboat racer, Joe Carstairs, whose exploits were celebrated in the 1926 fashion spread in *Eve* (figure 5); her biographer, Kate Summerscale, writes that "by 1930 a sour note was occasionally entering press reports about Carstairs. . . . [She] was perceived now as a comic or sinister would-be man. Characteristics never mentioned before—her continual gum-chewing, her tattoos, her spitting, her swearing—began to surface in the articles: 'She smokes incessantly,' reported one, 'not with languid feminine grace, but with the sharp decisive gestures a man uses.'"[105] Hall's reputation also foundered, and her last two novels received poor reviews. Likewise, the poet H.D. "and her lesbian friends were deeply disturbed by the outrage over Radclyffe Hall's court case and did not dare to 'call' themselves 'homosexuals.' ('We had to be very, very careful,' H.D.'s friend recalls.)"[106] Henceforth notices of "close companionship" between women such as Lady Ludlow and Miss Pryce would inevitably acquire other unsavory connotations. One way to deflect public attention away from the new sexual label was to shore up one's reputation as a public heterosexual, as Raitt suggests may have been the case with Vita Sackville-West.[107] Months after the obscenity trial, the lesbian Hilda Matheson, director of talks at the BBC, had no trouble in persuading Sackville-West and her homosexual husband, Harold Nicolson, to chat over the airwaves about marriage: "Though they agreed that marriage should be redefined and that women should be more independent, they of course said nothing in public about homosexuality within marriage."[108]

An explanatory model based on a dramatic "before" and "after" seems almost too seductive in its simplicity, but the simple—if, for some, lamentable—fact of the matter is that after the obscenity trial of *The Well* life changed utterly for *all* women who lived with other women, or *all* women drawn to masculine styles of dress, whether lesbian or not. Yet it would be misleading to assert that the outcome of the banning of *The Well* was irredeemably negative. To be sure, the subject of lesbianism, commented the *Saturday Review*, had "been dragged from the calm field of science to be perverted and distorted by the fascination or the repulsion of the taboo against obscenity."[109] At the same time, however, the possibility of denial—so convenient for those who knew but preferred not to—began to slip away: "The old sex taboos are dissolving. We are beginning to face openly the facts of sex, with a degree of intelligence and frankness which even a quarter of a century ago was impossible."

When the print media thrust Hall's image—sometimes ghastly and unflatter-ing—on innumerable front pages, some women thrilled to the possibility of self-recognition and even subcultural formation, as seen in the private sketch of Hall in Hepworth's diary (figure 1), or in the thousands of letters of sup-port Hall received during and after the obscenity trial, or in the imitation by admirers such as those kindred spirits in attendance at the Foyle's Luncheon. Just as Hall's first name became a byword for lesbian ("Mrs. Arthur is a . . . is a . . . well, you know, Radclyffe"[110]), so too did her distinctive appearance, published extensively in press reports, become the classic iconic type of the mannish lesbian. Photographs of Hall played a major part in the processes of mythologizing her fashion sense, literary career, savvy understanding of pub-licity in mass culture, and details of her life, lovers, and friends.

The events of the latter half of 1928 were a watershed in shattering the silence and invisibility surrounding the subject of female homosexuality. The trial was a crystallizing moment for gradual cultural and social change in mul-tiple sites: women's greater political autonomy (full suffrage in the same year) and access to previously male-dominated professions; technologies of self-imaging and changes in mass media and fashion; greater fluidity in gender roles; dissemination of sexual knowledge; and expansion of the reading pub-lic—in short, social changes we associate with modernity. Hall, "terribly Mod-ern & shingled & monocled," as Ellis remarked, was regarded by many in the print media before the trial as the very picture of "high-brow modernism," as was Gluck. In posing before the camera, Hall, Troubridge, Gluck, and Allen probably never imagined that, decades later, their visual images would be associated *exclusively* with lesbianism and lesbians. Such fashionable and innovative women flourished in the public culture of 1920s London because English modernity provided a space for experimentation in a number of dis-cursive realms: sexuality, sexual knowledge, fashion, and literary and visual representation. However inadvertently or fortuitously, these women were among the pioneers in the imaging of Sapphism in England, from the early years of the First World War to the publication of *The Well*. While the visual disclosure to the public that such women were lesbians damaged individual careers and undoubtedly foreclosed some promising directions in modern fashion and artistic production, it also made possible for the first time the con-struction of a public English lesbian subculture.

Notes

INTRODUCTION: "IT'S HARD TO TELL THEM APART TODAY"

1. Significantly, in an interview given during the uproar over her book, Hall referred to her earlier relationship with Mabel "Ladye" Batten with this language of companionship. Hall explains that she became "the intimate friend and constant companion of one of the most generous-minded and brilliant women that I have ever known. . . . I had the privilege of sharing a home until her death a few years ago." See *T.P.'s Weekly*, September 8, 1928, p. 587.

2. A member of the "new rich," Lady Ludlow was famous for lavish entertainment and conspicuous consumption. First the "widow of the financier and South African diamond magnate, Sir Julius Wernher," Lady Ludlow later remarried to become mistress of a London mansion, Bath House, and a country home, Luton Hoo, in addition to other properties. See Pamela Horn, *Women in the 1920s* (Stroud, Gloucestershire: Alan Sutton, 1995), p. 28.

3. The prosecution of *The Well of Loneliness* (published in July 1928) for obscene libel took place in November 1928 at Bow Street Police Court, London: "The Director of Public Prosecutions applied for an Order under the Obscene Publications Act of 1857 . . . [which] gave magistrates throughout the country statutory powers to order the destruction of 'any obscene publication held for sale or distribution on information laid before a court of summary jurisdiction.'" See Vera Brittain, *Radclyffe Hall: A Case of Obscenity?* (London: Femina Books, 1968), p. 86. The appeal in December 1928 against the order for destruction of copies seized was unsuccessful and the novel was banned in Britain until 1949, when it was republished by the Falcon Press (later Hammond, Hammond). See Michael Baker, *Our Three Selves: The Life of Radclyffe Hall* (New York: Morrow, 1985), p. 353.

4. Emily Hamer, *Britannia's Glory: A History of Twentieth-Century Lesbians* (London: Cassell, 1996), p. 84. In her important study of women in the interwar period Deirdre Beddoe refers to Hall's "bombshell" as "the classic lesbian novel, the 'lesbian Bible.' It remains the best known novel in English on the subject and

its role is seminal to the history of lesbianism in Britain." See *Back to Home and Duty: Women Between the Wars, 1918–1939* (London: Pandora, 1989), p. 29.

5. Jeffrey Weeks, *Coming Out: Homosexual Politics in Britain from the Nineteenth Century to the Present* (1977; reprint, London: Quartet Books, 1990), p. 101.

6. Alan Sinfield, *The Wilde Century: Effeminacy, Oscar Wilde, and the Queer Moment* (New York: Columbia University Press, 1994), p. 3. Emphasis mine. See also Ed Cohen, *Talk on the Wilde Side: Toward a Genealogy of a Discourse on Male Sexualities* (New York: Routledge, 1993).

7. Hall may have professed an allegiance to Ellis's theory of sexual inversion at the time of writing and publishing *The Well*, but in her own life, and even in *The Well* itself, she was far more eclectic, even incorporating competing notions advanced by others such as Edward Carpenter (see my chapter 5).

8. Because the language for what was clinically defined as "female sexual inversion" was still fluid and imprecise, it will be my practice to use such terms as "Sapphist," "lesbian," or "homosexual," interchangeably. Other terms, such as "spinster" or "man-hater," as we will see in chapter 2, were particularly useful to allude obliquely to mannish women or lesbians in that the code words could refer to independent women or feminists generally or to lesbians euphemistically. The term "butch" was not in use in Britain until the 1960s.

9. This passage is apparently taken from the publisher's own promotional material. James Douglas, "A Book That Must Be Suppressed," *Sunday Express*, August 19, 1928, p. 10. For this reason, several newspapers attempted to define "inversion" for their readers. See, for example, the *Manchester Guardian*, November 17, 1928, p. 18, and *The Times*, November 17, 1928, p. 5.

10. I suggest that the "vast majority of readers" falls into a group who preferred to "know-but-not-know" because, in the press coverage of the obscenity trial, several newspapers asserted that Hall thrust on British society "a disagreeable task which it has hitherto shirked." The topic seems to have been thought of but promptly dismissed as unthinkable. See the *Sunday Express*, August 19, 1928, p. 10.

11. *Morning Post*, November 17, 1928, p. 10. Emphasis mine. A similar point was made elsewhere: "The result of the publicity which has been directed to the offending novel recently has been to make tens of thousands talk about a subject which is ordinarily ignored." See the *Spectator*, September 1, 1928, p. 258. One of Hall's biographers, Sally Cline, describes novelist May Sinclair's shock upon learning that the relationship between Hall and Una, Lady Troubridge was not "platonic." Sinclair reportedly told a friend, "I don't believe what is said of them is true." See *Radclyffe Hall: A Woman Called John* (London: John Murray, 1997), p. 273.

12. *Daily Herald*, November 10, 1928, p. 1, and *Manchester Guardian*, November 10, 1928, p. 14. Both newspapers were quoting directly from the trial.

13. Alkarim Jivani, *It's Not Unusual: A History of Lesbian and Gay Britain in the Twentieth Century* (London: Michael O'Mara Books, 1997), p. 40. Irons recalls this conversation with her mother in an interview conducted for a 1997 documentary broadcast on BBC2.

14. The song "Masculine Women and Feminine Men" (written by Monaco and Leslie) was recorded on February 26, 1926, by the Savoy Havana Band.

15. Judith Halberstam, *Female Masculinity* (Durham, N.C.: Duke University Press, 1998), p. 85. For a reading of mannishness in women before the war, see Martha Vicinus, "Fin-de-Siècle Theatrics: Male Impersonation and Lesbian Desire" in Billie Melman, ed., *Borderlines: Genders and Identities in War and Peace, 1870–1930* (New York: Routledge, 1998), pp. 163–92.

16. Sinfield, *The Wilde Century*, p. 8.

17. A few exceptions should be mentioned. First, Sherrie A. Inness thoughtfully examines the lesbian in popular American culture in the twentieth century, but there is an unfortunate tendency to collapse the two decades of the interwar period. Inness reads Hall's novel against another provocative text of the 1920s (Edouard Bourdet's 1926 play, *The Captive*) and situates both against the "popular ideology about homosexuality," particularly medical literature. While Inness indicates an interest in the medical discourse of both the 1920s and 1930s, the medical resources she cites are drawn either from the prewar period or from the mid-1930s. The relationship between female masculinity and lesbianism changes so profoundly after the publication of *The Well* that commentary by medical observers of the mid-1930s cannot provide an accurate picture of readers' initial responses to the figure of Stephen Gordon, the novel's protagonist. The impact of Stephen's wardrobe, for instance, in relation to female inversion would have been quite different before and after the 1928 trial, as I argue in chapter 4. See *The Lesbian Menace: Ideology, Identity, and the Representation of Lesbian Life* (Amherst: University of Massachusetts Press, 1997), p. 20.

A second exception is Nicky Hallett's *Lesbian Lives: Identity and Auto/Biography in the Twentieth Century* (London: Pluto Press, 1999). In addition to a chronological specificity (juxtaposing the 1920s and 1930s against the 1980s and 1990s), Hallett situates her reading of auto/biography specifically in English culture.

Finally, historian Ruth Ford carefully scrutinizes the scrapbooks of Australian Monte (Ethel May) Punshon (1882–1989) and tracks shifts in lesbian subjectivity over several decades. See "Speculating on Scrapbook, Sex, and Desire: Issues in Lesbian History," *Australian Historical Studies* 27, no. 106 (1996): 111–26.

18. Newton's essay, originally published in *Signs: Journal of Women in Culture and Society*, was revised and reprinted in Martin Duberman, Martha Vicinus, and George Chauncey Jr., eds., *Hidden from History: Reclaiming the Gay and Lesbian Past* (New York: New American Library, 1989), pp. 281–93.

19. Newton, "The Mythic Mannish Lesbian," p. 283.

20. Carroll Smith-Rosenberg, *Disorderly Conduct: Visions of Gender in Victorian America* (New York: Knopf, 1985), p. 177.

21. Newton, "The Mythic Mannish Lesbian," p. 284.

22. See for instance, Martha Vicinus, " 'They Wonder to Which Sex I Belong': The Historical Roots of the Modern Lesbian Identity," *Feminist Studies* 18, no. 3 (fall 1992): 467–97 and Marylynne Diggs, "Romantic Friends or a 'Different Race of Creatures'? The Representation of Lesbian Pathology in Nineteenth-Century America," *Feminist Studies* 21, no. 2 (summer 1995): 317–40.

23. Terry Castle, *The Apparitional Lesbian: Female Homosexuality and Modern Culture* (New York: Columbia University Press, 1993), pp. 96, 106. The diaries of Anne Lister (1791–1840) were found and later transcribed by Helena Whitbread.

24. Halberstam, *Female Masculinity*, p. 85.

25. C[on] O'L[eary], "Breaking Silence," *T.P.'s & Cassell's Weekly*, August 11, 1928, p. 487.

26. Mica Nava, "Modernity's Disavowal: Women, the City, and the Department Store," in Mica Nava and Alan O'Shea, eds., *Modern Times: Reflections on a Century of English Modernity* (London: Routledge, 1996), p. 39.

27. Douglas Goldring, *The Nineteen Twenties: A General Survey and Some Personal Memories* (London: Nicholson and Watson, 1945), p. xvi.

28. To cite only one example, Hall, who moved in middlebrow literary and theater circles, never met Bryher and her modernist circle, or Gluck, who sometimes mixed with a different theater crowd (Lady Ludlow, incidentally, signed the guest book of Gluck's exhibit in 1932).

29. Although artist Dorothy Hepworth's diary was dated on the binding as 1927, information seems to have been recorded in it for several years thereafter, so it is difficult to date precisely when the sketch was drawn. On August 5, 1928, Hepworth wrote in her diary: "I have read of a book I want to get on the masculine woman. I should think it should be interesting. . . . It has a very good review in the Sunday Times. I should say it is well worth reading, and is about a subject that is not as a rule a discussed subject in England." Biographer Michael Dickens argues that Hepworth's diaries include entries and drawings by both Hepworth (1894–1978) and her life partner, the artist Patricia Preece (1894–1966). Although Dickens attributes the sketch in the diary, as well as a reading list of sexological works, to Preece, he believes the diary entry cited above is written

in Hepworth's hand. See Dickens, *Masquerade* (London: Fourth Estate, forthcoming). Preece apparently signed and exhibited Hepworth's work in an unusual collaborative arrangement. I am grateful to Christine Hepworth for allowing access to Hepworth's private papers.

30. My term is a modification of Shari Benstock's phrase "Sapphic Modernism." See "Expatriate Sapphic Modernism: Entering Literary History," in Karla Jay and Joanne Glasgow, eds., *Lesbian Texts and Contexts: Radical Revisions* (New York: New York University Press, 1990), pp. 183–203.

Some literary critics have found Benstock's formulation troubling, as seen in Erin G. Carlston's critique of Benstock's phrase: "The word 'Sapphic' in conjunction with 'Modernism' tends both to imply a transparent relation between biography and literary production and to apply an anachronistic conception of lesbian identity to the sexual cultures of the early twentieth century." See *Thinking Fascism: Sapphic Modernism and Fascist Modernity* (Stanford: Stanford University Press, 1998), p. 6.

31. Katy Deepwell, introduction to *Women Artists and Modernism*, ed. Katy Deepwell (Manchester: Manchester University Press, 1998), p. 6.

32. Alan O'Shea, "English Subjects of Modernity," in Mica Nava and Alan O'Shea, eds., *Modern Times: Reflections on a Century of English Modernity* (London: Routledge, 1996), p. 11.

33. Nava, "Modernity's Disavowal," p. 39.

34. Rita Felski, *The Gender of Modernity* (Cambridge: Harvard University Press, 1995), p. 20.

35. Comment made by the mother to her daughter, the lesbian journalist Evelyn Irons, in the autumn of 1928, reported in Jivani, *It's Not Unusual*, p. 40.

36. Alison Light, *Forever England: Femininity, Literature, and Conservatism Between the Wars* (London: Routledge, 1991), pp. 10–11. Nava also notes the tendency toward conservatism among middle-class Englishwomen who sought to escape the home by going into working-class areas of the city to educate poor women: "The visionary element in their activities was perhaps somewhat compromised by the fact that their personal freedom from the constraints of late Victorian domesticity was gained in the process of attempting to enforce it elsewhere, on the women of the poorer classes. But this contradiction need not undermine the *modernity* of their consciousness and experience." See "Modernity's Disavowal," p. 44.

It is not within the scope of this discussion to outline the extensive debate on women's exclusion from studies on modernity, but suffice it to say that the feminist academic project has worked assiduously to redefine modernity and clarify women's relationship to it. See especially Janet Wolff's ground-breaking essay,

"The Invisible *Flâneuse*: Women and the Literature of Modernity," in her *Feminine Sentences: Essays on Women and Culture* (Berkeley: University of California Press, 1990), pp. 34–50.

37. O'Shea, "English Subjects of Modernity," p. 8.

38. Bertha Harris, "The More Profound Nationality of their Lesbianism: Lesbian Society in Paris in the 1920s," in Phyllis Birkby et al., eds., *Amazon Expedition: A Lesbian Feminist Anthology* (Albion, Calif.: Times Change Press, 1973), p. 79.

39. See also Andrea Weiss, *Paris Was a Woman: Portraits from the Left Bank* (London: HarperCollins, 1995).

40. By the turn of the century, Paris, Shari Benstock explains, "had an international reputation as the capital of same sex love among women and was designated 'Paris-Lesbos.' " See *Women of the Left Bank: Paris, 1900–1940* (Austin: University of Texas, 1986), p. 47.

For a history of lesbian cultures and identities in a cross-cultural context, see Martha Vicinus's *Romantic Friendships: Lesbian Identities, 1800–1930* (work in progress).

41. Robert Graves and Alan Hodge, *The Long Weekend: A Social History of Great Britain, 1918–1939* (1940; reprint, New York: Norton, 1963), p. 101.

42. Goldring, *The Nineteen Twenties*, p. 228.

43. Beverley Nichols, *The Sweet and Twenties* (London: Weidenfeld and Nicolson, 1958), p. 104. By the phrase "the man in Harley Street," Nichols refers to physicians whose practices were (and still are) in this area of London. Hugh David describes Nichols as someone who "uniquely personifies what we might call the 'society homosexual' of the twenties." See *On Queer Street: A Social History of British Homosexuality, 1895–1995* (London: HarperCollins, 1997), p. 79.

44. Ross McKibbin, *Classes and Cultures: England, 1918–1951* (Oxford: Oxford University Press, 1998), p. 322.

45. Nava, "Modernity's Disavowal," pp. 38–9.

46. Among a handful of such editorialists was the Dean of St. Paul's, who argued: "In France there is much more liberty or licence than with us. In this country practically all publishers, librarians, and booksellers would be ashamed to assist in selling books of this kind. . . . I have seen several cheap books on Paris bookstalls the titles of which leave no doubt that they belong to this class. . . . In Germany there is, or was before the war, a sort of cult of abnormal practices, such as were partially condoned in Pagan antiquity. There is no doubt that public opinion in this country would not allow apologists for perversion to come out into the open." See W. R. Inge, "Where Should We Draw the Line?" *Evening Standard*, December 12, 1928, p. 5.

47. *Daily Express*, August 24, 1928, p. 8.

48. *Spectator*, September 1, 1928, p. 258. Emphasis mine.

49. In Hepworth's diary dated 1927 Preece listed works of sexology (by Richard von Krafft-Ebing, Havelock Ellis, and Iwan Bloch) as well as literary works by Sappho, Baudelaire, and Zola.

50. Although Mary Louise Roberts's meticulously researched study of postwar France does not engage fully with homosexuality, her work nevertheless demonstrates the power of an approach that focuses on a specific national culture and time frame. See *Civilization Without Sexes: Reconstructing Gender in Postwar France, 1917–1927* (Chicago: University of Chicago Press, 1994). Throughout this book I will usually refer to "England" rather than "Britain" because London was the primary site of most of the activities, events, and topics under consideration. Occasionally, a source in Scotland might be cited, but, in most every case, in relation to English culture.

51. Peter Osborne, "Modernity Is a Qualitative, Not a Chronological Category," cited by O'Shea, "English Subjects of Modernity," p. 8.

52. Sinfield, *The Wilde Century*, p. 3.

I. THE MYTHIC MORAL PANIC: RADCLYFFE HALL
AND THE NEW GENEALOGY

1. *Sunday Express*, August 19, 1928, p. 10. All subsequent quotations by Douglas are from this editorial unless otherwise indicated. The notorious reference to "prussic acid" apparently owes its origin not to Douglas's imagination but to legal history when a nineteenth-century pornography trial coincided with the introduction of a bill into the House of Lords to curtail the sale of poisons. The judge in the case, Lord Chief Justice Campbell, referred to the pornographic material as "a sale of poison more deadly than prussic acid, strychnine or arsenic." See Alec Craig, *The Banned Books of England* (London: Allen and Unwin, 1962), p. 22. Douglas's association of prussic acid and young children may have also been triggered by the huge headlines in the *Glasgow Weekly News* one week prior to the publication of his editorial. See "Renfrew Mystery Solved by Little Girl: Prussic Acid Used in Eaglesham Poison Case," August 11, 1928, p. 24.

2. Letter from Radclyffe Hall to Newman Flower, April 10, 1928; Correspondence—Publishers and Agents, vol. 4, Lovat Dickson Papers, MG 30, D 237, National Archives of Canada, Ottawa. (Hereafter all citations to the Lovat Dickson Papers refer to the collection held at the National Archives of Canada, Ottawa.)

3. Stan Cohen, *Folk Devils and Moral Panics*, quoted by Jeffrey Weeks, *Sex,*

Politics, and Society: The Regulation of Sexuality Since 1800 (London: Longman, 1989), p. 14.

4. Havelock Ellis, *Studies in the Psychology of Sex, Complete in Two Volumes.* (1902; reprint, New York: Random House, 1942), p. 261.

5. Letter to the Editor, *Lancet* 1 (June 22, 1918): 884. For information on women and the war, see Gail Braybon, *Women Workers in the First World War* (London: Routledge, 1989).

6. Jean Radford, "An Inverted Romance: *The Well of Loneliness* and Sexual Ideology," in Jean Radford, ed., *The Progress of Romance: The Politics of Popular Fiction* (London: Routledge, 1986), p. 98.

7. For an illuminating discussion of the role the press played in the controversy over the "flapper," see Billie Melman, *Women and the Popular Imagination in the Twenties: Flappers and Nymphs* (New York: St. Martin's Press, 1988), pp. 15–37. See also Sheila Jeffreys, *The Spinster and Her Enemies: Feminism and Sexuality, 1880–1930* (London: Pandora, 1985).

8. Melman, *Women and the Popular Imagination in the Twenties*, p. 36.

9. Joseph Bristow, *Sexuality* (London: Routledge, 1997), p. 53.

10. Diana Souhami, *The Trials of Radclyffe Hall* (London: Weidenfeld and Nicolson, 1998), pp. 183–4.

11. Nichols, *Sweet and Twenties*, p. 106.

12. The phrase "by-now-famous" appears in Leigh Gilmore's "Obscenity, Modernity, Identity: Legalizing *The Well of Loneliness* and *Nightwood*," *Journal of the History of Sexuality* 4, no. 4 (1994): 612. A number of critics have misquoted Douglas, either through minor omission of a word or reversing "boy" and "girl." The Douglas quotation appears in dozens of books and articles too numerous to list.

13. Beddoe, *Back to Home and Duty*, p. 28.

14. Notable exceptions include Gilmore's "Obscenity, Modernity, Identity" and Angela Ingram's " 'Unutterable Putrefaction' and 'Foul Stuff': Two 'Obscene' Novels of the 1920s," *Women's Studies International Forum* 9, no. 4 (1986): 341–54.

15. Ellen Bayuk Rosenman, "Sexual Identity and *A Room of One's Own*: 'Secret Economies' in Virginia Woolf's Feminist Discourse," *Signs: Journal of Women in Culture and Society* 14, no. 3 (spring 1989): 638, 639.

16. *Life and Letters* 1, no. 5 (October 1928): 313.

17. Of the reviews to appear after the Douglas editorial, four reviews were clearly written afterward, as they refer to the controversy: *Lancet* 2 (September 1, 1928): 484; *Life and Letters*, pp. 313–14; *Time and Tide* (November 23, 1928): 1124–25; and *British Journal of Inebriety* 26 (1928–29): 93–4.

18. Baker, *Our Three Selves*, p. 205.

19. A more elaborate discussion of Ellis's reputation can be found in chapter 5. Cape further exploited his own edited version of Ellis's statement by including extracts from it in all the newspaper advertisements promoting the novel. See, for example, the *Daily Telegraph*, July 27, 1928, p. 15.

20. Letter from Havelock Ellis to Bryher, September 18, 1928. GEN MSS 97, ser. 1, box 2, The Beinecke Rare Book and Manuscript Library, Yale University (hereafter referred to as the Beinecke).

21. Graves and Hodge, *Long Weekend*, p. 56, and *Morning Post*, August 10, 1928, p. 12. The *Post* praised the author's "powers of sensitive penetration and subtle expression . . . [and] skillful reserve."

22. Graves and Hodge, *Long Weekend*, p. 55, and *Times Literary Supplement* (hereafter referred to as the *TLS*), August 2, 1928, p. 566.

23. Quoted by Michael S. Howard, *Jonathan Cape, Publisher* (London: Jonathan Cape, 1971), p. 103.

24. Arnold Dawson, *Daily Herald*, August 22, 1928, p. 7. In an argument that Sir Chartres Biron would later recycle in his judgment at the end of the obscenity trial, Douglas argued that any literary virtues claimed by the novel's defenders, specifically Cape and Ellis, actually worked *against* the project because "adroitness and cleverness . . . intensifies its moral danger." To reinforce this point, Douglas incorporated both Cape's promotional blurb and Ellis's preliminary statement in toto into the editorial.

25. Joan Scanlon, "Bad Language vs. Bad Prose? Lady Chatterley and *The Well*," *Critical Quarterly* 38, no. 3 (1996): 5. As Ingram points out, "major reviews were generally favorable." See " 'Unutterable Putrefaction' and 'Foul Stuff,' " p. 342.

26. L. P. Hartley, *Saturday Review*, July 1928, p. 126, and Leonard Woolf, *Nation & Athenaeum*, August 4, 1928, p. 593.

27. *Daily Telegraph*, August 17, 1928, p. 13.

28. Ethel Mannin, *Confessions and Impressions* (London: Jarrolds, 1930), p. 226. Emphasis mine.

29. Margaret Lawrence, *We Write As Women* (London: Michael Joseph, 1937), p. 260.

30. I. A. R. Wylie, *Sunday Times*, August 5, 1928, p. 5.

31. Elsie M. Lang, *British Women in the Twentieth Century* (London: T. Werner Laurie, 1929), pp. 236–7.

32. *Glasgow Herald*, August 9, 1928, p. 4.

33. *Morning Post*, August 10, 1928, p. 12; Woolf, *Nation & Athenaeum*, August 4, 1928, p. 593; and *Glasgow Herald*, p. 4.

34. Bennett, *Evening Standard*, August 9, 1928, p. 7. Bennett's review of *The Well* also appeared on the same day in the *Liverpool Echo*, the *Glasgow Evening*

Citizen, and the *Manchester Evening News*. Numerous reviews praised Hall for her courage in tackling such a delicate subject.

35. Quoted by Q. D. Leavis, *Fiction and the Reading Public* (London: Chatto and Windus, 1932), p. 281. The claim on behalf of Bennett's powers was made by his own paper, the *Evening Standard*; another book with Bennett's approval had "cleared the first edition right out of existence and still the clamor goes on."

36. See Anthea Trodd, *Women's Writing in English: Britain, 1900–1945* (London and New York: Longman, 1998), p. 49. The terms "low-brow" and "high-brow" were imported from America by H. G. Wells. See Graves and Hodge, *Long Weekend*, p. 50.

37. Woolf, *Nation & Athenaeum*, August 4, 1928, p. 593, and Bennett, *Evening Standard*, August 9, 1928, p. 7

38. Virginia Woolf's letter "To the Editor of the 'New Statesman'" was written in 1932 but never sent. It is reprinted in *The Death of the Moth and Other Essays* (Harmondsworth, England: Penguin Books, 1961), p. 152.

39. Leavis, *Fiction and the Reading Public*, pp. 20–1.

40. Trodd, *Women's Writing in English*, p. 47. Trodd continues: "The middlebrow reader is the person whose reading habits are determined by reference to the whole intermediary apparatus of reviews, Books of the Month, prizes and subscription libraries. The highbrow reader can rely upon reviews in a distinctive and smaller selection of their own group journals . . . and the lowbrow reader is out of reach of any such apparatus and borrows from the twopenny libraries" (pp. 48–9).

41. Letter from Virginia Woolf to Vita Sackville-West, August 30, 1928, in Nigel Nicolson and Joanne Trautmann, eds., *The Letters of Virginia Woolf*, vol. 3, *1923–1928* (New York and London: Harcourt Brace Jovanovich, 1978), p. 520, and Naomi Jacob, *Me and the Swans* (London: William Kimber, 1963), pp. 120–1.

42. Howard, *Jonathan Cape, Publisher*, p. 106. One of "the books most in demand at the Times Book Club [was] . . . Well of Loneliness, by Radclyffe Hall." See the *Spectator*, August 25, 1928, p. 245.

43. Gillian Whitlock, " 'Everything Is Out of Place': Radclyffe Hall and the Lesbian Literary Tradition," *Feminist Studies* 13, no. 3 (fall 1987): 581, n. 16. A highbrow, according to Woolf, "is the man or woman of thoroughbred intelligence who rides his mind at a gallop across country in pursuit of an idea," while the equally honorable lowbrow, is "a man or a woman of thoroughbred vitality who rides his body in pursuit of a living at a gallop across life." Although subject to a "mind/body" split, the interests of the "high" and "low" were not antithetical but complemented one another. See Woolf, "To the Editor of the 'New Statesman,' " pp. 152–3. Leonard Woolf characterized the highbrow as "genuinely attracted by elements in literature . . . which may conveniently be called

aesthetic, and which are not primarily interesting or attractive to the great public." See *Hunting the Highbrow* (London: Hogarth, 1927), p. 20.

44. Letter from Woolf to Quentin Bell, November 1, 1928. See Woolf, *Letters of Virginia Woolf*, 3: 555, and Woolf, "To the Editor of the 'New Statesman,'" p. 155.

45. Rosenman, "Sexual Identity and *A Room of One's Own*," p. 642 and Virginia Woolf, *The Diary of Virginia Woolf*, vol. 3, *1925–1930*, ed. Anne Olivier Bell (London: Penguin Books, 1980), pp. 193, 207.

46. Hermione Lee, *Virginia Woolf* (London: Vintage, 1997), pp. 514–5.

47. Letter from Hall to Winifred Macy, June 13, 1926. Quoted by Souhami, *Trials of Radclyffe Hall*, p. 148.

48. Una Troubridge Diaries, vol. 2, April 11, 1927, Lovat Dickson Papers, MG 30, D 237.

49. Woolf, "To the Editor of the 'New Statesman,'" p. 155. Woolf and several of her fellow modernists lived in Bloomsbury. In 1928 Woolf called Rose Macaulay "a successful lady novelist" who had "lived with the riff raff of South Kensington culture for 15 years." See Woolf, *Letters of Virginia Woolf*, 3: 501.

50. McKibbin, *Classes and Cultures*, p. vi.

51. Quentin Bell, *Virginia Woolf: A Biography* (New York: Harcourt Brace Jovanovich, 1972), 2: 140, and Cline, *Radclyffe Hall*, p. 212.

52. Trodd, *Women's Writing in English*, p. 50.

53. Wylie, *Sunday Times*, August 5, 1928, p. 5.

54. Richard King, *Tatler*, August 15, 1928, p. 298.

55. Woolf, *Nation & Athenaeum*, p. 593 and *Life and Letters*, p. 314. Emphasis mine.

56. *British Journal of Inebriety*, pp. 93–4. Emphasis mine.

57. W. R. Gordon, *Daily News and Westminster Gazette*, August 23, 1928, p. 4.

58. *Life and Letters*, p. 313.

59. Gordon, *Daily News and Westminster Gazette*, p. 4.

60. Cyril Connolly, *New Statesman*, August 25, 1928, p. 615, and Gordon, *Daily News and Westminster Gazette*, p. 4.

61. Another instance of transferring qualities from *The Well*'s protagonist on to the author herself is seen in Rebecca West's comment: "Since Miss Radclyffe Hall is sincere and well bred, no financial gain would make the prosecution of *The Well of Loneliness* anything but a veritable martyrdom to her." See Rebecca West, *Ending in Earnest: A Literary Log* (Garden City, N.Y.: Doubleday, Doran, 1931), p. 119.

62. *Glasgow Herald*, August 9, 1928, p. 4.

63. *Life and Letters*, p. 313.

64. Gordon, *Daily News and Westminster Gazette*, p. 4.

65. Nichols, *Sweet and Twenties*, p. 106.

66. James Douglas, *Daily Express*, November 29, 1927, p. 8.

67. J. C. Cannell, *When Fleet Street Calls: Being the Experiences of a London Journalist* (London: Jarrolds, 1932), pp. 200–1.

68. Cline, *Radclyffe Hall*, p. 243.

69. Before the war Douglas published a collection of short essays recording his "impressions of Preachers." See James Douglas, *The Man in the Pulpit* (London: Methuen, 1905), p. 43. Douglas also wrote a novel entitled *The Unpardonable Sin* (1907).

70. Nichols, *Sweet and Twenties*, p. 106, and Gerard J. DeGroot, *Blighty: British Society in the Era of the Great War* (London: Longman, 1996), p. 32. DeGroot continues: "Manliness should not be confused with what today is called machismo, since it encompassed a raft of attributes including honor, duty, sacrifice, honesty, and of course physical strength and endurance. Good character was supposed to arise from a strong will, which was in turn a sign of a healthy mind."

71. James Douglas, "Back to the Puritans," *Sunday Express*, November 4, 1928, p. 14.

72. *New Adelphi* 2, no. 1 (September 1928): 5939.

73. West, *Ending in Earnest*, p. 118. In the reference to "orange juice" West may have been slyly alluding to Douglas's Ulster origins—George Bernard Shaw called Douglas "a raving Orangeman." See Arnold Dawson, "Literature and the Stunt Press," *Clarion* no. 1864 (December, 1928): 7. Ellis was even more blunt than Shaw: "I understand the 'Daily Express' man is, or has been, insane." See Letter from Havelock Ellis to Bryher, September 18, 1928. GEN MSS 97, ser. 1, box 2, Beinecke.

74. Souhami, *Trials of Radclyffe Hall*, p. 183.

75. Connolly too observed that "in August, the reviewer's desert, [novels] loom up larger than they are." See *New Statesman*, August 25, 1928, p. 614.

76. Raymond Williams, *The Long Revolution* (Harmondsworth, England: Penguin Books Books, 1980), p. 233, and John Stevenson, *British Society, 1914–45* (Harmondsworth, England: Penguin Books Books, 1984), p. 405.

77. *Tatler*, November 28, 1928, p. 408.

78. Arnold Dawson, "The Literary Censorship Danger," *Clarion* no. 1861 (September 1928): 15. What underscores this cynicism still further is the fact that while the *Express*, a Beaverbrook paper, was denouncing *The Well*, another Beaverbrook paper, the *Evening Standard*, was printing Bennett's respectful review.

79. Nicholas Rance, "British Newspapers in the Early Twentieth Century," in Clive Bloom, ed., *Literature and Culture in Modern Britain*, vol. 1, *1900–1929* (London and New York: Longman, 1993), p. 122.

80. Stephen Koss, *The Rise and Fall of the Political Press in Britain*, vol. 2, *The Twentieth Century* (London: Hamish Hamilton, 1984), p. 389, and Baker, *Our Three Selves*, pp. 223, 224.

81. *Daily Express*, August 18, 1928, p. 1.

82. *Sunday Express*, August 19, 1928, p. 1.

83. Brittain, *Radclyffe Hall*, p. 52.

84. *Sunday Express*, August 26, 1928, p. 6.

85. Ibid., and Baker, *Our Three Selves*, p. 224.

86. Letter to the Editor, *Spectator*, September 8, 1928, p. 295. I surveyed most major newspapers, including *The Times*, the *Daily Herald*, the *Daily Telegraph*, and the *Manchester Guardian*, as well as a number of journals, such as the *Spectator*, the *Saturday Review*, and the *Nation & Athenaeum*.

87. Dawson, "The Literary Censorship Danger," p. 15.

88. Dawson, "Literature and the Stunt Press," p. 7 and "The Literary Censorship Danger," p. 15.

89. Raymond Mortimer, *New Statesman*, August 25, 1928, p. 602.

90. Douglas himself recognized the dilemma such "advertising" posed in his attack on "modern sex-novelists": "If the critic pours his vitriol over you, he advertises you instead of inhibiting you." See *Daily Express*, November 29, 1927, p. 8.

Hall's defense lawyer, Norman Birkett, also offered a sensible critique of Douglas, noting that, thirty years on, everyone was reading the novel and no one was apparently dying. Rolph lamented that Hall's "beautifully written book was actually described at the time by a journalist of that day named James Douglas in ridiculously exaggerated language, expressly designed to attract readers and inflame public opinion." See C. H. Rolph, ed., *Does Pornography Matter?* (London: Routledge, 1961), p. 3.

91. *Yorkshire Post*, August 24, 1928, p. 8. As a result of the publicity the *Newcastle Daily Journal and North Star* reported the book "must have been pretty well sold out. Queues lined up for it at all the booksellers" (August 24, 1928, p. 8); and the *Manchester Daily Dispatch* noted: "It would be difficult, if not impossible, to buy a copy in the city at the moment" (August 22, 1928, p. 4).

92. *Nation & Athenaeum*, September 1, 1928, p. 696.

93. Bristow, *Sexuality*, p. 53. See *People*, August 19, 1928, p. 2, and *Sunday Chronicle*, August 19, 1928, p. 1.

94. See, for example, *Evening Standard*, August 20, 1928, p. 6; *Manchester Daily Dispatch*, August 22, 1928, p. 4; *Newcastle Daily Journal and North Star*, August 24, 1928, p. 8; and *Daily Mirror*, November 20, 1928, p. 9.

95. Memorandum from Sir George Stephenson to Sir William Joynson-Hicks, August 21, 1928. PRO HO144/22547/527705, Public Record Office, London (hereafter referred to as Public Record Office).

Hall may have been surprised to learn that her reputation had preceded her as the deputy from Public Prosecutions told Joynson-Hicks: "Incidentally it would appear to be clear that the authoress is herself what I believe is known as a homo-sexualist, or as she prefers to describe it an 'invert.' "

96. Howard, *Jonathan Cape, Publisher*, p. 105.

97. McKibbin, *Classes and Cultures*, p. 324, and Howard, *Jonathan Cape, Publisher*, p. 105.

98. Transcript of the Judgement of Sir Chartres Biron, chief magistrate, Bow Street Police Court, Home Office file on the prosecution of *The Well of Loneliness*, November 16, 1928. PRO HO144/22547/527705, Public Record Office.

99. Ronald Blythe, *The Age of Illusion: England in the Twenties and Thirties, 1914–1940* (London: Hamish Hamilton, 1963), p. 31.

100. Cate Haste, *Rules of Desire: Sex in Britain, World War I to the Present* (London: Chatto and Windus, 1992), p. 74. In *Young in the Twenties* Ethel Mannin described Joynson-Hicks as "aggressively puritanical . . . anti alcohol, nightclubs, gambling, the poems and paintings of D. H. Lawrence, 'obscene' books, and all things 'sinful,' " (London: Hutchinson, 1971), p. 55.

101. Souhami, *Trials of Radclyffe Hall*, p. 218.

102. Ingram, " 'Unutterable Putrefaction' and 'Foul Stuff,' " p. 353.

103. Newman Flower, ed., *The Journal of Arnold Bennett, 1921–1928* (London: Cassell, 1933), p. 271.

104. Cecil Roberts, *One Year of Life: Some Autobiographical Pages* (London: Hodder and Stoughton, 1952), p. 96.

105. West, *Ending in Earnest*, p. 118.

106. Radclyffe Hall, *The Well of Loneliness* (1928; reprint, New York: Anchor Books, 1990), p. 437.

107. *The Times*, March 16, 1926, p. 10. *The Times* described Leslie's novel as "a study of undergraduate life at Cambridge." In 1929 the publisher of Norah C. James's *Sleeveless Errand* was called to Bow Street Magistrate's Court to explain why a novel with "filthy language" and depicting "indecent situations" should be tolerated, again, by "decent-minded people." The publisher withdrew the book and, like Cape, published it in Paris. Excerpts quoted by Ingram, " 'Unutterable Putrefaction' and 'Foul Stuff,' " p. 346. Incidentally, James, who worked in publicity for Jonathan Cape, was asked by the publisher to a read the manuscript of *The Well*.

108. The books Biron reviewed were "by no means confined to the law—the one subject, it was uncharitably said by lawyers, that he knew least about." See Rolph, *Does Pornography Matter?*, p. 78, and *The Times*, March 16, 1926, p. 10.

109. Souhami, *Trials of Radclyffe Hall*, p. 218.

110. McKibbin, *Classes and Cultures*, p. 325, and Roberts, *One Year of Life*, p. 96.

111. Blythe, *Age of Illusion*, pp. 33, 32. Stephen Koss reports that both the *Daily Express* and the *Sunday Express* received letters to the editor complaining about the papers' "constant criticism of Joynson-Hicks." See Koss, *Rise and Fall of the Political Press in Britain*, p. 479. That Jix was more a source of amusement is suggested in Goldring's tongue-in-cheek comment that writers were asking desperately what they could do to be banned, so they too could increase sales, *Nineteen Twenties*, p. 229. See also Weeks, *Coming Out*, p. 108, Baker, *Our Three Selves*, p. 227, and Brittain, *Radclyffe Hall*, p. 23.

112. "Gadfly," *Daily Herald*, March 7, 1929, p. 7.

113. Sir William Joynson-Hicks, *Do We Need a Censor?* (London: Faber and Faber, 1929), pp. 13, 14.

114. Ibid., pp. 5, 13.

115. Woolf, *Letters of Virginia Woolf*, 3: 555.

116. Quoted by Jane Lewis, *Women in England, 1870–1950: Sexual Divisions and Social Change* (Brighton, Sussex: Wheatsheaf Books, 1984), p. 134.

117. *Liverpool Post and Mercury*, August 15, 1928, p. 4.

118. Mrs. Cecil Chesterton in the *Daily Herald*, August 23, 1928, p. 7.

119. C. H. Rolph, introduction to *Radclyffe Hall*, by Brittain, p. 14.

120. Roberts, *One Year of Life*, p. 96.

121. *Spectator*, September 1, 1928, p. 258.

122. Woolf, *Nation & Athenaeum*, August 4, 1928, p. 593. Woolf's phrase "rather strangely" suggests that he was unfamiliar with Ellis's important work on inversion.

123. *Liverpool Post and Mercury*, August 15, 1928, p. 4.

124. George Chauncey Jr., "From Sexual Inversion to Homosexuality: Medicine and the Changing Conceptualization of Female Deviance," *Salmagundi* 58–59 (fall 1982/winter 1983): 116, 119.

125. *Spectator*, September 1, 1928, p. 258. Incidentally, the *Spectator* ultimately declined to publish the review of *The Well* it had earlier solicited on the grounds, as explained in its editorial, that "the subject of sexual perversion is one which is better ignored."

126. *North Mail and Newcastle Chronicle*, August 11, 1928, p. 3.

127. *T. P.'s & Cassell's Weekly*, August 11, 1928, p. 487; *Evening Standard*, August 9, 1928, p. 7; *Eve: The Lady's Pictorial*, August 22, 1928, p. 363; *Liverpool Post and Mercury*, August 15, 1928, p. 4.

128. *Truth*, August 29, 1928, p. 381, and *Sunday Chronicle*, August 19, 1928, p. 1.

129. *Eve: The Lady's Pictorial*, August 29, 1928, p. 407.

130. *Daily Express*, August 21, 1928, p. 15. On p. 1 the newspaper ran a headline "Publishers' Ban on Woman's Novel" and explained that the book dealt with "a form of sexual abnormality."

131. *Daily Express*, August 21, 1928, p. 15. Emphasis mine. See chapter 4 for a fuller discussion of Hall's distinctive manner of dress as situated against the dominant fashions of the 1920s.

132. *Spectator*, September 1, 1928, p. 258. The three other publications to condemn the subject of Hall's novel were: *People*, the *Sunday Chronicle*, and, of course, the *Express*.

133. Letter from Bryher to H.D. [Hilda Doolittle], December 18?, 1929. YCAL MSS 24, ser. 1, box 3, Beinecke.

134. Gayle S. Rubin, "Thinking Sex: Notes for a Radical Theory of the Politics of Sexuality," in Linda S. Kauffman, ed., *American Feminist Thought at Century's End* (Cambridge: Blackwell, 1993), p. 32.

135. Sheila Jeffreys, "Women and Sexuality," in June Purvis, ed., *Women's History: Britain, 1850–1945* (London: UCL Press, 1995), p. 206.

136. King, *Tatler*, August 15, 1928, p. 298.

137. Interview with Radclyffe Hall in the *New York Telegram Magazine*, December 13, 1928, p. 2.

138. *Daily Herald*, November 17, 1928, p. 5.

139. Rebecca O'Rourke, *Reflecting on The Well of Loneliness* (London: Routledge, 1989), p. 94.

140. Weeks, *Sex, Politics, and Society*, p. 14.

141. Dawson, "The Literary Censorship Danger," p. 15.

142. See, for example, Alison Oram, *Women Teachers and Feminist Politics, 1900–1939* (Manchester: Manchester University Press, 1996), and Lillian Faderman, *Odd Girls and Twilight Lovers: A History of Lesbian Life in Twentieth-Century America* (New York: Penguin Books Books, 1992).

2. "THAT NAMELESS VICE BETWEEN WOMEN": LESBIANISM AND THE LAW

1. Travers Humphreys was quoted by the *Vigilante*, April 6, 1918, pp. 1–5, see esp. p. 1. Sir Ellis Hume-Williams was cited by *The Times*, November 19, 1920, p. 4. Unless otherwise indicated, subsequent references to the Allan trial can be found in this issue of the *Vigilante* (page numbers indicated in the text) and the Hall case can be found in this issue of *The Times*.

2. Twenty years earlier, Humphreys represented Oscar Wilde at a preliminary hearing at Bow Street. When Allan's case was taken over by the Crown and moved on to the Central Criminal Court, "it was decided that Travers Humphreys should be led by an elder." The "elder" was Sir Ellis Hume-Williams, who would represent Radclyffe Hall in the slander trial. See Philip Hoare, *Wilde's Last Stand: Decadence, Conspiracy, and the First World War* (London: Duckworth, 1997), pp. 95, 113.

3. Fox-Pitt, coincidentally, was a son-in-law of the Marquess of Queensberry, the man who called Wilde a "somdomite" [sic]. See Weeks, *Coming Out*, p. 105.

4. See Weeks's major studies: *Coming Out*, pp. 104–6 and *Sex, Politics and Society*, pp. 116–7. See also Alison Oram, " 'Embittered, Sexless, or Homosexual': Attacks on Spinster Teachers 1918–1939," in Lesbian History Group, ed., *Not a Passing Phase: Reclaiming Lesbians in History 1840–1985* (London: The Women's Press, 1989), pp. 99–118, especially 106, and Annabel Faraday, "Social Definitions of Lesbians in Britain, 1914–1939," unpublished Ph.D. thesis, University of Essex, 1985.

5. Only *The Times* actually mentions "lesbian" and "lesbianism" in the Maud Allan trial. See *The Times*, May 30 to June 8, 1918. Other newspapers, such as the *Daily Mirror*, the *Morning Post*, the *Daily Mail*, the *Manchester Guardian*, and the *Daily Chronicle* refer to the subject as "perversion," "moral weakness," "a mental disease," "unnatural vice," "sexual pervert," and "immoral." The *Sunday Chronicle* may have been the most coy in stating that the case concerned a "lady whose name was coupled with . . . that which was sometimes described as—(the remainder of the sentence was inaudible)," April 7, 1918, p. 4. The coverage by the *Daily Express* typifies the print media's response to Radclyffe Hall's case by describing how she was alleged to be "a grossly immoral woman" who "had come between Admiral Sir Ernest Troubridge and his wife, and had wrecked their home," November 19, 1920, p. 1. *The Times*, the *Daily Mail*, the *Manchester Guardian*, the *Daily Herald*, the *Morning Post*, and the *Daily Chronicle* repeated these allegations and also referred to "unnatural vice" and "sexual immorality."

6. Hoare has discovered another intriguing link between the two trials in that Admiral Troubridge's son by a previous marriage served as a political agent to Pemberton Billing. Hoare deduces from this association that Troubridge's son may have shared information about his step-mother's lesbianism with his employer: "It is likely that Billing knew about Una's lesbian relationships, already common knowledge by 1918 and further evidence of society decadence." We should be wary of Hoare's unsubstantiated assertion that Troubridge's lesbian relationships were "common knowledge." See *Wilde's Last Stand*, p. 123n.

7. Several newspapers were quick to point this out once Allan's trial was over. Thus the *Daily Mirror*'s editorial, entitled "Government by Hysterics," noted with regard to Pemberton Billing: "You have a plan, a project you think ought to be adopted by the Government. The Government pays no attention to you . . . what then do you proceed to do? . . . You can yourself scream your way through a court of law, and . . . emerge as a Great Hero for about a fortnight. . . . Government by hysteria pays." June 8, 1918, p. 8.

8. *The Times*, June 5, 1918, p. 7.

9. Ibid., May 31, 1918, p. 4.

10. *Sunday Times*, June 2, 1918, p. 6.

11. *The Times*, June 5, 1918, p. 7. The editorial further comments: "It is safe to say that no lawsuit of modern times has attracted such universal and painful interest. . . . Not only in London, but even more in the provincial towns and countryside, the daily reports have been read and discussed with almost as deep anxiety as the news of the war itself." Obviously, the trial is too complex to cover adequately in this chapter. For further information on the trial, see Lucy Bland, "Trial by Sexology? Maud Allan, *Salome*, and the 'Cult of the Clitoris' Case," in Lucy Bland and Laura Doan, eds., *Sexology in Culture: Labelling Bodies and Desires* (Chicago: University of Chicago Press, 1998), pp. 183–98; Regina Gagnier, Appendix A "Art as Propaganda in Wartime," in *Idylls of the Marketplace: Oscar Wilde and the Victorian Public* (Stanford: Stanford University Press, 1986); Hoare, *Wilde's Last Stand*; Michael Kettle, *Salome's Last Veil: The Libel Case of the Century* (London: Granada Publishing, 1977); and Jennifer Travis, "Clits in Court: *Salome*, Sodomy, and the Lesbian 'Sadist,'" in Karla Jay, ed., *Lesbian Erotics* (New York: New York University Press, 1995), pp. 147–63.

12. *Daily Chronicle*, November 20, 1920, p. 1; *The Times*, November 19, 1920, p. 4.

13. *The Times*, November 20, 1920, p. 11.

14. Ibid., June 5, 1918, p. 7.

15. Bland, "Trial by Sexology?," p. 191.

16. *Daily Herald*, November 20, 1920, p. 2.

17. *Morning Post*, November 19, 1920, p. 3. Mrs. Helen Salter, the second witness to Fox-Pitt's "slander," told the court that "when the defendant made that remark about Miss Radclyffe Hall's being a thoroughly immoral woman there was a change in his manner, and he showed some embarrassment." See *The Times*, November 20, 1920, p. 4.

18. Ibid., November 20, 1920, p. 4.

19. The Labouchère Amendment (Section 11) of the Criminal Law Amendment Act of 1885 reads: "Any male person who, in public or private, commits, or is a

party to the commission of, or procures or attempts to procure the commission by any male person of any act of gross indecency with another male person, shall be guilty of a misdemeanor, and being convicted thereof shall be liable at the discretion of the court to be imprisoned for any term not exceeding two years, with or without hard labor." See Criminal Law Amendment Act, 1885 (48 & 49 Vict. c. 69), sec. 11.

20. *Daily Mail*, November 20, 1920, pp. 7–8.

21. In fact, as Hume-Williams stated the phrase was "so indecent that no reputable paper in England has ever reproduced it in the course of the reporting of this case." See *Daily Express*, June 5, 1918, p. 1.

22. Bland, "Trial by Sexology?," p. 192.

23. Felix Cherniavsky, *The Salome Dancer* (Toronto: McCelland and Stewart, 1991), p. 247.

24. Cline, *Radclyffe Hall*, p. 179. Hall was awarded £500 in damages, but Fox-Pitt later won an appeal and the right for a new trial. Hall followed her lawyer's advice and dropped her case. For an excellent review of the case and a post-trial analysis of Hall's "hollow" victory, see especially pp. 164–68.

25. Travis observes perceptively, "Although Billing was the defendant in what became a criminal libel trial, Allan became the sexual subject under investigation." See "Clits in Court," p. 147. Hume-Williams, Allan's barrister, also recognized that in the end it would be the plaintiff who would suffer: "[Billing] must not march to success over the ruins of a woman's reputation." See *The Times*, June 5, 1918, p. 4.

26. Report by the Joint Select Committee of the House of Lords and the House of Commons. *Minutes of Evidence Taken Before the Joint Select Committee on the Criminal Law Amendment Bill* (London: HMSO, 1920), p. 936, para. 1479.

27. Weeks, *Coming Out*, p. 106.

28. Jeffreys, *Spinster and Her Enemies*, pp. 113–15.

29. Martin Pugh, *Women and the Women's Movement in Britain, 1914–1959* (London: Macmillan, 1992), p. 79. Pugh's account is misleading because he implies that lawmakers "preferred to lose the entire measure rather than pass it without the anti-lesbian clause." In fact, the opposite was true. The Lords refused to pass the CLA Bill with the antilesbian clause and sent it back to the Commons. Because of the lack of time before Parliament recessed, the bill was allowed to languish.

30. Cline advances the ahistorical view that in the autumn of 1920 Hall may have been influenced by "apprehensions . . . that a move was afoot to bring lesbian relations within the purview of the criminal law." Cline rightly observes that in 1920 there was a "growing public awareness of the subject," which would

in turn "increase the threat from Fox-Pitt's allegations." It is, however, unlikely that Hall could have peered as far ahead as August of 1921 when the subject of criminalizing lesbianism was raised in the Commons. See *Radclyffe Hall*, p. 164.

31. Judith Butler, *Gender Trouble: Feminism and the Subversion of Identity* (London: Routledge, 1990), p. 75. Emphasis mine.

32. The main concern of the Criminal Law Amendment Act of 1885 was to protect the young. The Act thus changed the age of consent for women from thirteen to sixteen (though the act allowed the age to remain at thirteen for indecent assault). Groups, such as the Association for Moral and Social Hygiene and the Criminal Law Amendment Committee (comprised of social purity activists and feminists), lobbied intensively for decades to strengthen and improve the 1885 Act. One major loophole was a clause that allowed men to defend themselves by claiming they had "reasonable cause to believe" a girl was over the age of sixteen.

33. *Hansard*, Commons, 5th ser., 145 (1921): 1799.

34. Philippa Levine, " 'Walking the Streets in a Way No Decent Woman Should': Women Police in World War I," *Journal of Modern History* 66 (1994): 34.

35. Joan Lock, *The British Policewoman* (London: Robert Hale, 1979), pp. 19–20. Margaret Damer Dawson (1874–1920), according to an obituary notice, was "a daughter of the late Mr. Richard Dawson . . . and of Agnes Lady Walsingham." Damer Dawson initially pursued an interest in music (attaining a gold medal and diploma from the London Academy of Music) before embarking on an activist career. She worked for more humane treatment for animals (earning awards and recognition in Denmark and Finland) and later labored on behalf of children and unwanted infants. See *Daily Telegraph*, May 22, 1920, Newspaper Cutting Collection, Millicent Garrett Fawcett Library, London (hereafter referred to as Fawcett Library).

36. Damer Dawson reports: "In February 1915 I was asked to resign by the Deputy Chief of the Corps of Policewomen, Miss Nina Boyle, to resign my position, because she said I had gone against women's interests [in enforcing curfew restrictions against women only]." See Mary S. Allen, *The Pioneer Policewoman*, ed. and arr. Julie Helen Heyneman (London: Chatto and Windus, 1925), p. 139.

37. The WPS initially sustained its activities through voluntary contributions solicited by Damer Dawson who lectured extensively, but in 1916 the government awarded a grant. See Allen, *Pioneer Policewoman*, pp. 20–1. About this time the group also received a fortune from an unnamed donor; Lock writes: "It must have been a great deal of money for they quickly took on new staff and moved to bigger and better premises." See *British Policewoman*, p. 52.

38. Mrs. Sophia Stanley was, like many of the early policewomen, a "lady of means," who was married to an "ex-Indian civil servant." See John Carrier, *The*

Campaign for the Employment of Women as Police Officers (Aldershot, England: Avebury, 1988), p. 36, and Joan Lock, "Downfall of the Ladylike Policewoman," *Police Review*, August 10, 1984, p. 1548.

39. Levine, " 'Walking the Streets,' " pp. 44–5.

40. Allen, *Pioneer Policewoman*, pp. 128–9. Mary Sophia Allen (1878–1964) was the daughter of "a former manager of the Great Western Railway." (See *Daily Telegraph*, December 18, 1964, Newspaper Cutting Collection, Fawcett Library.) Lock describes her as the "dutiful, nervous, and delicate daughter in a middle-class Bristol household," until she became a suffragette. (See Joan Lock, "The Extraordinary Life of Mary Allen," *Police Review*, June 29, 1984, p. 1266.) Isobel Goldingham was the daughter of the late John Dalrymple Goldingham of the India Civil Service. (See Allen, *Pioneer Policewoman*, p. 56.)

41. For detailed histories of the establishment and operations of women police in general during the First World War and after, the debates surrounding the establishment of the MWPP, and the WPS specifically, see Lucy Bland, "In the Name of Protection: The Policing of Women in the First World War," in Carol Smart and Julia Brophy, eds., *Women-in-Law* (London: Routledge, 1985), pp. 23–49; Carrier, *Campaign for the Employment*; Levine, " 'Walking the Streets' "; and Lock, *British Policewoman*. Levine in particular outlines the ways in which women's policing organizations were perceived by feminists and the public alike.

42. Levine, " 'Walking the Streets,' " p. 61. In a speech to the National Union of Societies for Equal Citizenship on June 27, 1921, Allen claimed that no WPS members were accepted (Astor Papers, 1416/1/1/943, Reading University). (Hereafter all citations to the Astor Papers refer to the collection held at Reading University.) Lock argues that while it is true that no WPS members were accepted in the first hiring, "many of the second [batch] were from the WPS." Elsewhere, however, Lock describes a Mrs. Hampton as "the only member of the WPS to be employed by the Metropolitan Police," and she was eventually dismissed by the Met "because a member of the Women Police Service was not desired." See *British Policewoman*, pp. 91, 99–100. In my review of fifty-six MWPP personnel records held at the Metropolitan Police Historic Museum in London, between February 1919 and August 1920, seven recruits listed the WPS as their former employer.

43. Not to be confused with the Joint Select Committee on the Criminal Law Amendment Bill, which was a parliamentary committee and was comprised of members of the Lords and Commons, the CLA Committee, as Levine explains, consisted of "a collection of social purity, feminist, and other activists committed to combating what it saw as a 'white slave trade' of young English girls into prostitution abroad." See " 'Walking the Streets,' " p. 38. " 'Social purity,' " Bland explains, "was the contemporary euphemistic term for 'sexual purity'—the

'purity' or 'sexual continence' of both sexes. The social purity movement was intent on changing society's sexual behavior and attitudes." See Lucy Bland, *Banishing the Beast: English Feminism and Sexual Morality* (London: Penguin Books, 1995), p. 52.

44. Criminal Law Amendment Committee pamphlet, August 7, 1914, PRO HO45/10806/309485, Public Record Office.

45. Lock, "The Extraordinary Life of Mary Allen," p. 1266.

46. Bland, "In the Name of Protection," p. 27.

47. Carrier, *Campaign for the Employment*, p. 18.

48. Baird Committee, *Report of the Committee on the Employment of Women on Police Duties*, Cmnd. 887 (London: HMSO, 1920), p. 19, para. 179.

49. Sir Nevil Macready, *Annals of an Active Life* (London: Hutchinson, 1924), p. 416.

50. Levine, " 'Walking the Streets,' " pp. 47–8.

51. Speech by Mary Allen to an Emergency Conference of NUSEC, June 27, 1921, Astor Papers, 1416/1/1/943.

52. Levine notes: "When the WPS calculated the socioeconomic backgrounds of the 1,080 women it had 'trained and equipped' between 1914 and 1919, 411 (about 40 percent) had private means." See " 'Walking the Streets,' " p. 46.

53. Allen, *Pioneer Policewoman*, pp. 131-2.

54. *Daily Mail* newspaper cutting, October 4, 1918, PRO HO45/111067/370521, Public Record Office.

55. *Daily Telegraph*, May 22, 1920.

56. *The Women's Auxiliary Service: A Report of Work Accomplished During the Year 1920–1921*, p. 14, ADM 1/11/2, Metropolitan Police Historic Museum, London.

Macready's willingness to spend more money to train fresh recruits did not go unobserved—the *Daily Chronicle* interviewed a WPS inspector who argued that such a policy was "a glaring waste of labor and public money." See newspaper cutting, November 23, 1918, PRO HO45/111067/370521, Public Record Office.

57. Carrier, *Campaign for the Employment*, p. 29.

58. Lock, *British Policewoman*, p. 85.

59. Memorandum by Sir Leonard Dunning, Inspector of Constabulary at the Home Office, January 30, 1917, PRO HO45/10806/309485, Public Record Office.

60. Letter from Sir Nevil Macready to Sir Edward Troup, January 29, 1920, PRO HO45/111067/370521, Public Record Office.

Allen was less successful with the Joint Select Committee. When she asked Astor to address the committee, Astor drafted a letter on October 29, 1920, to Muir Mackenzie that she did not send: "I should like very much to have one or two experienced policewomen called as witnesses. . . . I do not think [Allen's] point of view is perhaps quite so valuable, but I understand that she is very anxious to give evidence." See Astor Papers, 1416/1/1/930. Letter marked "not sent." Stanley, however, was invited to testify at the Met's request.

61. Note by Alker Tripp, September 22, 1920, PRO HO45/11067/370521, Public Record Office.

62. Astor Papers, 1416/1/1/930.

63. *Women Police Service: Report for 1916*, ADM 1/11/7, Metropolitan Police Historic Museum, London.

64. Carrier, *Campaign for the Employment*, p. 104.

65. Baird Committee, *Report*, p. 58, para. 979.

66. Bridgeman Report, *Appendix to Report of the Departmental Committee on the Employment of Policewomen*, Cmnd. 2224 (London: HMSO, 1924), p. 407.

67. Carrier, *Campaign for the Employment*, p. 76.

68. Lock, "Downfall of the Ladylike Policewoman," p. 1548.

69. Lock, *British Policewoman*, p. 59.

70. Letter from Sir William Horwood to Mary S. Allen, September 21, 1921, PRO HO45/11067/370521, Public Record Office.

71. Letter from Sir William Horwood to Sir Edward Troup, September 21, 1920, PRO HO45/11067/370521, Public Record Office.

72. Report by the Joint Select Committee, *Minutes of Evidence*, pp. 936–7, paras. 1479–1501. All subsequent citations to Chapman's testimony before the committee and the discussion that testimony generated can be found on these pages in the report.

73. Lock, *British Policewoman*, pp. 130–1. See also Allen, *Pioneer Policewoman*, p. 81. Chapman's support for women in policing continued through the 1920s, as evidenced first by a letter of congratulations he sent on the launch of the *Policewoman's Review* and, second, by an article he contributed on women police, where he observes, "Nobody wants to turn women into men, but everybody knows by this time that nothing has hindered the progress of the world so much as man's reluctance to admit women to an equal share of its management." See *Policewoman's Review* 1, no. 1 (May 1927): 5 and 1, no. 2 (June 1927): 10.

74. "Note Supplied by a Shorthand Writer," April 12, 1921, PRO HO45/11067/370521, Public Record Office.

75. Angela V. John's work recuperates men's contribution to the suffrage campaign. See Claire Eustance, Joan Ryan, and Laura Ugolini, eds., "Between the Cause and the Courts: The Curious Case of Cecil Chapman," in *A Suffrage Reader: Charting Directions in British Suffrage History* (London: Leicester University Press, 2000), pp. 145–61. John further notes that on October 8, 1910, the *Vote* characterized Chapman as "one of the most important and convincing

speakers to be had on any suffrage platform." I would like to thank Angela John for sharing her work in progress on Chapman.

76. Private Correspondence, April 19, 1996.

77. *Woman's Leader* (publication of the National Union of Societies for Equal Citizenship), August 12, 1921, pp. 401–2.

78. Jeffreys, *Spinster and Her Enemies*, p. 55.

79. Margaret Jackson, *The* Real *Facts of Life: Feminism and the Politics of Sexuality, c. 1850–1940* (London: Taylor and Francis, 1994), p. 42.

80. George Ives Diary, July 9, 1914. vol. xxi, p. 112, 6695, British Sexological Society Collection, Harry Ransom Humanities Research Center, The University of Texas at Austin. Chapman was elected to membership in the BSSSP in 1914. On July 8, 1914, Chapman chaired the Inaugural Meeting of the BSSSP during which Laurence Housman, E. B. Lloyd, and Edward Carpenter addressed "the less recognized characteristics of sexual inversion." I am grateful to Lesley Hall for this information.

81. Carrier, *Campaign for the Employment*, p. 17.

82. After a conversation with Mary Allen in 1931, Una Troubridge recorded in her diary that the London Met seemed only interested in "fluffy policewomen." See Baker, *Our Three Selves*, p. 267.

83. *Hansard*, Commons, 5th. ser., 145 (1921): 1799–1806. See especially p. 1800.

84. Jeffreys, "Women and Sexuality," pp. 193–216, esp. p. 205.

85. Jackson, Real *Facts of Life*, pp. 121, 108.

86. Faderman, *Odd Girls and Twilight Lovers*, p. 48.

87. Richard von Krafft-Ebing, *Psychopathia Sexualis With Especial Reference to the Antipathic Sexual Instinct: A Medico-Forensic Study* (1886; reprint, New York: Stein and Day, 1965), p. 262.

88. August Forel, *The Sexual Question: A Scientific, Psychological, Hygienic, and Sociological Study for the Cultured Classes* (1906; reprint, New York: Rebman Company, 1908), p. 274–5. Ellis also opens his chapter on "Sexual Inversion in Women" with the assertion, "It has been found, under certain conditions, to abound among women in colleges and convents and prisons, as well as under the ordinary conditions of society." The choice of the word "abound" is strategic, for his purpose here is to establish that inversion is as common in women as in men. See Havelock Ellis, *Studies in the Psychology of Sex*, vol. 2, *Sexual Inversion* (Philadelphia: F. A. Davis, 1928), p. 195.

89. Forel, *Sexual Question*, p. 251–2. Emphasis mine.

90. Albert Moll, *Perversions of the Sex Instinct: A Study of Sexual Inversion* (1891; reprint, Newark: Julian Press, 1931), pp. 231, 233.

91. In this paper, published six years later, Browne advocates an acceptance of female sexual inversion well ahead of her time: "Let us recognize this force

[female sexual inversion], as frankly as we recognize and reverence the love between men and women." See F. W. Stella Browne, "Studies in Feminine Inversion," *Journal of Sexology and Psychanalysis* [sic] (1923): 54–5. Lesley Hall kindly alerted me to Chapman's association with the BSSSP.

92. Krafft-Ebing, *Psychopathia Sexualis*, pp. 263, 262. Emphasis mine.

93. Ellis, *Sexual Inversion*, p. 214.

94. *Hansard*, Lords, 5th ser., 14 (1921): 565–577. See especially p. 572.

95. Michel Foucault, *The History of Sexuality*, vol. 1, *An Introduction* (1976; reprint, London: Penguin Books, 1990), pp. 10, 3.

96. Ibid., pp. 17–18.

97. Ibid., p. 35.

98. *Hansard*, Commons, 5th ser., 145 (1921): 1799.

99. *Hansard*, Lords, 5th. ser., 14 (1921): 568.

100. *Hansard*, Commons, 5th Ser., 146 (1921): 1596.

101. *Hansard*, Lords, 5th ser., 14 (1921): 574. Emphasis mine.

102. Jackson notes that "The Cavendish-Bentinck Library . . . [supplied] suffragists with books they could not procure in the ordinary way." See Real *Facts of Life*, p. 179.

103. *Hansard*, Lords, 5th ser., 14 (1921): 573.

104. *Hansard*, Commons, 5th ser., 146 (1921): 1606.

105. Forel, *Sexual Question*, p. 247.

106. In a letter to the *Lancet*, Lionel A. Weatherly, M.D. made a similar claim following Maud Allan's trial. According to Weatherly, lesbianism was a major cause in the decline of birthrates. See *Lancet* 1 (June 22, 1918): 884–5.

107. Arabella Kenealy, *Feminism and Sex Extinction* (London: T. Fisher Unwin, 1920), pp. 246, 253, 263.

108. W. C. D. Whetham and C. D. Whetham, *The Family and the Nation: A Study in Natural Inheritance and Social Responsibility* (London: Longmans, Green, 1909), p. 199.

109. Ellis, *Sexual Inversion*, p. 262.

110. Bland, *Banishing the Beast*, p. 264.

111. The Scientific Humanitarian Committee, *The Social Problem of Sexual Inversion* in Mark Blasius and Shane Phelan, eds., *We Are Everywhere: A Historical Sourcebook of Gay and Lesbian Politics* (London: Routledge, 1997), p. 140.

112. *Hansard*, Lords, 5th ser., 14 (1921): 570. It is important to mention that, due to class differences, the tenor of the debate in the Lords, where the clause was rejected, is entirely different, as the Lords generally refer to the sexual activities between women as this "particular subject." Twice the topic is called "disgusting" and once "polluting," but overall references to the subject are quite restrained in comparison to the discourse of the House of Commons.

113. Forel, *Sexual Question*, pp. 247, 404.

114. Letter (dated October 22, 1921) addressed to Lord Aberdeen from Lady Astor, Astor Papers, 1416/1/1/550. *Time and Tide* describes the enemies of the bill as "the usual little group . . . [whose] speeches were of the usual type, though somewhat fuller of repetition than is usual" (August 12, 1921, p. 757).

115. Richard Davenport-Hines argues that none of the three men who sponsored the clause "commanded respect" in the House of Commons. Macquisten's "views seldom carried any weight" and Wild's voice was often heard but with little effect. See *Sex, Death, and Punishment: Attitudes to Sex and Sexuality in Britain Since the Renaissance* (London: Collins, 1990), p. 151.

116. Hilda Matheson, Astor's political secretary, was a lesbian; one of her lovers in the late 1920s was Vita Sackville-West. It is not clear whether or not Alison Neilans was a lesbian, though if not homosexual she was most certainly homosocial. Neilans lived with Ethel (Madge) Turner for the last twelve years of her life and named Turner the major beneficiary of her will. I would like to thank Hilary Frances for sharing her research on Neilans with me.

117. This letter, on AMSH letterhead, was among Lady Astor's private papers and dated August 5, 1921. It is unclear whether it was written before the Commons debate or hours after. If before, the letter demonstrates that Neilans felt they had won; if after, Neilans was as yet unaware that the addition of the antilesbian clause meant that the bill would probably be rejected by the Lords. Astor Papers, 1416/1/2/32. Astor was "most bitterly disappointed" with the Bill's rejection in the Lords. See Letter from Hilda Matheson to Mr. Robinson, M.P., August 18, 1921, Astor Papers, 1416/1/1/546.

118. Letter by Alison Neilans for the AMSH, August 12, 1921, Astor Papers, 1416/1/1/546.

119. *Church Militant* (publication of the League of the Church Militant), September 1921, p. 63.

120. *Shield*, November/December, 1921, pp. 203–4. "The new clause dealing with indecency between females is on [the] right lines in so far as it equalizes the sexes in this respect," though the article recognizes the danger of blackmail. See *Woman's Leader*, August 12, 1921, p. 401.

121. *Seventh Report of the Association for Moral and Social Hygiene*, April 1, 1921–March 31, 1922, p. 23, Fawcett Library.

122. Letter sent by Pat Dansey and quoted by Diana Souhami, *Mrs. Keppel and Her Daughter* (London: Flamingo, 1997), p. x.

123. Chauncey, "From Sexual Inversion to Homosexuality," p. 115.

124. This key difference in the law concerning male and female homosexuality accounts for the slower development of lesbian visibility: "It is clear that by the end of the nineteenth century a recognizably 'modern' male homosexual iden-

tity was beginning to emerge, but it would be another generation before female homosexuality reached a corresponding level of articulacy." See Weeks, *Sex, Politics, and Society*, p. 108.

3. OUTRAGING THE DECENCIES OF NATURE?
UNIFORMED FEMALE BODIES

1. Nigel Nicolson, *Portrait of a Marriage* (1973; reprint, London: Weidenfeld and Nicolson, 1990), p. 99. Emphasis mine. All references to the events on April 18, 1918, can be found on this page, except where otherwise indicated.

2. Sackville-West's own mother declared that her daughter "looks so charming in her corduroy trousers. She ought to have been a boy!" See Victoria Glendinning, *Vita: The Life of V. Sackville-West* (London: Weidenfeld and Nicolson, 1983), p. 93. The phrase "women-on the-land" refers to the Women's Land Army, "a new kind of 'army,' a 'land army' that would supplement their men's efforts. . . . The Land Army sought specifically and often explicitly to attract single women of the educated, middle-classes." See Susan R. Grayzel, "Nostalgia, Gender, and the Countryside: Placing the 'Land Girl' in First World War Britain," *Rural History* 10, no. 2 (1999): 155–170, especially 156, 157.

3. *Daily Express*, June 10, 1918, p. 2.

4. *Sphere*, June 15, 1918, p. iv.

5. Angela Woollacott, "Dressed to Kill: Clothes, Cultural Meaning, and World War I Women Munitions Workers," in Moira Donald and Linda Hurcombe, eds., *Gender and Material Culture*, vol.2, *Representations of Gender from Prehistory to the Present* (London: Macmillan, 2000). I am grateful to Angela Woollacott for sharing her manuscript with me.

For another interesting discussion of women and the uniform, see Susan R. Grayzel, " 'The Outward and Visible Sign of Her Patriotism': Women, Uniforms, and National Service During the First World War," *Twentieth Century British History* 8, no. 2 (1997): 145–64.

6. Marchioness of Londonderry, *Retrospect* (London: Frederick Muller, 1938), pp. 127–8.

7. Naomi Jacob, *Me in War-Time* (London: Hutchinson, 1940), p. 208.

8. Mary Agnes Hamilton, "Changes in Social Life," in Ray Strachey, ed., *Our Freedom and Its Results* (London: Hogarth Press, 1936), p. 250.

9. *Daily Express*, June 6, 1918, p. 2.

10. "A Sergeant's Letter," *Our Own Gazette* [YWCA] 36 (January 1918), p. 29. Woollacott cites this letter as an example of how "at least some women were perceived as becoming more like men." See "Dressed to Kill."

11. *Punch*, May 29, 1918, p. 344. A satirical weekly magazine "based on the middle-class prejudices," *Punch* lampooned a range of cultural stereotypes, from upper-class dandies and effeminate men to suffragettes and flappers. While *Punch* can be seen as a cultural barometer of such "middle-class prejudices," it also worked hard to promote them. See Leavis, *Fiction and the Reading Public*, p. 11.

12. *Daily Mail*, June 4, 1918, p. 2. The Women's Land Army were a corps of agricultural workers who, among their other duties, cut down trees.

13. *Daily Express*, June 10, 1918, p. 2. The scene conveyed by the letter-writer bears a remarkable resemblance to the picture shown in a January 31, 1917, *Punch* cartoon called "Our Land-Workers" (p. 76). Four young women who lounge around a sitting room have their hands in their pockets; three of the women smoke and one whistles. One has placed her feet on the mantelpiece and sprawls out lazily. The caption reads: "Mabel (discussing a turn for the village Red Cross Concert): 'What about getting ourselves up as girls?' Ethel: 'Yes—but have we the clothes for it?' "

14. *Punch*, January 15, 1919, p. 46.

15. See Angus McLaren, *The Trials of Masculinity: Policing Sexual Boundaries, 1870–1930* (Chicago: University of Chicago Press, 1997), pp. 207–31.

16. In light of this historical project I will refer to Barker by female pronouns rather than male. In 1929 Barker was tried as a woman, Valerie Arkell-Smith, and the newspaper coverage of this trial also regarded her as such.

17. Cannell, *When Fleet Street Calls*, p. 204. Barker was arrested for contempt of court on February 28, 1929, because she had failed to respond to a summons on a charge of bankruptcy. Her biological sex was discovered by the medical doctor at Brixton Prison and she was subsequently transferred to the women's prison at Holloway. For further discussion of Barker's story, see Julie Wheelwright, *Amazons and Military Maids: Women Who Dressed as Men in the Pursuit of Life, Liberty, and Happiness* (London: Pandora, 1989), p. 2. The following newspapers presented the most extensive coverage of Barker's trial in March and April 1929: the *Daily Express*; the *Daily Herald*; the *Daily Mail*; *Reynolds's Illustrated News*; and the *Sunday Dispatch*.

18. Sir Ernest Wild's judgment was reported by several newspapers, including *Reynolds's Illustrated News*, April 28, 1929, p. 17.

19. Macready, *Annals of an Active Life*, p. 416.

20. On one of the Metropolitan Police (Women Patrols) enrollment forms I found a handwritten note by Mrs. Stanley reaffirming with evident irritation that "the 'Women Police Service' is an unofficial and unauthorized body" (August 27, 1920). Metropolitan Police Historic Museum, London.

21. *Report of the Commissioner of Police of the Metropolis for the Years 1918 and 1919*, Cmnd. 543 (London: HMSO, 1918–19).

22. Ibid.

23. This information is contained in a large file on the Women Police Service collected by the London Metropolitan Police. PRO HO45/11067/370521, Public Record Office.

24. Carrier, *Campaign for the Employment*, p. 89.

25. Baird Committee, *Report*, p. 20, para. 180. Emphasis mine.

26. Allen, *Pioneer Policewoman*, p. 25. Emphasis mine. The hat was designed by another early member of the organization, Miss St. John Partridge.

27. For an extended discussion of the cultural significance of khaki in particular, and of the uniform and gender more generally, see Susan R. Grayzel, *Women's Identities at War: Gender, Motherhood. and Politics in Britain and France During the First World War* (Chapel Hill: University of North Carolina Press, 1999). See also Angela Woollacott, " 'Khaki Fever' and its Control: Gender, Class, Age, and Sexual Morality on the British Homefront in the First World War," *Journal of Contemporary History* 29 (1994): 325–47.

28. Letter to the Editor, *Policewoman's Review*, 2, no. 20 (December 1928): 159.

29. Jennifer Craik, *The Face of Fashion: Cultural Studies in Fashion* (London: Routledge, 1994), p. 2.

30. This comment was cited by Alan Bestie in "My Lifetime Crusade," an undated newspaper cutting in the Women Police file at the Metropolitan Police Historic Museum, London.

31. Carrier, *Campaign for the Employment*, p. 46.

32. Levine, " 'Walking the Streets,' " p. 71.

33. This quotation is from an unidentified newspaper cutting, dated April 12, 1921. PRO HO45/11067/370521, Public Record Office.

34. Diana Condell and Jean Liddiard, *Working for Victory? Images of Women in the First World War, 1914–1918* (London: Routledge, 1987), p. 115.

35. Allen, *Pioneer Policewoman*, p. 22.

36. Carrier, *Campaign for the Employment*, p. 46.

37. Joanne Finkelstein, *The Fashioned Self* (Philadelphia: Temple University Press, 1991), p. 139.

38. Mary Allen, *Lady in Blue* (London: Stanley Paul, 1936), p. 71.

39. Allen, *Pioneer Policewoman*, p. 84.

40. Elizabeth Lutes Hillman, "Dressed to Kill? Uniforms, Gender, and Sexuality." Paper presented at the Berkshire Conference on Women's History, June 9, 1996.

41. Lock, *British Policewoman*, p. 150.

42. Allen, *Lady in Blue*, p. 70.

43. This excerpt was in a file on the WPS in the Metropolitan Police Historic Museum, London. The typescript was entitled *Women Police: Extracts from "Guardians of the Queen's Peace" by George Howard*. In pencil the document provides the following publication details, London: Odhams Press Ltd., 1953, p. 4. The presence of this typescript suggests that the Metropolitan Police carefully monitored information about women's policing organizations.

44. Pugh, *Women and the Women's Movement*, p. 34.

45. Hamer, *Britannia's Glory*, p. 47.

46. Jacob, *Me and the Swans*, pp. 157–8.

47. Forel, *Sexual Question*, p. 254.

48. For the first major study on transvestism, see Magnus Hirschfeld's *Transvestites*, trans. Michael A. Lombardi-Nash (1910; reprint, Buffalo: Prometheus Books, 1991). Dave King offers an illuminating discussion of the distinctions between homosexuality and transvestism in his "Gender Blending: Medical Perspectives," in Richard Ekins and Dave King, eds., *Blending Genders: Social Aspects of Cross-dressing and Sex-changing* (London and New York: Routledge, 1996), pp. 78–98. Weeks also clarifies how Ellis "regarded transvestism as an essentially heterosexual phenomenon. Here he followed closely Magnus Hirschfeld's massive work on transvestism. Ellis was striving . . . to emphasize that 'inverts' were essentially 'ordinary' people in all but their sexual behavior." See *Coming Out*, p. 63.

49. Hall, *Well of Loneliness*, p. 271.

50. Allen, *Pioneer Policewoman*, p. 18. Lock cites Allen's physical description of Damer Dawson and then writes, "such fulsomeness might suggest a homosexual affection, particularly since the writer was, by now, grotesquely masculine in appearance. It is perfectly possible that this was so, but, of course, writing did tend more to the purple in those days." See *British Policewoman*, p. 128.

51. Hall, *Well of Loneliness*, p. 271.

52. This reference was provided by Joan Lock, private correspondence, April 1996.

53. Baker, *Our Three Selves*, p. 267.

54. Bridgeman Report, *Report of the Departmental Committee on the Employment of Policewomen*, Cmnd. 2224 (London: HMSO, 1924), p. 207.

55. Havelock Ellis, "Sexual Inversion in Women," *Alienist and Neurologist*, 16 (1895): 153.

56. Macready, *Annals of an Active Life*, p. 415.

57. *Women's Auxiliary Service*, p. 25. ADM 1/11/2, Metropolitan Police Historic Museum, London.

58. Memorandum by Sir Leonard Dunning. PRO HO45/10806/309485, Public Record Office. The chief constable at Grantham, incidentally, was the first to make use of the services of the WPS.

59. Macready, *Annals of an Active Life*, p. 415.

60. The *News of the World* reported that Colonel Barker once wore a sword in public, "clad in full ceremonial dress as a colonel, with sword and medal ribbons" (March 10, 1929, p. 9).

61. I am grateful to Lucy Bland for explaining the sword's significance among different suffrage groups. The cover illustration I refer to here is reprinted in Bland, *Banishing the Beast*, p. 255.

62. Macready, *Annals of an Active Life*, p. 165.

63. Allen, *Pioneer Policewoman*, p. 131.

64. Letter from Sir Edward Troup to Sir Nevil Macready, January 29, 1920. PRO HO45/11067/370521, Public Record Office. Emphasis mine.

65. Letter from Sir Nevil Macready to Sir Edward Troup, January 29, 1920. PRO HO45/11067/370521, Public Record Office.

66. McLaren explains that while transvestism was not illegal for either sex, such behavior was more dangerous for men than for women: "A woman who dressed as a man was not viewed as particularly threatening," but a man could be accused of "gross indecency." See McLaren, *Trials of Masculinity*, pp. 230, 210.

67. Met file on the WPS. PRO HO45/11067/370521, Public Record Office.

68. Lock, *British Policewoman*, p. 130.

69. Allen, *Pioneer Policewoman*, p. 136.

70. "Note Supplied by a Shorthand Writer." PRO HO45/11067/370521, Public Record Office. Emphasis mine. All subsequent quotations from this hearing can be found in this April 12, 1921, document.

71. Memorandum on Interview with the Secretary of State, April 15, 1921. PRO HO45/11067/370521, Public Record Office.

72. Allen, *Pioneer Policewoman*, p. 177.

73. Memorandum on Interview with the Secretary of State. PRO HO45/11067/370521, Public Record Office.

74. Allen, *Pioneer Policewoman*, p. 179.

75. McLaren, *Trials of Masculinity*, p. 207.

76. No one has explored "female masculinity" more thoroughly than the cultural critic Judith Halberstam. In her historically nuanced examination of "masculinity without men," Halberstam notes: "Female masculinity is a particularly fruitful site of investigation because it has been vilified by heterosexist and feminist/womanist programs alike; unlike male femininity . . . female masculinity is generally received by hetero- and homo-normative cultures as a pathological sign of misidentification and maladjustment, as a longing to be and to have a power

that is always just out of reach. Within a lesbian context, female masculinity has been situated as the place where patriarchy goes to work on the female psyche and reproduces misogyny within femaleness." See *Female Masculinity*, p. 9.

77. *Empire News and Sunday Chronicle*, February 26, 1956, p. 2.

78. *Daily Mail*, April 25, 1929, p. 5.

79. Hallett, *Lesbian Lives*, p. 55.

80. James Vernon, " 'For Some Queer Reason': The Trials and Tribulations of Colonel Barker's Masquerade in Interwar Britain," *Signs: Journal of Women in Culture and Society* 26, no. 1 (autumn 2000). James Vernon kindly shared his work in progress with me.

81. Allen, *Lady in Blue*, p. 71.

82. Lock, *British Policewoman*, p. 150.

83. Allen, *Lady in Blue*, p. 74.

84. Lock, *British Policewoman*, p. 150.

85. *Daily Sketch*, March 28, 1929, p. 2, and *Sunday Dispatch*, March 31, 1929, p. 18.

86. *Sunday Dispatch*, p. 18.

87. *Daily Mail*, March 7, 1929, p. 14.

88. Ibid., March 6, 1929, p. 14.

89. *Daily Herald*, March 7, 1929, p. 1.

90. *Daily Mail*, March 6, 1929, p. 14.

91. *Empire News and Sunday Chronicle*, February 19, 1956, p. 2.

92. Ibid., February 26, 1956, p. 2.

93. Ibid., March 4, 1956, p. 2.

94. Marjorie Garber, *Vested Interests: Cross-Dressing and Cultural Anxiety* (New York: Routledge, 1992), p. 69.

95. McLaren, *Trials of Masculinity*, p. 215.

96. *Daily Mail*, March 8, 1929, p. 14.

97. *Empire News and Sunday Chronicle*, March 4, 1956, p. 2.

98. Allen, *Pioneer Policewoman*, p. 17.

99. Allen, *Lady in Blue*, p. 25.

100. Lock, *British Policewoman*, p. 150.

101. Before becoming Colonel Victor Barker, "Miss Barker was one of the first girls in the neighborhood to wear an Eton crop and ride a motor-bike." See *Daily Mail*, March 8, 1929, p. 14.

102. Allen, *Lady in Blue*, p. 73.

103. Carrier, *Campaign for the Employment*, p. 149.

104. Letter to Lord Muir Mackenzie from Lady Astor, October 29, 1920 (marked in blue pencil "not sent"), Astor Papers, 1416/1/1/930.

105. *Daily Chronicle*, March 8, 1929, p. 4.

106. Ibid., March 7, 1929, p. 3.

107. *Empire News and Sunday Chronicle*, March 11, 1956, p. 2. During Vita Sackville-West's brief spell of playful experimentation with the uniform, she also aspired to greater heights of impersonation, and before the ruse was over she was swapping war reminiscences with a Frenchman who took her for a fellow officer. Flamboyance in dress led to more daring and outrageous acts. See Nicolson, *Portrait of a Marriage*, p. 105.

108. *Daily Herald*, March 6, 1929, p. 1.

109. *Empire News and Sunday Chronicle*, February 19, 1956, p. 2.

110. *News of the World*, March 10, 1929, p. 9.

111. The popular press reacted to Barker's stunning impersonation as a male with amazement, as the headlines indicate. The *News of the World* referred to her "Amazing Impersonation" (March 10, 1929, p. 9); the *Daily Mail* proclaimed "Masquerade Woman's Biggest Exploit" (March 7, 1929, p. 13); the *Daily Express* referred to Barker's "astonishing story" and "astounding masquerade" (March 6, 1929, p. 1); and finally, the *Daily Mirror* cited "Woman's Amazing Masquerade as an Army Officer" (March 6, 1929), p. 3.

112. Baker, *Our Three Selves*, p. 254. All references to Hall's response to Barker can be found on this page.

113. *Daily Herald*, April 25, 1929, p. 5. Sir Ernest Wild was one of the most vociferous supporters in the House of Commons of the clause to criminalize lesbianism. Homosexuality "sent the Recorder of London, Sir Ernest Wild, into paroxysms of rage in which he browbeat his victims, professing he could not believe his ears, though these had been hearing, ad nauseam, the same evidence for twenty years. Perhaps his name added heat to his horror." See Roberts, *One Year of Life*, p. 96.

114. *Daily Herald*, April 26, 1929, p. 5. Wild exclaimed that Barker had "prostituted" marriage: "Perhaps there are not many who look so much like a man as Mrs. Arkell-Smith, but I suppose others prostitute marriage in this way." See *Reynolds's Illustrated News*, March 10, 1929, p. 1.

115. *Daily Mail*, April 25, 1929, p. 5.

116. *Daily Herald*, April 26, 1929, p. 5. Hall was equally indignant about Barker's lack of respect for the institution of marriage: "After having married the woman if [Barker] doesn't go and desert her!" See Baker, *Our Three Selves*, p. 254.

117. *Manchester Guardian*, November 10, 1928, p.14.

118. Hall's use of sexology is highly selective. She does not refer, for instance, to the work of Magnus Hirschfeld on transvestism.

119. Hallett argues that Barker was "treated with hostility in the press in 1929 because she had used her disguise to perpetrate sexual fraud, and had been married to a woman for three years." See *Lesbian Lives*, p. 55.

120. *Daily Chronicle*, April 25, 1929, p. 11.

121. For an illuminating study of transsexuality, see Jay Prosser, "Transsexuals and the Transsexologists: Inversion and the Emergence of Transsexual Subjectivity," in Bland and Doan, eds., *Sexology in Culture*, pp. 116–31.

122. *Daily Herald*, April 26, 1929, p. 5.

123. Halberstam, *Female Masculinity*, p. 28.

124. *Daily Express*, April 26, 1929, p. 11.

125. King, "Cross-Dressing, Sex-Changing, and the Press," pp. 134–5.

126. Vern L. Bullough and Bonnie Bullough, *Cross Dressing, Sex, and Gender* (Philadelphia: University of Pennsylvania Press, 1993), p. 163.

127. In the *Empire News and Sunday Chronicle* (February 26, 1956, p. 2) Barker writes: "During the quarrels [her second husband] would seize me by the hair and beat me up." Haward testified in court that Barker said her husband was "rather rough at times." When asked, "Wasn't there a scene once in your flat when he came and knocked her about . . . and it was after being knocked about by him in your flat that she ran away from him?" Haward replied, "Yes." See *The Times*, March 28, p. 11.

128. Havelock Ellis, *Studies in the Psychology of Sex*, vol. 7: *Eonism and Other Supplementary Studies*, in Lucy Bland and Laura Doan, eds., *Sexology Uncensored: The Documents of Sexual Science* (Chicago: University of Chicago Press, 1998), p. 259.

129. *Sunday Dispatch*, March 31, 1929, p. 18.

130. *Daily Herald*, March 7, 1929, p. 1.

131. During Barker's trial the court heard that "no normal relations [were possible] because she [Miss Haward] believed the defendant had been wounded in the war." See *Daily Herald*, April 25, 1929, p. 5.

132. *Daily Express*, March 28, 1929, p. 1.

133. *Daily Mail*, March 26, 1929, p. 11.

134. *Daily Sketch*, March 26, 1929, p. 2.

135. *Daily Express*, April 26, 1929, p. 11.

136. Captain A. H. Henderson-Livesey, *The Women Police Question* (London: The League of Womanhood, 1925), pp. 15, 9. Emphasis mine. The League of Womanhood, according to a statement at the end of the pamphlet, was dedicated to advancing "the view of the modern woman who dissents from the feminist creed. . . . The League will only seek to represent those women who regard motherhood and marriage as the best and highest walk of life that a woman can

follow, and who regard all other occupations—however desirable in themselves—as second best." A copy of this pamphlet is in the Fawcett Library.

137. Henderson-Livesey, *Women Police Question*, p. 9. Such a position is reminiscent of a June 9, 1915 *Punch* cartoon (p. 449) that depicts a cocky young man, in the clothing of a dandy with a straw boater, declaring: "It's all very well to talk about policewomen. But what could they do against us men?" The fellow is apparently a shirker, for one of the ladies replies: "I suppose the authorities think that they would be quite a match for those who have remained at home." The only person lower on the evolutionary scale than a cross-dressing female policewoman is a man who has not signed up.

138. Carrier, *Campaign for the Employment*, p. 148.

139. Henderson-Livesey, *Women Police Question*, p. 7.

140. *Sunday Dispatch*, March 31, 1929, p. 18.

141. Barker claimed that her membership in the extremist group the National Fascisti was almost the result of an accident: "A wrongly-addressed envelope led to my becoming a member." When Barker dropped round to deliver the letter, she was invited to join: " 'Why not?' I wondered. The role would help me in my pose as a man." As a member of this group, Barker rose in rank from captain to colonel; still, she confesses, "I entered into my military role with more enthusiasm than discretion." See *Empire News and Sunday Chronicle*, March 25, 1956, p. 11.

Barker's involvement with the Fascisti landed her in court in 1927 for an offense against the Firearms Act: "On that occasion . . . this masquerade as a man was used, and the prisoner came into court with eyes bandaged, led into the dock by a friend. It was explained to the Court that Barker had previously suffered temporary blindness owing to war wounds." See *Reynolds's Illustrated News*, April 28, 1929, p. 17.

In *Lady in Blue* Allen describes her visit in 1934 to Germany where she met with Hitler and Goering. In Hitler, Allen declares, "I discovered a patriot whose sincerity and faith in his country's future enables [sic] him to mould the passions of somewhere near a hundred million people." Allen was delighted with these words from Goering: " 'No one can do official work without the right to wear uniform,' he said. 'It inspires confidence and ensures authority. It divides the policewoman from the agent provocateur and the spy.' That exactly sums up my own views on the subject, which is one of the most controversial matters concerning policewomen all over the world. I left Germany much impressed with the new régime and its bearing on the enrollment of Women Police." Allen eventually joined the British Union of Fascists and in 1940 shared a platform with the British fascist leader, Sir Oswald Mosley. See *Lady in Blue*, pp. 151, 155. Also see R. M. Douglas, *Feminist Freikorps: The British Voluntary Women Police, 1914–1940* (New York: Greenwood Press, 1999).

142. *Empire News and Sunday Chronicle*, April 15, 1956, p. 4. Like Barker, the male transvestite Austin Hull explained in court that when he dressed in accordance with his biological sex, "he was often taken for a woman. When attired in male clothes people followed and stared at him." See McLaren, *Trials of Masculinity*, p. 211.

This dilemma is represented by Hall in *The Well* in the character of Wanda, a "Polish painter": "If she dressed like a woman she looked like a man, if she dressed like a man she looked like a woman." See *Well of Loneliness*, p. 353.

143. *Sunday Dispatch*, 10 March 10, 1929, p. 1.

144. *Daily Mail*, March 26, 1929, p. 11.

145. In calling for the evolution of "new sexual vocabularies," Halberstam argues that concepts such as female masculinity "acknowledge sexualities and genders as styles rather than life-styles, as fictions rather than facts of life, and as potentialities rather than as fixed identities." See Judith Halberstam, "F2M: The Making of Female Masculinity," in Laura Doan, *The Lesbian Postmodern* (New York: Columbia University Press, 1994), pp. 210–11.

146. Baker, *Our Three Selves*, p. 254.

147. In a January 9, 1931, diary entry, Troubridge writes: "C. Allen & Tagart [Allen's partner] . . . staid [sic] & dined with us & we had a deeply interesting & to me very heartening evening. To feel that they are in sympathy with Johns [sic] aims & mine is good indeed for they are fine citizens." See Una Troubridge Diaries, vol. 2, Lovat Dickson Papers, MG 30, D 237.

148. For a full-length study of this phenomenon, see Wheelwright, *Amazons and Military Maids*. In "A Woman's View" (*Britannia*, March 22, 1929, p. 443), Rosita Forbes positions Barker in a tradition that dates back to Pope Joan. The article also discusses the case of a woman who had served fourteen years as a man in the Foreign Legion.

4. PASSING FASHIONS: READING FEMALE MASCULINITIES IN THE 1920S

1. Letter from Radclyffe Hall to Audrey Heath, March 19, 1929; Correspondence—Publishers and Agents, vol. 4, Lovat Dickson Papers, MG 30, D 237. Emphasis mine.

This chapter develops from a paper delivered at the June 1996 Tenth Berkshire Conference on the History of Women ("Female Boyishness and Visualizing Sapphic Desire"), which was later published in *Feminist Studies* (1998) under the same title as the chapter heading. I am grateful to several scholars who helped me to focus my argument, especially Judith Halberstam, Sue Lanser, and Martha Vicinus.

2. *Daily Herald*, March 7, 1929, p. 1; *News of the World*, March 10, 1929, p. 9.

3. *Daily Herald*, March 9, 1929, p. 1.

4. Benstock, *Women of the Left Bank*, p. 173.

5. Judith Halberstam observes a similar shutting down of possibilities in "sexual discourse": "the sexual discourse we have settled for is woefully inadequate when it comes to accounting for the myriad practices which fall beyond the purview of conventionally gendered hetero- and homosexuality." See "Lesbian Masculinity, or Even Stone Butches Get the Blues," *Women and Perfornance: A Journal of Feminist Theory* 8, no. 2 (1996): 70.

6. Garber, *Vested Interests*, p. 390.

7. The shingle, one of several popular hairstyles, was so de rigueur some women would insist on it even if it made them look "as if [they] had just served fifteen years in prison." See *Daily Express* April 7, 1924, p. 5. The same year saw the introduction of the close-fitting cloche hat: "This was extremely important, because when it had imposed itself on the fashion it almost compelled women to wear their hair short. Those who would not cut off their locks were condemned to wear the only possible hat on the tops of their heads, where it gave a very ridiculous appearance. Within a couple of years of the first appearance of the cloche 99 percent. of the young women of Western Europe had short hair." See James Laver, *Taste and Fashion from the French Revolution to Today* (London: George G. Harrap, 1937), p. 130.

8. Sandra M. Gilbert and Susan Gubar, *No Man's Land: The Place of the Woman Writer in the Twentieth Century*, vol. 2, *Sexchanges* (New Haven: Yale University Press, 1989), p. 327.

9. "Female cross-dressing . . . was restricted by an ordinance passed in 1800 and, at the turn of the century, strictly enforced by Lépine, the Paris prefect of police." See Benstock, *Women of the Left Bank*, p. 48.

10. Valentine Ackland, *For Sylvia: An Honest Account* (London: Chatto and Windus, 1985), p. 88. Gay Wachman kindly alerted me to this passage.

11. Benstock, *Women of the Left Bank*, p. 181.

12. See also Weiss, *Paris Was a Woman*.

13. Elizabeth Wilson, *Adorned in Dreams: Fashion and Modernity* (London: Virago, 1985), p. 164.

14. Jivani, *It's Not Unusual*, p. 27.

15. An examination of Troubridge's diaries and the biographies on Hall by Michael Baker and Sally Cline indicates that the couple spent about two days in

Paris in 1921, seven days in 1922, eight days in 1924, and three to four days in 1927. The couple apparently did not visit Paris at all in 1923, 1925, or 1928. The exception was the extended visits in 1926 to obtain information for *The Well* (about five days in August and September, followed by a sustained visit from October 5 to November 2). See Una Troubridge Diaries, vols. 1 and 2, Lovat Dickson Papers, MG 30, D 237; Baker, *Our Three Selves*; and Cline, *Radclyffe Hall*. Claudia Stillman Franks notes too that Hall's "contact with [Brooks and Barney, among others on the French scene] was exclusively social. She saw them too sporadically for them to play any major part in her life, and similarly, she played no part in theirs." See *Beyond 'The Well of Loneliness': The Fiction of Radclyffe Hall* (Amersham, England: Avebury, 1982), p. 33.

16. Cline, *Radclyffe Hall*, p. 230.

17. Ibid. "When [Hall] needed to relax several British friends were visiting Paris."

18. Ibid. Alternatively, the myth surrounding Hall's connection with Paris may have developed because some readers thought Hall's art was following her life: the hero of *The Well*, Stephen Gordon, went into exile in Paris. I suspect that Hall chose Paris as Stephen's destination because she realized that writing a novel in support of sexual inverts was risky, so it would be better not to draw on a scene closer to home, in London. By putting the spotlight on Paris, where many in Britain already thought homosexual culture thrived, Hall successfully deflected the focus from London's own "fashionable artistic night-clubs and . . . rowdy lesbian bars." See Cline, *Radclyffe Hall*, p. 174.

19. Cline writes that Hall "was eccentric and her fashions bizarre." See *Radclyffe Hall*, p. 311.

20. In 1924 the *Daily Express* ran an article entitled "Masculine Note in Fashion," which indicated that many of the details of the new tailored look "were associated with the early [tailors] of the nineties" (April 8, 1924, p. 5).

21. This verse appeared originally in *Woman*, September 26, 1894. Emphasis mine.

22. Joel Kaplan and Sheila Stowell, *Theatre and Fashion: Oscar Wilde to the Suffragettes* (Cambridge: Cambridge University Press, 1994), p. 61.

23. Eliza Lynn Linton, "Girl of the Period" from March 14, 1868, quoted by Herbert van Thal, *Eliza Lynn Linton: The Girl of the Period* (London: George Allen and Unwin, 1979), p. 81.

24. Cline, *Radclyffe Hall*, p. 112.

25. Richard von Krafft-Ebing, *Psychopathia Sexualis with Especial Reference to the Antipathetic Sexual Instinct. A Medico-Forensic Study* (1886; reprint, Brooklyn: Physicians and Surgeons Book Co., 1908), pp. 334–35, 355.

26. Havelock Ellis, *Sexual Inversion* (1897; reprint, Philadelphia: F. A. Davis, 1927), p. 250.

27. Mannin, *Confessions and Impressions*, p. 227. The longer quotation is from Austin Harrison's *Pandora's Hope* and was cited by book reviewer Edith Shackleton in the *Sunday Express*, November 23, 1925, p. 11.

28. *Daily Mail*, August 17, 1921, p. 9.

29. Katrina Rolley, "Cutting a Dash: The Dress of Radclyffe Hall and Una Troubridge," *Feminist Review* 35 (1990): 55.

30. Hall (1880–1943) was the daughter of "a monied Victorian gentleman," who had attended Eton and Oxford and, after separation from Hall's mother, a young American widow, provided his daughter "with a very large annual allowance for maintenance and education." See Baker, *Our Three Selves*, p. 10; Una, Lady Troubridge, *The Life and Death of Radclyffe Hall* (London: Hammond, Hammond, 1961), p. 14. On coming of age Hall inherited a fortune from her grandfather (see Cline, *Radclyffe Hall*, p.43). Hall never received a formal education, but instead was taught by a series of nannies and governesses. Una Troubridge (1887–1963) grew up in a genteel but modest upper-middle class family. Since her father was in the consular service, Troubridge's childhood was spent in a "cultured and cosmopolitan atmosphere"; she was educated by a Belgian governess (see Baker, p. 62). At thirteen, she "won a scholarship to the Royal Academy of Art" (p. 63). Gluck (born Hannah Gluckstein, 1895–1978) was born into a wealthy business family, founders of the famed J. Lyons and Co., which, among several other enterprises, owned the fashionable Trocadero Restaurant. She attended the St. Paul's Girls' School in Hammersmith, but rather than go on to university she chose to attend the St. John's Wood Art School. See Diana Souhami, *Gluck: Her Biography* (London: Pandora Press, 1989), pp. 22, 34, 37.

31. Valerie Steele, *Fashion and Eroticism: Ideals of Feminine Beauty from the Victorian Era to the Jazz Age* (New York: Oxford University Press, 1985), p. 237.

32. Beddoe, *Back to Home and Duty*, p. 23; see also the entry for "flapper" in the *Oxford English Dictionary*, vol. 5 (Oxford: Oxford University Press, 1989). For further information on the flapper fashion see Steele, *Fashion and Eroticism*; Cecil Beaton, *The Glass of Fashion* (London: Weidenfeld and Nicolson, 1954); and Melman, *Women and the Popular Imagination in the Twenties*.

33. The first women in England to cut their hair short in the prewar era were young students at the Slade School of Art, who considered it almost a rite of passage. As a student there in 1911, Carrington sported a boblike cut, and Dorothy Hepworth was, upon her arrival in January 1918, "frightfully disappointed so few girls wear their hair short," according to biographer Kenneth Pople (interview conducted in Bristol, England, in May 1996).

34. Phyllis Tortora and Keith Eubank, *A Survey of Historic Costume* (New York: Fairchild Publications, 1989), p. 299. One must be careful about referring interchangeably to these three popular hairstyles of the 1920s because the styles evolved (and overlapped) over the decade. The first short haircut was the bob, which appeared just before and during the war; it reached full fashion in 1924. The shingle was introduced in about 1923 and was in full fashion in 1925; finally, the Eton crop appeared in 1926 and reached full fashion in 1927. See Georgine de Courtais, *Women's Headdress and Hairstyles in England from AD 600 to the Present Day* (London: B. T. Batsford, 1973), p. 150.

35. Hamilton, "Changes in Social Life," p. 234. Hamilton reflects on the impact of social change for women in the early years after the First World War. For a good discussion of the evolution of ready-made clothing, see Wilson, *Adorned in Dreams*.

36. *The Times*, August 8, 1921, p. 9.

37. I checked the letters to the editor for several weeks after the article "The Boyette: Seaside Girls Who Dress Like Boys" appeared. *Daily Mail*, April 19, 1927, p. 7. Emphasis mine.

38. James Laver, *A Concise History of Costume* (London: Thames and Hudson, 1969), p. 233. Emphasis mine.

39. Quentin Crisp, *The Naked Civil Servant* (New York: New American Library, 1983), p. 21. Emphasis mine.

40. H. Montgomery Hyde, *The Other Love: An Historical and Contemporary Survey of Homosexuality in Britain* (London: Mayflower Books, 1972), p. 197.

41. David Pryce-Jones, *Cyril Connolly: Journal and Memoir* (London: Collins, 1983), pp. 131, 149. Horatia Fisher was the daughter of Sir William Fisher, commander of the Mediterranean fleet, and niece of Desmond MacCarthy.

42. Humphrey Carpenter, *The Brideshead Generation: Evelyn Waugh and His Friends* (London: Faber and Faber, 1989), p. 176. Bakewell told Connolly that she and another woman were lesbians (apparently untrue); Connolly found this "disclosure" sexually exciting and became all the more interested. I am grateful to Lorraine Naylor for alerting me to this information.

43. Ibid., p. 177. The Honorable Evelyn Gardner was the the daughter of the first Baron Burghclere, and the granddaughter of the fourth Earl of Carnarvon.

44. Ruth Adam, *A Woman's Place: 1910–1975* (London: Chatto and Windus, 1975), p. 98.

45. The new popularity of unisex clothing was another alarming development. The ever vigilant *Daily Mail* noted that "coats are cut in almost exactly the same way for men and for women, while the woman often wears with it a light grey silk jumper collar, and tie resembling a man's shirt collar and tie. Soft grey felt hats, worn by man and woman alike, increase the similarity of costume, and the

woman's shingle or Eton crop completes her manlike aspect." Quoted in the magazine *Urania*, 71–72 (1928): 10.

46. *Daily Mail*, January 18, 1921, p. 9.

47. *Eve: The Lady's Pictorial*, August 24, 1927, p. 367.

48. Women in khaki "assumed mannish attitudes, stood with legs apart while they smote their riding whips, and looked like self-conscious and not very attractive boys." See "Letter to the Editor," *Morning Post*, July 1916. Quoted by Susan Kingsley Kent, *Making Peace: The Reconstruction of Gender in Interwar Britain* (Princeton: Princeton University Press, 1993), p. 37.

49. C. Willett Cunnington, *English Women's Clothing in the Present Century* (London: Faber and Faber, 1952), p. 163.

50. *Punch*, January 26, 1927, p. 98.

51. Ibid., January 5, 1921, p. 15.

52. Cunnington, *English Women's Clothing in the Present Century*, p. 163.

53. Mannin, *Young in the Twenties*, p. 72.

54. *Punch*, June 15, 1921, p. 470.

55. Richard Klein, *Cigarettes Are Sublime* (Durham: Duke University Press, 1993), p. 117.

56. Souhami, *Gluck*, pp. 35–6.

57. Laver, *Taste and Fashion from the French Revolution to Today*, p. 130.

58. Women most often appeared in trousers or breeches in public for sporting activities, such as skiing and riding. *Punch*, May 11, 1927, p. 517.

59. Cunnington, *English Women's Clothing in the Present Century*, p. 147. Emphasis mine.

60. *Tatler*, January 13, 1926, p. 92. Rolley points out too that Hall's pearl earrings were important signifiers of her femininity: "In a period of fashionable androgyny, signifiers of gender such as earrings become extremely important." See "Cutting a Dash," p. 65.

61. Garber, *Vested Interests*, p. 161.

62. Cline, *Radclyffe Hall*, p. 294.

63. Allen, *Lady in Blue*, pp. 73–4.

64. Richard Corson, *Fashions in Eyeglasses* (London: Peter Owen, 1967), p. 202.

65. Elaine Showalter, *Sexual Anarchy: Gender and Culture at the Fin de Siècle* (London: Virago Press, 1992), p. 169.

66. Baker, *Our Three Selves*, p. 118.

67. *Eve: The Lady's Pictorial*, July 13, 1927, p. 72.

68. Ibid., August 29, 1928, p. 407.

69. Cline, *Radclyffe Hall*, p. 219.

70. *Newcastle Daily Journal and North Star*, August 22, 1928, p. 8. Incidentally, Hall would not have worn an Eton crop in 1928. By then that style was

"not nearly so popular" and was displaced by the "long shingle vogue." See *Daily Express*, August 16, 1928, p. 5 and August 23, 1928, p. 3.

71. *Birmingham Post*, April 11, 1927, p. 13.

72. Mannin, *Confessions and Impressions*, p. 227.

73. Benstock, *Women of the Left Bank*, p. 177.

74. A diary entry by Troubridge for June 17, 1927 reads: "I with her [Hall] to Weatherill, and to Harrods where we got me a calfskin coat." Later that year, in November 1927: "Then to Weatherill and Burlington Arcade." See Una Troubridge Diaries, vol. 2, Lovat Dickson Papers, MG 30, D 237.

Weatherill between the wars was a fairly expensive place to shop and carried very distinctive clothing for women. Apparently it was quite evident to onlookers when someone wore a Weatherill suit.

75. *Eve: The Lady's Pictorial*, March 31, 1926, p. B (advertising supplement). I would argue that the popularity of the "severely masculine mode" in the mid-1920s complicates Steele's contention that the "feminine ideal" in the 1920s "was not so much 'boyish' as youthful." See *Fashion and Eroticism*, p. 239.

For other examples of the "severely masculine mode," see *Eve: The Lady's Pictorial* April 28, 1926, p. H and *Tatler*, June 16, 1926, p. c (advertising supplement).

76. Gilbert and Gubar, *No Man's Land*, 2:354, and Elizabeth Wilson, "Deviant Dress," *Feminist Review*, 35 (1990), p. 69.

77. Terry Castle, *Noël Coward and Radclyffe Hall: Kindred Spirits* (New York: Columbia University Press, 1996), p. 31. Castle is the first to note that Coward and Hall were indeed "kindred spirits," but Hall wore "slick and satiny" masculine clothing as early as 1920, predating Coward by a few years.

78. Alison Adburgham, *A Punch History of Manners and Modes: 1841–1940* (London: Hutchinson, 1961), p. 311.

79. Rolley, "Cutting a Dash," p. 57.

80. Baker, *Our Three Selves*, p. 203.

81. Ibid., p. 164.

82. *Tatler*, February 27, 1924, p. 402.

83. Ibid., June 2, 1926, p. aa (advertising supplement) and March 15, 1922, p. 386. Another *Tatler* article stated: "Capes will be accepted for evening wear [including] . . . those of black satin lined with wonderful brocades." January 25, 1922, p. 136. Capes were still going strong two years later: "And, of course, the cape . . . is another popular feature of the present fashions." See *Eve: The Lady's Pictorial*, June 11, 1924, p. 356.

84. *Tatler*, June 23, 1926, p. 468.

85. The photograph of Knight appeared in *Eve: The Lady's Pictorial*, September 19, 1928, p. 577. A photo of an unidentified woman in a Spanish hat,

looking extremely feminine, can be seen in the September 9, 1928, edition of the very paper that led to the obscenity trial, the *Sunday Express*.

86. This quotation is my more detailed transcription of the interview with Evelyn Irons in the spring 1997 BBC documentary, "It's Not Unusual." Alkarim Jivani's book of the same title was written to accompany the three-part series, and an edited version of the interview with Irons appears on p. 28.

87. Baker, *Our Three Selves*, p. 132. Cline also compares Hall's "exotic kiss curl" to "sideburns." See *Radclyffe Hall*, p. 148. Incidentally, to have one's hair shingled at Harrods was an expensive proposition, costing about four guineas. Alan Jenkins, *The Twenties* (London: Book Club Associates, 1974), p. 56.

88. Cline, *Radclyffe Hall*, p. 220.

89. *Manchester Daily Journal*, July 14, 1927, in Cline, *Radclyffe Hall*, p. 221. Emphasis mine.

90. *Eve: The Lady's Pictorial*, March 31, 1926, p. 629.

91. Benstock links Hall with the Marquise de Belbeuf and argues that "female cross-dressing was not only a mark of aristocracy, it was sister to the dandyism of the period." See *Women of the Left Bank*, p. 180.

92. *Daily Chronicle*, March 7, 1929, p. 3.

93. *Eve: The Lady's Pictorial*, June 9, 1926, p. 511.

94. Baker, *Our Three Selves*, p. 132.

95. April 23, 1923, and July 4, 1923. Una Troubridge Diaries, vol. 2, Lovat Dickson Papers, MG 30, D 237.

96. Richard Ormrod, *Una Troubridge: The Friend of Radclyffe Hall* (New York: Carroll and Graf, 1985), p. 153.

97. Baker, *Our Three Selves*, p. 166.

98. Meryle Secrest, *Between Me and Life: A Biography of Romaine Brooks* (London: Macdonald and Jane's, 1976), p. 199.

99. *Daily Express*, April 8, 1924, p. 5.

100. Ibid., March 25, 1924, p. 7.

101. *Tatler*, February 27, 1924, p. 402.

102. A "severely masculine woman" is virtually synonymous for contemporary readers with lesbian. We should remember that in fashion terms, however, as defined by the *Oxford English Dictionary*, "severe" refers to a style "sober, restrained, austerely simple or plain." See *Oxford English Dictionary* (Oxford: Oxford University Press, 1971).

103. Bridget Elliott and Jo-Ann Wallace, *Women Artists and Writers: Modernist (Im)Positionings* (New York: Routledge, 1994), p. 51.

104. *Daily Mirror*, October 18, 1924. Newspaper cutting from the private papers in the collection of Roy Gluckstein, London. (Hereafter referred to as Gluckstein.)

105. *Westminster Gazette*, undated newspaper cutting, Gluckstein.

106. *Tatler*, April 21, 1926; *Daily Graphic*, October 14, 1924, Gluckstein.

107. *Sketch*, April 21, 1926, p. 146.

108. *The Concise Oxford Dictionary of Current English* (Oxford: Clarendon Press, 1995), p. 1052. Emphasis mine.

109. *Punch*, November 3, 1926, p. 483.

110. Plus-fours, incidentally, were the first article of male clothing Barker purchased and wore in public. *Eve: The Lady's Pictorial* informs readers that "winter sports give the enterprising feminine enthusiast plenty of opportunities for wearing the most dashing masculine apparel [plus fours]." January 14, 1925, p. 47.

111. "Why She Feels Better in Men's Clothes," undated and unidentified newspaper cutting, Gluckstein. This sentiment echoes a comment Barker made about trousers: "I know that dressed as a man I did not, as I do now that I am wearing skirts again, feel hopeless and helpless." See *Sunday Dispatch*, March 31, 1929, p. 18.

112. *Morning Post*, April 12, 1926, Gluckstein.

113. "Why She Feels Better in Men's Clothes," Gluckstein.

114. *Daily Graphic*, April 9, 1926, Gluckstein.

115. Blythe, *Age of Illusion*, p. 38.

116. Pugh, *Women and the Women's Movement in Britain 1914–1959*, p. 180.

117. Carrier, *Campaign for the Employment*, p. 149.

118. Cline, *Radclyffe Hall*, p. 219.

119. Gluck seems to be an obvious exception to the rule, for although she was an artist, journalists did indeed play "guess the gender." By patronizing men's tailors and shops and wearing breeches, plus-fours, and trousers in London, Gluck pushed the boundaries of female masculinity even further than Hall.

120. *Eve: The Lady's Pictorial*, August 29, 1928, p. 409.

121. *Sunday Times*, August 5, 1928, p. 12.

122. *Britannia*, March 8, 1929, p. 357. In early 1929 *Eve: The Lady's Pictorial* became *Britannia*, but by May of 1929 the magazine was renamed yet again to become the monthly *Britannia and Eve*.

123. *Britannia*, May 1929, p. 66.

124. Blythe, *Age of Illusion*, p. 38.

125. *Manchester Daily Dispatch*, November 21, 1928, p. 5.

126. "It's Not Unusual," BBC documentary. Irons, a journalist who worked on the women's page of the *Daily Mail*, and her partner often joined Hall and Troubridge for first nights in the mid-1920s. While acknowledging that Hall's novel helped "a great many people who had been desperately unhappy," "I simply thought that it was drawing too much attention to what had been going on for a long time. And we didn't want to be disturbed. That was the main thing." Irons notes too that she felt there was a real danger of losing her job.

127. Jivani, *It's Not Unusual*, p. 40.

128. Baker, *Our Three Selves*, p. 247.

129. As I have mentioned in the introduction, n. 29, both Hepworth and Preece seem to have recorded information and sketched in the diaries.

130. At the time of the obscenity trial in late 1928, Hall was forty-eight years old.

131. Journalist J. C. Cannell, who attended the trial at the Old Bailey, declared: "What surprises me is *not* that 'Colonel' Barker should have been successful in posing as a man, but that no one discovered 'his' claims to being a colonel or even a soldier to be fraudulent." See Cannell, *When Fleet Street Calls*, p. 207.

132. Annette Kuhn, *The Power of the Image: Essays in Representation and Sexuality* (London: Routledge, 1985), p. 53; *Empire News and Sunday Chronicle*, February 19, 1956, p. 2.

133. Roberts, *One Year of Life*, p. 96. On March 17, 1932, Troubridge notes in her diary that there were "nearly 700 people and [Hall] spoke most admirably. After luncheon she signed books for nearly an hour. Robert Allan [sic] and [Helen] Tagart were our guests and Tony [Clare Atkins] and Christopher [St. John] there & many friends." "Friends" here seems to refer to lesbians. Una Troubridge Diaries, vol. 3, Lovat Dickson Papers, MG 30, D 237.

134. Rolley, "Cutting a Dash," p. 57.

5. LESBIAN WRITERS AND SEXUAL SCIENCE:
A PASSAGE TO MODERNITY?

1. Rita Felski, introduction to *Sexology in Culture*, ed. Bland and Doan, p. 1.

2. Quoted by Baker, *Our Three Selves*, p. 203.

3. Letter from Radclyffe Hall to Havelock Ellis, July 19, 1928, Havelock Ellis Papers, ADD70539, British Library.

4. Quoted by Arthur Calder-Marshall, *Havelock Ellis: A Biography* (London: Rupert Hart-Davis, 1959), p. 263.

5. Troubridge, *The Life and Death of Radclyffe Hall*, p. 81.

6. Baker, *Our Three Selves*, p. 203.

7. Bennett, *Evening Standard*, August 9, 1928, p. 7. Bennett was also the author of a novel that treated the subject of lesbianism, *The Pretty Lady* (London: Cassell, 1918).

8. Beverley Brown, " 'A Disgusting Book When Properly Read': The Obscenity Trial," *Hecate* 10, no. 2 (1984): 13.

9. Bryher, *The Heart to Artemis: A Writer's Memoirs* (London: Collins, 1963), p. 199.

10. Felski, "Introduction," p. 1. Richard von Krafft-Ebing (1840–1902) was a professor of psychiatry at the University of Vienna; Havelock Ellis (1859–1939) was the most influential sexologist in Britain from the late nineteenth to the early twentieth century.

11. The full title of Faderman's second chapter is "A Worm in the Bud: The Early Sexologists and Love Between Women," *Odd Girls and Twilight Lovers*, p. 37.

12. Newton, "The Mythic Mannish Lesbian," p. 288.

13. Alison Hennegan, introduction to *The Well of Loneliness* (1928), by Radclyffe Hall (London: Virago, 1982), p. vii.

14. Harry Oosterhuis, "Richard von Krafft-Ebing's 'Step-Children of Nature': Psychiatry and the Making of Homosexual Identity," in Vernon A. Rosario, ed., *Science and Homosexualities* (New York: Routledge, 1997), p. 72.

15. Jay Prosser, *Second Skins: The Body Narratives of Transsexuality* (New York: Columbia University Press, 1998), p. 139.

16. Vicinus, " 'They Wonder to Which Sex I Belong,' " p. 485.

17. Suzanne Raitt, "Sex, Love, and the Homosexual Body in Early Sexology," in Bland and Doan, eds., *Sexology in Culture*, p. 161.

18. Baker, *Our Three Selves*, p. 216. On p. 217 Baker informs us that Hall read Émile Zola, Guy de Maupassant, Marcel Proust, Natalie Barney's *Pensées d'une Amazone*, and Colette's *Claudine* novels. It is likely that the English writers under consideration in this chapter read other literary works that dealt with lesbianism, including Clemence Dane's *Regiment of Women* (1917), Arnold Bennett's *Pretty Lady*, and Rosamond Lehmann's *Dusty Answer* (1927).

19. Felski, *The Gender of Modernity*, p. 14.

20. Editorial on Havelock Ellis's *Sexual Inversion*, *Lancet* 2 (November 19, 1896): 1344. In the wake of Oscar Wilde's conviction, any manuscript that dealt with a subject as controversial as sexual inversion would not have easily found a publisher in England.

As Weeks explains, *Sexual Inversion* became entangled in political intrigue when copies were displayed in the offices of the radical Legitimation League. The league was under surveillance by Scotland Yard for suspected connections with anarchists, and "the police obviously felt that a book on 'sexual inversion' . . . would provide a convenient hammer with which to crush the society." The organization's secretary, George Bedborough, "was arrested and eventually brought to trial in October 1898 for selling 'a certain lewd, wicked, bawdy, scandalous libel,' namely, Ellis's *Sexual Inversion*. Ellis himself was not charged, nor indeed was the book itself on trial as such. . . . Ellis determined that future editions of his *Studies* would not be published in Britain." See *Sex, Politics, and Society*, p. 181.

21. From the outset the designated readership of sexological literature included

professionals in the medical and legal fields. See Jackson, Real *Facts of Life*, p. 159.

Krafft-Ebing's study *Psychopathia Sexualis* was "written for lawyers and doctors discussing sexual crimes in court," and Ellis, in his foreword to *Studies in the Psychology of Sex*, specified that copies of his work be sold "only to professional readers." See Oosterhuis, "Richard von Krafft-Ebing's 'Step-Children of Nature,' " p. 70; Ellis, *Studies in the Psychology of Sex, Complete in Two Volumes*, p. xxii.

22. Letter from Havelock Ellis to Miss Ellerman (Bryher), March 3, 1919, GEN MSS 97, ser. 1, box 2, Beinecke.

23. Letter from Bryher to H.D., March 20, 1919, YCAL MSS 24, ser.1, box 3, Beinecke.

24. Letter from Ellis to Bryher, March 3, 1919. GEN MSS 97, ser. 1, box 2, Beinecke. *Sexual Inversion* was the second volume of what was in 1919 a six-volume set.

25. *Hansard*, Lords, 5th ser., 14 (1921): 574.

26. Browne, "Studies in Feminine Inversion," p. 55. As mentioned in an earlier chapter, this paper was presented to the British Society for the Study of Sex Psychology in 1917.

27. Brittain, *Radclyffe Hall*, p. 60.

28. Sonja Ruehl, "Inverts and Experts: Radclyffe Hall and the Lesbian Identity," in Rosalind Brunt and Caroline Rowan, eds., *Feminism, Culture, and Politics* (London: Lawrence and Wishart, 1982), p. 16.

29. George Piggford, " 'Who's That Girl?': Annie Lennox, Woolf's *Orlando*, and Female Camp Androgyny," *Mosaic* 30, no. 3 (September 1997): 49. Emphasis mine.

30. Newton, "The Mythic Mannish Lesbian," p. 285. See also Judy Greenway's essay on Otto Weininger for an examination of feminist negotiation of misogynist sexologies, "It's What You Do With It That Counts: Interpretations of Otto Weininger," in Bland and Doan, eds., *Sexology in Culture*, pp. 27–43.

31. Margaret Haig Mackworth, *This Was My World* (London: Macmillan, 1933), p. 127.

32. Melman, *Women and the Popular Imagination in the Twenties*, p. 3.

33. Brittain explains: "In 1928, sex phenomena were classified in two simple categories, 'nice' and 'nasty.' 'Nice' applied to love, marriage, legitimate babies and respectable romance. . . . 'Nasty' was reserved for almost everything else." See *Radclyffe Hall*, p. 58.

34. Glendinning, *Vita*, p. 405.

35. This excerpt appears in a 1920 diary entry. See Nicolson, *Portrait of a Marriage*, p. 102. For a good close reading of this diary passage, see Raitt, "Sex, Love, and the Homosexual Body in Early Sexology," p. 155.

36. Troubridge's misspelling of Ferenczi's name in the day-books has been a source of confusion for biographers and critics. Ferenczi wrote on telepathy, psychoanalysis, sexuality, and homosexuality. Troubridge mentions no specific works, but Ferenczi did produce an essay in 1911 on "The Role of Homosexuality in the Pathogenesis of Paranoia." I am grateful for Nina Arzberger's kind assistance.

37. Dr. Jacobus X was the pseudonym of Louis Jacolliot, a French army surgeon whose works on sexuality and psychology included *Medico-legal Examination of the Abuses, Aberrations, and Dementia of the Genital Sense* (1900) and *The Ethnology of the Sixth Sense: Studies and Researches into its Abuses, Perversions, Follies, Anomalies, and Crimes* (1899). I am grateful to Lesley Hall for providing this information.

In her "Notes from 'Sexual Inversion,'" Hall listed several other names associated with theorizing sexual inversion, including: Ulrichs, Krafft-Ebing, and Carpenter. Radclyffe Hall/Lady Una Troubridge Collection, box 12, folder 5, Harry Ransom Humanities Research Center, The University of Texas at Austin. I am grateful to Joanne Glasgow for referring me to this information.

38. Letter from H.D. to Bryher, dated 1919, probably early April. GEN MSS 97, ser. 1, box 13, Beinecke.

39. Roy Porter and Lesley Hall, *The Facts of Life: The Creation of Sexual Knowledge in Britain, 1650–1950* (New Haven: Yale University Press, 1995), p. 259.

40. Raitt, "Sex, Love, and the Homosexual Body in Early Sexology," p. 153.

41. Hall, *Well of Loneliness*, p. 26. All further quotations from this edition will be cited by page number in the text. See Hubert Kennedy's informative article, "Karl Heinrich Ulrichs: First Theorist of Homosexuality," in Vernon A. Rosario, ed., *Science and Homosexualities* (New York: Routledge, 1997), pp. 26–45, especially p. 26.

42. The diary is among the private papers of Dorothy Hepworth.

43. Letter from Norman Douglas to Bryher, July 13, 1922, GEN MSS 97, ser. 1, box 9, Beinecke.

44. Goldring, *The Nineteen Twenties*, p. 62.

45. Elsa Lanchester, *Elsa Lanchester, Herself* (New York: St. Martin's Press, 1983), p. 70. In the mid-1920s Lanchester was introduced to Krafft-Ebing's work "for laughs" by the novelist Mary Butts (p. 65).

46. Mannin, *Young in the Twenties*, pp. 31–2.

47. Cline, *Radclyffe Hall*, p. 163.

48. Goldring, *The Nineteen Twenties*, pp. 145, 147.

49. The exclamation point at the end of his sentence underscores how times had changed between his recollection of the more radical early 1920s and the time of writing the memoirs in 1945. The lecturer was probably James Strachey who, according to Virginia Woolf, spoke on "Onanism" at the 1917 Club on No-

vember 21, 1918. See Virginia Woolf, *The Diary of Virginia Woolf*, vol.1, *1915–1919*, ed. Anne Olivier Bell (London: Penguin Books Books, 1977), p. 221. I am grateful to Lucy Bland for this reference, and also the information that James Strachey wore a beard and round glasses.

50. Letter from Ellis to Bryher, March 3, 1919, GEN MSS 97, ser. 1, box 2, Beinecke.

51. Letter from H.D. to Bryher, April 22, 1919, GEN MSS 97, ser. 1, box 13. Beinecke.

52. Havelock Ellis, *Studies in the Psychology of Sex*, vol. 2, *Sexual Inversion* (1897; reprint, Philadelphia: F. A. Davis, 3d ed., 1921), p. 229.

According to critic Joseph Bristow, Ellis's collaborator, the homosexual John Addington Symonds wrote that he "wished to distance these documents [the case histories] from the type commonly used by sexologists." Symonds told Ellis that his case histories were "quite different from those collected by physicians." Bristow observes: "Doubtless [Symonds] believed that his particular sympathies for homosexuality produced franker and thus more reliable insights into the phenomenon." See "Symonds' History, Ellis's Heredity: Sexual Inversion," in Bland and Doan, eds., *Sexology in Culture*, pp. 94–5.

53. The phrase "under the ban of society," here attributed to Krafft-Ebing, can also be found in a pamphlet (intended for private circulation only) by Edward Carpenter: "It is difficult . . . for outsiders not personally experienced in the matter to realize the great strain and tension of nerves under which those persons grow up from boyhood to manhood—or from girl to womanhood—who find their deepest and strongest instincts under the ban of the society around them." See Edward Carpenter, *Homogenic Love, and Its Place in a Free Society* (Manchester: Labour Press, 1894), p. 29.

54. Edward Carpenter, *The Intermediate Sex: A Study of Some Transitional Types of Men and Women* (1908; reprint, London: Allen and Unwin, 1916), p. 55. Carpenter (1844–1929), a homosexual, socialist, and ardent supporter of feminism, was not a sexologist as such, although he produced a large body of influential work on sexuality. For more about Carpenter, see Weeks, *Coming Out*, pp. 68–83.

55. Letter from Kathlyn Oliver to Edward Carpenter, October 25, 1915, Carpenter Collection, MSS 386/262, Sheffield Archives, Sheffield. (Hereafter referred to as Carpenter Collection.)

56. Ellis, *Sexual Inversion*, p. 229.

57. Prosser, *Second Skins*, p. 139.

58. *Lancet*, p. 1344.

59. Ellis, *Sexual Inversion*, p. 82.

60. Oosterhuis, "Richard von Krafft-Ebing's 'Step-Children of Nature,'" p. 70.

61. See, for example, Rosenman, "Sexual Identity and *A Room of One's Own*," p. 645.

62. Oosterhuis traces these important shifts in Krafft-Ebing's thought to his last writings for Hirschfeld's *Jahr für sexuelle Zwischenstufen*, namely an article entitled "Neue Studien auf dem Gebiete der Homosexualität." See "Richard von Krafft-Ebing's 'Step-Children of Nature,' " p. 79.

63. Carpenter, *Intermediate Sex*, p. 23.

64. The influence of the degeneration model lingered in interwar Britain, despite the emergence of other theories; for example, "both Carpenter and Weininger argued that homosexuality was natural and rejected the prevalent pathological models." See Greenway, "It's What You Do With It That Counts," p. 36.

65. Ellis, *Sexual Inversion*, p. 317.

66. Whitlock, " 'Everything Is Out of Place,' " p. 572.

67. Ellis, *Sexual Inversion*, p. 317.

68. In *Despised and Rejected* Allatini also observes that "suffering must inevitably accompany realization." See "A. T. Fitzroy" (Rose Allatini), *Despised and Rejected* (1918; reprint, London: Gay Mens Press, 1988), p. 221.

69. Hall, *Well of Loneliness*, p. 205. Hall later transforms Stephen's internalized "mark of Cain" into a proud and "honorable" war wound—a scar on her cheek—"as a mark of her courage," p. 293.

70. Carpenter, *Intermediate Sex*, pp. 14, 38.

71. Although Hall included Carpenter's name among several others mentioned by Ellis in her "Notes from 'Sexual Inversion,' " Carpenter's theories on the "intermediate sex" are rarely associated directly or extensively with Hall in biographies or in the critical literature. Since Troubridge kept careful note of books read it would seem that Carpenter's name would appear in the diaries, but it doesn't. This may be due to the fact that during the years when Carpenter's work was most influential, Troubridge seems to have destroyed the diaries (none exist between 1914 and 1917, the period covering the courtship and first sexual experience between Hall and Troubridge). Hall's list appears in her handwritten "Notes from 'Sexual Inversion.' " Radclyffe Hall/Lady Una Troubridge Collection, box 12, folder 5, Harry Ransom Humanities Research Center, The University of Texas at Austin.

72. Bland, *Banishing the Beast*, p. 263.

73. *British Medical Journal*, June 29, 1909, newspaper cutting, Carpenter Collection, NC623.

74. The volume was *Love's Coming-of-Age: A Series of Papers on the Relation of the Sexes*, which first appeared in 1896. Keith Nield, "Edward Carpenter: The Uses of Utopia," in Tony Brown, ed., *Edward Carpenter and Late Victorian Radicalism* (London: Frank Cass, 1990), p. 20.

75. Nield, "Edward Carpenter," pp. 26–7. In 1911 one admirer, L. D. Abbott, called him "the greatest man of Modern England" who "whether as mystic or scientist, prophet or poet, critic or appreciator, religionist or idol-breaker, scholar or workman, disciple or teacher, health-giver to the body or light-giver to the soul, is always masterly and always easily great." See L. D. Abbott, *The Free Comrade*, June, 1911, Carpenter Collection, C per 37.

76. Letter from Hall to Ellis, July 19, 1928, ADD70539, British Library.

77. Adam Parkes, "Lesbianism, History, and Censorship: *The Well of Loneliness* and the SUPPRESSED RANDINESS of Virginia Woolf's *Orlando*," *Twentieth Century Literature* 40, no. 4 (Winter 1994): 441.

78. Gilbert and Gubar, *No Man's Land*, 2:354.

79. Ellis excused himself from the court proceedings by telling Hall that he did not perform well in the witness box and also, as the author of a book (*Sexual Inversion*) "judicially condemned," he was " 'tarred with the same brush.' " Quoted by Cline, *Radclyffe Hall*, p. 256.

80. *Lancet* 2 (September 1, 1928): 484. This explains the reviewer's assessment that the novel, "to which Mr. Havelock Ellis contributes a preface, is certainly not effective as a presentation of the case for social toleration of an abnormal habit of life."

81. Hennegan, "Introduction," pp. xiv-xv.

82. Ruehl, "Inverts and Experts," p. 20. Whitlock too proposes that "rather than merely reproducing Ellis's theories, Hall transformed them into a quite different discourse that generates quite different effects." See " 'Everything Is Out of Place,' " p. 560. See also Jean Radford who, in perhaps the most thorough investigation of Ellis's theory of inversion, claims that "the co-existence of contradictory discourses about homosexuality" constitutes a " 'reverse' discourse." See "An Inverted Romance," p. 106.

83. Critics often note, for instance, that the notion of the "third sex" was developed by various sexologists. See Newton, "The Mythic Mannish Lesbian," p. 289 and Claire Tylee, *The Great War and Women's Consciousness* (Iowa City: University of Iowa Press, 1990), p. 175.

84. Bonnie Kime Scott, *Refiguring Modernism: The Women of 1928*, vol. 1 (Bloomington: Indiana University Press, 1995), p. 249.

85. Ruehl, "Inverts and Experts," p. 20.

86. Bryher, *Development* (New York: Macmillan, 1920) and *Two Selves* (Paris: Contact Publishing, 1923); letter from H.D. to Bryher, April 10, 1919. GEN MSS 97, ser. 1, box 13, Beinecke. Bryher's two early novels have been reprinted in a single volume, with a useful introduction by editor Joanne Winning. See Bryher, *Two Novels: Development and Two Selves* (Madison: University of Wisconsin Press, 2000).

87. Letter from Ellis to Bryher, December 19, 1918, GEN MSS 97, ser. 1, box 2, Beinecke.

88. Letter from Bryher to H.D., March 20, 1919. YCAL MSS 24, ser. 1, box 3, Beinecke.

89. Ellis, *Sexual Inversion*, p. 244. This passage appears in an earlier version but without the reference to "boyishness," suggesting that Ellis had begun to consider a wider range of female masculinities. See "Sexual Inversion in Women," p. 152.

90. Ellis, *Sexual Inversion*, p. 251. Sally Mitchell writes: "Many women who were girls at the turn of the century had longed intensely not to be. . . . I wanted so much to be a boy that I did not dare to think about it at all, for it made me feel quite desperate to know that it was impossible to be one.'" See Mitchell, *The New Girl: Girls' Culture in England, 1880–1915* (New York: Columbia University Press, 1995), p. 103.

91. Browne, "Studies in Feminine Inversion," p. 55.

92. Allatini's *Despised and Rejected* was originally published in 1918 but was prosecuted for sedition under the provisions of Defence of the Realm Act (DORA) and banned as "likely to prejudice the recruiting of persons to serve in His Majesty's Forces, and their training and discipline." The novel ambitiously tackles the issues of conscientious objection and Uranism, Carpenter's preferred term for homosexuality. See Jonathan Cutbill, introduction to *Despised and Rejected*, by Allatini, no page numbers.

Tylee describes this novel as having "great cultural interest," but it has thus far received scant scholarly attention. See *The Great War and Women's Consciousness* for an interesting discussion, pp. 121–9, especially p. 122.

93. Bryher, *Development*, pp. 6–7.

94. Gilmore, "Obscenity, Modernity, Identity," p. 610.

95. Allatini, *Despised and Rejected*, p. 162. Nancy and Stephen also beg to have their hair cut short. Nancy cries "Couldn't I have my hair cut short?" (*Two Selves*, p. 34), and Stephen asks, "May I cut off my hair?" (Hall, *Well of Loneliness*, p. 57).

96. *TLS*, June 24, 1920, p. 401.

97. *Athenaeum*, July 30, 1920, GEN MSS 97, ser. 2, box 82, Beinecke. Unless otherwise noted, all reviews of *Development* can be found in this box of press cuttings, usually with no page number.

98. *The Bookman*, August 1920, Beinecke. Emphasis mine.

99. *London Opinion*, July 17, 1920, Beinecke.

100. *Daily Telegraph*, July 16, 1920, Beinecke.

101. *Today*, August 19, 1920, and *Daily Telegraph*, July 16, 1920, Beinecke; Ellis, *Sexual Inversion*, pp. 318–9.

102. "Mr. Polygon Amor," *Literary Review*, Beinecke. Emphasis mine.

103. Ellis, *Sexual Inversion*, p. 317.

104. Thus, by strategically shifting the terms of comparison from color-blindness to color-hearing, Ellis proposes a bold new perspective that rejects morbidity: "Color-hearing, while an abnormal phenomenon . . . cannot be called a diseased condition. . . . All such organic variations are abnormalities." See *Sexual Inversion*, p. 318.

105. Bryher, *Two Selves*, p. 72.

106. Bryher, *Development*, p. 57. Through Ellis, Bryher came to regard inversion as "as natural as breathing."

107. Ibid., p. 163. Emphasis mine. Stephen too is separated from others by her intense "sensitivity to beauty." See Hall, *Well of Loneliness*, p. 15.

108. In a passage from *Development*, reminiscent of Stephen's revelation ("there are so many of us—thousands"), the narrator characterizes Nancy's difference as "fairly prevalent": "While . . . not common to every one, as she had at first imagined, it was not confined to the few, but was, in one form or another, fairly prevalent." See Hall, *Well of Loneliness*, p. 204, and Bryher, *Development*, p. 163.

109. Carpenter, *Intermediate Sex*, p. 134. Emphasis mine. Carpenter quotes from the 1901 edition of Ellis's *Sexual Inversion*. Ellis also wrote that inversion "occurs with special frequency" among "women of high intelligence." See *Sexual Inversion*, p. 262. Inverts too were preoccupied with the numbers game, as is evident from an entry in the back of Troubridge's 1928 diary: "*Statistics*: 15 in a 1000—1.5 per cent," figures she has apparently obtained from Hirschfeld's *A Manual of Sexual Science*. See Una Troubridge Diaries, vol. 2, Lovat Dickson Papers, MG 30, D 237.

110. Weeks, *Coming Out*, p. 64.

111. Again, this passage from Ellis's 1901 edition is cited by Carpenter. See *Intermediate Sex*, p. 138.

112. Carpenter, *Intermediate Sex*, p. 128. Carpenter often used a number of terms interchangeably to refer to the invert, including "homogenic," "homosexual," "intermediate sex," and "Uranian." He did not use the terms "lesbian" or "Sapphist."

113. Connolly, *New Statesman*, p. 615

114. Claire Buck, " 'Still Some Obstinate Emotion Remains': Radclyffe Hall and the Meanings of Service," in Suzanne Raitt and Trudi Tate, eds., *Women's Fiction and the Great War* (Oxford: Clarendon Press, 1997), p. 186.

115. Forel, *Sexual Question*, p. 242.

116. In general, the British medical establishment did not hold sexology in high regard. *British Medical Journal*, June 29, 1909, newspaper cutting, Carpenter Collection, NC623.

117. Browne, "Studies in Feminine Inversion," p. 57.

118. Rebecca West, *Time and Tide*, March 15, 1929: 284.

119. Transcript of the Judgement of Sir Chartres Biron, chief magistrate, Bow Street Police Court, Home Office file on the prosecution of *The Well of Loneliness*, November 16, 1928. PRO HO144/22547/527705, Public Record Office.

120. Baker, *Our Three Selves*, p. 219; Hall, *Well of Loneliness*, p. 406.

121. *Glasgow Herald*, July 6, 1920, Beinecke.

122. Catharine R. Stimpson argues that "both Ellis and Hall give their inverts some compensations: intelligence and talent." See "Zero Degree Deviancy: The Lesbian Novel in English," *Critical Inquiry* 8, no. 2 (winter 1981): 370.

123. Ruehl, "Inverts and Experts," pp. 26–7.

124. Carolyn Burdett, "The Hidden Romance of Sexual Science: Eugenics, the Nation, and the Making of Modern Feminism," in Bland and Doan, eds., *Sexology in Culture*, p. 44.

125. Carpenter, *Intermediate Sex*, p. 41.

126. Carpenter, *Homogenic Love, and Its Place in a Free Society*, p. 51; Carpenter, *Intermediate Sex*, p. 14.

127. *Athenaeum*, July 30, 1920, Beinecke. Nancy's color-hearing registers here as a marker of sex rather than of inversion and effectively neutralizes her apparent masculinity.

128. Allatini, *Despised and Rejected*, pp. 348, 349.

129. Carpenter, *Intermediate Sex*, pp. 37–8. Carpenter invokes a mind/body split in his discussion of the "homogenic" woman. Externally she is "thoroughly feminine and gracious," but inwardly she has assumed the very male characteristics that, in Carpenter's view, inhibit the evolutionary improvement of the human race (pp. 35–6). The female Uranian appears "thoroughly feminine" on the outside, but her "inner nature is to a great extent masculine": "a temperament active, brave, originative, somewhat decisive, not too emotional; fond of out-door life, of games and sports, of science, politics, or even business" (pp. 38, 36).

130. Beverly Thiele, "Coming-of-Age: Edward Carpenter on Sex and Reproduction," in Tony Brown, ed., *Edward Carpenter and Late Victorian Radicalism* (London: Frank Cass, 1990), pp. 109–10.

131. Carpenter, *Intermediate Sex*, p. 109.

132. Ibid., p. 109.

133. Carpenter cites an early version of Ellis: "There are . . . certain occupations to which inverts are specially attracted. Acting is certainly one of the chief of these." See *Intermediate Sex*, p. 110.

134. Allatini, *Despised and Rejected*, pp. 217–18. Bryher and Hall both emphasize too the naturalness of inversion. Bryher speaks of color-hearing (her metaphor for inversion) as being "as natural as breathing," and Hall describes

Stephen's same-sex desire "as much a part of herself as her breathing." See *Development*, p. 163, and *Well of Loneliness*, p. 146.

135. Carpenter, *Intermediate Sex*, p. 24.

136. Weeks, *Coming Out*, p. 76. Carpenter writes: "with [Uranians'] extraordinary gift for, and experience in, affairs of the heart—from the double point of view, both of the man and of the woman—it is not difficult to see that these people have a special work." See *Intermediate Sex*, p. 14.

137. Allatini, *Despised and Rejected*, p. 349. Carpenter believed that the Uranian "may be destined to form the advance guard of that great movement which will one day transform the common life by substituting the bond of personal affection and compassion for the monetary, legal and other external ties which now control and confine society." See *Intermediate Sex*, p. 116. G. Bernard Shaw observed that for Carpenter Uranians were "a chosen race." See Shaw, preface *Salt and His Circle*, by Stephen Winsten (London: Hutchinson, 1951), p. 9.

138. Antoinette possesses several telling signifiers of female inversion, including her name and her glaring ineptitude for needlework. Terry Castle credits Allatini with being one of the first writers "to invoke Marie Antoinette specifically as a lesbian icon. . . . Antoinette cannot escape . . . from her fateful name—or from the powerful homoerotic emotion with which it is so obviously associated." Antoinette's name, Castle provocatively continues, "might thus be said to function as a kind of proleptic hint to the reader—as the cipher, or symbolic intimation, of Antoinette's own emerging lesbian desires." See *The Apparitional Lesbian*, pp. 141, 142.

Another tell-tale sign of Antoinette's lesbianism is the fact that "Antoinette could do neither cross-stitch nor crochet, wherefore her grandmother argued that there must be something radically wrong with her." See *Despised and Rejected*, p. 62. As Ellis indicated, in female inverts "there is . . . a dislike and sometimes incapacity for needle-work and other domestic occupations." See *Sexual Inversion*, p. 250.

139. Allatini, *Despised and Rejected*, p. 348. Angela Ingram also refers to Stephen's role as an "intercessor" in the reproductive process. See "Un/Reproductions: Estates of Banishment in English Fiction after the Great War," in Mary Lynn Broe and Angela Ingram, eds., *Women's Writing in Exile* (Chapel Hill: University of North Carolina Press, 1989), p. 333.

140. Hall, *Well of Loneliness*, p. 417. Teresa de Lauretis explains Stephen's relinquishing of Mary as "a repudiation of lesbianism as such." See *The Practice of Love: Lesbian Sexuality and Perverse Desire* (New York: Routledge, 1994), p. 211.

For a bold alternative reading to mine, see Prosser's chapter on *The Well*, in which he argues: "That Stephen gives up Mary to Martin Hallam in spite of Mary's devotion to her indicates that the invert functions not as a figure for lesbianism—a lure or a construct—but precisely as its refusal. Through her passing over Mary (both passing over her and passing her over to Martin), Stephen affirms her identification with the heterosexual man. More powerfully than any moment in the novel—and certainly more troublingly for the transsexual critic recuperating *The Well* as a transsexual novel—this act highlights her disidentification with women and locates her in a masculinist economy in which women are to be exchanged (given up/sacrificed/courted)." See *Second Skins*, p. 166.

141. Carpenter, *Intermediate Sex*, p. 27. "[M]any are fine, healthy specimens of their sex, muscular and well-developed in body, of powerful brain, high standard of conduct, and with nothing abnormal or morbid of any kind observable in their physical structure or constitution. . . . They may have an important part to play in the evolution of the race" (pp. 23, 24).

142. Carpenter, *Intermediate Sex*, p. 29. By 1914 Carpenter significantly modified this typology: "As we have seen that the varieties of human type, intermediate and other, are very numerous, almost endless, so we shall do well to keep in mind that the varieties of love and sex-relation between individuals of these types are almost endless, and cannot be dispatched in sweeping generalizations— whether such relations be normal or homosexual." See *Intermediate Types Among Primitive Folk: A Study in Social Evolution* (London: George Allen, 1914), p. 164.

143. Ellis, *Sexual Inversion*, p. 222; Hall, *Well of Loneliness*, p. 285.

144. Newton, "The Mythic Mannish Lesbian," p. 292.

145. Hall, *Well of Loneliness*, pp. 299, 297.

146. Carpenter, *Intermediate Sex*, pp. 37–8.

147. Hall, *Well of Loneliness*, p. 149; Ellis, *Sexual Inversion*, pp. 216, 219.

148. Loralee MacPike likewise observes that Mary does not conform to Ellis's conceptualization of the "pseudohomosexual": Mary "is someone new. . . . [She] is a member of a group . . . [of] lesbians who for social reasons create heterosexual (or heterosexual-appearing) unions while retaining a primary attraction to, and often an emotional commitment to, women. Mary's conflicting history suggests that she is one of them, but this does not mean she is not a true invert. . . . Martin's attraction to Mary is in fact an indication that *she* is a true invert." See "Is Mary Llewellyn an Invert? The Modernist Supertext of *The Well of Loneliness*," in Elizabeth Jane Harrison and Shirley Peterson, eds., *Unmanning Modernism: Gendered Re-Readings* (Knoxville: The University of Tennessee Press, 1997), pp. 85, 87n.

149. Newton, "The Mythic Mannish Lesbian," p. 292; Carpenter, *Intermediate Sex*, pp. 35–6.

150. Weeks, *Coming Out*, p. 75.

151. Hall, *Well of Loneliness*, pp. 101, 98; Whitlock, " 'Everything Is Out of Place,' " p. 571, and Carpenter, *Intermediate Sex*, pp. 32–3.

MacPike similarly argues that because Martin "seems to be attracted to inverts and to inverts alone . . . [he] is excludable from the ranks of 'ordinary men.'" See "Is Mary Llewellyn an Invert?" pp. 87–8n.

152. Christopher E. Shaw, "Identified with the One: Edward Carpenter, Henry Salt, and the Ethical Socialist Philosophy of Science," in Tony Brown, ed., *Edward Carpenter and Late Victorian Radicalism* (London: Frank Cass, 1990), p. 35. Of all natural objects, Martin fixates on trees "because [he] love[s] them and the element they stand for." This preoccupation echoes Carpenter's, for whom "the real tree exists and can be seen in the resplendent light of the universal consciousness; but the tree which we ordinarily look upon is only the merest aspect of its infinitude, a few isolated thoughts or relations which the botanist or the woodman may happen to separate off and *call* the tree." See *Well of Loneliness*, p. 93, and Carpenter, *The Art of Creation: Essays on the Self and Its Powers* (London: George Allen, 1904), p.61.

153. Hall, *Well of Loneliness*, p. 94; Shaw, "Identified with the One," p. 34.

154. Alan Sinfield, *The Wilde Century*, p. 115.

155. Thiele, "Coming-of-Age," p. 110.

156. Forel, *Sexual Question*, p. 439.

157. Hall, *Well of Loneliness*, pp. 437, 83. I am influenced here by Gilbert and Gubar's discussion of Olive Schreiner in *No Man's Land*, 2:79. Carpenter writes that only through "long experience and devotion, as well as by much suffering—will [the intermediate] have an important part to play in the transformation" of the race into "a higher form." See *Intermediate Sex*, pp. 122–3.

158. Hall, *Well of Loneliness*, p. 431. Ingram perceptively observes that "at the end of the novel Stephen becomes a mother . . . of the whole homosexual race." See "Un/Reproductions," p. 333.

159. Quoted in Gilbert and Gubar, *No Man's Land*, 2:79. Letter to Havelock Ellis, November 9, 1888.

160. Buck, "Radclyffe Hall and the Meanings of Service," p. 186. "Miss Ogilvy" was in some respects a first draft for some of the ideas Hall would develop more fully in *The Well*, including the invert's place within the evolutionary stages.

161. Weeks, *Coming Out*, p. 72.

162. Edward Carpenter, *Angels' Wings: A Series of Essays on Art and Its Relation to Life* (London: Swan Sonnenschein, 1898), pp. 6–7, and Carpenter, *Art of Creation*, p. 60.

163. Hall, *Well of Loneliness*, pp. 92, 93. Shaw explains that Carpenter saw "primitive harmony" as "deficient in its lack of human self-awareness." See "Identified with the One," p. 35.

164. Carpenter, *Art of Creation*, p. 61.

165. Carpenter, *Intermediate Sex*, p. 32.

166. Carpenter, *Art of Creation*, p. 60, and Hall, *Well of Loneliness*, p. 437.

167. Felski, *Gender of Modernity*, p. 14.

168. Carpenter, *Intermediate Sex*, p. 70.

169. Allatini, *Despised and Rejected*, p. 69.

170. Whitlock, " 'Everything Is Out of Place,' " p. 559; Hall, *Well of Loneliness*, p. 390.

6. PORTRAIT OF A SAPPHIST? FIXING THE FRAME OF REFERENCE

1. *Punch*, October 6, 1926, p. 383.

2. Graham Clarke, introduction to *The Portrait in Photography*, ed. Graham Clarke (London: Reaktion Books, 1992), p. 1.

3. Roland Barthes, *Camera Lucida: Reflections on Photography*, trans. Richard Howard (1980; reprint, New York: Hill and Wang, 1993), p. 89.

4. Hamer, *Britannia's Glory*, pp. 102, 48.

5. Newton, "The Mythic Mannish Lesbian," pp. 281–2.

6. Mandy Merck, *Perversions: Deviant Readings* (New York: Routledge, 1993), p. 86.

7. Halberstam, *Female Masculinity*, p. 109. Suzanne Raitt also argues that at this time, "Lesbianism was not a political identity. In fact, it may not have been an *identity*, a place in which the self was found at all. Conceived as an intermittent sexual or emotional orientation, it could flourish happily in the interstices of heterosexual existence, hardly threatening at all." See *Virginia and Vita*, pp. 6–7.

8. Marx Wartofsky, "Cameras Can't See: Representation, Photography, and Human Vision," *Afterimage* 7, no. 9 (April 1980): 8.

9. Clarke, "Introduction," p. 1.

10. Lock, *British Policewoman*, p. 167. Hamer, more generously, characterizes Allen's "public role as the face of police women in Britain." See *Britannia's Glory*, p. 48. Studio photographers who produced official WPS portraits were usually identified; however, no information is available about other WPS photographs, which could have been taken by a professional, someone within the ranks of the WPS, or a sympathetic supporter.

11. Lisa Tickner, *The Spectacle of Women: Imagery of the Suffrage Campaign, 1907–1914* (London: Chatto and Windus, 1987), p. ix.

12. Allen, *Lady in Blue*, p. 74. Allen also attributes her excellence in public speaking to her work with the suffrage movement: "I was thanked several times for a clearness of enunciation that I had learned in Suffragette street-corner meet-

ings. Indeed, I have never ceased being thankful that I was a rebel against law and order before I became head of an organization of policewomen."

13. Tickner, *Spectacle of Women*, p. xi.

14. According to Lock, such photographs "served the growing megalomania of Mary Allen. Subscribers [to the *Policewoman's Review*]were treated to an endless flow of photographs of her strutting around the world." See *British Policewoman*, p. 167. Supporters, however, were obviously not put off by this format, as evident in Viscountess Rhondda's letter: "The idea of publishing such a review seems to me quite an excellent one . . . from a propaganda point of view." See *Policewoman's Review*, I, no. 2 (June 1927): 14.

15. This photograph is reproduced in Allen's *Pioneer Policewoman*.

16. Mick Gidley, "Hoppé's Impure Portraits: Contextualizing the American Types," in Clarke, ed., *The Portrait in Photography*, p. 139.

17. Tickner, *Spectacle of Women*, p. xi.

18. Lock, *British Policewoman*, caption for illustration 14, no page number.

19. Allen, *Pioneer Policewoman*, p. 240. Emphasis mine.

20. Halberstam describes this photo as "a remarkable image of the power of female masculinity," one almost guaranteed to exacerbate a " 'child's confusion and terror.' " See *Female Masculinity*, p. 108. Hamer describes this publicity shot as "a shockingly lesbian image." See *Britannia's Glory*, p. 53.

21. John Tagg, *The Burden of Representation: Essays on Photographies and Histories* (1988; reprint, Minneapolis: University of Minnesota Press, 1995), p. 100.

22. There is no proof that the photograph Macready presented in his testimony was in fact either of the two photographs in the narrative sequence depicting WPS officers dealing with a "Case," but it is likely. See Lock's discussion of the incident in *British Policewoman*: "I came across a picture of them [Allen and Damer Dawson] 'arresting' a rather odd-looking 'man' " (p. 110).

23. Tagg has tracked how the "early years of the development of the photographic process coincided approximately with the period of the introduction of the police service" in Britain, "and for more than a hundred years the two have progressed together." See *Burden of Representation*, p. 74.

24. Deborah Bright, introduction to *The Passionate Camera: Photography and Bodies of Desire*, ed. Deborah Bright (London: Routledge, 1998), p. 5.

25. Baird Committee, *Report*, p. 20, para. 180.

26. Tagg, *Burden of Representation*, p. 100.

27. The WPS's repudiation of Macready's accusation appeared in their own report, *Women's Auxiliary Service*, p. 14, ADM 1/11/2, Metropolitan Police Historic Museum.

28. Ibid.

29. Letter from Macready to Troup, January 29, 1920, PRO HO45/11067/370521, Public Record Office.

30. Tickner, *Spectacle of Women*, p. x. Despite their own roots in militant suffragism, the WPS came into existence as a result of splitting off from a women's policing group that refused to put women's needs second. For further discussion on the WPS's relationship with early suffragism, see chapter 2.

31. Jacqueline Rose, "Sexuality and Vision: Some Questions," in Hal Foster, ed., *Vision and Visuality* (Seattle: Bay Press, 1988), p. 116.

32. Wartofsky, "Cameras Can't See," p. 8.

33. See, for example, Jacob, *Me and the Swans*, pp. 157–8.

34. Janet Lyon, "Women Demonstrating Modernism," *Discourse* 17, no. 2 (Winter 1994–5): 14.

35. Cline, *Radclyffe Hall*, p. 199. The photo also appeared in the *Bookman*, with the caption "Miss Radclyffe Hall, author of 'The Unlit Lamp.' " See *Bookman*, November, 1924, p. 112.

36. It would be misleading to suppose that Gluck and Hall sought out Coster solely because of his reputation as the "photographer of men." Although the photographer initially promoted himself in this way when he first opened his studio in 1926, he soon moved beyond his "men only" policy to include notable women, such as the novelists Sheila Kaye-Smith (who sat for Coster in 1930), Mary Borden (1931), and Margaret Kennedy (1931). The catalogue of photographs by Coster held by the National Portrait Gallery in London also lists Vita Sackville-West, Winifred Ashton [Clemence Dane], and Rebecca West (who all sat in 1934), as well as other women who sat in the late 1920s and early 30s who were known for their writing or work in the theater. See Terence Pepper, *Howard Coster's Celebrity Portraits: 101 Photographs of Personalities in Literature and the Arts* (London: National Portrait Gallery, 1985), pp. 103, 107.

37. Eric Homberger, "J. P. Morgan's Nose: Photographer and Subject in American Portrait Photography," in Clarke, ed., *The Portrait in Photography*, p. 115.

38. Clarke, "Introduction," p. 1.

39. Tagg, *Burden of Representation*, p. 37.

40. Cline, *Radclyffe Hall*, p. 212.

41. By comparison, an undated photograph of Gluck by Coster accentuates the subject's face, but the lower angle of the portrait—shot from the waist level looking up—captures a completely different aspect of the artist, one altogether more relaxed in her sporty, light cotton jacket and open, zippered top. Further contributing to the cool air of the photograph is Gluck's downward glance, eyes nearly closed, unbuttoned cuffs, and thumb tucked casually into the jacket, holding a cigarette. In contrast, Hall's portrait by Coster, who specialized in work-

ing with "those who he felt were people of consequence and achievement," is rather more formal. By 1932, with her sexuality known throughout the English-speaking world, Hall poses confidently in a sartorial style now associated with her and women like her: bow-tie, monocle, tailored-jacket, short haircut. See Pepper, *Howard Coster's Celebrity Portraits*, p. vii.

42. Bill Jay, "Emil Otto Hoppé, 1878–1972," *Studies in Visual Communication* 11 (1985): 6.

43. Gidley, "Hoppé's Impure Portraits," p. 133 and E. O. Hoppé, "As Others See Us," *Royal Magazine* 57, no. 338 (December 1926): 107–14.

44. Gidley, "Hoppé's Impure Portraits," p. 133, and Tagg, *Burden of Representation*, p. 37.

45. Hoppé, "As Others See Us," p. 107.

46. Ibid., p. 114, and Susan Sontag, *On Photography* (1973; reprint, New York: Farrar, Straus and Giroux, 1977), pp. 120–1.

47. Hoppé, "As Others See Us," pp. 110, 113.

48. Interestingly, the Gluck portrait Hoppé selected for the spread in the *Royal Magazine* de-emphasizes her male clothing by foregrounding her face. Another portrait taken at the same sitting (Hoppé believed that "six pictures made at the same sitting will often show a different aspect of the sitter") depicts Gluck in a fedora and coat, with upturned collar—far more masculine attire. See Hoppé, "As Others See Us," p. 110.

49. *Evening News*, April 10, 1926, Gluckstein.

50. *Daily Mirror*, October 18, 1924, Gluckstein.

51. Elizabeth Ponsonby is "believed to have been the original of Agatha Runcible in *Vile Bodies*," a comic novel published in 1930 by Evelyn Waugh. See Jenkins, *The Twenties*, p. 30.

52. Victor Burgin, "Looking at Photographs," in Victor Burgin, ed., *Thinking Photography* (1982; reprint, London: Macmillan, 1994), p. 142.

53. This information appears in an in-house publication on Fox Photos. I am grateful to Angela Minshull of London's Hulton Getty Picture Collection for allowing me access to this material.

54. Bloom, *Literature and Culture in Modern Britain*, p. 15. The *Bookman* and *Eve: The Lady's Pictorial*, for instance, regularly featured photographs (usually studio portraits) of popular writers.

55. Una Troubridge Diaries, vol. 2, April 12, 1927, Lovat Dickson Papers, MG 30, D 237.

56. Hall, *Well of Loneliness* p. 214.

57. Trodd, *Women's Writing in English*, pp. 37, 36.

58. *Daily Mirror*, April 13, 1927, p. 24. Souhami mistakenly reports that upon winning the Femina Prize, photographs of "Miss Radclyffe Hall and Colette were

printed side by side." See *Trials of Radclyffe Hall*, p. 148. Hall also visited the studio of Peter North around this time, and his portrait of her appeared in the *Graphic* on April 30, 1927. Another studio portrait used in the *Bookman* in May would be picked up by the *Daily Mail* in its story about the banning of *The Well*, November 17, 1928. These cuttings can be found in the files on the banning of *The Well* in the Public Record Office, London.

59. Cline, *Radclyffe Hall*, p. 219.

60. This article appeared originally in the *Bookman* in West's "Letters from Europe" (1929–30). See West, *Ending in Earnest*, p. 6.

61. Lee, *Virginia Woolf*, p. 468. While Bloomsbury was not averse to publicity, my point here is that Woolf herself did not manipulate self-imaging to promote her career. For an insightful discussion of the commercialization of the Bloomsbury group, see Jane Garrity, "Selling Culture to the 'Civilized': Bloomsbury, British *Vogue*, and the Marketing of National Identity," *Modernism/Modernity* 6, no. 2 (April 1999): 29–58.

62. The phrase "schoolgirl antics" refers to conflicts Brooks experienced in painting Gluck's portrait. See Bridget Elliott, "Performing the Picture or Painting the Other: Romaine Brooks, Gluck, and the Question of Decadence in 1923," in Katy Deepwell, ed., *Women Artists and Modernism* (Manchester: Manchester University Press, 1998), p. 80. I am grateful to Bridget Elliott for generously sharing her work in progress.

63. This newspaper cutting is undated and includes no publication information. Gluckstein.

64. Rudolph de Cordova, "Women in the News," *Eve: The Lady's Pictorial*, September 15, 1926, p. 551. The *Bulletin and Scots Pictorial* ran one of the Douglas portraits in their announcement concerning the Femina Prize (April 13, 1927, p. 2).

65. *Eve: The Lady's Pictorial*, July 13, 1927, p. 72. Hall was sketched by several artists and these images were sometimes used by the print media, instead of studio portraits. See, for example, Kathleen Shackleton's sketch of Hall in the *Bookman* in April, 1926, p. 33.

66. *Eve: The Lady's Pictorial*, May 12 and 19, 1926, pp. 328–9.

67. Troubridge, *Life and Death of Radclyffe Hall*, p. 95.

68. Clarke, "Introduction," p. 1.

69. Una Troubridge diaries, vol. 2, August 5, 1927, Lovat Dickson Papers, MG 30, D 237.

70. In-house publication of the Hulton Getty Picture Collection.

71. Hallett, *Lesbian Lives*, p. 185. Hallett devotes a chapter to what she terms "the iconography of lesbian visual representation, formulated within 'established'

(heterosexual, structurally denigrated) identification, yet developed a strategy of such 'subversion through inversion,'" p. 178.

72. *Eve: The Lady's Pictorial*, July 13, 1927, p. 72.

73. *Sunday Times*, March 21, 1926, p. 11, and *Observer*, March 14, 1926, p. 9.

74. *Illustrated Sunday Herald*, March 21, 1926, p.4.

75. Barthes, *Camera Lucida*, p. 98.

76. Gale MacLachlan and Ian Reid, *Framing and Interpretation* (Carlton, Victoria: Melbourne University Press, 1994), p. 23.

77. See Walter Benjamin's 1936 essay, "The Work of Art in the Age of Mechanical Reproduction," in *Illuminations: Essays and Reflections* (New York: Schocken Books, 1968), p. 220.

78. Brittain, *Radclyffe Hall*, p. 52.

79. Baker, *Our Three Selves*, p. 223. This cropping may explain Hamer's rather odd claim that "when Hall posed for portraits she ensured that they were carefully constructed to represent her as more masculine than she actually was." See *Britannia's Glory*, p. 113.

80. Cline, *Radclyffe Hall*, p. 243.

81. Souhami, *Trials of Radclyffe Hall*, p. 178.

82. Tagg, *Burden of Representation*, p. 98. This exchange of one interpretive framework for another emerges from the very dynamics of reading photography, whereby viewers "are unshaken in their belief in the photograph as a direct transcription of the real. The falsifications that can occur—cropping, retouching, interference with the negative—are only perversions of this purity."

83. Burgin, "Looking at Photographs," pp. 146–7.

84. Roland Barthes, *Image Music Text*, trans. Stephen Heath (New York: Hill and Wang, 1977), p. 15.

85. *Daily Express*, August 24, 1928, p. 1.

86. Ibid., December 15, 1928, p. 9.

87. *Sunday Chronicle*, August, 26, 1928, p. 2. The *Yorkshire Post* also ran the same photograph. Their caption, however, merely noted that Hall's novel had been withdrawn from publication (August 24, 1928, p. 11).

88. *Sunday Chronicle*, November 18, 1928, p. 1.

89. *Daily Herald*, August 21, 1928, p. 1. See also *Evening News*, November 11, 1928, cutting from the Home Office file.

90. *Bulletin and Scots Pictorial*, August 22, 1928, p. 11.

91. *Eve: The Lady's Pictorial*, August 29, 1928, p. 407.

92. Ibid., September 12, 1928, p. 499.

93. Cline, *Radclyffe Hall*, p. 276.

94. *London Calling*, September 8, 1928, p. 20.

95. *Daily Herald*, November 10, 1928, p. 1.

96. *Sunday Express*, August 19, 1928, p. 10.

97. Goldring, *The Nineteen Twenties*, p. 228.

98. *Sunday Express*, August 19, 1928, p. 10.

99. Souhami, *Gluck*, p. 103.

100. MacLachlan and Reid, *Framing and Interpretation*, p. 28.

101. Souhami, *Gluck*, p. 103.

102. MacLachlan and Reid, *Framing and Interpretation*, p. 23.

103. Souhami, *Gluck*, p. 110.

104. Sinfield, *The Wilde Century*, p. 3, *Evening Standard*, November 16, 1828, pp. 2, 3; *Manchester Guardian*, November 10, 1928, p. 14.

105. Kate Summerscale, *The Queen of Whale Cay* (London: Fourth Estate, 1997), pp. 113–4.

106. Interview by Susan Friedman with Sylvia Dobson in December 1990. Quoted by Cassandra Laity in her introduction to H.D.'s *Paint It Today* (New York: New York University Press, 1992), p. xx.

107. Raitt, *Vita and Virginia*, p. 7.

108. Lee, *Virginia Woolf*, p. 489.

109. *Saturday Review*, November 17, 1928, p. 643.

110. Letter from Bryher to H.D., December 18?, 1929, YCAL MSS 24, ser. 1, box 3, Beinecke.

Bibliography

ARCHIVAL SOURCES

The Beinecke Rare Book and Manuscript Library, Yale University, New Haven, Conn.
  Bryher Papers
  H.D. Papers. Yale Collection of American Literature
British Library Department of Manuscripts, London
  Havelock Ellis Papers
The Fawcett Library, London Guildhall University, London
  Newspaper Cutting Collection
  Association for Moral and Social Hygiene Collection
Harry Ransom Humanities Research Center, The University of Texas at Austin
  British Sexological Society Collection
  Radclyffe Hall/Lady Una Troubridge Collection
Imperial War Museum, London
  Women at Work Collection
Metropolitan Police Historic Museum, London
  Collection on Metropolitan Women Police Patrols and Women Police Service
  Press Cuttings Collection
National Archives of Canada, Ottawa
  Lovat Dickson Papers
Public Record Office, London
  Home Office Records (HO 45, HO 144)
Reading University, Reading, England
  Astor Papers, Papers of Nancy Astor 1879–1964
Sheffield City Archives, Sheffield, England
  Carpenter Collection

NEWSPAPERS AND PERIODICALS

Athenaeum
Birmingham Post
Bookman
Britannia
British Journal of Inebriety
British Medical Journal
Bulletin and Scots Pictorial
Church Militant
Clarion
Daily Chronicle
Daily Express
Daily Graphic
Daily Herald
Daily Mail
Daily Mirror
Daily News and Westminster Gazette
Daily Sketch
Daily Telegraph
Empire News and Sunday Chronicle
Eve: The Lady's Pictorial
Evening News
Evening Standard
Glasgow Herald
Glasgow Weekly News
Illustrated Sunday Herald
Lancet
Life and Letters
Literary Review
Liverpool Post and Mercury
London Calling
London Opinion
Manchester Daily Dispatch
Manchester Daily Journal
Manchester Guardian
Morning Post
Nation & Athenaeum
New Adelphi
New Statesman
New York Telegram Magazine

Newcastle Daily Journal and North Star
News of the World
North Mail and Newcastle Chronicle
Observer
Our Own Gazette
People
Policewoman's Review
Punch
Reynolds's Illustrated News
Saturday Review
Shield
Sketch
Spectator
Sphere
Sunday Chronicle
Sunday Dispatch
Sunday Express
Sunday Times
T.P.'s & Cassell's Weekly
Tatler
Time and Tide
The Times
Times Literary Supplement
Today
Truth
Urania
Vigilante
Vote
Woman's Leader
Yorkshire Post

PUBLISHED SOURCES

Adam, Ruth. *A Woman's Place: 1910–1975*. London: Chatto and Windus, 1975.

Adburgham, Alison. *A Punch History of Manners and Modes, 1841–1940*. London: Hutchinson, 1961.

Allatini, Rose [A. T. Fitzroy, pseud.]. *Despised and Rejected*. 1918. London: Gay Mens Press, 1988.

Allen, Mary S. *Lady in Blue*. London: Stanley Paul, 1936.

————. *The Pioneer Policewoman*. Edited and arranged by Julie Helen Heyneman. London: Chatto and Windus, 1925.

Baird Committee. *Report of the Committee on the Employment of Women on Police Duties*. London: HMSO, 1920.

Baker, Michael. *Our Three Selves: The Life of Radclyffe Hall*. New York: Morrow, 1985.

Barthes, Roland. *Camera Lucida: Reflections on Photography*. 1980. Trans. Richard Howard. New York: Hill and Wang, 1993.

————. *Image Music Text*. Trans. Stephen Heath. New York: Hill and Wang, 1977.

Beaton, Cecil. *The Glass of Fashion*. London: Weidenfeld and Nicolson, 1954.

Beddoe, Deirdre. *Back to Home and Duty: Women Between the Wars, 1918–1939*. London: Pandora, 1989.

Bell, Quentin. *Virginia Woolf: A Biography*. 2 vols. New York: Harcourt Brace Jovanovich, 1972.

Benstock, Shari. "Expatriate Sapphic Modernism: Entering Literary History." In Karla Jay and Joanne Glasgow, eds., *Lesbian Texts and Contexts: Radical Revisions*. New York: New York University Press, 1990.

————. *Women of the Left Bank: Paris, 1900–1940*. Austin: University of Texas, 1986.

Bland, Lucy. *Banishing the Beast: English Feminism and Sexual Morality*. London: Penguin Books, 1995.

————. "In the Name of Protection: The Policing of Women in the First World War." In Carol Smart and Julia Brophy, eds., *Women-in-Law*. London: Routledge, 1985.

————. "Trial by Sexology? Maud Allan, *Salome*, and the 'Cult of the Clitoris' Case." In Lucy Bland and Laura Doan, eds., *Sexology in Culture: Labelling Bodies and Desires*. Chicago: University of Chicago Press, 1998.

Bland, Lucy and Laura Doan, eds. *Sexology Uncensored: The Documents of Sexual Science*. Chicago: University of Chicago Press, 1998.

Bloom, Clive, ed. *Literature and Culture in Modern Britain*. Vol. 1, *1900–1929*. London and New York: Longman, 1993.

Blythe, Ronald. *The Age of Illusion: England in the Twenties and Thirties, 1914–1940*. London: Hamish Hamilton, 1963.

Bridgeman Report. *Appendix to Report of the Departmental Committee on the Employment of Policewomen*. London: HMSO, 1924.

Bright, Deborah, ed. *The Passionate Camera: Photography and Bodies of Desire*. London and New York: Routledge, 1998.

Bristow, Joseph. *Sexuality*. London: Routledge, 1997.

————. "Symonds' History, Ellis's Heredity: Sexual Inversion." In Lucy Bland

and Laura Doan, eds., *Sexology in Culture: Labelling Bodies and Desires*. Chicago: University of Chicago Press, 1998.

Brittain, Vera. *Radclyffe Hall: A Case of Obscenity?* London: Femina Books, 1968.

Brown, Beverley. " 'A Disgusting Book When Properly Read': The Obscenity Trial." *Hecate* 10, no. 2 (1984).

Browne, F. W. Stella. "Studies in Feminine Inversion." *Journal of Sexology and Psychanalysis* [sic] (1923).

Bryher [Winifred Ellerman]. *Development*. New York: Macmillan, 1920.

———. *The Heart to Artemis: A Writer's Memoirs*. London: Collins, 1963.

———. *Two Selves*. Paris: Contact Publishing, 1923.

Buck, Claire. " 'Still Some Obstinate Emotion Remains': Radclyffe Hall and the Meanings of Service." In Suzanne Raitt and Trudi Tate, eds., *Women's Fiction and the Great War*. Oxford: Clarendon Press, 1997.

Bullough, Vern L. and Bonnie Bullough. *Cross Dressing, Sex, and Gender*. Philadelphia: University of Pennsylvania Press, 1993.

Burgin, Victor. "Looking at Photographs." In Victor Burgin, ed., *Thinking Photography*. 1982. London: Macmillan, 1994.

Butler, Judith. *Gender Trouble: Feminism and the Subversion of Identity*. London: Routledge, 1990.

Calder-Marshall, Arthur. *Havelock Ellis: A Biography*. London: Rupert Hart-Davis, 1959.

Cannell, J. C. *When Fleet Street Calls: Being the Experiences of a London Journalist*. London: Jarrolds, 1932.

Carpenter, Edward. *Angels' Wings: A Series of Essays on Art and Its Relation to Life*. London: Swan Sonnenschein, 1898.

———. *The Art of Creation: Essays on the Self and Its Powers*. London: George Allen, 1904.

———. *Homogenic Love, and Its Place in a Free Society*. Manchester: Labour Press, 1894.

———. *The Intermediate Sex: A Study of Some Transitional Types of Men and Women*. 1908. London: Allen and Unwin, 1916.

———. *Intermediate Types Among Primitive Folk: A Study in Social Evolution*. London: George Allen, 1914.

Carpenter, Humphrey. *The Brideshead Generation: Evelyn Waugh and His Friends*. London: Faber and Faber, 1989.

Carrier, John. *The Campaign for the Employment of Women as Police Officers*. Aldershot, England: Avebury, 1988.

Castle, Terry. *The Apparitional Lesbian: Female Homosexuality and Modern Culture*. New York: Columbia University Press, 1993.

———. *Noël Coward and Radclyffe Hall: Kindred Spirits*. New York: Columbia University Press, 1996.

Chauncey Jr., George. "From Sexual Inversion to Homosexuality: Medicine and the Changing Conceptualization of Female Deviance." *Salmagundi* 58–59 (fall 1982/winter 1983).

Cherniavsky, Felix. *The Salome Dancer*. Toronto: McCelland and Stewart, 1991.

Clarke, Graham, ed. *The Portrait in Photography*. London: Reaktion Books, 1992.

Cline, Sally. *Radclyffe Hall: A Woman Called John*. London: John Murray, 1997.

Condell, Diana and Jean Liddiard. *Working for Victory? Images of Women in the First World War, 1914–1918*. London: Routledge, 1987.

Corson, Richard. *Fashions in Eyeglasses*. London: Peter Owen, 1967.

Craig, Alec. *The Banned Books of England*. London: Allen and Unwin, 1962.

Craik, Jennifer. *The Face of Fashion: Cultural Studies in Fashion*. London: Routledge, 1994.

Crisp, Quentin. *The Naked Civil Servant*. New York: New American Library, 1983.

Cunnington, C. Willett. *English Women's Clothing in the Present Century*. London: Faber and Faber, 1952.

Davenport-Hines, Richard. *Sex, Death, and Punishment: Attitudes to Sex and Sexuality in Britain Since the Renaissance*. London: Collins, 1990.

Deepwell, Katy, ed. *Women Artists and Modernism*. Manchester: Manchester University Press, 1998.

DeGroot, Gerard J. *Blighty: British Society in the Era of the Great War*. London: Longman, 1996.

Elliott, Bridget. "Performing the Picture or Painting the Other: Romaine Brooks, Gluck, and the Question of Decadence in 1923." In Katy Deepwell, ed., *Women Artists and Modernism*. Manchester: Manchester University Press, 1998.

Elliott, Bridget and Jo-Ann Wallace. *Women Artists and Writers: Modernist (Im)Positionings*. New York: Routledge, 1994.

Ellis, Havelock. "Sexual Inversion in Women." *Alienist and Neurologist* 16 (1895).

———. *Studies in the Psychology of Sex*. 7 vols. 1897. Philadelphia: F. A. Davis, 3d ed., 1921.

———. *Studies in the Psychology of Sex, Complete in Two Volumes*. 1902. New York: Random House, 1942.

Faderman, Lillian. *Odd Girls and Twilight Lovers: A History of Lesbian Life in Twentieth-Century America*. New York: Penguin Books, 1992.

Faraday, Annabel. "Social Definitions of Lesbians in Britain, 1914–1939." Unpublished Ph.D. thesis, University of Essex. 1985.

Felski, Rita. *The Gender of Modernity*. Cambridge: Harvard University Press, 1995.

———. "Introduction." In Lucy Bland and Laura Doan, eds., *Sexology in Culture: Labelling Bodies and Desires*. Chicago: University of Chicago Press, 1998.

Finkelstein, Joanne. *The Fashioned Self*. Philadelphia: Temple University Press, 1991.

Flower, Newman, ed. *The Journal of Arnold Bennett: 1921–1928*. London: Cassell, 1933.

Forel, August. *The Sexual Question: A Scientific, Psychological, Hygienic, and Sociological Study for the Cultured Classes*. 1906. New York: Rebman Company, 1908.

Foucault, Michel. *The History of Sexuality*. 3 vols. 1976. Reprint, London: Penguin Books, 1990.

Franks, Claudia Stillman. *Beyond "The Well of Loneliness": The Fiction of Radclyffe Hall*. Amersham, England: Avebury, 1982.

Gagnier, Regina. *Idylls of the Marketplace: Oscar Wilde and the Victorian Public*. Stanford: Stanford University Press, 1986.

Garber, Marjorie. *Vested Interests: Cross-Dressing and Cultural Anxiety*. New York: Routledge, 1992.

Garrity, Jane. "Selling Culture to the 'Civilized': Bloomsbury, British *Vogue*, and the Marketing of National Identity." *Modernism/Modernity* 6, no. 2 (April 1999).

Gidley, Mick. "Hoppé's Impure Portraits: Contextualizing the American Types." In Graham Clarke, ed., *The Portrait in Photography*. London: Reaktion Books, 1992.

Gilbert, Sandra M. and Susan Gubar. *No Man's Land: The Place of the Woman Writer in the Twentieth Century*. Vol. 2, *Sexchanges*. New Haven: Yale University Press, 1989.

Gilmore, Leigh. "Obscenity, Modernity, Identity: Legalizing *The Well of Loneliness* and *Nightwood*." *Journal of the History of Sexuality* 4, no. 4 (1994).

Glendinning, Victoria. *Vita: The Life of V. Sackville-West*. London: Weidenfeld and Nicolson, 1983.

Goldring, Douglas. *The Nineteen Twenties: A General Survey and Some Personal Memories*. London: Nicholson and Watson, 1945.

Graves, Robert and Alan Hodge. *The Long Weekend: A Social History of Great Britain, 1918–1939*. 1940. New York: Norton, 1963.

Grayzel, Susan R. "Nostalgia, Gender, and the Countryside: Placing the 'Land Girl' in First World War Britain." *Rural History* 10, no. 2 (1999).

———. *Women's Identities at War: Gender, Motherhood, and Politics in Britain and France During the First World War*. Chapel Hill: University of North Carolina Press, 1999.

H. M. Government. *Minutes of Evidence Taken Before the Joint Select Committee on the Criminal Law Amendment Bill*. London: HMSO, 1920.

———. *Report of the Commissioner of Police of the Metropolis for the Years 1918 and 1919*. London: HMSO, 1918–19.

Halberstam, Judith. "F2M: The Making of Female Masculinity." In Laura Doan, ed., *The Lesbian Postmodern*. New York: Columbia University Press, 1994.

———. *Female Masculinity*. Durham and London: Duke University Press, 1998.

———. "Lesbian Masculinity, or Even Stone Butches Get the Blues." *Women and Performance: A Journal of Feminist Theory* 8, no. 2 (1996).

Hall, Radclyffe. *The Well of Loneliness*. 1928. Reprint, New York: Anchor Books, 1990.

Hallett, Nicky. *Lesbian Lives: Identity and Auto/Biography in the Twentieth Century*. London: Pluto Press, 1999.

Hamer, Emily. *Britannia's Glory: A History of Twentieth-Century Lesbians*. London: Cassell, 1996.

Hamilton, Mary Agnes. "Changes in Social Life." In Ray Strachey, ed., *Our Freedom and Its Results*. London: Hogarth Press, 1936.

Hansard. Official Reports, 5th Series, *Parliamentary Debates, House of Commons*, vols. 145 and 146 (1921).

———. Official Reports, 5th Series, *Parliamentary Debates, House of Lords*, vol. 14 (1921).

Harris, Bertha. "The More Profound Nationality of their Lesbianism: Lesbian Society in Paris in the 1920s." In Phyllis Birkby et al., eds., *Amazon Expedition: A Lesbian Feminist Anthology*. Albion, Calif.: Times Change Press, 1973.

Haste, Cate. *Rules of Desire: Sex in Britain, World War I to the Present*. London: Chatto and Windus, 1992.

Henderson-Livesey, Captain A. H. *The Women Police Question*. London: The League of Womanhood, 1925.

Hennegan, Alison. "Introduction." In Radclyffe Hall, *The Well of Loneliness*. 1928. London: Virago, 1982.

Hoare, Philip. *Wilde's Last Stand: Decadence, Conspiracy, and the First World War*. London: Duckworth, 1997.

Homberger, Eric. "J. P. Morgan's Nose: Photographer and Subject in American Portrait Photography." In Graham Clarke, ed., *The Portrait in Photography*. London: Reaktion Books, 1992.

Hoppé, E. O. "As Others See Us." *Royal Magazine* 57, no. 338 (December 1926).

Horn, Pamela. *Women in the 1920s*. Stroud, Gloucestershire: Alan Sutton Publishing, 1995.

Howard, Michael S. *Jonathan Cape, Publisher*. London: Jonathan Cape, 1971.

Hyde, H. Montgomery. *The Other Love: An Historical and Contemporary Survey of Homosexuality in Britain*. London: Mayflower Books, 1972.

Ingram, Angela. "Un/Reproductions: Estates of Banishment in English Fiction after the Great War." In Mary Lynn Broe and Angela Ingram, eds., *Women's Writing in Exile*. Chapel Hill: University of North Carolina Press, 1989.

———. " 'Unutterable Putrefaction' and 'Foul Stuff': Two 'Obscene' Novels of the 1920s." *Women's Studies International Forum* 9, no. 4 (1986).

Inness, Sherrie A. *The Lesbian Menace: Ideology, Identity, and the Representation of Lesbian Life*. Amherst: University of Massachusetts Press, 1997.

Jackson, Margaret. *The Real Facts of Life: Feminism and the Politics of Sexuality, c. 1850–1940*. London: Taylor and Francis, 1994.

Jacob, Naomi. *Me and the Swans*. London: William Kimber. 1963.

———. *Me in War-Time*. London: Hutchinson, 1940.

Jay, Bill. "Emil Otto Hoppé, 1878–1972." *Studies in Visual Communication* 11 (1985).

Jeffreys, Sheila. *The Spinster and Her Enemies: Feminism and Sexuality, 1880–1930*. London: Pandora, 1985.

———. "Women and Sexuality." In June Purvis, ed., *Women's History: Britain, 1850–1945*. London: UCL Press, 1995.

Jenkins, Alan. *The Twenties*. London: Book Club Associates, 1974.

Jivani, Alkarim. *It's Not Unusual: A History of Lesbian and Gay Britain in the Twentieth Century*. London: Michael O'Mara Books, 1997.

John, Angela V. "Between the Cause and the Courts: The Curious Case of Cecil Chapman." In Claire Eustance, Joan Ryan, and Laura Ugolini, eds., *A Suffrage Reader: Charting Directions in British Suffrage History*. London: Leicester University Press, 2000.

Joynson-Hicks, Sir William. *Do We Need a Censor?* London: Faber and Faber, 1929.

Kenealy, Arabella. *Feminism and Sex Extinction*. London: T. Fisher Unwin, 1920.

Kent, Susan Kingsley. *Making Peace: The Reconstruction of Gender in Interwar Britain*. Princeton: Princeton University Press, 1993.

Kettle, Michael. *Salome's Last Veil: The Libel Case of the Century*. London: Granada Publishing, 1977.

Koss, Stephen. *The Rise and Fall of the Political Press in Britain*. Vol. 2, *The Twentieth Century*. London: Hamish Hamilton, 1984.

Krafft-Ebing, Richard von. *Psychopathia Sexualis With Especial Reference to the Antipathic Sexual Instinct. A Medico-Forensic Study*. 1886. Reprint, New York: Stein and Day, 1965.

Lanchester, Elsa. *Elsa Lanchester, Herself*. New York: St. Martin's Press, 1983.

Lang, Elsie. *British Women in the Twentieth Century*. London: T. Werner Laurie, 1929.

Laver, James. *A Concise History of Costume*. London: Thames and Hudson, 1969.

————. *Taste and Fashion from the French Revolution to Today*. London: George G. Harrap, 1937.

Lawrence, Margaret. *We Write As Women*. London: Michael Joseph, 1937.

Leavis, Q. D. *Fiction and the Reading Public*. London: Chatto and Windus, 1932.

Lee, Hermione. *Virginia Woolf*. London: Vintage, 1997.

Levine, Philippa. " 'Walking the Streets in a Way No Decent Woman Should': Women Police in World War I." *Journal of Modern History* 66 (1994).

Lewis, Jane. *Women in England, 1870–1950: Sexual Divisions and Social Change*. Brighton, England: Wheatsheaf Books, 1984.

Light, Alison. *Forever England: Femininity, Literature, and Conservatism Between the Wars*. London and New York: Routledge, 1991.

Lock, Joan. *The British Policewoman*. London: Robert Hale, 1979.

————. "Downfall of the Ladylike Policewoman." *Police Review*. August 10, 1984.

————. "The Extraordinary Life of Mary Allen." *Police Review*. June 29, 1984.

Lyon, Janet. "Women Demonstrating Modernism." *Discourse* 17, no. 2 (winter 1994–5).

Mackworth, Margaret Haig. *This Was My World*. London: Macmillan, 1933.

MacLachlan, Gale and Ian Reid. *Framing and Interpretation*. Carlton, Victoria: Melbourne University Press, 1994.

MacPike, Loralee. "Is Mary Llewellyn an Invert? The Modernist Supertext of *The Well of Loneliness*." In Elizabeth Jane Harrison and Shirley Peterson, eds., *Unmanning Modernism: Gendered Re-Readings*. Knoxville: The University of Tennessee Press, 1997.

Macready, Sir Nevil. *Annals of an Active Life*. London: Hutchinson, 1924.

Mannin, Ethel. *Confessions and Impressions*. London: Jarrolds, 1930.

————. *Young in the Twenties*. London: Hutchinson, 1971.

Marchioness of Londonderry. *Retrospect*. London: Frederick Muller, 1938.

McKibbin, Ross. *Classes and Cultures: England 1918–1951*. Oxford: Oxford University Press, 1998.

McLaren, Angus. *The Trials of Masculinity: Policing Sexual Boundaries, 1870–1930*. Chicago: University of Chicago Press, 1997.

Melman, Billie. *Women and the Popular Imagination in the Twenties: Flappers and Nymphs*. New York: St. Martin's Press, 1988.

Merck, Mandy. *Perversions: Deviant Readings*. New York: Routledge, 1993.

Moll, Albert. *Perversions of the Sex Instinct: A Study of Sexual Inversion*. 1891. Newark: Julian Press, 1931.

Nava, Mica. "Modernity's Disavowal: Women, the City, and the Department Store." In Mica Nava and Alan O'Shea, eds., *Modern Times: Reflections on a Century of English Modernity*. London and New York: Routledge, 1996.

Newton, Esther. "The Mythic Mannish Lesbian: Radclyffe Hall and the New

Woman." In Martin Duberman, Martha Vicinus, and George Chauncey Jr., eds., *Hidden from History: Reclaiming the Gay and Lesbian Past*. New York: New American Library, 1989.

Nichols, Beverley. *The Sweet and Twenties*. London: Weidenfeld and Nicolson, 1958.

Nicolson, Nigel. *Portrait of a Marriage*. 1973. London: Weidenfeld and Nicolson, 1990.

Nield, Keith. "Edward Carpenter: The Uses of Utopia." In Tony Brown, ed., *Edward Carpenter and Late Victorian Radicalism*. London: Frank Cass, 1990.

Oosterhuis, Harry. "Richard von Krafft-Ebing's 'Step-Children of Nature': Psychiatry and the Making of Homosexual Identity." In Vernon A. Rosario, ed., *Science and Homosexualities*. New York: Routledge, 1997.

Oram, Alison. " 'Embittered, Sexless or Homosexual': Attacks on Spinster Teachers 1918–39." In Lesbian History Group, ed., *Not a Passing Phase: Reclaiming Lesbians in History, 1840–1985*. London: The Women's Press, 1989.

———. *Women Teachers and Feminist Politics, 1900–1930*. Manchester: Manchester University Press, 1996.

Ormrod, Richard. *Una Troubridge: The Friend of Radclyffe Hall*. New York: Carroll and Graf, 1985.

O'Rourke, Rebecca. *Reflecting on "The Well of Loneliness"*. London: Routledge, 1989.

O'Shea, Alan. "English Subjects of Modernity." In Mica Nava and Alan O'Shea, eds., *Modern Times: Reflections on a Century of English Modernity*. London: Routledge, 1996.

Parkes, Adam. "Lesbianism, History, and Censorship: *The Well of Loneliness* and the SUPPRESSED RANDINESS of Virginia Woolf's *Orlando*." *Twentieth Century Literature* 40, no. 4 (winter 1994).

Pepper, Terence. *Howard Coster's Celebrity Portraits: 101 Photographs of Personalities in Literature and the Arts*. London: National Portrait Gallery, 1985.

Piggford, George. " 'Who's That Girl?': Annie Lennox, Woolf's *Orlando*, and Female Camp Androgyny." *Mosaic* 30, no. 3 (September 1997).

Porter, Roy and Lesley Hall. *The Facts of Life: The Creation of Sexual Knowledge in Britain, 1650–1950*. New Haven: Yale University Press, 1995.

Prosser, Jay. *Second Skins: The Body Narratives of Transsexuality*. New York: Columbia University Press, 1998.

———. "Transsexuals and the Transsexologists: Inversion and the Emergence of Transsexual Subjectivity." In Lucy Bland and Laura Doan, eds., *Sexology in Culture: Labelling Bodies and Desires*. Chicago: University of Chicago Press, 1998.

Pryce-Jones, David. *Cyril Connolly: Journal and Memoir*. London: Collins, 1983.

Pugh, Martin. *Women and the Women's Movement in Britain, 1914–1959*. London: Macmillan, 1992.

Radford, Jean. "An Inverted Romance: *The Well of Loneliness* and Sexual Ideology." In Jean Radford, ed., *The Progress of Romance: The Politics of Popular Fiction*. London: Routledge, 1986.

Raitt, Suzanne. "Sex, Love, and the Homosexual Body in Early Sexology." In Lucy Bland and Laura Doan, eds., *Sexology in Culture: Labelling Bodies and Desires*. Chicago: University of Chicago Press, 1998.

Rance, Nicholas. "British Newspapers in the Early Twentieth Century." In Clive Bloom, ed., *Literature and Culture in Modern Britain*. Vol. 1, *1900–1929*. London and New York: Longman, 1993.

Roberts, Cecil. *One Year of Life: Some Autobiographical Pages*. London: Hodder and Stoughton, 1952.

Roberts, Mary Louise. *Civilization Without Sexes: Reconstructing Gender in Postwar France, 1917–1927*. Chicago: University of Chicago Press, 1994.

Rolley, Katrina. "Cutting a Dash: The Dress of Radclyffe Hall and Una Troubridge." *Feminist Review* 35 (1990).

Rolph, C. H., ed. *Does Pornography Matter?* London: Routledge, 1961.

Rose, Jacqueline. "Sexuality and Vision: Some Questions." In Hal Foster, ed., *Vision and Visuality*. Seattle: Bay Press, 1988.

Rosenman, Ellen Bayuk. "Sexual Identity and *A Room of One's Own*: 'Secret Economies' in Virginia Woolf's Feminist Discourse." *Signs: Journal of Women in Culture and Society* 14, no. 3 (spring 1989).

Ruehl, Sonja. "Inverts and Experts: Radclyffe Hall and the Lesbian Identity." In Rosalind Brunt and Caroline Rowan, eds., *Feminism, Culture, and Politics*. London: Lawrence and Wishart, 1982.

Scanlon, Joan. "Bad Language vs. Bad Prose? Lady Chatterley and *The Well*." *Critical Quarterly* 38, no. 3 (1996).

The Scientific Humanitarian Committee. *The Social Problem of Sexual Inversion*. In Mark Blasius and Shane Phelan, eds., *We Are Everywhere: A Historical Sourcebook of Gay and Lesbian Politics*. London: Routledge, 1997.

Scott, Bonnie Kime. *Refiguring Modernism: The Women of 1928*. Vol. 1. Bloomington: Indiana University Press, 1995.

Secrest, Meryle. *Between Me and Life: A Biography of Romaine Brooks*. London: Macdonald and Jane's, 1976.

Shaw, Christopher E. "Identified with the One: Edward Carpenter, Henry Salt, and the Ethical Socialist Philosophy of Science." In Tony Brown, ed., *Edward Carpenter and Late Victorian Radicalism*. London: Frank Cass, 1990.

Showalter, Elaine. *Sexual Anarchy: Gender and Culture at the Fin de Siècle*. London: Virago, 1992.

Sinfield, Alan. *The Wilde Century: Effeminacy, Oscar Wilde, and the Queer Moment*. New York: Columbia University Press, 1994.

Smith-Rosenberg, Carroll. *Disorderly Conduct: Visions of Gender in Victorian America*. New York: Knopf, 1985.

Sontag, Susan. *On Photography*. 1973. New York: Farrar, Straus and Giroux, 1977.

Souhami, Diana. *Gluck: Her Biography*. London: Pandora Press, 1989.

——. *Mrs. Keppel and Her Daughter*. London: Flamingo, 1997.

——. *The Trials of Radclyffe Hall*. London: Weidenfeld and Nicolson, 1998.

Steele, Valerie. *Fashion and Eroticism: Ideals of Feminine Beauty from the Victorian Era to the Jazz Age*. New York: Oxford University Press, 1985.

Stevenson, John. *British Society, 1914–1945*. Harmondsworth, England: Penguin Books, 1984.

Stimpson, Catharine R. "Zero Degree Deviancy: The Lesbian Novel in English." *Critical Inquiry* 8, no. 2 (winter 1981).

Summerscale, Kate. *The Queen of Whale Cay*. London: Fourth Estate, 1997.

Tagg, John. *The Burden of Representation: Essays on Photographies and Histories*. 1988. Reprint, Minneapolis: University of Minnesota Press, 1995.

Thiele, Beverly. "Coming-of-Age: Edward Carpenter on Sex and Reproduction." In Tony Brown, ed., *Edward Carpenter and Late Victorian Radicalism*. London: Frank Cass, 1990.

Tickner, Lisa. *The Spectacle of Women: Imagery of the Suffrage Campaign 1907–1914*. London: Chatto and Windus, 1987.

Tortora, Phyllis and Keith Eubank. *A Survey of Historic Costume*. New York: Fairchild Publications, 1989.

Travis, Jennifer. "Clits in Court: *Salome*, Sodomy, and the Lesbian 'Sadist.'" In Karla Jay, ed., *Lesbian Erotics*. New York: New York University Press, 1995.

Trodd, Anthea. *Women's Writing in English: Britain, 1900–1945*. London: Longman, 1998.

Troubridge, Una, Lady. *The Life and Death of Radclyffe Hall*. London: Hammond, Hammond, 1961.

Tylee, Claire. *The Great War and Women's Consciousness*. Iowa City: University of Iowa Press, 1990.

Vernon, James. " 'For Some Queer Reason': The Trials and Tribulations of Colonel Barker's Masquerade in Interwar Britain." *Signs: Journal of Women in Culture and Society* 26, no. 1 (autumn 2000).

Vicinus, Martha. "Fin-de-Siècle Theatrics: Male Impersonation and Lesbian Desire." In Billie Melman, ed., *Borderlines: Genders and Identities in War and Peace, 1870–1930*. New York: Routledge, 1998.

——. " 'They Wonder to Which Sex I Belong': The Historical Roots of the Modern Lesbian Identity." *Feminist Studies* 18, no. 3 (fall 1992).

Wartofsky, Marx. "Cameras Can't See: Representation, Photography, and Human Vision." *Afterimage* 7, no. 9 (April 1980).

Weeks, Jeffrey. *Coming Out: Homosexual Politics in Britain from the Nineteenth Century to the Present.* 1977. Reprint, London: Quartet Books, 1990.

———. *Sex, Politics, and Society: The Regulation of Sexuality since 1800.* London: Longman, 1989.

West, Rebecca. *Ending in Earnest: A Literary Log.* Garden City, N.Y.: Doubleday, 1931.

Wheelwright, Julie. *Amazons and Military Maids: Women Who Dressed as Men in the Pursuit of Life, Liberty, and Happiness.* London: Pandora, 1989.

Whetham, W. C. D. and C. D. Whetham. *The Family and the Nation: A Study in Natural Inheritance and Social Responsibility.* London: Longmans, Green, 1909.

Whitlock, Gillian. " 'Everything Is Out of Place': Radclyffe Hall and the Lesbian Literary Tradition." *Feminist Studies* 13, no. 3 (fall 1987).

Williams, Raymond. *The Long Revolution.* Harmondsworth, England: Penguin Books, 1980.

Wilson, Elizabeth. *Adorned in Dreams: Fashion and Modernity.* London: Virago, 1985.

———. "Deviant Dress." *Feminist Review* 35 (1990).

Woolf, Leonard. *Hunting the Highbrow.* London: Hogarth, 1927.

Woolf, Virginia. *The Death of the Moth and Other Essays.* Harmondsworth, England: Penguin Books, 1961.

———. *The Diary of Virginia Woolf.* Edited by Anne Oliver Bell. Vol. 1, *1915–1919.* London: Penguin Books, 1977.

———. *The Diary of Virginia Woolf.* Edited by Anne Olivier Bell. Vol. 3, *1925–1930.* London: Penguin Books, 1980.

———. *The Letters of Virginia Woolf.* Edited by Nigel Nicolson and Joanne Trautmann. Vol. 3, *1923–1928.* New York and London: Harcourt Brace Jovanovich, 1978.

Woollacott, Angela. "Dressed to Kill: Clothes, Cultural Meaning, and World War I Women Munitions Workers." In Moira Donald and Linda Hurcombe, eds., *Gender and Material Culture.* Vol. 2, *Representations of Gender from Prehistory to the Present.* London: Macmillan, 2000.

———. " 'Khaki Fever' and its Control: Gender, Class, Age, and Sexual Morality on the British Homefront in the First World War." *Journal of Contemporary History* 29 (1994).

Index

Ackland, Valentine, 98

"Acts of indecency by females" clause (1920), 32, 35, 36–37, 45–49, 51, 54, 58, 60, 220*n*120. *See also* Criminal Law Amendment Bill (1921); Joint Select Committee

Adam's Breed (Hall), 177, 183, 186, 190; and Femina Prize, 8, 11, 110, 111; sales of, 12, 182

Allan, Maud, 31–34, 36–37, 45, 50, 213*n*25

Allatini, Rose Laure ("A. T. Fitzroy"), 147, 148, 162; and Carpenter, 143, 153–55 passim; and sexology, 127, 130, 144, 146. *See also Despised and Rejected*

Allen, Mary Sophia, xvii, 39, 43, 68, 85, 104, 182, 215*n*40; fascism, 93, 229*n*141; vs. Metropolitan Police, 67, 80, 81; use of photography, 165–73, 174–76, 181, 183, 184; sexuality, 44, 76–77, 83, 108, 194, 224*n*50; as suffragette, 40, 78–79, 86–87, 168, 252*n*12; uniform, 71–72, 73–76, 82–84, 87–88, 92–94, 120, 173–74; Women Police Service, 41, 42

America (United States), 2, 81, 84, 108, 120; New York City, 83

Annals of an Active Life (Macready), 77

Arkell-Smith, Lieutenant Harold, 86

Association for Moral and Social Hygiene (AMSH), 35, 214*n*32

Astor, Nancy, Lady, 35, 45, 48, 61, 87, 88, 169, 216*n*60, 220*n*117

Athenaeum, 148, 152

Baird Committee, 40, 43, 70, 79, 173, 174

Baker, Michael, 19, 89, 109, 115, 116, 151, 188

Bakewell, Jean, 104, 234*n*42

Baldwin, Mrs. Stanley, 184

Bannerman, Miss, 115

Barker, Valerie (alias Colonel Victor Barker and Valerie Arkell-Smith), 68, 83, 104, 166, 222*n*17; clothing and gender identity, 82, 84–86, 88–90, 225*n*60, 238*n*111, 239*n*131; cross-dressing, 91–92, 93–94, 115; fascism, 93, 229*n*141; press coverage of, 90, 94, 95–96, 120, 227*n*111; Hall on, 89–90, 95, 124, 125

Barnes, Djuna, 97

Barney, Natalie Clifford, xvi, xix, 98

Barthes, Roland, 164, 189

Batten, Mabel ("Ladye"), 32, 100, 185, 195*n*1

Baudelaire, Charles, xxii

Beaverbrook, Lord, 17

Beddoe, Deirdre, 4, 195n4
Bennett, Arnold, 9, 22, 127, 128, 204n35, 239n7
Benstock, Shari, 96, 98, 99, 106, 111, 115, 199n30, 200n40
Best, Edna, 109
Birkett, Norman, 207n90
Birmingham Post, 111
Biron, Sir Chartres, 1, 21–24 passim, 43, 44, 80, 151, 203n24
Bland, Lucy, 33, 34, 143, 215n43
Bloch, Iwan, 59, 135
Bloomfield, Paul, 184
Blythe, Ronald, 119, 122
Bodkin, Sir Archibald, 21, 22, 24
Boyette, 102, 103, 105
Boyishness, 97, 99, 102–106, 118, 124, 147–48
Boyle, Nina, 38, 214n36
Bright Young People, xvii, 122, 135–36, 180
Bristow, Joseph, 4, 243n52
Britannia, 121–22
British Journal of Inebriety, 13, 25
British Medical Journal, 143
British Society for the Study of Sex Psychology (BSSSP), 48, 52, 53, 59, 135, 218n80
Brittain, Vera, 24, 132, 133, 188
Brooks, Romaine, 96, 98, 116, 117, 183
Browne, F. W. Stella, 52, 53, 132, 134, 147, 151, 218n91
Bryher (Winifred Ellerman), 28, 130, 133–34, 144, 146–49, 150, 151, 162; Carpenter, 143, 152–53; class background, xvii, xx, 135; Ellis, 7, 127–28, 131, 137; sexology, 127, 132. *See also Development; Two Selves*

Buck, Claire, 160–61
Bulletin and Scots Pictorial, 190
Bullough, Vern L. and Bonnie, 91
Burdett, Carolyn, 152
Burgin, Victor, 188
Butch and femme, xv, 113, 166, 167, 180, 181, 186, 196n8
Butler, Judith, 36, 38

Cannell, J. C., 15, 16, 239n131
Cantab, The (Leslie), 22
Cape, Jonathan, 6–8, 10, 18, 21, 28, 127, 203n24, 208n107
Carlston, Erin G., 199n30
Carpenter, Edward, 53, 59, 129, 134, 160, 218n80, 243n53, 243n54, 245n75; Ellis, 145, 146, 149–50, 163; intermediate sex, 26, 138, 141, 142–43, 146, 152–57, 159, 161, 162, 244n71, 247n112; on nature, 158; superiority doctrine, 150–51, 152, 155. *See also* Uranian
Carrier, John, 40, 70, 93
Carstairs, Marion Barbara ("Joe"), 105, 122, 193
Castle, Terry, xvi, 112, 249n138
Cather, Willa, xvi, xix, 97
Cavendish-Bentinck Library, 133
Chapman, Cecil Maurice, 72, 217n73, 218n80; Joint Select Committee witness, 37, 38, 44, 45–49, 51–58 passim; as magistrate in WPS uniform dispute, 73, 77–78, 80; suffragist supporter, 217n75
Chauncey, George Jr., 26, 62
Cherniasky, Felix, 34
Chesterton, Mrs. Cecil, 209n118
Christie, Agatha, 12
Cigarettes. *See* Smoking

Clarion, 19

Clarke, Graham, 164

Cline, Sally, 99, 120, 213*n*30; on
    Allen, 108; on James Douglas,
    15–16; on Hall's appearance, 100,
    110, 113–16 passim, 188

Clothing. *See* Fashion

Cohen, Stan, 1, 30

Colette, xxii

Color-hearing, 146, 148–49, 153,
    162, 247*n*104, 248*n*127, 248*n*134

Condell, Diana, 73

Connolly, Cyril, 104, 150, 234*n*42

Cookson, Sybil, 122

Coster, Howard, 176, 254*n*36,
    254*n*41

Country Life, 101

Coward, Noël, 112, 236*n*77

Criminal Law Amendment Act
    (1885), 35, 46, 213*n*19, 214*n*32.
    See also Labouchère Amendment

Criminal Law Amendment Bill
    (CLA) (1921), 32, 35, 36–37; de-
    bate in parliament, 48, 49, 51, 53,
    55–58, 60–62, 132, 213*n*29. *See
    also* "Acts of indecency by fe-
    males" clause; Joint Select Com-
    mittee

Criminal Law Amendment Bill
    (1922), 61

Criminal Law Amendment Commit-
    tee, 40, 214*n*32, 215*n*43

Crisp, Quentin, 104

Cross-dressing, 66, 146, 231*n*9,
    237*n*91; Barker, 88, 91–92, 96,
    115; concept of, xxii, 94, 97, 98,
    100, 125; Gluck, 179–80, 181;
    Women Police Service, 80, 174–75

"Cult of the Clitoris," 31, 32, 34

Cunnington, C. Willett, 107

Daily Express. *See Express*

Daily Graphic, 118, 119

Daily Herald, xiii, 19, 23, 29, 85,
    95, 190, 191

Daily Mail, 3, 17, 41, 66, 101, 123;
    Barker, 84–85, 92; boyette, 103,
    105; Irons, 123, 191

Daily Mirror, 182, 185

Daily News and Westminster Gazette,
    xi

Daily Sketch, 92

Daily Telegraph, 8, 148

Damer Dawson, Margaret, xvii,
    38–44 passim, 70, 71, 73, 76, 78,
    80, 168–76 passim, 214*n*35,
    224*n*50

Darling, Justice (Charles John), 33

Dawson, Arnold, 19, 30

de Belbeuf, Marquise, 96, 237*n*91

Deepwell, Katy, xviii

Desart, Lord, 55, 57, 58

Despised and Rejected (Allatini),
    130, 153, 154–55, 246*n*92

Development (Bryher), 130, 146–49

Dickens, Michael, 198*n*29

Dixon, A. L., 43

Douglas, 176, 177, 183, 190, 191

Douglas, James, 22, 206*n*73; on Bry-
    her's fiction, 148; editorialist tech-
    niques, 14–16, 207*n*90; "prussic
    acid" editorial, 1–6, 7, 8, 10, 12–
    21 passim, 25–30 passim, 187,
    188, 189, 191, 203*n*24

Douglas, Norman, 135

Dunning, Sir Leonard, 42

East, William Norwood, 134

Ellerman, Sir John, 133

Ellerman, Winifred. *See Bryher*

Elliott, Bridget, 183

Ellis, Havelock, 53, 56, 61, 128–29, 130, 135, 136, 148, 153, 224*n*48, 240*n*10; Bryher, 127–28, 131, 134, 137, 162; case histories, 131, 137–39, 147, 166, 243*n*52; color-hearing, 149; "Commentary," 6–7, 9, 126, 143, 144, 203*n*24; cross-dressing, 91; Hall, 89, 112, 134, 143, 145, 163, 194, 196*n*7, 254*n*79; influence on *The Well of Loneliness*, 127, 141–46 passim, 156, 157; Krafft-Ebing, 132, 140, 141; sexual inversion, xii, 2, 25, 59, 62, 76, 77, 100–101, 147, 150, 218*n*88. *See also Sexual Inversion*; *Studies in the Psychology of Sex*

Empire News and Sunday Chronicle, 115

Eugenics, 152

Eve: The Lady's Pictorial, 96, 101, 105, 114, 121, 122, 193; Hall, 27, 110, 183–84, 185, 187, 190

Evening News, 179, 190

Evening Standard, 17, 127

Express, 6, 13, 20, 23, 25, 188, 191–92; *Daily Express*, xxii, 3, 17, 27, 65, 66, 92, 116–17, 185, 189; *Sunday Express*, 1, 2, 4, 5, 8, 16–19 passim, 28, 187

Faderman, Lillian, 50, 128, 137

Fashion, 183; gender ambiguity, xviii, 96–125, 174, 175; sexual identity, xiii, 14, 27, 71, 90, 95–126; twenties style, xiii-xiv, xix, xxi-xxii

Felski, Rita, 126, 128, 130, 162

Female masculinities, xxi, 181; Allen and Women Police Service, 87,

169, 174, 175; as fashion, 95–99 passim, 120, 125; Gluck, 117, 177; Halberstam on, 90, 225*n*76, 230*n*145; Hall, 111, 112, 177; lesbianism, 90, 124, 197*n*17

Female sexual inversion/invert. *See* Sexual inversion

Femina Vie Heureuse Prize, 8, 11, 110, 111, 114, 120, 181–85 passim, 188, 190

Feminism, xix, 2, 3, 40, 50, 51, 59

Feminism and Sex Extinction (Kenealy), 35

Ferenczi, Sándor, 134, 242*n*36

Fine Art Society, 118, 192

Finkelstein, Joanne, 74

First World War: as opportunity for women, xviii-xix, 2, 24, 85, 107; women in uniform, 64, 76, 82, 83; women police, 38–39

Fisher, Horatia, 104, 234*n*41

Flapper, xvii, 3, 4, 102, 105, 106, 119, 122, 164, 185, 202*n*7

Forel, August, 52, 58, 59, 60, 76, 134, 151, 160

Forster, E. M., 8, 143

Foucault, Michel, 54, 55, 56

Fox Photos, 185

Fox-Pitt, St. George Lane, 31–32, 33–34, 63, 211*n*3, 213*n*24

Foyle's Bookshop, 22, 124, 194

France, xiii, xix, 2, 28, 200*n*46; Paris, xx, 54, 97, 98, 123, 200*n*40, 232*n*18

Freud, Sigmund, 128–35 passim

Galsworthy, John, 178

Galsworthy, Mrs. John, 114

Galton, Francis, 152

Garber, Marjorie, 86, 96, 108, 109

Gardner, Evelyn, 104, 234n43
Germany, 2, 81, 200n46; Berlin, xx
Gilbert, Sandra M., 96, 98, 112, 144
Gilmore, Leigh, 147
Glasgow Herald, xi, 9, 151
Gluck (Hannah Gluckstein), xvii,
  111, 122; family background,
  101, 233n30; fashion and self-
  presentation, 107, 117–19, 120,
  238n119; Gluck frame, 192; pho-
  tography, xxii, 99, 165, 166–67,
  176–84, 194, 254n41, 255n48
Goldingham, Isobel, 39, 43, 73, 77,
  169, 174, 215n40; as suffragette,
  40, 78, 168
Goldring, Douglas, xx, 136–37, 191
Gordon, W. R., xi, 14
Graves, Robert, xx
Gritten, Howard, 35
Gubar, Susan, 96, 98, 112, 144

H.D. (Hilda Doolittle), 133, 134,
  137, 146, 147, 193
Haire, Norman, 134
Hairstyles, xiv, 96, 97, 100, 104,
  105, 119, 123, 156, 164, 233n33;
  Eton crop, 102, 106, 108, 121,
  234n34; shingle, 102, 106, 111,
  113, 231n7, 234n34
Halberstam, Judith, 90, 166,
  225n76, 230n145, 253n20
Hall, Lesley, 46
Hall, Radclyffe, 23, 29, 77, 104,
  136, 147, 176, 193, 205n61,
  208n95, 233n30; appearance of,
  13, 95, 96, 97, 100, 101, 107,
  110–16 passim, 119–25 passim,
  166, 177, 194, 235n60; on Barker,
  89–90, 94, 95, 124, 125; byword
  for lesbianism, 28, 123, 194;

lesbianism, xv, xxii, 112, 113, 123,
  124, 145, 188, 194; libel suit
  (1920), 31–37 passim, 45, 50; as
  middlebrow, 8, 10, 11, 12, 187;
  modernity and, xix, xxiii, 27, 112,
  177, 186, 187; and Paris, xx,
  98–99, 231n15; photographs of,
  xiii, xiv, xvi, xxii, 5, 18, 27, 99,
  122, 123, 165, 166–67, 176– 77,
  181–92 passim, 194, 255n42,
  256n59; position in lesbian
  history, xii, xvi, xvii, xxiii, 3; self-
  presentation, xv, xvi, 27, 90, 117,
  123, 165; and sexology, xv, xvi,
  xxii, 7, 128, 130, 133–35 passim,
  140–46 passim, 152, 154, 155,
  160; sexual inversion, xvi, 1, 8, 76,
  79, 89–90, 122, 125, 141, 142,
  151, 161, 187. *See also Adam's
  Breed*; Femina Prize; "Miss Ogilvy
  Finds Herself"; *Unlit Lamp, The*;
  Well of Loneliness, The
Hallett, Nicky, 83, 90, 197n17,
  228n119, 256n71
Hamer, Emily, 75, 165, 166, 252n10
Hamilton, Mary Agnes, 65, 102
Hardy, Thomas, 178
Harris, Bertha, xix, 98
Hartley, L. P., 8, 9
Haward, Elfrida, 89, 90, 91
Hegal, G. W. F., 161
Henderson-Livesey, Captain A. H.,
  92–93
Hennegan, Alison, 141
Henry, Sir Edward, 80–81
Hepworth, Dorothy, xvii, xx, 123,
  135, 194, 198n29, 233n33
Heyer, Georgette, 12
Highbrow, 5, 9–12, 25, 204n40,
  204n43

Hillman, Elizabeth Lutes, 74
Hirschfeld, Magnus, 59, 76, 129, 150
History of Human Marriage, The
  (Westermarck), 134
Hodge, Alan, xx
Homogenic, xiii, 153, 154, 159, 161,
  248n129
Homophobia, xxiii, 3, 4, 5, 12, 28,
  49, 152. *See also* Moral panic
Homosexualität des Mannes und des
  Weibes, Die (Hirschfeld), 234
Homosexuality, 57, 142, 193; codes
  of, 119; as concept, xiv, xx, 24,
  26; Ellis, 157; female, 25, 34, 35,
  59, 118, 122; knowledge of, 131,
  132; male, xii, xxi, 7, 61, 159,
  194; sexological explanations, 129,
  139, 143, 144, 163, 244n64; su-
  periority of, 142, 146, 149, 150–
  55, 162; terms for, xiii; Ulrichs,
  135. *See also* Lesbianism; Sexual
  inversion
Hoppé, E. O., 176, 178–79, 255n48
Horwood, Sir William, 43, 44, 45,
  80
Houston Chronicle, 120
Howard, George, 75
Hume-Williams, Sir Ellis, 31, 211n2
Humphreys, Travers, 31, 34, 211n2
Huxley, Aldous, 16
Hyde, H. Montgomery, 104

Ingram, Angela, 21, 249n139,
  251n158
Inness, Sherrie A., 197n17
Inskip, Sir Thomas, 21
Intermediate sex, xiii, 160, 161, 162;
  Carpenter, 26, 138, 141, 142–43,
  146, 150, 152–55, 156, 157, 159,
  244n71, 250n142

Intermediate Sex, The (Carpenter),
  134, 142, 143, 151
Intersexes, The (Mayne), 135
Inversion. *See* Sexual inversion
Irons, Evelyn, xiii, 113, 123, 191,
  238n126

Jackson, Charles Kains, 158
Jackson, Margaret, 50
Jacob, Naomi, 10, 65, 75–76, 104,
  176
James, Norah C., 208n107
James Tait Black Memorial Prize, 8
Jeffreys, Sheila, 29, 35–36, 47, 50
Jivani, Alkarim, 98
John, Angela, 46, 217n75
Joint Select Committee on the Crimi-
  nal Law Amendment Bill (1920),
  37, 44–49 passim, 51, 53–55,
  215n43. *See also* "Acts of inde-
  cency by females" clause; Criminal
  Law Amendment Bill (1921)
Joyce, Nora, 137
Joynson-Hicks, Sir William ("Jix"),
  1, 10, 21–24 passim, 28–29,
  208n95, 208n100, 209n11

Kenealy, Arabella, 35, 59, 60
Kensington, Bishop of, 43
King, Dave, 91
King, Richard, 12, 29
Klein, Richard, 107
Knight, Laura, 113
Krafft-Ebing, Richard von, 51–52,
  56, 128, 129, 132, 135, 156,
  240n10; Ellis, 89, 136, 139–40,
  141; influence of, 137–38, 139,
  142, 143, 145; and lesbianism,
  100
Kuhn, Annette, 124

Labouchère Amendment (in Criminal Law Amendment Act, 1885), xviii, 34, 35, 48, 49, 51, 212n19

Lady in Blue (Allen), 167, 168, 169

Lancashire Daily Post, 110

Lancet, 2, 131, 139, 145

Lanchester, Elsa, 136, 242n45

Lane, Sir William Arbuthnot, 22

Laver, James, 104

Lavery, Lady Hazel and Sir John, 178

Law, 31–63; lesbianism and, xii, xviii, xxi, 32, 35, 45, 51; male homosexuality and, xii, 7

Lawrence, D. H., 143, 208n100

Lawrence, Margaret, 8

Lawrence, Susan, 119

League of Womanhood, The, 228n136

Leavis, Q. D., 9

Lee, Hermione, 11

Legitimation League, 240n20

Lesbianism, xix, xxii, 5, 13, 37, 50, 108, 180, 211n5; concept of, xvii, 9, 26, 29–30, 33, 34, 63, 96, 107, 110, 129, 152, 197n17; fear of, 2, 4, 36; Hall and, 123, 124, 145, 187, 194; increase of, 6, 45–46, 48, 59, 60; knowledge of, xiv–xv, 24–25, 27, 55–56, 193, 213n30; predatory lesbian, 49, 52; terms for, xiii, xx–xxi, 44, 53, 62. *See also* Homosexuality, female; Mannish lesbian

Leslie, Shane, 22–23

Levine, Philippa, 38, 39, 41, 73

Liddiard, Jean, 73

Life and Letters, 13, 14, 25

Light, Alison, xiv

Lister, Anne, xvi

Literary Review, 148

Liverpool Post and Mercury, 25, 26

Lock, Joan, 38, 44, 75, 83, 167, 171, 215n42

London Calling, 191

Londonderry, Marchioness of, 65

London Public Morality Council, 21

Lowbrow, 9, 10, 12, 204n40, 204n43

Lowther, Barbara ("Toupie"), 123

Ludlow, Lady, xi, 193, 195n2, 198n28

Macaulay, Rose, 205n49

Mackworth, Margaret Haig (Vicountess Rhondda), 133, 137–38

Macpherson, Lady, 28

Macquisten, Frederick A., 35, 37, 50, 55, 57, 58, 59, 220n115

Macready, General Sir Nevil, 39, 40–44, 68–71, 75, 77–80, 93, 173–75, 176

Malmesbury, Lord, 48, 55, 60

Manchester Daily Dispatch, 122

Manchester Guardian, xiii

Mannin, Ethel, 8, 106, 111, 136

Mannish lesbian, 99, 165–67; Gluck, 117, 180; Hall, xv, xvi, xxiii, 112, 113, 125, 188, 194; stereotype of, 106, 120. *See also* Homosexuality, female; Lesbianism

Mansfield, Katherine, 16

Manual of Sexual Science, A (Hirschfeld), 134, 247n109

Married Love (Stopes), 126, 133

Marx, Karl, 161

Masculine woman, xiii, xiv, 82, 102, 177, 180, 181; as lesbian, 26, 44, 71, 99, 106, 237n102

"Masculine Women and Feminine Men" (1926 song), xiv, 180

Matheson, Hilda, 35, 193, 220n116
Mayne, Xavier (Edward Irenaeus
  Prime Stevenson), 135
McKibbin, Ross, 11, 21
McLaren, Angus, 67, 82, 86
Men's League for Women's Suffrage,
  46
Merck, Mandy, 165
Metropolitan Police (Met), xxi, 38,
  63, 65; vs. Women Police Service,
  38, 41–44, 45, 46, 49, 69–71, 77,
  80–82, 166, 168. See also Hor-
  wood, Sir William; Macready,
  General Sir Nevil
Metropolitan Women Police Patrols
  (MWPP), 40, 42, 72, 77, 93, 94,
  170; origins, 39, 41, 68; vs.
  Women Police Service, 68–69,
  70–71, 80, 173, 175, 215n42
Middlebrow, 5, 9–12, 187, 204n40
"Miss Ogilvy Finds Herself" (Hall),
  161
Mitford, Nancy, 104
Modern Girl, 99, 102–106, 118–19,
  122
Modernity, xxiii, 131, 175, 176, 194;
  conservative, xix; defined, xviii,
  xxi, 148, 152, 199n36; Hall and,
  27, 112, 177, 186, 187; lesbian
  and, 162, 163. See also Sapphic
  modernity
Moll, Albert, 52, 134
Monocle, xiv, 96, 97, 106, 108–10,
  115
Moore-Brabazon, Lieutenant-Colonel
  J. T. C., 60
Moral panic, xx, xxi, 1–2, 3, 6, 28,
  29, 30. See also Homophobia
Morning Post, 7, 26
Mortimer, Raymond, 19–20

Muir Mackenzie, Lord, 37, 54, 88,
  216n60
Murry, John Middleton, 16
Mussolini, Benito, 178

Nation, 8, 20
National Union of Societies for Equal
  Citizenship (NUSEC), 41, 215n42
National Union of Women Workers
  (NUWW), 39, 41, 44
National Vigilance Association
  (NVA), 21, 40
Nava, Mica, 199n36
Neilans, Alison, 35, 61, 63,
  220n116, 220n117
Newcastle Daily Journal and North
  Star, 111
Newspapers. See Print media
New Statesman, 19, 25
News of the World, 88
Newton, Esther, xv-xvi, 128, 157,
  165, 166
Newton, Isabel, 32, 34, 134
New Woman, xiii, xv-xvi, 99–100,
  102, 105, 106, 162, 181
Nichols, Beverley, xx, 15, 200n43
Nicolson, Harold, 64, 134, 193
Nield, Keith, 143
Nightclubs, 135, 136–37
North, Peter, 190, 256n58
North Mail and Newcastle Chronicle,
  26

Obscene Publications Act (1857), 3,
  22, 195n2
Observer, 23, 186
Oliver, Kathlyn, 138
Orlando (Woolf), 11, 132
Ormrod, Richard, 116, 119
Oosterhuis, Harry, 129, 141

Parkes, Adam, 144
Passage to India, A (Forster), 8
Passing, 82, 88, 96, 118, 122, 125
Pearce-Crouch, Ernest, 86
Pemberton Billing, Noel, 31, 32–33, 63, 213n25
People, 20, 110, 113
Perversion, 26, 28, 89–90, 138, 173–74, 179, 211n5
Peto, Dorothy, 44, 88
Photography, 186, 188, 189; Gluck, xxii, 165, 176–78, 179–80, 181; Hall, xv, xxii, 165, 176–77, 181–92 passim, 194; photographic frame, 187, 190, 192; portraiture, 164–65, 166–67, 169–70, 175, 176–77; as propaganda, 170–73; and Women Police Service, 79–80, 165, 167–76
Piggford, George, 132
Pioneer Policewoman, The (Allen), 73, 87, 88, 167, 169, 171
Police Federation, 40
Policewoman's Review, The, 167, 217n73
Ponsonby, Elizabeth, 180, 255n51
Preece, Patricia, xvii, xxii, 135, 198n29
Print media, xvii, 16–17, 24, 29, 175, 183; anti-suffrage, 3–4; Hall, 6, 187, 188; homosexuality, discussion of, xxii, 20, 28, 32, 33, 34, 120, 179, 180
Prosser, Jay, 129, 139, 249n140
Proust, Marcel, xxii
Pryce, Margaret Eleanor, xi, xii, 193
Psychopathia Sexualis (Krafft-Ebing), 56, 135, 138, 140, 241n21
Pugh, Martin, 36, 213n29

Punch, 66, 105–108 passim, 111, 118, 121, 164, 177, 222n11

Queensberry, Marquess of, 211n3

Radford, Jean, 3, 245n82
Raitt, Suzanne, 129, 193, 252n7
Representation of the People Equal Franchise Bill, 3, 4, 29
Roberts, Cecil, 22, 23
Roberts, Mary Louise, 201n50
Rolley, Katrina, 101, 112, 235n60
Rolph, C. H., 25, 207n90
Romantic friendship, xi, xvi
Rose, Jacqueline, 175
Rosenman, Ellen Bayuk, 5, 10
Rousseau, Jean-Jacques, 161
Royal Magazine, 178, 255n48
Rubin, Gayle S., 28
Ruehl, Sonja, 132, 152

Sackville-West, Vita, xx, 61–62, 97, 129, 220n116; class background, xvii; homosexuality within marriage, 193; in masculine clothing, 64, 107, 221n2; passing, 67–68, 227n107; sexological works, 133, 134, 135
Sapphic modernity, xvii-xviii, xix, xxiii. *See also* Modernity
Sapphist/sapphism, xiii, xx, 24, 25, 194
Sargent, John Singer, 185
Sassoon, Siegfried, 143
Saturday Review, 9, 193
Saunders, Inspector, 171
Schreiner, Olive, 160
Scott, Bonnie Kime, 145
Sex, Politics, and Society (Weeks), 1
Sex and Character (Weininger), 134

Sexology (sexual science), xv, xvi, 33, 50, 52–55, 59–61, 90, 123; dissemination into public culture, 101, 126, 131–44; feminist critique of, 50–51, 128; homosexual response to, 137–40; lesbian writers and, xxii, 129–30, 137, 140–63; methodology of, 6, 51, 163; in parliamentary debate, 56–58, 91; status of, 127–28, 129, 130–31; as tool of political control, xxi, xxiii, 18–19, 36, 37, 51, 62–63

Sexual inversion/invert, xiii, xv, xx, xxii, 3, 93, 127, 129, 196n8; Browne, 132, 218n91; Ellis, 6–7, 53, 62, 100–101, 126, 128, 144, 146, 147, 149, 150 156, 157, 162; Forel, 52, 76, 160; Hall, 1, 8, 89–90, 122–25 passim, 141, 142, 151, 161, 187; knowledge of, 24, 25–26, 101, 130, 135, 137, 163, 179; Krafft-Ebing, 138, 139, 143

Sexual Inversion (Ellis), 131, 137, 139, 143, 144, 240n20

Sexual Life of Our Time, The (Bloch), 135

Sexual Question, The (Forel), 52, 76

Shaw, Christopher E., 158, 251n163

Shaw, George Bernard, 178, 206n73

Shield, 61

Shortt, Edward, 43, 81

Showalter, Elaine, 109

Sinclair, May, 196n11

Sinfield, Alan, xii, xiv

Sketch, 109, 118

Smoking, 106–107; flappers, 102, 164; Gluck, 117, 118; as sign of masculinity or lesbianism, 96, 97, 101, 105, 106, 108, 110, 111, 122

Smith-Rosenberg, Carroll, xvi

Social Problem of Sexual Inversion, The (BSSSP), 59, 135

Social purity, 215n43

Society for Psychical Research (SPR), 31–32, 35, 134

Souhami, Diana, 4, 16, 21, 23, 188

Spectator, xxii, 26, 28, 209n125

Sphere, 64

Spinster and Her Enemies, The (Jeffreys), 35–36

Stanley, Sophia, 39, 40, 42, 44, 68, 72, 77, 170, 214n38, 222n20

Steadman, Myra, 76–77

Steele, Valerie, 102

Stein, Gertrude, xvi, xix, 97, 111–12

Stephenson, Sir George, 20, 21

Stopes, Marie, 126, 133

"Studies in Feminine Inversion" (Browne), 132, 147

Studies in the Psychology of Sex (Ellis), 131–32, 133, 134, 137

Suffrage, xviii, 3, 29, 40, 46, 69, 86, 133, 168, 170, 175, 194

Suffragette, 78

Suffragettes, 40, 41, 49, 79, 87, 168, 252n12

Suggia, Madame Guilhermina, 178

Summerscale, Kate, 193

Sunday Chronicle, 20, 189–90

Sunday Dispatch, 84

Sunday Express. See Express

Sunday Times, 121, 123

Symonds, John Addington, 149, 150, 155, 243n52

Tagart, Helen, 77, 169, 230n147

Tagg, John, 174

Tancred, Edith, 88

Tatler, 12, 17, 26, 101, 108, 113, 117

Terry, Ellen, 178
Thiele, Beverly, 153
Tickner, Lisa, 168
Times, The, 32, 33, 102, 106
Times Literary Supplement (TLS), 4, 7, 9, 25
Time and Tide, 25, 220n114
To the Lighthouse (Woolf), 11
Transsexuality, 90, 129
Transvestism, 76, 119, 224n48
Trefusis, Violet, 64, 134
Tripp, Alker, 43
Trodd, Anthea, 10
Troubridge, Admiral Sir Ernest, 32, 116, 211n5
Troubridge, Una, Lady, 77, 126, 165, 176, 187, 233n30; appearance of, 100, 101, 106, 109, 110, 112–17 passim, 119, 185–86; Femina Prize, 11, 181; Hall, xvii, 32, 33, 35, 98, 183, 184, 190; as lesbian, 111, 123, 124, 136, 194; sexology reading list, 134, 244n71
Troup, Sir Edward, 43, 44, 80
Trousers, 84, 107, 109, 113, 117; boyette, 103; plus-fours, 118, 238n10; regulatory legislation for women, 97–98; sign of lesbianism, 106, 107, 110. *See also* Uniforms
Two Selves (Bryher), 130, 146, 149

Ulrichs, Karl Heinrich, 129, 135, 139, 145, 150, 151
Uniforms, xviii, xxi, 64–68, 72–74; Women Police Service and, 43, 46, 67, 68–82
Unlit Lamp, The (Hall), xvi, 176
Uranian, 59, 150, 152, 154, 155, 157–58, 161, 163, 248n129, 249n136, 249n137

Vernon, James, 83
Vicinus, Martha, 129
Vigilante, 31, 32
Vivien, Renée, 97
Votes for Women, 168

Warner, Sylvia Townsend, 98
Waugh, Evelyn, 104, 255n51
Wedekind, Frank, xxii
Wedgwood, Colonel, 55–56, 60
Weeks, Jeffrey, 35, 36, 59, 63; on Carpenter, 154, 158, 161; on Ellis, 150; moral panic, 1, 29
Weininger, Otto, 134, 244n64
Well of Loneliness, The (Hall), 24, 76, 79, 126, 130, 163, 186, 194; ban of, xv, 4, 13, 21, 22, 29, 30, 95, 110, 111, 151, 190, 195n2; Carpenter's influence on, 141, 142–43, 152–63 passim, 196n7; James Douglas's editorial on, xxii, 1–3, 4, 5, 6, 15, 17–20 passim, 27; Ellis's "Commentary," 6–7, 9, 126, 143, 144, 203n24; Ellis's influence on, 127, 128, 145, 156, 157, 196n7, 245n79; influences on, xxii, 98, 129; obscenity trial of, xii, xiii, xvii, xix, xx-xxii passim, 1, 5, 22, 23, 29, 80–90, 110, 120, 122, 124, 151, 192, 196n10; reception and reviews of, 1–2, 5, 6–14, 25–26, 27, 28, 122, 127, 128, 150, 184, 191; sales figures for, 10, 18; social and cultural impact of, xii, 96, 122, 124, 127, 132, 187, 193; Stephen Gordon, xv, 13, 14, 133, 134, 140–48 passim, 151–62 passim, 181, 197n17, 249n134, 249n140
Wemyss, Lord, 54

West, Rebecca, 151, 182, 205n61
Westermarck, Edward, 134, 135
Westminster Gazette, 117
Whetham, William and Catherine, 59
Whitlock, Gillian, 10, 142, 158, 245n82
Whitman, Walt, 158
Wild, Sir Ernest, 35, 56–59, 89–91, 220n115, 227n113
Wilde, Oscar, xii, xxiii, 27, 31, 32, 211n2, 240n20
Wilkinson, Mrs. Tudor, 180
Wilson, Elizabeth, 98
Wolff, Janet, 199n36
Women of the Left Bank (Benstock), 98
Women Police Question, The (Henderson-Livesey), 92
Women Police Service (WPS), 37, 38–46, 49, 67, 68–82, 83, 165, 166, 167–76, 215n42, 222n20, 254n30

Women Police Volunteers (WPV), 38, 39
Women's Auxiliary Service, 81, 167. *See also* Women Police Service
Women's Freedom League, 47
Women's Land Army, 64, 66, 221n2, 222n12
Women's Social and Political Union (WSPU), 40, 78, 168
Woolf, Leonard, 8, 9, 25
Woolf, Virginia, 9–12, 24, 96, 132, 182, 183, 256n61
Woollacott, Angela, 64
Wyles, Lilian, 72
Wylie, I. A. R., 12

X, Dr. Jacobus (Louis Jacolliot), 134, 242n37

Yorkshire Post, 20, 190
Young in the Twenties (Mannin), 106

Zola, Émile, xxii

Between Men ~ Between Women
Lesbian and Gay Studies

Lillian Faderman and Larry Gross, Editors

Richard D. Mohr, *Gays/Justice: A Study of Ethics, Society, and Law*

Gary David Comstock, *Violence Against Lesbians and Gay Men*

Kath Weston, *Families We Choose: Lesbians, Gays, Kinship*

Lillian Faderman, *Odd Girls and Twilight Lovers: A History of Lesbian Life in Twentieth-Century America*

Judith Roof, *A Lure of Knowledge: Lesbian Sexuality and Theory*

John Clum, *Acting Gay: Male Homosexuality in Modern Drama*

Allen Ellenzweig, *The Homoerotic Photograph: Male Images from Durieu/Delacroix to Mapplethorpe*

Sally Munt, editor, *New Lesbian Criticism: Literary and Cultural Readings*

Timothy F. Murphy and Suzanne Poirier, editors, *Writing AIDS: Gay Literature, Language, and Analysis*

Linda D. Garnets and Douglas C. Kimmel, editors, *Psychological Perspectives on Lesbian and Gay Male Experiences*

Laura Doan, editor, *The Lesbian Postmodern*

Noreen O'Connor and Joanna Ryan, *Wild Desires and Mistaken Identities: Lesbianism and Psychoanalysis*

Alan Sinfield, *The Wilde Century: Effeminacy, Oscar Wilde, and the Queer Moment*

Claudia Card, *Lesbian Choices*

Carter Wilson, *Hidden in the Blood: A Personal Investigation of AIDS in the Yucatɨn*

Alan Bray, *Homosexuality in Renaissance England*

Joseph Carrier, *De Los Otros: Intimacy and Homosexuality Among Mexican Men*

Joseph Bristow, *Effeminate England: Homoerotic Writing After 1885*

Corinne E. Blackmer and Patricia Juliana Smith, editors, *En Travesti: Women, Gender Subversion, Opera*

Don Paulson with Roger Simpson, *An Evening at The Garden of Allah: A Gay Cabaret in Seattle*

Claudia Schoppmann, *Days of Masquerade: Life Stories of Lesbians During the Third Reich*

Chris Straayer, *Deviant Eyes, Deviant Bodies: Sexual Re-Orientation in Film and Video*

Edward Alwood, *Straight News: Gays, Lesbians, and the News Media*

Thomas Waugh, *Hard to Imagine: Gay Male Eroticism in Photography and Film from Their Beginnings to Stonewall*

Judith Roof, *Come As You Are: Sexuality and Narrative*

Terry Castle, *Noel Coward and Radclyffe Hall: Kindred Spirits*

Kath Weston, *Render Me, Gender Me: Lesbians Talk Sex, Class, Color, Nation, Studmuffins . . .*

Ruth Vanita, *Sappho and the Virgin Mary: Same-Sex Love and the English Literary Imagination*

René C. Hoogland, *Lesbian Configurations*

Beverly Burch, *Other Women: Lesbian Experience and Psychoanalytic Theory of Women*

Jane McIntosh Snyder, *Lesbian Desire in the Lyrics of Sappho*

Rebecca Alpert, *Like Bread on the Seder Plate: Jewish Lesbians and the Transformation of Tradition*

Emma Donoghue, editor, *Poems Between Women: Four Centuries of Love, Romantic Friendship, and Desire*

James T. Sears and Walter L. Williams, editors, *Overcoming Heterosexism and Homophobia: Strategies That Work*

Patricia Juliana Smith, *Lesbian Panic: Homoeroticism in Modern British Women's Fiction*

Dwayne C. Turner, *Risky Sex: Gay Men and HIV Prevention*

Timothy F. Murphy, *Gay Science: The Ethics of Sexual Orientation Research*

Cameron McFarlane, *The Sodomite in Fiction and Satire, 1660–1750*

Lynda Hart, *Between the Body and the Flesh: Performing Sadomasochism*

Byrne R. S. Fone, editor, *The Columbia Anthology of Gay Literature: Readings from Western Antiquity to the Present Day*

Ellen Lewin, *Recognizing Ourselves: Ceremonies of Lesbian and Gay Commitment*

Ruthann Robson, *Sappho Goes to Law School: Fragments in Lesbian Legal Theory*

Jacquelyn Zita, *Body Talk: Philosophical Reflections on Sex and Gender*

Evelyn Blackwood and Saskia Wieringa, *Female Desires: Same-Sex Relations and Transgender Practices Across Cultures*

William L. Leap, ed., *Public Sex/Gay Space*

Larry Gross and James D. Woods, eds., *The Columbia Reader on Lesbians and Gay Men in Media, Society, and Politics*

Marilee Lindemann, *Willa Cather: Queering America*

George E. Haggerty, *Men in Love: Masculinity and Sexuality in the Eighteenth Century*

Andrew Elfenbein, *Romantic Genius: The Prehistory of a Homosexual Role*

Gilbert Herdt and Bruce Koff, *Something to Tell You: The Road Families Travel When a Child Is Gay*

Richard Canning, *Gay Fiction Speaks: Conversations with Gay Novelists*